D1564876

Blacks in the New World

Edited by August Meier
and John H. Bracey

*A list of books in the series
appears at the end of this book.*

Indians at Hampton Institute, 1877–1923

Indians at Hampton Institute, 1877–1923

Donal F. Lindsey

University of Illinois Press   *Urbana and Chicago*

DISCARDED

WIDENER UNIVERSITY
WOLFGRAM
LIBRARY
CHESTER, PA.

WIDENER UNIVERSITY

© 1995 by the Board of Trustees of the University of Illinois
Manufactured in the United States of America
C 5 4 3 2 1

This book is printed on acid-free paper.

Library of Congress Cataloging-in-Publication Data

Lindsey, Donal F.
    Indians at Hampton Institute, 1877–1923 / Donal F. Lindsey.
      p.   cm. — (Blacks in the New World)
    Includes bibliographical references and index.
    ISBN 0-252-02106-1 (alk. paper)
      1. Indians of North America—Virginia—Hampton—Education (Higher)
2. Hampton Institute—History. 3. Indians of North America—
Government relations. 4. African Americans—Virginia—Hampton—
Education (Higher). 5. Multicultural education—Government policy—
Virginia—Hampton. I. Title. II. Series
    E97.65.V8L56 1995
    378.755'412—dc20
                                              93-45510
                                                   CIP

To my mother, Aïda Lindsey,
    and to the memories of
my father, Donal O. Lindsey, and Elliott M. Rudwick

Contents

Illustrations follow page 90

Preface

Near colonial Williamsburg, Hampton University, in Hampton Virginia, lies on the peninsula between the James and York Rivers at the mouth of Chesapeake Bay. Founded in 1868 during Reconstruction, as a normal school primarily for the industrial education of blacks, Hampton Institute began a much smaller program to educate Indians in 1877. This program lasted for almost a half century with more than 120 Indians attending each year between 1883 and 1902. Overall 1,388 Indian students passed through Hampton's doors, although just 160 graduated, and only an average of 31 attended during its last decade.

Yet Hampton's influence on Indian policy, Indian education, and Indian race relations with both whites and blacks was disproportionate to the small number of Indians involved. The Hampton Indian program recruited its students from 65 tribes, and left records that move beyond local issues to illuminate the still shadowy history of relations between the United States and the American Indian tribes surviving both disease and conquest. Besides Hazel W. Hertzberg's classic study on Pan-Indianism and the recent works of Robert A. Trennert, Jr., and Frederick Hoxie, few scholars of Native American history have focused on the 1890s–1920s era; even fewer have looked at federal policy or its formation.

Moreover, Hampton offers a unique opportunity to examine, within a single institutional setting over an extended period of time, the attitudes of prominent white reformers toward the two racial minorities whose experiences most defined the shape of American history. Just as important, Hampton records yield a rare glimpse into how blacks and Indians themselves compared their collective experiences. Where other histories of their relations deal with the Five Civilized Tribes removed to Oklahoma's Indian Territory and with small racially mixed communities scattered through the eastern United States, a study of Hampton's biracial program examines an upper crust of white policymakers and a "picked body" of black and Indian students, interacting in a metropolitan area within reach of the nation's capital.

Historians have never conducted a large-scale examination of all three races at Hampton, despite its excellent archives, voluminous publications, and strong ties to major organizations concerned with both minorities. Instead historians have largely focused on one racial group while ignoring the school's other minority. Yet revisionist histories of black education at Hampton raise questions relevant to Indian education there and elsewhere: not asking them reinforces the long-standing isolation of the study of Indians, as a specialty of the western frontier, anthropology, and folklore, separated from expanding urban-oriented disciplines directed at other minorities. Conversely, the more numerous studies of blacks at Hampton have overlooked the possibility that a detailed knowledge of the school's Indian program could open new perspectives on black education.

In fact, no complete picture can emerge from a split image view of either red or black at Hampton. Its principals and staff dealt on a daily basis with the issues raised by bringing blacks and Indians together. Their thinking about one minority unavoidably and demonstrably textured their thinking about the other, not only on campus but also in the national arena. This study, therefore, will consider the Indian program at Hampton Institute in full context, extensively comparing the two sides of the equation as a major means of analysis.

Most evidence about Hampton shows not only whites but many Indians and blacks verbalizing Eurocentric themes. At a school whose educational philosophy was among the nation's most accommodationist, independent thinking by blacks and Indians was usually unwanted and thus its expression rarely preserved, although at times candid remarks of both races rocked white staff and changed school operations.

Moreover, reliance on Hampton sources alone masks the consistent desire of Native American peoples for self-determination and nationhood, as confirmed by treaties with the United States. The existence of these sacred agreements has led historian Vine Deloria, Jr. (Sioux), to argue that the modern civil rights movement was irrelevant to Indians. It was not until the mid-1960s, when Stokely Carmichael and the black power movement demanded self-determination and peoplehood, that the struggle of African Americans began to make sense to Indians. Before what Vincent Harding calls this search for "black history through Indian eyes," many Indians believed that blacks were just imitating whites whose own American dream seemed uncharted and mysterious, in its technological means without spiritual ends.

Much of Hampton's history and influence is closely tied to Samuel Chapman Armstrong, its charismatic founder and first principal. It was Armstrong who shaped its curriculum as well as its attitudes toward race relations, and who influenced both national reform and government policy. Understanding Armstrong's ideas on race relations at Hampton requires examination of his upbringing in Hawaii, his education at Williams College, and his service in the Freedmen's Bureau, while familiarity with the outline of federal Indian policy is required to assess the influence of Hampton's Indian program. Therefore the introductory first chapter provides a brief biography of Armstrong— from his birth in 1839 through the founding and early expansion of Hampton Institute (1868–72)—as well as a capsule history of federal Indian policy.

The study proper is more thematically than chronologically organized, although the second chapter traces the growth of Armstrong's interest in Indians and its translation into what he hoped would be a permanent Indian program at Hampton—a program challenged by other school officials, neighboring whites, local blacks, and black students. School officials often claimed that Indians were foisted on Hampton, since their commitment to the industrial education of Negroes might be questioned if Indian students were seen as deliberately recruited. And since the introduction into Hampton of the Indian prisoners held at Fort Marion in St. Augustine, Florida, drew together Samuel Armstrong and another influential leader of mainstream opinion on Indians, Captain Richard Henry Pratt, both Pratt's racial views and activities at the Institute and his subsequent disillusionment with Armstrong are described.

Chapter 3 examines Armstrong's views on Indian reform and their influence in a variety of arenas, as Hampton's Indian program quickly made the general a major figure in the Indian "assimilation" movement of the late nineteenth century. The Indian program's role in sectional reconciliation and the effect of black emancipation on Indian reform emerge as central to Armstrong's involving Hampton in Indian education.

Thus begins a comparative analysis whose various dimensions are discussed in the next four chapters. In chapter 4, I shift the focus from Armstrong's statements contrasting the black and Indian experiences as a tool influencing national legislation, to the use made at Hampton itself of comparisons between the two races toward molding student behavior. The often misunderstood extent of segregation at Hampton is examined in chapter 5: were segregated arrangements made on racial grounds alone, as writers on both groups have usually assumed, or did practical considerations complicate this picture? Chapter 6 explores personal relations between blacks and Indians at Hampton, and the forces shaping those relations: was friction between the groups minor or significant, and were its causes external or intrinsic?

Chapter 7 completes the comparative analysis by juxtaposing Hampton's stated policy of studying and preserving its students' respective cultures with Thomas Jesse Jones's "social studies" curriculum, which seemed to contradict this policy.

The last two chapters deal with changes over time within the Indian program itself and with the diverse forces leading to its eventual collapse. Chapter 8 places the various and changing composition of the Indian student body in the context of controversies: over the questioned long-term retention of European education by Indian students and over the 1887 investigation by Thomas S. Childs of Hampton's treatment of Indians, clearly the most important challenge to the program. The last chapter examines additional factors helping to end Hampton's Indian program. Internal factors would come into sharp relief beginning with Armstrong's succession in 1893 by Hollis Burke Frissell. Of New Armenia, New York, Yale University, and the Union Theological Seminary, Frissell had begun his career as Hampton's chaplain in 1880. He found that external factors against the Indian program had been building almost since its beginning. After discussing this whipsaw of forces, the chapter provides a final assessment or overview of the historical importance of Hampton's Indian program.

Acknowledgments

A great debt of thanks is owed to many who contributed to this project. I am deeply grateful to Kent State University professors August Meier, Henry B. Leonard, Frank L. Byrne, and Mark F. Seeman for overseeing the preparation of the dissertation on which this book is based. The untimely death of Professor Elliott M. Rudwick in 1985 deprived me of his generous support of my research.

Many individuals assisted in the research for this study, which I must emphasize is about the past and cannot be construed as applying to present-day Hampton University. My first thanks goes to Fritz J. Malval, the archivist of the Hampton University Archives, and his staff members Donzella S. Willford and Cynthia G. Poston. Robert M. Kvasnicka of the National Archives and Research Administration, Karen D. Drickamer of Williams College Library, and Linda A. Burroughs of Kent State University Library also provided valuable help. Two private individuals deserve my gratitude for their unexpected assistance: Arthur Howe, Jr., sent me boxes of material belonging to his grandfather, S C. Armstrong, and Julia Graham Lear, the daughter of Edward Kidder Graham, sent me a copy of her father's well-written manuscript on Hampton Institute.

Numerous other individuals have helped me complete this book. Walter L. Williams, now of the University of Southern California, introduced me to Indian history when I was an undergraduate at the University of Cincinnati, and since that time has given me a decade of encouragement and advice. I am indebted to my grandmother, Cornelia T. Lindsey, who financed much of my research. David Wallace Adams of Cleveland State University, Wilbert H. Ahern of the University of Minnesota at Morris, and Daniel F. Littlefield, Jr., of the University of Arkansas at Little Rock saved me from making a handful of errors, as did David K. Eliades of Pembroke State University and other members of Theda Perdue and Michael Green's NEH Summer Seminar on Southeastern Indians. Finally, I wish to thank the indexer, Theresa J. Schaefer, and to express deep gratitude to Karin G. Rabe and Judith M. Daniels, who critically read the manuscript and lent their enormous editing expertise.

Abbreviations

ABCFM	American Board of Commissioners for Foreign Missions
AMA	American Missionary Association
ARCIA	*Annual Report of the Commissioner of Indian Affairs*
BTW	Booker T. Washington
HBF	Hollis Burke Frissell
HUA	Hampton University Archives
IRA	Indian Rights Association
LMC	*Proceedings of the Lake Mohonk Conferences for the Indian*
NARA	National Archives Research Administration
NEA	*The Journal of Proceedings and Addresses of the National Education Association*
NEC	National Education Committee
RHP	Richard Henry Pratt
SAI	Society of American Indians
SCA	Samuel Chapman Armstrong
SW	*Southern Workman*
T&T	*Talks and Thoughts* (of the Hampton Indian Students)

Indians at Hampton Institute, 1877–1923

1

General Samuel Chapman Armstrong, the Founding of Hampton Institute, and Federal Indian Policy

Since specialists in Native American history may be unfamiliar with General Armstrong and the founding of Hampton Institute, and specialists in African American history with federal policy toward Indians, a brief overview of each will help lay a foundation for the history of Hampton's Indian program.

Samuel Chapman Armstrong

The charismatic founder of Hampton Institute, Samuel Chapman Armstrong, was born in Wailuku, Maui, on January 30, 1839, the sixth of Richard and Clarissa Armstrong's ten children. He later asserted that "it meant something to the Hampton School, and perhaps to the ex-slaves of America, that, from 1820 to 1860, the distinctly missionary period, there was worked out in the Hawaiian Islands, the problem of the emancipation, enfranchisement and Christian civilization of a dark-skinned Polynesian people in many respects like the Negro race."[1]

The American Board of Commissioners for Foreign Missions (ABCFM), founded in 1810, first began missionary work in Hawaii in 1819. Soon after Irish Protestant Richard Armstrong graduated from Princeton Theological Seminary and married Clarissa Chapman, of Puritan descent, the couple left New Bedford, Massachusetts, in 1831, as members of the third party of ABCFM missionaries to the Pacific. The new missionaries spent a year stationed in the Marquesas and in Maui, before Richard was transferred to the central mission at Honolulu and became the spiritual advisor of King Kamehameha III. Eight years later Richard was made minister of public instruction and a member of both the House of Nobles and the Privy Council, posts he held until his death in 1860.[2]

Rather than feeling honored by these positions, Richard believed that it was he who did honor to the Hawaiians. Unmoved by the Hawaiians' astonishing eagerness for American institutions, he wrote that the "king himself is as near to being an animal as man can well be & most of the high chiefs are ignorant, lazy, & stupid." As a remedy, Richard proposed to improve "the *heart,* the *head* & the *body* at once. This is a lazy people & if they are ever to be made industrious the work must begin with the young. So I am making strenuous efforts to have some sort of manual labor connected with every school . . . without industry they cannot be moral." Samuel Armstrong's biographer, Suzanne C. Carson, asserts that "Hampton Institute was the direct heir to this philosophy of education," which itself had European roots in the methods of Johann Heinrich Pestalozzi and Philipp Emmanuel von Fellenburg.[3]

The young Samuel accompanied his father on school inspections throughout the islands, and later mentioned two specific schools as Hampton's inspiration. The first, Lahainaluna, was a normal school, founded in 1831 after Hawaii's effort to establish common schools had almost collapsed for want of trained native teachers; it was the first school in Hawaii to incorporate manual labor into an academic curriculum. Samuel was even more impressed by David B. Lyman's Hilo Boarding and Manual-Labor School, established in 1836. This school recruited students in rural areas and continued to emphasize industrial skills after they had been discontinued at Lahainaluna. Samuel credited Hilo as inspiring many of Hampton's methods, saying that while Lahainaluna "turned out more brilliant; the latter [produced] less advanced but more solid men."[4]

Samuel Armstrong's daughter would later note that her father "saw that the cases of the Hawaiian and the Negro, although similar, were not parallel, and their needs not identical. There was a small and decadent people: here a large and rapidly growing one, and a people related in a peculiar way to their neighbors." In 1872, while addressing the National Education Association (NEA) in Boston, Armstrong himself commented that for Negro education, "an imitation of northern models will not do [for] right methods at the South must be created, not copied."[5]

His own formal education began at the Royal School in Honolulu, which had been founded in 1840 to educate the children of the Hawaiian nobility. From there he advanced to Punahou School in 1854, just as its rechartering as Oahu College marked the pinnacle of his father's effort to educate leaders able to create a "puritan commonwealth in the tropics." Although white settlers had established Punahou for their own children, both the Royal and Punahou schools ultimately included children of both races. However, the missionaries attempted to discourage their outnumbered children from fraternizing with the Hawaiians. Fearful that her eldest daughter was "constantly exposed to the natives & imitates *all* they do," Clarissa made sure that her new house had "high walls around it." Samuel's classmates at Royal included a future king and queen—Kalakaua and his sister Liliuokalani—but he assured his older brother William Nevins that the "half whites and natives . . . do not trouble us."[6]

On September 23, 1860, only two weeks after Richard Armstrong died of injuries sustained in a riding accident, Samuel fulfilled his father's wishes by leaving Hawaii to study at Williams College in northwestern Massachusetts, the mecca for missionaries' sons. By coming to Williams, Armstrong completed a circle that had begun when an earlier Williams student, ABCFM founder Samuel J. Mills, trained a Hawaiian student at the Cornwall, Connecticut "heathen" school (1817–27). This student, Henry Obookiah, inspired the ABCFM's missionary work in Hawaii.[7]

One of Samuel's first friends at Williams was Archibald Hopkins, son of Mark Hopkins, president of both Williams (1836–72) and the ABCFM (1857–87). Within two months of his arrival, Samuel had moved out of the dorms and into the "Prex'" residence as Archibald's roommate. There the elder Hopkins, one of the nation's most acclaimed moral philosophers, introduced Samuel to conservative metaphysics, including the beliefs that philosophical inquiry ultimately confirms old truths, that piety prevails over intellect and scholarship, that education is the only possible social equalizer, and that private property qualified one for spiritual stewardship—a tenet soon to be called the "gospel of wealth." Above all, Hopkins believed that an individual's duty in a complex but harmonious universe was "not merely to find unity produced by God, [but actively] to seek to produce unity." Although many of Hopkins's views were ones Samuel already had learned from his missionary father, Armstrong later claimed that "whatever good teaching I may have done has been Mark Hopkins teaching through me."[8]

Graduating fourth in his class, Armstrong joined the Union army in August 1862 without waiting for commencement exercises or the naturalization process that would make him an American citizen. He was commissioned captain of Company D of the 125th New York Regiment, in return for recruiting its members. Within a month, however, Armstrong's troops were prisoners of war, "bagged" along with more than twelve thousand other Union soldiers by Stonewall Jackson at Harper's Ferry. Sent on parole to Camp Douglas in Chicago, the regiment was reactivated through an exchange of prisoners in late

1862 and engaged in minor skirmishes for six months before taking part in the battle of Gettysburg. Armstrong was promoted to major for having led the repulse of Pickett's charge on July 3, 1863, which contributed to the northern victory. He was then sent on recruiting duty to New York, where some prominent citizens attempted to raise a Negro regiment for him. When state authorities foiled this plan, Armstrong applied for reassignment to an existing Negro regiment and a return to active duty.[9]

Thereafter Armstrong rose rapidly through the ranks. On the basis of his military record, high examination scores, and recommendations (from his uncle, Massachusetts Chief Justice Reuben A. Chapman, from Hopkins, and from the ABCFM's Rufus Anderson), he was appointed in November 1863 as Lieutenant Colonel of the Ninth Regiment United States Colored Troops (USCT) at Fort Benedict, Maryland.[10] There he took charge of a makeshift school for black troops in a Confederate's tobacco barn. After five inactive months restationed at Hilton Head, South Carolina, the impatient Armstrong led his black troops North to fight at Deep Bottom, Virginia, in August 1864, and was subsequently promoted to Colonel of the Eighth Regiment, USCT. In March 1865 President Lincoln made the twenty-six-year-old a brevet Brigadier General. Armstrong's black regiment was blocking the only escape road when Lee surrendered; he was present at Appomattox on the ninth of April. Before being mustered out of the army in November 1865, Armstrong patrolled the Texas border against Maximilian, and gained his American citizenship by having served in the army for three years.[11]

Despite his obvious bravery and leadership qualities, Armstrong had fought at first with malice toward none, jesting to Archibald Hopkins, "Bozaris when dying shouted, 'Strike for your altars and your fires.' That's all poppycock. I say *strike,* in order that you may get $100 or so per month, see the country, wear soldiers' clothes, save the land from anarchy, rescue the Constitution and punish the rebels—long live the Republic! At this point please sing at the top of your voice 'My country 'tis of Thee!' I wish I were a parrot or a monkey that I might not be troubled by mortal cares any more." He later admitted that the "Union is to me little or nothing. I see no great principle necessarily involved in it." On the contrary, Armstrong found the "secesh army" to be "bone of our bone"; he engaged in "pleasant and cordial intercourse" with Confederate soldiers when he was their captive, telling his mother that "they shamed us; they fought, they said, not for money but for their homes, and wanted the war to cease. . . . few of us really know what we are fighting for."[12]

In effect he told Archibald Hopkins in December 1862 that his concern for slaves arose more out of religious conviction than concern for social justice: "I am sort of an abolitionist, but I have not learned to love the Negro. I believe in universal freedom; I believe the whole world cannot buy a single soul. The Almighty has set, or rather limited, the price of one man, and until worlds can be paid for a single soul, I do not believe in selling or buying them, more on account of their souls than their bodies." Four days later he told his brother Baxter that "these Negroes—as far as I've seen—are worse than the Kanakas, and are hardly worth fighting for." In his book, *Education for Life,* Francis Greenwood Peabody, dean of the Harvard Divinity School and vice president of the Hampton Board of Trustees, attributed Armstrong's insensitivity to the evils of servitude to the fact that he "was still a Hawaiian, and his judgments of Negro slavery were softened by his recollection of the gentle paternalism which he had witnessed among the natives of the Pacific, where the harsher methods of the southern states had been unknown." Neither of Armstrong's mentors—his father nor Hopkins—had been an abolitionist.[13]

Nevertheless, after President Lincoln's Emancipation Proclamation, which accorded well with his religious principles, Armstrong embraced the northern cause with a true sense of mission. He wrote his mother that the "first day of January (1863) is at hand—possibly the greatest day in American history—when the sons of Africa shall be free. . . . Then I shall know for what I am contending—for freedom and for the oppressed. . . . If this proclamation shall be cancelled in any way, I think I shall resign." When leading black troops he asserted that he "felt the high duty and sacredness of my position. . . . I would be nowhere else if I could." He explained to her that

> The African race is before the world, unexpectedly to all; and all mankind are looking to see whether the African will show himself equal to the opportunity. . . . to demonstrate to the world that he is a man. . . . All men must respect heroism and military prowess. . . . the star of Africa is rising, her millions now for the first time catching the glimpse of the glorious dawn—auroral gleams are lighting up the horizon of their future, and their future . . . rests largely upon the success of the Negro troops in this war. . . . it will yet be a grand thing to have been identified with this Negro movement.

But even on the day of northern victory, Armstrong remained ambivalent: he "felt a sadness—a feeling that the colored soldier had not done enough [to have] been sufficiently proved." Indeed, although Armstrong felt his work with blacks was his greatest calling, his statements are startlingly inconsistent, leading biographer Robert Schneider to view Armstrong as "acting independently of any clearly defined ideology." Schneider argued that "abstractions such as the integrity of the Union or the freedom of the sons of Africa meant little to him except as a means to fulfilling the sense of mission in his life."[14]

Called by historian James M. McPherson the "greatest educational salesman" of the nineteenth century, Armstrong had a commanding presence and a unique way of aligning polarities of racial consciousness into a "workable" whole, which struck one as either negative or positive. Five foot ten with thick, dark brown hair that grayed prematurely, he excelled at everything "manly" he tried. Whether as boxer, sailor, horseman, or soldier his spirited sense of abandon aimed to shame "cowardice" out of fellows. But a cut off the same log as Hopkins, he lacked any noticeable worldly satisfaction in "winning." He is said to have spoken in a not unpleasant rapid-fire tenor voice that timed pitch with facial expression, a faculty unrevealed in snapshots of this islander taken at various ages, all of which show the same stern but aloof stare. In a penmanship that one friend "stood on my head to read," for years Armstrong tenderly encouraged his family to write one another on the anniversary of the days his father and brother had died. Two black aides remembered him as the white man who gave the hungriest pupil his own cut of meat, picked up the bags of another whenever his were carried, and patronized the poorest taxi driver.

In 1890 at the age of fifty-one, soon after his second marriage, to Mary Alice Ford, a massive stroke paralyzed the left side of his body during his speech in New England on behalf of his work. The public drama of this break in the health of a beloved, once vibrant man, and the common knowledge of his final three years as an invalid, spawned the legend that he had given his life for blacks and Indians. A powerful Armstrong cult developed among whites, despite his assertion that "I have not sacrificed anything in my life." Having requested a simple soldier's funeral, he was laid to rest in the school cemetery in the plot prepared for the next Hampton student to die. On Armstrong's grave stood a block of volcanic rock from Hawaii and another of icy granite from the Berkshires, symbolically uniting the halves of his early life that had brought him to Hampton. As he requested, the "simple headstone" bore "no text or sentiment, only name and date."[15]

The Founding of Hampton Institute

In pursuit of a mission, Armstrong had planned to join the Freedmen's Bureau even before leaving the army. In February 1866, after an interview with Freedmen's Bureau Commissioner Oliver Otis Howard, he was appointed superintendent of the Ninth Subdistrict of

Virginia, a sprawling domain of nine counties headquartered at Hampton. There, he would oversee seven officers, thirty-four female missionaries from the North, abandoned land, and all matters relating to freedmen. Howard told Armstrong that his post was the "most delicate" in the bureau.[16]

Howard was evidently referring to several factors that made Hampton unique. Because the area around Fortress Monroe was under Union control throughout the war, local whites had burned and then abandoned the town. Deserted Hampton thus became a city of refuge for the first mass escape of slaves, many of whom occupied and cultivated the outlying vacant lands. The peninsula's black population quadrupled during the war from 10,000 to 40,000; the village of Hampton alone held 7,000 blacks, whereas all of Elizabeth City County had contained only 2,600 in 1861 (see map 1). The large number of blacks drew northern missionaries, members of the American Missionary Association (AMA), to make Hampton their first station for ex-slaves. Its size would prove to be second only to that of the Port Royal "experiment" on the South Carolina Sea Islands.[17] But precisely because Hampton offered an unusual opportunity for carrying out Radical Reconstruction, it became the scene of deep rifts among bureau agents, missionaries, and freedmen.

Armstrong replaced an abolitionist superintendent who had been dismissed and court-martialed for attempting to subvert President Andrew Johnson's conservative reconstruction plans. Captain C. B. Wilder had hoped to distribute the abandoned land among former slaves, as Howard, in accord with provisions of the congressional act creating the Freedmen's Bureau, had initially directed him to do in Circular Order Thirteen of July 28, 1865. Although Armstrong's utterances about Johnson were critical enough to gain notice from some local white and black radicals, he nevertheless obediently implemented the three main goals of the president's program.[18] He restored property to the former rebels, enforced labor contracts between freedmen and their former owners, and tried to remove the "excess" black population from his jurisdiction, withdrawing their rations as a last resort.[19]

As federal policy broke promises the government had made to freedmen, Armstrong increasingly gloried in the fact of emancipation itself. Unlike the Radical Reconstructionist goal of changing southern white society, Armstrong's became one of fitting the Negro to take his place in it. He concluded that "the right point of contact between Northern aid and Southern need is the normal school."[20]

In May 1866, two months after arriving at Hampton, Armstrong wrote to the AMA's general superintendent of schools, Samuel Hunt, of the need to "prepare colored teachers for southern schools; teach-

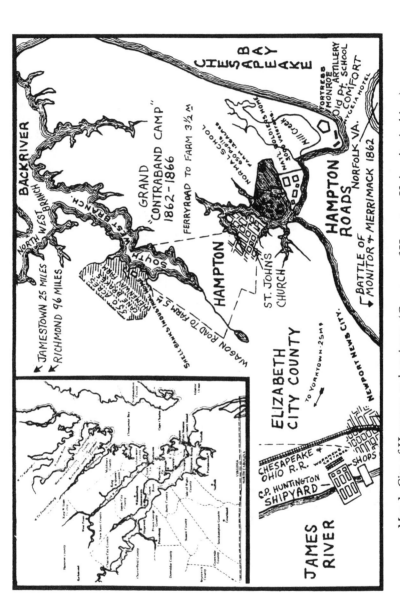

Map 1. City of Hampton and environs. (Courtesy of Hampton University Archives)

ers who will cost much less than whites; who can live the year through in one place, thus saving expense of transportation; who, in fact, can make a living out of their schools, and, after being started, support themselves [through augmenting their low salaries with money earned through manual skills learned at school]; who will penetrate the country and, singly, occupy isolated & remote places where our [northern white] ladies could never go."[21] Armstrong noted that putting Negro education in the hands of former Confederates would be a "sham." He wanted a centrally located school for black students supported and operated by northern whites, one where not only the liberal arts of the AMA schools but agricultural and mechanical skills would be taught to round out instruction in a "whole circle of living." His plan aimed to develop all teachers and leaders of the Negro race for life in society *as it was.*[22]

During this period when numerous schools were being founded for the newly freed slaves—the AMA established eight in 1867–68—Armstrong quickly located a site for his new school, a 125-acre plot of abandoned land. From Hampton's April 1868 beginning, Armstrong sought independence from the AMA in order to develop his own plan of education, which he believed if successful would guarantee a "dozen more like it in the South."[23] In 1869 Hampton was endorsed by a hand-picked party of visitors that included Mark Hopkins, Daniel Coit Gilman (then of Yale College), and future president James A. Garfield. Although Armstrong retained six officers of the AMA as Hampton trustees, by 1870 he had replaced most of the teachers appointed by the AMA with a staff personally loyal to him. In 1872 the former Union officer and Freedmen's Bureau agent convinced white moderates and blacks in the Virginia General Assembly to allocate a third of the state's Morrill Act Land Grant Funds to Hampton, which made the school financially solvent. Such support persuaded the AMA in 1879 to relinquish its deed on the property to a fifteen-member board of trustees selected by Armstrong, who then convinced the state of Virginia to charter the Hampton Normal and Agricultural Institute (see map 2).[24] Having obtained autonomy, Armstrong was set to begin his struggle to convert northern missionaries, southern whites, and Negroes to his accommodationist industrial program. His later work for Indians would contribute to the accomplishment of this goal.

An Introduction to Federal Indian Policy

The context in which Hampton's Indian program developed was the federal government's haphazardly implemented plan for "civilizing"

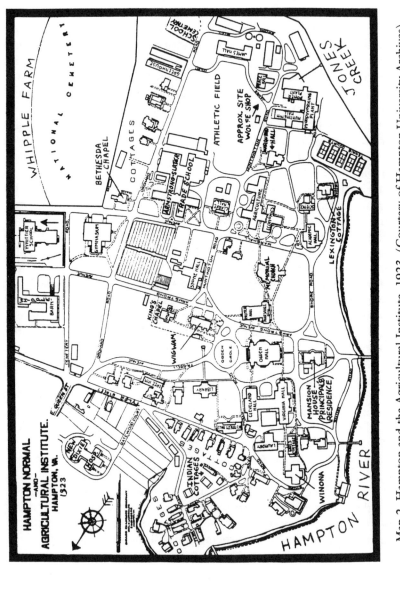

Map 2. Hampton and the Agricultural Institute, 1923. (Courtesy of Hampton University Archives)

the Native American. Founded in 1824, the United States Office of Indian Affairs emerged organizationally weak from the Civil War, and by the late 1860s transcontinental railroads laden with white settlers were shattering the Indian removal policy conceived by Jefferson and carried out by Jackson. The distinct, "permanent" Indian frontier was gone. Thus President Grant recast the removal policy to concentrate as many of the western tribes as possible onto reservations within two large tracts of land, one north of Nebraska and the other south of Kansas, near the removed eastern tribes.

By 1870 all three components of Grant's "Peace Policy" had come together: the placing of all Indians on reservations, the nomination of Indian agents by Christian churches rather than by political patronage, and the presidential appointment of a nine-man Board of Indian Commissioners. The reservation system served to separate whites and Indians, clear the path for westward expansion, and force Indians into a settled lifestyle that would allow their eventual "civilization." The selection of agents by religious boards began when Grant, having been deprived by the House of power to appoint military officers as Indian agents, retaliated by using the boards to deny the House its eagerly anticipated congressional patronage. Grant charged the Board of Indian Commissioners with supervising the Indian Office's expenditure of funds, inspecting its field agencies, and generally advising the office, as well as informing the public about the conduct of Indian affairs. In short, Indians off the reservation were to be dealt with by the army, those on the reservation by the missionary, with the commissioners monitoring both overseers.

But Grant's Indian policy was weakened by public protests and jurisdictional disputes. The plan to concentrate Indians at a couple of central locations was abandoned after the controversial removals of the Ponca, Northern Cheyenne, and Nez Perce, while southwestern and Pacific Coast tribes were being surrounded by whites in place. At the same time, many religious boards were unprepared to assume the burden of appointing agents even as they bickered among themselves over real or imagined slights in the number of agencies considered to be within their respective jurisdictions. Especially after the Battle of the Little Bighorn in 1876, the tenure of religious boards was jeopardized by the public clamor to transfer Indian Affairs from the Interior Department back to the War Department, as before 1849. In 1881 the secretary of the interior officially stopped relying on the religious boards to select agents and returned to patronage appointments. And the Board of Indian Commissioners, its powers never clearly defined, exercised a nebulous "joint control over Indian affairs with the Interior Department."

Nevertheless, although the Peace Policy was formally repudiated by the end of President Hayes's administration, it did not fail totally or end abruptly. In 1871 the negotiation of treaties recognizing Indian tribes as distinct nations had been officially abandoned. Individual guardianship subverted tribal autonomy. Increasingly, as Indians were subdued and brought within range of "civilizing," missionaries paid close attention to Indian affairs, and members of the Board of Indian Commissioners became spokesmen in newly formed organizations for Indian reform. The appointment of field inspectors in 1873 and special investigators in 1879 improved supervision over agencies. There were successful experiments employing Indians to help the agents— after 1872 as their own police, after 1877 as freighters, and after 1883 as judges in a Court of Indian Offenses that ruled against such traditional practices as the Sun Dance, medicine-making, polygamy, and the sale of wives.

By 1880 the disintegration of the Plains Indian roving culture had created a unique opportunity for white reformers. An assemblage of ideas that had been applied to a few tribes much earlier—the replacement of tribal identification by identification with race and American citizenship, of communal landholdings by individual homesteads and private property, of native languages by English, and of the Great Mystery by Christianity—came to the forefront of Indian reform. Behind this policy was a commitment to "education" as the vehicle for a complete cultural transformation of the Indian.[25] According to historian Paul Stuart, after 1865 "Congress and the Indian Office established a reservation system for American Indians and subsequently created a mechanism for destroying it. Education and the allotment of Indian lands, they thought, would end the reservation system and assure the civilization of the Indians."[26]

The policy of having whites educate Indians had appealed to governing officials at least since 1775, when the Continental Congress appropriated $500 for the schooling of Indian youth at Dartmouth College. In 1793 the U.S. government subsidized a small educational project among the Six Nations of New York. A $10,000 "Civilization Fund" was established in 1819 and the next year the government first provided for Indian education in treaties, a practice that became increasingly common. Mechanical training for Indians was incorporated into an academic curriculum at the Choctaw Academy in Scott County, Kentucky (1834) and soon became an integral part of all educational programs for Indians. Five years later the first manual labor school west of the Mississippi was founded at Fort Leavenworth, Kansas, and in 1860 a reservation boarding school opened its doors on the Yakima reservation in Washington. But not until 1870 did the federal government make a general appropriation for Indian education, and even then, much of that money remained unspent.[27]

The federal commitment to school Indians mushroomed after 1880. Between 1877, the year of Congress's first *annual* general appropriation for Indian education, and 1900, the number of Indian schools increased from 150 to 296, school attendance multiplied by five, and the annual funding increased from $20,000 to $2,936,080.[28]

Yet the administration of Indian schools lagged behind the growing educational program and increased federal expenditures. In 1882 Congress created the position of superintendent of Indian Schools without specifying the position's powers. Applicants for appointment to Indian schools did not require qualifications as teachers until 1885. Finally in 1890 a field supervisor of Indian schools was appointed and rules for Indian schools with a uniform course of study codified. In 1891 virtually all school employees were removed from the patronage of the agents and placed under civil service, and between 1897 and 1908 the agents themselves gave way to bonded school superintendents. For the first time the commissioner of Indian Affairs, who was highly enough placed to be subject to public scrutiny, gained the power to appoint Indian agents from among civil service candidates. But even with these developments in federal Indian education, as late as 1923 only Haskell Institute in Lawrence, Kansas, offered a full high school course to Indians.[29]

The founding of Hampton Institute coincided with the beginnings of the Grant Peace Policy, and Armstrong's interest in Indians emerged within a year. While the Indian program at Hampton would take seven years to germinate, it would reach maturity long before the end of its forty-six-year tenure. Its influence was largely over by the 1920s, as critics of assimilation—led by John Collier, President Franklin Roosevelt's future commissioner of Indian Affairs—were marshaling their forces for an "Indian New Deal" that saw value in Indian culture.[30]

Notes

1. SCA, "From the Beginning," in Hampton Institute, *Twenty-Two Years' Work of the Hampton Normal and Agricultural Institute at Hampton, Va., Records of Negro and Indian Graduates and Ex-Students* (Hampton, 1893), p. 1.

2. Thomas C. Richards, *Samuel J. Mills: Missionary Pathfinder, Pioneer and Promoter* (Boston, 1906). This biographical introduction utilizes the following standard works: Helen W. Ludlow, "Personal Memories and Letters of General S. C. Armstrong," 1408 typewritten pages, 1898, Williamsiana Col-

lection, Williams College (hereafter cited as "Personal Memories"); Edith Armstrong Talbot, *Samuel Chapman Armstrong: A Biographical Study* (New York, 1904); Francis G. Peabody, *Education for Life: The Story of Hampton Institute* (1918; reprint, College Park, 1969); Suzanne C. Carson, "Samuel Chapman Armstrong: Missionary to the South" (Ph.D. diss., Johns Hopkins University, 1952); and Robert F. Schneider, "Samuel Chapman Armstrong and the Founding of the Hampton Institute" (Honors thesis, Williams College, 1973), hereafter "Founding Hampton." See also Fritz J. Malval, *A Guide to the Archives of Hampton Institute* (Westport, 1985).

3. Richard Armstrong to Reuben A. Chapman, Feb. 18, 1840, Sept. 8, 1848, Richard Armstrong Papers, Library of Congress, cited in Carson, "Samuel Chapman Armstrong," pp. 18–20.

4. SCA in *Twenty-Two Years' Work,* p. 2; SCA, "Reminiscences," an address given at Oahu College, June 25, 1891, SCA speeches, HUA, pp. 90–91; Schneider, "Founding Hampton," pp. 13–14.

5. Talbot, *Samual Chapman Armstrong,* p. 155; SCA, "Normal School Work among the Freedmen," paper delivered before the NEA at Boston, Aug. 6, 1872, pp. 3–5, in Carson, "Samuel Chapman Armstrong," p. 205.

6. Schneider, "Founding Hampton," pp. 8–10, for quote see Carson, "Samuel Chapman Armstrong," p. 1; Clarissa C. Armstrong to Chapman, Apr. 1, 1836, and SCA to William Nevins Armstrong, Mar. 11, 1854, in Richard Armstrong Papers, in Carson, "Samuel Chapman Armstrong," pp. 21, 31. See also Talbot, *Samuel Chapman Armstrong,* p. 28.

7. Richards, *Samuel J. Mills,* p. 94.

8. Peabody, *Education for Life,* p. 65. For Hopkins see Frederick Rudolph, *Mark Hopkins and the Log: Williams College, 1836–1872* (New Haven, 1956), esp. pp. 23, 48, 184, 237; John Denison, *Mark Hopkins: A Biography* (New York, 1935); Mark Hopkins, "The Living House or God's Method of Social Unity," *Twenty Baccalaureate Sermons,* Aug. 3, 1862, p. 6, in Schneider, "Founding Hampton," pp. 49–50, and SCA in *Twenty-Two Years' Work,* p. 1.

9. Account of Chaplain Ezra D. Simons, New York Monument Commission, *Final Report on Gettysburg and Chattanooga,* 2:890, cited in Everette T. Tomlinson and Paul G. Tomlinson, *A Leader of the Freedmen: The Life and Story of Samuel Chapman Armstrong,* Army and Navy Edition (Philadelphia, 1917), pp. 32–33.

10. Chapman to General L. Thomas, Oct. 12, 1863; M. Hopkins to Thomas, Oct. 12, 1863; Rufus Anderson to Thomas, Oct. 13, 1863, all in Carson, "Samuel Chapman Armstrong," p. 102.

11. Talbot, *Samuel Chapman Armstrong,* pp. 129–32; Carson, "Samuel Chapman Armstrong," pp. 188–92.

12. SCA to A. Hopkins, July 21, 1862, to C. C. Armstrong, Aug. 30, 1864, and to Clara Armstrong, Oct. 5, 10, 1862, all in Ludlow "Personal Memories," pp. 286, 394–96, 262 respectively.

13. SCA to A. Hopkins, Dec. 8, 1862, and to Richard Baxter Armstrong, Dec. 12, 1862, both in Ludlow, "Personal Memories," pp. 282–83, 285; Peabody, *Education for Life,* p. 67.

14. SCA to C. C. Armstrong, Mar. 4, 1864 (published letter), Dec. 20, 1862, Nov. 17, 1863, and Apr. 9, 1865, all in Ludlow "Personal Memories," pp. 286, 352, 435–37; Schneider, "Founding Hampton," pp. 59, 61.

15. For views of Armstrong's personality in addition to those in the standard biographical works listed above see Lyman Abbott, "Snapshots of My Contemporaries: General Samuel Chapman Armstrong—Educational Pioneer," *Outlook* (Aug. 17, 1894): 613–16; Robert C. Ogden, "Samuel Chapman Armstrong: A Sketch," address given at Hampton Institute Founder's Day, Jan. 28, 1894 (New York, 1894); Francis G. Peabody, "Address on Founder's Day," *SW* 27 (Mar. 1898), p. 51; impressions of Armstrong by two black students, William H. Daggs and Robert R. Moton, Misc. Box, Armstrong Family Papers, Williamsiana Collection, Williams College. See also SCA, "Memorandum," Armstrong Papers, HUA.

16. SCA to Richard Baxter Armstrong, Mar. 3, 1866, in Ludlow, "Personal Memories," p. 537.

17. Robert F. Engs, *Freedom's First Generation: Black Hampton, Virginia, 1861–1890* (Philadelphia, 1979), esp. pp. xvii, 45, 85, 164. On Port Royal, see especially Willie Lee Rose, *Rehearsal For Reconstruction: the Port Royal Experiment* (New York, 1964).

18. Examples of Armstrong's more radical statements are "Take the [Freedmen's Bureau] away, and the Negroes might as well be hanged at once," and "rebel politicians exasperate all good men by their abuse and palpable spirit of treason." He found the prospect of President Johnson's impeachment as "better than absolutism to which his temper would have led him." See SCA to C. C. Armstrong, Mar. 15, 1866, and SCA to Mary Jane Armstrong, Apr. 5, 1868, in Ludlow, "Personal Memories," pp. 540, 678, 580 respectively.

19. Engs, *Freedom's First Generation*, pp. 100–19.

20. SCA, "Normal School Work among the Freedmen," paper delivered before the NEA at Boston, Aug. 6, 1872, pp. 3–5, in Carson, "Samuel Chapman Armstrong," p. 205.

21. SCA to Samuel Hunt, May 15, 1866, Va files, frame HI-8907, AMA MSS cited in Edward Kidder Graham, "A Tender Violence: The Life of Hampton Institute in Relation to Its Times (1868–1968)," chap. "The Heavenly City of Samuel Chapman Armstrong," p. 24. Citations below denote that Graham paginated each chapter separately. A copy of this excellent manuscript has been graciously provided to me by the author's daughter, Julia Graham Lear.

22. "An Act to Incorporate the Hampton Normal and Agricultural Institute by the General Assembly of the State of Virginia, Approved June 4, 1870," in Peabody, *Education for Life*, appendix two, pp. 336–39; Carson, "Samuel Chapman Armstrong," p. 185; Schneider, "Founding Hampton," pp. 86–87.

23. Graham, "Tender Violence: Heavenly City," pp. 25–27. The Freedmen's Bureau would contribute over $50,000 to Hampton over the next two years. SCA to C. C. Armstrong, Jan. 26, 1868, in Ludlow, "Personal Memories," pp. 626–28; "An Act to Incorporate" in Peabody, *Education for Life*,

appendix two, pp. 336–39; Carson, "Samuel Chapman Armstrong," pp. 185–87.

24. Engs, *Freedom's First Generation*, pp. 145–48; Carson, "Samuel Chapman Armstrong," pp. 196–98. Southern moderates like Virginia's Superintendent of Public Instruction William H. Ruffner and Robert W. Hughes of the Richmond *Dispatch* supported Hampton, as did Daniel Norton, the black physician from Williamsburg. "An Act to Incorporate" in Peabody, *Education for Life*, pp. 336–39; Carson, "Samuel Chapman Armstrong," pp. 185–87.

25. Standard studies on federal Indian Policy after the Civil War include Robert W. Mardock, *The Reformers and the American Indian* (Columbia, Mo., 1969); Henry E. Fritz, *The Movement for Indian Assimilation, 1860–1890* (Philadelphia, 1963); Loring Benson Priest, *Uncle Sam's Stepchildren: The Reformation of United States Indian Policy, 1865–1877* (Lincoln, 1975); William T. Hagan, *Indian Police and Judges: Experiments in Acculturation and Control* (New Haven, 1966); Robert H. Keller, Jr., *American Protestantism and United States Indian Policy, 1869–1882* (Lincoln, 1983); Francis Paul Prucha, *American Indian Policy in Crisis: Christian Reformers and the Indian, 1865–1900* (Norman, 1976) and *The Great Father: The United States Government and the American Indian* (Lincoln, 1984), 1:485–606, 2: to 779; Frederick E. Hoxie, *A Final Promise: The Campaign to Assimilate the Indians, 1880–1920* (Lincoln, 1984).

26. Paul Stuart, *The Indian Office: Growth and Development of an American Institution, 1865–1900* (Ann Arbor, 1978), p. 15.

27. Evelyn C. Adams, *American Indian Education: Government Schools and Economic Progress* (New York, 1946), pp. 29–37.

28. *ARCIA* 1900, p. 54.

29. Relevant general works on Indian education include Alice C. Fletcher, *Indian Education and Civilization,* Sen. Ex Doc. 95, 48th Cong., 2nd sess. ser. 2264 (Washington, D.C., 1888). This, the first federal study on Indian schools, sums up previous efforts of whites to educate the Indian and then compiles extracts from recent primary government and missionary reports from each state or territory. Since 1946 Adams's *American Indian Education* has served as a primer on the subject. Published at the end of Commissioner John Collier's pluralistic tenure in Indian Affairs, it spans Indian education from European colonial efforts to those of America until 1945. Nevertheless, the book's brevity (108 pages) and lack of footnotes means that it must be supplemented by primary sources like the *ARCIA,* especially its "Reports of the Superintendent of Indian Schools" (after 1884). See also David Wallace Adams, "The Federal Indian Boarding School: A Study of Environment and Response" (Ph.D. diss., Indiana University, 1975); *Rules for Indian Schools, With Courses of Study, Lists of Text Books, and Civil Service Rules* (Washington, D.C., 1892), and William N. Hailmann, *Education of the Indian,* Monographs on Education in the U.S., No. 19 (St. Louis, 1904). Useful material on federal Indian education also appears in Hoxie, *A Final Promise,* esp. pp. 189–210.

Studies of other Indian schools puts Hampton's Indian program in perspective. The oldest and best known study is Elaine Goodale Eastman's biography, *Pratt: The Red Man's Moses* (Norman, 1935). Eastman supported the assimilationist views of this founder of the famous Carlisle Indian School rather than Collier's pluralistic ones. While Collier believed Native Americans had as much to teach whites as to learn in return, Pratt blamed government corruption and duplicity for the Indians' apparent rejection of integration. Other works include Richard Henry Pratt, *Battlefield and Classroom: Four Decades with the American Indian, 1867–1904*, ed. with an intro. by Robert M. Utley (New Haven, 1964); Carmelita Ryan, "The Carlisle Indian Industrial School" (Ph.D. diss., Georgetown University, 1962); Robert L. Brunhouse, "History of the Carlisle School" (Masters thesis, University of Pennsylvania, 1935); and Solon G. Ayers, "An Investigation of Terminal Vocational Education at Haskell Institute" (Ph.D. diss., University of Kansas, 1952).

Robert A. Trennert, Jr., *The Phoenix Indian School* (Norman, 1988), analyzes the mixed results of a government school, focusing on the interaction of its five career superintendents with local boosters and acculturationist federal Indian policymakers. Of course, Phoenix was not biracial, nor eastern, and thus was not a major force in national racial reform (its *Native American* often reprinted material from eastern schools). Phoenix had a larger number of Indian students with more full-bloods than Hampton, but recruited among fewer tribes, mostly those from Arizona. Phoenix's records, much like those compiled at Hampton, preclude sophisticated cultural or intertribal analysis because white administrators ignored Indian viewpoints that challenged their commitment to acculturation.

Guides through the literature on whites educating Indians include Frederick J. Dockstader, *The American Indian in Graduate Studies: A Bibliography of Theses and Dissertations* (New York, 1957); Brewton Berry, *The Education of the American Indian: A Survey of the Literature* (Washington, D.C., 1968); and Francis Paul Prucha, *A Bibliographical Guide to the History of Indian-White Relations in the United States* (Chicago, 1977).

For background on the many ways Native Americans educated their children long before white-run schools like Hampton endeavored to do so, see the introduction of Margaret Connell Szasz's *Indian Education in the American Colonies, 1607–1783* (Albuquerque, 1988). See Forrest Carter, *The Education of Little Tree* (Albuquerque, 1976), an unforgettable but challenged "autobiography" describing Cherokee education.

30. See Lawrence C. Kelly, *The Assault on Assimilation: John Collier and the Origins of Indian Policy Reform* (Albuquerque, 1983) and Hazel W. Hertzberg, *The Search for an American Indian Identity: Modern Pan-Indian Movements* (Syracuse, 1971), pp. 179, 200–205.

2

The Rise of Hampton's Indian Program

The opening sentence of the 1872 premier issue of Hampton's monthly magazine, the *Southern Workman*, acknowledged the importance of Indians to the history of the Virginia peninsula. Indians had welcomed John Smith to the "hallowed" ground around Hampton in 1607. Here, "at the birth place of English civilization in North America," the Indian, the Anglo, and the African had first encountered each other. Three years after landing at Old Point Comfort, Captain Smith had established on the site of an Indian village, "Kecoughtan," the town of Hampton, making it "the oldest contiguous settlement" of Englishmen in the New World; nine years later, in 1619, a Dutch man-o-war had introduced Negro slavery.[1]

The Hampton region continued to be the site of events helping to shape American history. During the Civil War, it was at Hampton that General Benjamin F. Butler issued the famous order declaring slaves "contraband" of war, and the final siege against Richmond was staged from Fortress Monroe. The ironclad ships, the *Monitor* and the *Merrimac*, ushered in modern naval warfare near Hampton Roads. On the very ground where the institute would later stand, Mary Peake, a free Negro, established the first school anywhere for freedmen.

Hampton tradition maintains that its Indian program arose in reply to the "Macedonian cry" for refuge from a group of Plains Indian prisoners under the charge of Captain Richard H. Pratt. When this group of Indians arrived at Hampton on April 14, 1878, General Armstrong viewed the occasion as a recreation of the original meeting of red, black, and white. Seeing himself as the architect of this reunion, he wrote to his wife, Emma, "Indians working beautifully—a millennial dawn—those races at peace. . . . I shall creep like Alex the Great.—I will die at peace like Gen. Wolfe.—I will 'still live' like Noah Webster." Armstrong perceived this moment as providential: since both the displacement of the Indian and the enslavement of the black by the English on this continent had begun in the Hampton area, it seemed only fitting that the whites' "civilizing" efforts begin there as well. In mundane terms, it was Armstrong's own long interest in Indians that now brought them to Hampton, as will be seen. Certainly the arrival at Hampton of Pratt and his St. Augustine prisoners from Fort Marion created a new and significant public awareness of the presumed need to educate Indians to white society. Hampton Institute—and under Pratt's guidance its daughter institution, the Carlisle Indian Industrial School—led the way to the development of the modern Indian school system.[2]

The Roots of Armstrong's Interest in Indians

General Armstrong apparently first became interested in Indians through the influence of Edward Parmelee Smith, corresponding secretary of the AMA and a member of the Hampton Institute Board of Trustees. After Smith was appointed commissioner of Indian Affairs in 1870, Armstrong wrote him that missionary work among Indians was a "great field requiring not so much wise methods as skillful execution." Should the opportunity for serving Indians arise, he added, "please give me a chance for I can ride & throw a lasso and get along gloriously with savages." Quick to see a challenge in the Indians' "snare of injuries and revenge," Armstrong expressed a "lurking fondness for savage life, [for it] requires remarkably keen men to get moral ascendency over them, [and] only miraculous grace can get them." Nevertheless, the general's early interest in Indians was a secondary one; when Smith offered him an unnamed post in the Indian Service, Armstrong declined. He had no intention of leaving Hampton, but observed that "men who crusade for the darky want to do for the Indian."[3]

The general's interest in working with Indians may also have been reinforced by an experiment at Howard University in Washington, D. C., where a few Indians were being educated in the early 1870s. Arapaho Philip Sheridan Labaree of the Wind River reservation, Squaxon Charles Robertson, and Emmunuska, or Minnie Tappan, a Cheyenne, attended Howard.[4] These three Indians were to be part of a more ambitious scheme for Indian education at Howard, or so assumed Samuel F. Tappan. Tappan, the sponsor of namesake Minnie Tappan and a member of the Indian Peace Commission, was also an abolitionist and a second cousin to AMA founders Lewis and Arthur Tappan. Armstrong undoubtedly had the Howard experiment in mind when in 1872 he wrote Emma, "I am on the track of some more money—it will be necessary to prove that the darky is an Indian in order to get it: but I can easily do that. . . . Keep dark and send me your thoughts on the identity of the Indian and the darky—SAME THING, aren't they?"[5]

However, Armstrong at this point was still not entirely convinced that educating Indians at Hampton would pay or that the students could be "civilized." Editorials in the *Southern Workman,* his mouth-piece, show this uncertainty. For example, he urged in the May 1873 issue that "we cease to trust to the reason and honor of a faithless and barbarous enemy." Referring to the sums Congress spent on Indian education, he concluded that "our present relations with the Indians are so expensive that a dozen such institutions as Hampton might be endowed from the outlay of a single year, an outlay too, which is ap-parently entirely profitless."[6] Nevertheless, Armstrong's willingness to educate at least a few Indians clearly predated the arrival of Pratt's charges. Indeed, fully six months before the captives arrived in April 1878 and three months before the start of negotiations in January, Hampton had already enrolled its first Indian pupil, Peter Johnson.

Johnson's presence at Hampton was the culmination of a sequence of events that began three years earlier in September 1874, when a trio of Indians was brought East by John Wesley Powell, a moving force behind the United States Geological Survey. Powell's pioneering eth-nological work among western Indians would lead to his founding of the Smithsonian Institution's Bureau of Ethnology in 1879. While con-ducting geological surveys in Utah, Powell had employed the Indian interpreter Richard D. Komas to help persuade the Utes to remove to Unitah Agency, away from Mormon influence. Three Utes—Komas, Johnson, and John Patterson—accompanied Powell when he returned to the East. The three were placed at Lincoln University, a prominent black liberal arts college in Chester County, Pennsylvania, and there they attended classes with blacks. After Patterson left for home and Komas died, Johnson found himself sole testament to Indian recep-tivity to "civilized" eastern education. Even though Principal I. W. Randall reported that Johnson was doing well, the Indian Office re-fused to pay his bills. Consequently, Johnson was transferred to the tidewater school by his scholarship donor, New Yorker William E. Dodge of Phelps Dodge & Co., whose philanthropy connected him to numerous organizations serving blacks or Indians.[7]

Johnson arrived at Hampton on October 31, 1877. For the next twenty months—the length of his mutually unsatisfactory stay—Johnson pleaded with the Indian Office for permission to return home, but was told by Commissioner Ezra A. Hayt that he must first show sufficient progress. Johnson was unhappy because his refusal to per-form manual labor prompted Armstrong, feeling that the "trouble is we have no basis for good discipline for Indians," to suspend him, first from school and then from rations. The principal wrote Hayt that "corporal punishment will never do and being sent home is being sent to an earthly Paradise. For this reason I would like to try Military prisoners like the Nez Perce."[8]

In fact, in the fall of 1877, before negotiating with Pratt over the St. Augustine prisoners, the general had attempted to capitalize on public interest in Chief Joseph's heroic trek to reach Canada. Armstrong had made two proposals to Secretary of Interior Carl Schurz for bringing captive Nez Perce from Fort Leavenworth, Kansas, to Hampton. The first proposition offered to board, clothe, and educate the entire Nez Perce tribe, or "not less than 150 Indians of all ages, for a period of three years, at a per annum rate of $250 each for the first year and $220 for the remaining two years." It is likely that Armstrong intended to colonize the tribe at Shellbanks, a property five miles from Hampton that was soon to become the school farm. The second and more modest proposition was to educate twenty-five Nez Perce youth, accompanied by an army officer and an interpreter, at Hampton for three years at an average cost of $238 per annum. He offered to construct a building, not to exceed $6,500 in cost for the purpose, and promised the cooperation of the authorities at Fortress Monroe in disciplining recalcitrant Indians.[9]

Armstrong spoke to President Hayes about these schemes, and had the chairman of the House Committee on Indian Affairs, Alfred Scales, bring the appropriation before his committee in November 1877. But the attempt to duplicate Captain Pratt's reputed success in domesticating Indian prisoners of war foundered because no government agency agreed to fund his Nez Perce project. During the next year, Armstrong would unsuccessfully try, with Pratt's assistance, to add the Nez Perce to the St. Augustine prisoners then at Hampton.[10]

As the preceding discussion has shown, the first eastern boarding schools to enroll Indian students were not Hampton and Carlisle, but Howard and Lincoln universities. Because they educated few Indians and garnered little publicity, however, Howard and Lincoln were not recognized as precedent setting. Neither institution formulated an organized, well-developed plan leading to the proliferation of Indian schools; nevertheless they set the stage for the larger and more successful endeavors at Hampton and Carlisle.

Indian education at Hampton arose neither through providence nor accident but rather through the calculation and design of the principal. Using Peter Johnson as his guinea pig, Armstrong had clearly begun envisioning a program of Indian education at Hampton even before the "Macedonian cry" from Fort Marion rang out. In wooing the Nez Perce, Armstrong had merely looked in the wrong direction; Pratt's plea put Armstrong on the right road. Thus Pratt played an important role in the inception of Hampton's Indian program. Yet later he would become one of its most vocal critics, countering Armstrong's racial views with his own convictions.

The Racial Views of Captain Pratt

Of humbler origins than Armstrong, Richard Henry Pratt was born on December 6, 1840, in Rushford, New York, the eldest son of Richard and Mary Herrick Pratt. In 1846 the Pratts moved to Logansport, Indiana. When Richard the younger was nine years old, his father was murdered by a fellow prospector in the California Gold Rush. Raised in Indiana by his mother, a devout Methodist, Richard received only two years of formal education before going to work to help support his family. The mature Pratt was a solidly built and physically fit six feet. His kindly looking face, pitted from smallpox, showed the supreme confidence generally born from a healthy ignorance of one's own shortcomings. Having served for four years as a corporal during the Civil War, he was promoted to lieutenant in 1864. Mustered out in 1865, Pratt spent an unhappy year in the hardware business in Logansport before reenlisting. In the spring of 1867 he was stationed at Fort Arbuckle, Indian Territory. Commissioned as a second lieutenant of the newly formed Tenth Cavalry, he rose to captain in 1873. This, the first black cavalry regiment, was largely composed of recently freed slaves who had been recruited in Little Rock, Arkansas. The unit had white officers and Indian scouts—Cherokee, Choctaw, Osage, and Tonkawa.

This juxtaposition of black, white, and red was crucial in generating the unchanging racial philosophy Pratt would soon crystallize. Pratt had been at Fort Arbuckle only a few days when a conversation with Major Amos S. Kimball led him to consider the legal position of blacks and Indians for the first time, and to realize that he, as a white officer over them, might soon face a serious and enduring moral dilemma. Inasmuch as Lieutenant Pratt had sworn "to support and defend the Constitution," he believed that, should the pending Fourteenth Amendment become part of the Constitution, the "Negro could not be relegated in army service to the Negro units of enlisted men solely, and the Indian could not continue to be imprisoned on separate tribal reservations."[11] His approval of the Fourteenth Amendment underscored the compromising position in which its ratification placed him, and he commented in later life that army units "composed entirely by colored men, officered by white officers, [violated] the Constitution of the United States, and I have ever since held that this violation by the Government of its Constitution has been full example and even warrant for all the 'Jim Crow' car and other harsh enactments of States and communities in denial of equal rights to the colored race."[12] Pratt also supported the Fifteenth Amendment and Negro voting.

Perhaps because he led black cavalrymen and Indian scouts on the frontier, Pratt made decisions with racial implications in a more flexible and practical manner than his superiors may have. Although on the one hand he supported the conquering of Indian peoples at any cost, on the other he could look beyond race when dealing with "civilized" individuals. After Custer massacred Indian families on the Washita River in 1868, soldier Pratt enthusiastically wrote his wife that the Indians had been badly whipped, "General Sheridan being determined to give them a thrashing." On another occasion, however, when a white and a black private clashed over which one of them would be the colonel's orderly, Pratt settled the dispute without reference to race. After making both men remove their shoes and trousers, he gave the job to the black private on the basis of cleaner socks and underwear.[13]

The key to Pratt's racial attitude was his heartfelt belief in the Protestant ethic and the American creed. He argued that the "violation of these principles has caused about all our Negro and Indian problems." Given this belief system and his direct and varied exposure to both blacks and Indians on the frontier, he came to view racial and cultural differences as environmental impediments that could be rather simply overcome through individual assertion and education. Years later, in reporting the events that led to the establishment of Carlisle, Pratt underlined his experience with black soldiers:

> I found many of the men of the command most capable. [George Washington] Williams, since the able historian of the colored race and American minister to Haiti, was a 1st sergeant in one of the companies. I often commanded Indian scouts, took charge of Indian prisoners and performed other Indian duty which led me to consider the relative conditions of the two races. The negro, I argued, is from as low a state of savagery as the Indian, and in 200 years' association with Anglo-Saxons he has lost his languages and gained theirs; has laid aside the characteristics of his former savage life, and, to a great extent, adopted those of the most advanced and highest civilized nation in the world, and has thus become fitted as a fellow citizen among them. This miracle of change came from association with the higher civilization. Then, I argued, it is not fair to denounce the Indian as an incorrigible

savage until he has had at least the equal privilege of association. If millions of black savages can become so transformed and assimilated . . . there is but ONE PLAIN DUTY RESTING UPON US with regard to the Indians, and that is to relieve them of their savagery and other alien qualities by the same methods used to relieve the others.

Thus Pratt's view was that Indian education should be built upon what he saw as the lessons of the black experience in America, and the success that Negro assimilation of American civilization represented. Pratt said of blacks, "Comparing their condition, their rights and privileges, their numbers, and the position to which many of them have attained in the country with their condition before they came to this country, two hundred and fifty years ago, it is evident we have an example to guide us in forming a conclusion in regard to our Indians."[14]

Not until the late 1870s did the precedent set by the black American experience provide a practical model for Indian reform. At this time, the Plains Wars, the destruction of the buffalo, and the encroachments of great numbers of white squatters onto tribal lands forced many of the western tribes to make some accommodation to white society. When many Americans believed that the only good Indians were dead ones, Pratt turned to the black experience to argue by analogy that a dark-skinned people bearing a "foreign" culture did not have to face extermination or starvation when inundated by Anglo-Saxon civilization. Unlike immigrants from Europe, neither blacks nor Indians had become associated with the Republic through choice; it was also sometimes assumed that they had shared similar lifestyles in their indigenous state because both lived in tribal arrangements. Both faced color prejudice, and their acculturation, much less assimilation, was generally viewed as a rural rather than an urban "problem."

Pratt's belief in the Indians' potential equality and in association with whites as a means of achieving it was not born of an egalitarian impulse in the modern pluralistic sense; he had no respect for either traditional African or Indian cultures. His approach, as might be expected from a career soldier, was forceful. In numerous addresses, Pratt contrasted the segregation and isolation forced upon Indians through the reservation system with what he termed the comparatively humane school of slavery, which made indispensable workers, devoted Christians, and English-speaking citizens out of exotic Africans. Pratt asserted that "I look upon slavery for the Negro as exemplifying a higher quality of Christianity than any scheme that either Church or State has originated and carried out in massing, controlling and supervising the

Indians. Slavery did not destroy the Negro race, but increased it. Yet slavery took away all the Negro's many languages, broke up his tribal relations and his old life absolutely and at once; [the slave received] in the main, kindly care, supervision, and direction, while the Indians' case has been the exact opposite." Pratt believed that the element of force, or "assimilation under duress," would also be needed to transform Indians culturally, because nothing else would ensure their necessary constant contact and intimate association with whites.[15]

Pratt saw that the different treatment received by blacks and Indians arose from the greed of the white man: "Greed made the Negro property, and brought him into the country as an article of commerce; scattered him over the land, and placed him under individual civilizing influences. Because he was property it was policy to increase his industrial capacity, to multiply his numbers, to make him forget his own tongue and learn that of the country. . . . On the contrary, the Indian had nothing of this value in him. . . . Finding enslavement impracticable, the white man . . . found in the lands [the Indian] possessed all the commercial value to be derived from him."[16]

To obtain Indian land it was not necessary to establish direct contact with the Indian; indeed what settlers wanted was the land without the Indian. Thus the Indian was "thrown back upon himself" and denied participation in mainstream society. Pratt never suggested a mechanism comparable to greed through which Indian absorption could be consummated, although he contended the reason Indians "have not become civilized and incorporated in the nation is entirely our fault." Later reformers viewed Pratt's failure to recognize that most tribal Indians resisted assimilation as his biggest delusion. The young Pratt's experience of having had to "contribute something to the support of a widowed mother, or suffer disgrace in the poor house or starve," led him to believe that the difficult circumstances of his childhood were "the greatest blessing that could have come to me. The Indians in their old estate face exactly the same condition." Because he never blamed the Indians themselves for their separation from whites, Pratt was respected by Indians of varying opinions.[17]

Pratt's objective of immediate and complete integration of Indians as individuals into white society stood out impressively in his analysis of Indian reform. His single-mindedness withstood opposition from an environment in which virtually every institution implicitly dealt with Indians en bloc as a separate people. Pratt considered it useless to attempt to "uplift" masses of Indians on reservations. To achieve success as Americans, talented blacks had been forced to separate themselves as individuals from African tribes and southern plantations. He pointed out that "Frederick Douglass lifted up his race by escaping from it and going out into the midst of our best civilization. So the Indian to stand alone or to lift up his race must escape from the slavery of reservation life."[18] Returning from eastern schools to home conditions would mean slowing, if not halting, the development toward "civilization." Although he envisioned the sunset of Native American cultures, Pratt considered himself a "friend of the Indian," and never gave any sign of regarding Indians as inherently inferior to whites.

Given Pratt's objective, it is not surprising that he was hostile to the reservation and to all those he saw as contributing to its survival. Thus he identified as enemies to Indian development people whom others often viewed as the Indians' friends. In Pratt's eyes, white missionaries, anthropologists, merchants who sold native crafts, most reformers, and employees of the Office of Indian Affairs had vested interests in the continuation of the reservation system and therefore retarded, if not opposed, Indian assimilation. He viewed the Office of Indian Affairs as a paternalistic bulwark for preserving treaties with provisions for subsidies and annuities that condemned Indians to live in idleness as a special people.

Not only did Pratt ignore the fact that annuities were payments for Indian land given up by treaty but he also drew another debatable analogy from black history when he asserted that the "early death of the 'Freedmen's Bureau,' with its 'forty acres and a mule,' was an infinite blessing to the negro himself. . . . Far better for the Indians had they never been placed under such a bureau system. Then the great law of necessity and self-preservation would have led the individual Indian to find his true place [within white society], and his real emancipation would have been speedily consummated." If the policy adopted for Indians "had been pursued by this government in its treatment of the colored race," Pratt said, "we would now have conditions in the Southern states similar to that upon our Indian reservations."[19]

Yet the captain's strongest bias was not racial but cultural; he desired a multiracial society where everyone acted like Anglo-Saxons of the Judeo-Christian persuasion. He firmly opposed black colonization, nationalism, group economy, and even milder race identifications such as mutual benefit societies, and race pride. Pratt asserted that all separate organizations and schools hindered racial advancement "because such schemes inevitably and always lack in largest liberty of opportunity and the necessary inspiration of highest example and achievement."[20] For both Indians and blacks, "equal ability comes when the same education and training is enforced during association."[21] Although Pratt typically blamed white racism for the black's inferior position in society, he also argued that "if the negro would step away from all that [singing of spirituals and retaining items of race pride] and settle down to work in all lines, and pay no attention to the fact that he is a negro . . . the prejudice against him would pretty soon disappear; but everywhere throughout the land he is paraded as a negro, and that is his greatest drawback." Regarding Indians Pratt maintained, "If you project any course of education for the Indian that does not in the fullest sense kindly invite him to disintegrate his tribes, enter into and be one with us [working in all occupations] you will block the way to his salvation. . . . All else is conflict. . . . Separate peoples and languages in one home beget suspicions and antagonisms."[22]

Pratt's reliance on black precedents for Indian reform carried an implicit affirmation of the African saga in America. Yet he was never a spokesman on behalf of blacks, even though insisting that until the Negro has a "full, fair and equal chance to develop all his best powers to the highest extent . . . all assertion of lower order and incompetence is baseless." After 1900, however, when the position of blacks in America had declined, he began emphasizing immigrants rather than blacks as role models for Indians, and resented Indians being classed with blacks.[23]

Pratt believed that Indians had received worse treatment from whites than had blacks, although "the Indians are a nobler race than the Africans, and will make a more valuable addition to our nation's life." What he expected this Indian contribution to be was unclear, however, since he saw no value in the cultures in which that nobility expressed itself. Always more pro-Indian than antiblack, the captain openly called for the amalgamation of Indians and whites, but only refused to condemn liaisons between black men and white women. Pratt did speak out publicly against lynching blacks and against defining mulattoes as Negro, and rejected charges that blacks were immoral.[24] In short, he typically defended Indians and blacks against whites, but sided with the Indian against the black when he found himself placed in a position between them, as was often the case after the Fort Marion prisoners came to Hampton Institute.

The Coming of Pratt's St. Augustine Prisoners to Hampton Institute

In April 1875, after two centuries of pushing Indians west, a new solution to the "Indian problem" was attempted by sending them east for punishment. General Philip H. Sheridan ordered that seventy-two

Kiowas, Comanches, Cheyennes, and Arapahos imprisoned at Fort Sill (in present day Oklahoma) be transported to St. Augustine, Florida. Pratt, who had arrested the men for "murders and depredations" on the frontier, was assigned to accompany them to Florida as their jailer. While they were still at Fort Sill, the attorney general's office declared Sheridan's plan to try the Indians under a military commission illegal: a nation could not declare a state of war on its own wards.[25]

Thus at the time the captives were transported by train from Fort Sill to St. Augustine, not one of them had had his guilt or innocence tested in any court, either military or civilian. Pratt lamented that "they were not tried. The Constitution of the U.S. which provides that no man 'shall be deprived of life, liberty and property without due process of law' was not observed in their case. I [transported the prisoners] under military orders. I felt uncomfortable about it and did what I could to ameliorate their condition." Nevertheless, one Cheyenne died en route and another soon after arrival: Grey Beard was shot by a guard after jumping from the moving train, and Lean Bear starved himself, both incidents testifying to the desperate state of mind of some members of the group.[26]

Once at St. Augustine, Pratt removed the prisoners' shackles and staked his military commission on permitting the Indians to police themselves. He gave them liberal visiting privileges in town and fostered a semblance of independence by establishing an Indian court, which, however, depended on his approval of its verdicts. To teach the Indians self-support, Pratt had them polish sea-beans, work in orange groves and packing houses, and clear palmetto groves abandoned by black laborers. According to Pratt, the Indians posed such keen competition to local white workers that a senator from Florida introduced a resolution in Congress to limit Indian labor.

The prisoners were also given the rudiments of an English education by two northern women: Miss Sarah Mather, who had previously taught at an AMA industrial training school for black girls in St. Augustine, and Miss Perrit, who had operated a young women's boarding house during the war. Pratt judged that good treatment greatly changed the Indians. In 1878, after the Indians had been confined for three years, "they wanted to quit their tribes and abandon their old lives forever, and asked to have their women and children sent to them and to remain in Florida . . . [in order to] make good civilized uses of their lives."[27] Their request was denied by Washington.

The chain of events resulting in the St. Augustine prisoners' transfer to Hampton Institute began in November 1877 when Sheridan and the War Department finally endorsed the recommendation of Indian Commissioner Hayt to release the Indians. Afraid that returning them to the reservation would undo the supposed benefits achieved by associating with whites, Pratt looked for alternatives. Although Pratt's first choice was to place his younger charges in some northern white agricultural and mechanical school, no school agreed to take them. By early January 1878 Pratt turned to a school for blacks and wrote to Armstrong, an acquaintance of the captain's principal teacher, Sarah Mather. At first neither she nor Pratt was able to persuade Hampton to take more than one of the St. Augustine prisoners. Armstrong faced opposition from Hampton board members, like his former Sunday school teacher in Hawaii and present institute treasurer James F. B. Marshall, the "tail on Armstrong's kite," who claimed that he and the majority of the trustees had little faith in the capacity of the red man. Feeling that the general already was shouldering too much responsibility, they opposed the admittance of Indians.[28]

A second factor may have contributed to Armstrong's reluctance. As Pratt's Indians now dressed, spoke, behaved, and worked much like whites, they lacked the attraction of the colorfully "wild" Nez Perce, whose "taming" would have brought glory to Hampton. In addition, Pratt's Indians had been refused government money for further education and had not recently received much attention in the newspapers. Pratt said that only after "considerable persuasion" did Armstrong agree to take "not over six of the Indians." But later, when "he found the distinction of the people who were willing to pay for this education, it influenced him to take all he could get."[29]

Foremost among the notable Americans who were involved with the Fort Marion Indians was Episcopal Bishop Henry B. Whipple of Minnesota, who preached Sunday sermons for the prisoners.[30] He wrote an editorial on their behalf in the New York *Tribune,* saying the inmates hung on his words "as if I were a messenger of life." Although four were supposed to join Whipple's school in Faribault, Minnesota, a visit to Hampton convinced him to ask Armstrong to keep the Indians. The general courted the bishop and his powerful Episcopal constituency by placing Hampton Indians under the care of Reverend J. J. Gravatt, the rector of old St. John's Church in Hampton. Armstrong informed Whipple that in the seventeenth century this church had solemnized the first Protestant baptism of Indians in America. Pratt later recalled this occurrence as epitomizing a central characteristic of Armstrong's leadership—that "his plans always contemplate owning men and their consciences." The general told Pratt that through Gravatt he would "capture" the influence of Whipple and Bishop William Hobart Hare, another powerful Episcopalian interested in Indians. In this chess game of missionary advantage, Pratt reported Armstrong told him that "Gravatt can take care of the Bishops and I'll add hundred or two dollars to his pay: that will catch him: he is human."[31] Whipple and Hare became lifelong supporters of Hampton's Indian program.

Other important northerners, some of whom wintered in St. Augustine, a popular resort town, also expressed interest in the prisoners. Harriett Beecher Stowe taught a few of the prisoners' classes and was so impressed by the Indians' transformation that she wrote of it in the *Christian Union* and attempted to place some of them in Amherst Agricultural School.[32] Mrs. Joseph Larocque and Dr. Horace Curuthers of New York took some Indians into their homes. General John Eaton, a former assistant commissioner of the Freedmen's Bureau and then commissioner of education, praised the effort.

All but five of the twenty-two Indians who requested to remain in school in the East ended up at Hampton; northern friends and local residents in Florida raised money for their transportation and scholarships. Pratt, setting aside his disdain for things Indian, told Armstrong that the Indians had made over $5,000 selling native arts and crafts.[33] In fact several of these Indians, including Bear's Heart, Cohoe, and Squint Eyes among the Cheyenne, and Koba and Etahdleuh among the Kiowa, were major artists in the Plains tradition of picture writing. When the AMA picked up the tab for thirteen of Pratt's Indians, including some of these artists, to enter Hampton, Armstrong realized that there was clearly more to be gained than to be lost by the Indian presence.[34]

Thus Pratt arrived with the surviving sixty-two of his Indians at Hampton on Sunday, April 14, 1878. Fifteen of these Indians were to remain at Hampton, later to be joined by two more. Pratt was temporarily assigned to assist Armstrong, while General J. H. O'Bierne escorted the main party of prisoners to tribal encampments in the West. During this first exposure to Armstrong and his ideas about biracial education, Pratt praised Hampton's industrial system with its "plain English book course," and stated that its moral and religious training met the needs of blacks and Indians alike. He was "unable to find any school so nearly meeting my views for Indian education." He sought to calm anticipated fears, informing the largely black audience in his introductory speech that there would be no race war at Hampton: the Indians had come to work. Then Minimic, the former war chief of the Cheyenne, broke the ice by telling his listeners, as Pratt interpreted, that the "skins of the people he meets here are just alike, colored, and these young men here all say to you, 'How do ye do?'"[35]

Although it would later be feared that Indians and blacks might become intimate, or unite against whites, the initial concern of school officials was the possibility of red against black or against white. In the unabashed style Armstrong reserved for friends, he wrote to Robert Curtis Ogden (the partner in John Wanamaker's famous Philadelphia store who was a Hampton trustee and later a moving force behind the Southern Education Board) that Pratt's Indians were "terrible cutthroats once but are said to be tamed. Now & then they will try to scalp a darky but their war hatchets won't make much impression on him." One white teacher said that many of her female colleagues "got rather panicky" when dealing with unruly Indians.[36] Apparently even some of the black students were fearful of the Indian newcomers. Rumors spread that Hampton Indians had gone on the warpath; indeed on one occasion after the next group of Indians arrived, the entire Indian population briefly left Hampton, intending to camp for the winter near Yorktown. Such trepidation about the St. Augustine prisoners proved excessive, however. Although these four separate tribes had once united against whites on the Plains, their defeat and subsequent confinement had rendered them the most tractable group of Indians that the institute was to have for many years. Nevertheless, real fear induced Armstrong to hire the Indians' jailer in Indian Territory, Lieutenant Henry Romeyn, as commandant of the school, and to depend on the might of Fortress Monroe in case of emergency.[37]

Despite fears of Indian wildness, however, the history of contact between colonists and Indians in the vicinity of Hampton had left a residue of concern for Indian welfare, visible largely as a glorification of colonial heritage. A few of the Virginians were, and many others pretended to be, the descendants of Pocahontas and John Rolfe. The institute hoped to capitalize on this vanity, but at first such blue bloods, while supporting federal Indian education, resented those of their own stock being educated with their former slaves. The *Southern Workman* of October 1879 reported that "the arrival of Indians at this school for Negroes was naturally not well received by many who had very different ideas of the two races."[38]

Even before the Indians came to Hampton the Richmond *Dispatch* had complained about the proposed biracial program, claiming that Indians and blacks were as distinct as blacks and whites. Any association of the two races "must result in discord, conflict, and retardation of improvement, population, and thrift." The *Dispatch* would not "break the spirit" of the original owner of the soil and "subdue the manhood of his nature by bringing him into an alliance [with the Negro] which will endow him with no valuable quality." Thus the initial reaction of the Virginians was to maintain a clear separation of

Indians from blacks. By the mid-1920s, however, so much intermarriage between the two groups had occurred in the tidewater that the Race Integrity Law classed all of the state's Indians as Negroes.[39]

Although not sharing any of the white Virginians' idea of Indian superiority, even radical local blacks at first opposed the admission of Indians to Hampton. John W. Cromwell, the militant editor of the *Virginia Star,* charged Armstrong with attempting to turn the institute into a reform school for Indian criminals, inasmuch as the first Indians were prisoners and, he argued sarcastically, its strict military discipline and denial of personal freedom made the school admirably suited as a penal institution. Cromwell had long believed that Hampton's reliance on industrial training would relegate Negroes to a second class citizenship. He now asked his black readers, "Are we wards?" (American Indians having been defined as such by the Supreme Court's 1831 decision in *The Cherokee Nation v. The State of Georgia.*)[40] In truth, Indians were not entitled to be citizens, voters, or jurors. As members of "domestic dependent nations," Indians owed no allegiance to the United States or its flag. Thus Cromwell felt the admission of Indians was a further tacit disavowal of the black contribution to national life, and of the freedom and rights blacks had won.

At the same time, the more conservative blacks attending Hampton viewed the new arrivals as interlopers. Booker T. Washington reported that "he and most of the student body believed that since Hampton was established for the benefit of the Negro, the Indian should not have been permitted to come in."[41] James C. Robbins, Hampton's first black teacher of Indians, believed that black students doubted Armstrong's commitment to their education, thinking that "in time this institution will be wholly for the Indians." This opinion did not appear entirely baseless. In 1881 the general's aunt implored him to admit enough Indians to gain a 50-50 ratio between black and Indian students, as a way to increase contributions from whites. In December 1881 J. D. W. Giles, a Hampton teacher, reported that, along with some other black students, Sarah Gerdiner was to be discharged in order to make room for additional Indian pupils because there was not enough room at Hampton to accommodate them all.[42] Although few blacks were in fact replaced by Indians, it did not take many such dismissals to provoke black protest. Armstrong reacted strongly to quell the fears of black students that Hampton was changing its mission, pointing out that Negro enrollment was greater than ever before. And he built additional quarters for Indians partly to allay the assertion that Negroes were being crowded out.[43]

Yet students were not alone in wondering whether Armstrong was becoming more interested in Indians than blacks. At this time, the bulk of Armstrong's personal correspondence and published articles concerned Indians rather than blacks. Even as Hampton trustee and fundraiser Thomas K. Fessenden agreed to approach railroad magnate Collis P. Huntington for funds to start Hampton's Indian program, he reminded Armstrong to give equal time to the Negro interest. He told the general that the latter "is by far the most important interest, and is that for which Hampton is designed, and it makes by far the strongest foundation for you *in the long run*. I think it would be a mistake to make it secondary. The great mass of our good people feel that the Indian effort at Hampton is comparatively unimportant and short lived." Fessenden concluded that the division of Armstrong's interests and energies diminished his effectiveness as a reformer for blacks, working against the purpose of the school and the wishes of its trustees. Fessenden asked Armstrong not to enlarge the Indian Department without the expressed approval of the executive committee. Commandant Romeyn wrote Fessenden in agreement, saying that Armstrong "should not divert any more funds or attention from what was the intention of the friends of the Institute at the time it was founded."[44]

Armstrong denied that Hampton was conceived as a school for blacks only, pointing out that its charter from the state of Virginia in 1870 did not mention race in its mandate "for the instruction of youth." Presumably for legal purposes, as a contingency in case nonblacks came, the general had in fact attempted to include the phrase "without distinction of color" in Hampton's charter. When Virginia's House of Delegates refused to grant the charter with such wording, Armstrong interpreted not mentioning color to mean "without distinction" just the same. In *Twenty-Two Years' Work,* Armstrong defined Hampton's mission as being for the "despised races" of the nation and further asserted that "while chiefly for the Negro, [it] is really for all who need it." Even as he claimed consistency with the institute's original purpose, Armstrong calmed those fearing an "Indian takeover" by saying occasionally that the Indian work at Hampton was "incidental" or "illustrative rather than exhaustive."[45] In truth, however, the fact that overall only about one in six of Hampton's students would be Indian revealed little about Armstrong's relative interest in the two races.

The Expansion of the Indian Program and the Outing System

The St. Augustine prisoners had not been at Hampton a month when Armstrong, ignoring those opposed to biracial education there, developed a bold concept for its expansion, "so long as" the administration in Washington "understood that the success of the experiment would . . . lead to important and extended efforts for the Indian race."[46] From the start, growth was envisioned as a matter not only of bringing more Indians to Hampton but of sending them forth from it to summer employment in the North.

Armstrong sought no less than a national commitment to Indian education. First, to showcase Hampton's Indians, he used the president's wife, Lucy Ware Webb Hayes, as a conduit for bringing a "choice and noble company" to the May 1878 commencement, which included President Hayes, Secretary of Interior Carl Schurz, and other members of the cabinet. Armstrong now persuaded the administration, in principle, to finance the education of fifty Indians per year at $167 each, although the money for each year would require a separate vote of approval by the House Appropriations Committee.

Still interested in the Nez Perce, Armstrong once more attempted to recruit about fifty of them. With the sanction of Secretary of War George W. McCrary, Pratt was sent to parley with Chief Joseph at Fort Leavenworth. In one of the few failures of his career, Pratt returned without a single child; the Nez Perce vetoed his plan, wanting first to know the fate of the adults. Pratt blamed the outcome on General John Pope, whose aide had been ordered to confer with the Indians, and so must have prejudiced them against the school.[47]

On his return to Washington, Pratt asked McCrary to send him elsewhere to present his case without any interference. The Sioux then were chosen, largely because they were the most "troublesome" of all of the Plains tribes whose subjugation on reservations was not yet certain. Consequently, Pratt canvassed six Sioux agencies along the banks of the Missouri River: Standing Rock, Cheyenne River, Crow Creek, Lower Brule, Spotted Tail, and Yankton. The experiment gained support in Washington because the authorities openly admitted that the children, once voluntarily relinquished, would act as hostages for the good behavior of their parents.[48] Educational success among these "warlike" Indians would also dramatically refute the prevailing national opinion that Indians could not be "civilized." Moreover, Secretary Schurz had promised Congress that if the Sioux were transferred from the War Department to his Interior Department, and the scheme for removing them to Indian Territory was abandoned, these Indians would make satisfactory progress in a few years toward self-support through farming. It was a bad omen, however, that the captain failed to recruit any students from the bands that government authorities most desired to subdue. These "turbulent" brethren of Red Cloud and

Spotted Tail did not want their children sent to school because "white people were all thieves and liars, and they did not want their children to learn such things."[49]

Not only did Armstrong hope to prove the success of his educational methods on a group of "wild" Indians but he also hoped to demonstrate the benefits of coeducation by recruiting an equal number of both sexes. Coeducation would break new ground in government Indian education. Although this concept remained controversial even for white adolescents, at least one long forgotten private attempt at coeducating Indians had occurred during the colonial period. But Armstrong himself had seen the concept work with good results among Hampton blacks. The general assured Schurz, who became his strongest supporter, that "an experience of ten years in educating together negro adults of both sexes, many of them being of the poorest class, is evidence that the co-education of Indian youth will succeed."[50] In his attempt to muster support for Indian coeducation, Armstrong credited as his inspiration Hayes's statement at a Hampton commencement that "the condition of women is the true gauge of civilization." He contended the educated Indian male would regress unless he found a mate to uphold his new values. But Commissioner of Indian Affairs Hayt argued that coeducation had traditionally failed because the girls inevitably "relapse into barbarism."[51] In this, the first of the skirmishes to plague his relations with every commissioner, Armstrong triumphed.

Pratt's first effort to recruit Indian girls was disappointing; there were only nine among the forty-nine Native Americans comprising Hampton's second group. Generally, Indians resisted sending girls because they usually did the more indispensible labor on reservations, whereas the males, who had lost their traditional role as warriors, were often at loose ends. Ironically, when Pratt managed to enlist a female contingent at Cheyenne River, the girls were dissuaded from going at the final moment by missionaries who feared intermarriage would result at a black institution. Although he encountered this racist attitude in varying degrees among whites at all the Indian agencies, Pratt "found no prejudice against the colored race existing naturally among the Indians anywhere."[52]

Pratt and his party of Indians boarded the last steamer before the Missouri River froze, carrying with them, at Armstrong's request, the Indians' "wild barbarous things" in order to "work that photograph business well."[53] Making use of the adage "clothes make the man," the general envisioned the now famous "before" and "after" photographs of new arrivals at Hampton as a publicity stunt to increase revenue.

The arrival of this group of Indian students on November 5, 1878, transformed Hampton's Indian Department. The new Indians came directly from their aboriginal societies, had little or no previous English schooling, and had not been subdued as prisoners of war. The already partially acculturated St. Augustine prisoners were to act in the words of both Armstrong and Pratt, "leaven for the lump."

There were now actually three cultural groups of Indians at Hampton. For besides thirty-six Sioux, Pratt brought thirteen Hidatsas, Mandans, and Arikaras from the Fort Berthold Agency. Unlike the nomadic and "warlike" Sioux, the Three Affiliated Tribes were peaceful and successful agriculturalists who had remained friendly to the United States throughout the Plains Wars. Pratt found these Indians living at Like-a-fishhook village "more industrious and nearer to self-support in their original state than any others." But the Sioux were their traditional enemies, and this ancient rivalry produced intertribal hostility on campus. The Fort Berthold Indians complained to J. C. Robbins that the Sioux threatened them and carried knives in their moccasins. Consequently, the new building erected to house the Indians had to be permanently partitioned above the first floor.[54] Management became even more difficult because four of the Sioux at Protestant Hampton came from Standing Rock, a Catholic agency. Sectarian issues, added to intertribal tensions, would trouble the Indian program.

Moreover, white staff at Hampton believed tension between blacks and Indians increased when the Sioux came, as it did between Hampton and the community. According to one teacher, "if the contact with the first group of Indians in military array struck terror in the hearts of the black students, one can understand their reactions when they came face to face with forty bronzed, disheveled, long-haired wild men from the far west." The first meeting of blacks and Sioux was one of "fear and reprehension" on both sides: the "awe and dismay" of blacks upon hearing the "terrible tales of these bloodthirsty" Indians, and the Sioux having "almost as wild [a] picture of the black man." Not only did white fear of interracial conflict increase, but coeducation raised the spectre of miscegenation, evoking more protest by white Virginians against biracial education at Hampton.[55]

At the same May 1878 commencement where the general enlisted the aid of the presidential party in bringing a second group of Indians to Hampton, Armstrong and Pratt spoke to Alexander Hyde of Lee, Massachusetts, about securing employment for Indians on thrifty New England farms during the summer. This conversation led to the famous "outing system," and ever since that time partisans have debated which man deserved credit for its founding.[56]

There is no question that Armstrong played a great role in implementing the outing system, by finding an area from which the system could be run, the local families who would participate by boarding Indians, and the man who would direct its operations. Through family and friendships at Williams College and in the ABCFM, Armstrong had ties to the Berkshire Hills, where Lee is located, which he used as a network for outing placements. Hyde, the local director, was a member of Hampton's board of trustees, the uncle of Armstrong's first wife, Emma Walker, and the president of the State Board of Agriculture, which was a useful position for coordinating the outing system. Armstrong also could draw on the experience of having sent about one thousand blacks to Boston for employment during his tenure as district supervisor of the Freedmen's Bureau.[57] Not only was it widely believed that Hampton's summers were too hot and humid for western Indians but Armstrong could not afford to keep them when, except for blacks engaged in agricultural production, the school was practically closed. On outing, it was hoped that Indians would learn "self-sufficiency" and create public sentiment for Hampton, and the need to monitor interracial contact when most of the white staff was away would not exist.

But to credit Armstrong for making the outing system work still leaves unsettled the question of who first conceived the idea. Although Hamptonians often credited the general with the outing system, Armstrong himself never took credit for its conception, despite Pratt's cynical comments that the "constant habit at Hampton of gobbling everything" was occasionally "nauseous." Furthermore, the case for the outing system being the invention of Pratt is strong. The captain asserted that he interested Armstrong in the outing system and spoke to Hyde about it in the general's presence. Pratt could have been inspired by the similar practice of hiring out Indians on reservations. He had in fact found employment among whites for his St. Augustine prisoners in Florida, and a few of these Indians went to live with northern families while others were attending Hampton. The captain himself claimed the black experience of slavery as his model, believing that the domestic and industrial habits of "civilized" Christian life, learned by blacks during slavery, could be duplicated with Indians under the milder system of outing.[58]

The outing system had conceptual links to Pratt's fundamental tenet that Indians should mingle, live, and compete with productive members of white rather than black society. Pratt saw the outing system at Hampton as a way of keeping Indians from being associated in the public mind with blacks. Weaving together red and white interests might even lead to Indians entering the public schools. Somewhat inconsistently, Pratt also believed that the degree of separation between blacks and Indians on school grounds was counterproductive. He complained that racial integration at Hampton "has not been carried out as I suggested, for you have always had an Indian boys' reservation and an Indian girls' reservation permanently established on the school grounds." Apparently Pratt felt that Indians at Hampton were denied the benefit that real association with blacks as a largely acculturated people would bring, while being forced into an artificial association with them as a despised minority. The fully integrated society the captain envisioned would include the equal association of all races.

And it is clear that he was the driving force that saved the outing system at its inception. When Hyde sent back to Hampton the discouraging news that only one patron had volunteered to take an Indian and that the local public was fearful, Pratt told Armstrong that he would take with him to Lee one of the best (i.e., least troublesome) of the Florida boys, Kiowa Etahdleuh, to speak to the farmers. Armstrong shot back, "That's it. Go."[59] Pratt and Etahdleuh arrived in Lee the next evening in time for a missionary meeting of the Congregational church. In two days all of the Indians selected to go on outing were provided for. To what extent they welcomed the experience is unclear, but one of Armstrong's successors said that "some of our Indian boys . . . looked sometimes with a feeling well-nigh akin to disgust on the struggling farmers of rocky New England, [who] seemed to them as mean and small in their dealings."[60] In any event, despite Pratt's ambivalence about the nature of racial contact at Hampton, his determination to implement the outing system may have delayed his open criticism of Hampton and his subsequent departure.

The Departure of Pratt

Captain Pratt's departure from Hampton's Indian program seems in retrospect to have been inevitable from the start, although it did not happen until the end of the 1879 school year. As Armstrong's subordinate, the captain perhaps feared, correctly, that the general's admirers would claim for him the title of founding father of Indian as well as black education. In any case, from at least as early as August 1878 Pratt wanted to begin his own school for Indians. By then he had been told by a reluctant Armstrong that Commissioner "Hayt is anxious to be spending more of the $60,000 given by Congress to educate the Indians at special schools & he is likely to believe you to be the man for him."[61] Pratt's quest for an undisputed arena to work out his particular racial convictions ultimately made it impossible for him to maintain a cooperative venture with Armstrong. Although it is uncertain how sharply Pratt had defined his own goals for Indian education while at Hampton, he could not have reconciled its program with the one he later devised at Carlisle, as a way station for Indians into public education and permanent residence in mainstream American society.

Armstrong never publicly criticized Pratt and apparently valued their relationship, but while at Hampton the captain chafed at losing control of what he considered to be "his" Indians. In early 1879 Pratt notified Secretary of War McCrary that he had fulfilled his mission to remain at Hampton until the Sioux and Fort Berthold Indians were accustomed to life at school and interested in white education. Since Commandant Romeyn, a regular army officer with Indian experience, was already detailed at Hampton (complying with the Morrill Act's detachment of an officer to state agricultural schools), Pratt asked to be returned to his regiment.[62]

But at that point Armstrong actively attempted to prevent Pratt's departure. Since the Indians were now used to Hampton, he warned McCrary that "we may expect new tendencies and forms of trouble to appear," particularly without the captain to enforce labor and discipline. Armstrong even lied a little to highlight his helplessness without Pratt, telling McCrary that he himself "never saw a live Indian until last April."[63] Employing a stratagem devised by McCrary, Armstrong tried to block Pratt's departure by convincing John Goode, the congressman serving the Hampton district, to insert a clause in the annual army appropriations bill that would detail an army officer not above the rank of captain to Indian education. Pratt's name was mentioned. Pratt justly accused Armstrong of attempting to fix his stay at Hampton and plainly told him he was not satisfied there.[64]

Next, the principal proposed that Pratt establish a separate Indian school as a branch of Hampton on the school's back bay farm. However, after surveying the property, Pratt concluded that the proximity to impoverished black "contraband" left during the Civil War and the remoteness of the location from influential whites made the plan unfeasible.[65]

The limits of his considerable persuasiveness exhausted, Armstrong at last acquiesced; accepting his loss with good grace, he even did his best to make Pratt's effort a success.[66] Meanwhile, the captain, blessed by General Sherman, consulted Schurz and McCrary about establishing an Indian school at Carlisle barracks in Pennsylvania.

Since Pratt bluntly reported that he left the institute because he opposed the education of Indians in a school for Negroes, he has been widely but too absolutely regarded as antiblack. In fact, it was Hampton's manner of associating blacks and Indians, under what Pratt believed were segregated circumstances that "fostered [the] principles of raceism [*sic*] and exclusivism," which he always detested for both races. By contrast, in February 1880, a few months after his departure from Hampton, Pratt supported the plan to introduce Indians into Berea College in Kentucky, most likely because the school was integrated. Pratt invited Berea's principal, John G. Fee, to visit Carlisle, where he attempted to convince Fee that Berea could broaden the outlook of the white, black, and red races with the concept of the brotherhood of man.[67]

In later years Pratt recalled his departure from Hampton in the light of what had subsequently become his fully developed view of race relations. He emphasized the differences in historical circumstances between Indians and blacks, which he felt precluded Indians being educated at a black school. The bias against Indians, he contended, was a "ficticious prejudice on both sides," a transitory ignorance arising from attempts on the frontier to isolate Indians from settlers. This bias had become institutionalized in the removal and reservation policies. Southern prejudice against blacks, on the other hand, was exacerbated by the "change in the South from slavery to freedom under circumstances destructive to the resources and wealth of the Southern people." In other words, he felt that, lacking a substantive foundation, the prejudice against Indians would vanish easily through contact, but race antipathy toward blacks would linger with the dislocations of the postbellum southern economy. Pratt asserted that unlike the eight million blacks, "the small number of Indians in the United States [then given at 260,000] rendered their problem a very short one." He claimed that by actively assimilating blacks and immigrants while hesitating over a few Indians, the nation was, in the phrase of Mississippi Senator Lucius Q. C. Lamar "swallowing a camel and straining at a gnat."[68]

Some Advantages for Hampton of an Indian Program

What did Armstrong and the school gain by establishing a permanent Indian program, considering the hostility to Indian education at Hampton felt by many—local southerners, blacks, trustees of the school, and ultimately Pratt? On the most basic level, those supporting Hampton's Indian project were more wealthy, influential, and powerful than its opponents. Thus Hampton's Indian work received special mention in the four annual messages of President Hayes. These were the first presidential pronouncements about Hampton Institute. Armstrong credited President Hayes, who visited Hampton twice, as the first public personality to take an interest in this project.[69]

Certainly Hampton's pathbreaking effort for Indians was an important, although perhaps not always decisive, reason for presidential visits. At Williams College, Armstrong had known James Garfield, who had become a Hampton trustee in 1877. In 1881 President Garfield's last public address before being mortally wounded en route to Williams's commencement was given at Hampton's graduating exercises. Although only Garfield had shown interest in Hampton before its Indian program, Ulysses S. Grant visited Hampton after his presidency and William McKinley before his term in the White House. Cabinet members, senators, congressmen, missionaries, educators, anthropologists, philanthropists, and numerous others, sometimes over 20,000 a year, visited the institute, often coming to see Indians but leaving with Armstrong's view of industrial education for blacks. Other notables asked the general to give a personal account of his Indian work. A petition signed by J. P. Morgan, Cyrus Field, Peter Cooper, Samuel J. Tilden, Whitelaw Reid, Morris Jesup, and other elite New Yorkers asked Armstrong to discuss his Indian work at the New York City Chamber of Commerce.[70]

The additional prestige Hampton received through its Indian work translated into pecuniary advantage, although never as much as anticipated. By establishing an Indian program at Hampton, Armstrong had hoped to recapture some of the earlier enthusiasm and money that had marked his efforts for blacks, whose education survived on charity. From as early as 1871, Armstrong had believed that public interest in black reform was waning: "people had got tired of the negro question, and wind and tide are against me. It's fearful to throw oneself against the popular current, and it is the most exhausting thing I ever tried."[71]

Statistical evidence suggests that Hampton's Indian program did indeed help to keep the school financially solvent. Until 1885 the federal government paid approximately $16,000 yearly to educate 100 Indians at Hampton, and from 1886 to 1912 up to $20,040 for 120 Indians—most years at the rate of $167 each.

Nevertheless, Armstrong was never satisfied with the amount of the government appropriation for Hampton's Indians, especially when Carlisle received $225 per student. However, it does not seem reasonable to believe that educating an Indian student cost a great deal more than a black student, a cost estimated by the school at $154 per annum. The absence of the Indian students on summer outings provided them with money for amenities at school and relieved Hampton financially. Food, clothing, and furniture cost Hampton very little because they were produced by its students. Transportation for Indians was paid directly by the government and during the first several years the Office of Indian Affairs bought several thousand dollars worth of wagons and harnesses made by Hampton Indians. Moreover, school authorities estimated that they received twice as much for the education of Indians from charity as from the government.[72] Figures reported by Pratt for 1880–84 alone show that charity contributed $102,853 to Hampton's Indian program.[73]

Although only about half of Hampton's subsequent increase in revenue can be directly attributed to its new Indian program, several benefactions were specifically tied to its needs. The eight years after 1878 witnessed the most massive building activity in Hampton's history, as the institute took on its modern appearance.[74] Some of the brick and mortar philanthropy that made Hampton the most expensively equipped educational facility serving blacks anywhere was inspired by its Indian program. Only a few weeks after the St. Augustine prisoners arrived, Armstrong proposed constructing a permanent facility to lodge Indian boys. He made this proposal a commitment in the government contract for instructing the Sioux. The Wigwam, completed in 1879, was financed largely by small contributions amounting to $12,000. This three-story edifice, made from bricks blasted by the students, served as the boys' dormitory for the duration of the Indian program, and still exists as an office building listed on the register of historic landmarks.[75] When the second party of Indians included girls, two new corridors were added to the black girls' dormitory, Virginia Hall, at the cost of $1,800 and the price of furnishing twenty-two rooms.[76]

This arrangement at Virginia Hall was temporary, however. Master political strategist Armstrong induced the administration to send more Indian girls to Hampton by planning a new building for them. He secured President Garfield's services to lay the cornerstone of an Indian girls' dormitory in May 1881, and got Secretary of War Robert Lincoln to break ground for a new industrial training building for blacks. The Boston Indian Citizenship Committee helped Armstrong engage abolitionist Thomas Tibbles of "Bleeding" Kansas fame and "Bright Eyes," Omaha Susan LaFlesche, as fundraisers for the Indian girls' building. (These two, along with Ponca Chief Standing Bear, had inaugurated the Indian reform movement in 1879 by publicizing the Ponca controversy.)[77] However, most of the money for the building was raised at a meeting in New York City's YMCA Hall, attended by Schurz, Pratt, General Nelson A. Miles, and Bishop Henry Potter.

Completed in 1882, Winona Lodge, meaning "elder sister," cost $30,000. Although Secretary of Interior Henry Teller had objected to Armstrong's tactic of erecting a building for Indian girls in order to force the government to fill it, he now "gladly complied."[78]

The Indians' presence at Hampton produced another school facility—housing for a health care program. Because most black students had been in good physical health, Hampton had needed no such program until confronted by the ills of its Indian students. While a portion of Olivia and Caroline Phelps-Stokes's $2,000 contribution for Winona was devoted to two rooms intended for an Indian girls' hospital, Hampton Trustee Henry W. Foote of Boston suggested that Armstrong raise money through a fair there, to build a hospital room for Indian boys. Armstrong induced Agent John G. Gasmann of Crow Creek to contribute Indian handicrafts to the fair, whose high point was the auctioning of a coat belonging to the White Ghost, the elderly principal chief of the Lower Brule Sioux. Armstrong persuaded Foote to direct the event and to build an entire hospital, by suggesting that the edifice might commemorate Foote's recently deceased daughter. Named for the Boston church whose donations financed its construction, the King's Chapel Hospital was opened in 1886 and dedicated to Mary Foote. The $6,000 facility included four rooms for Indians and four for blacks.[79]

In 1878, at the cost of $11,000, Mary Tileston Hemenway purchased for the school a 400-acre farm, Shellbanks.[80] The farm was bought for the Indians' benefit, to teach them to care for European livestock while providing some semblance of the outdoor life they had known in the West. In 1880 another property of 250 acres, purchased for $4,500 largely with the legacy of Boston abolitionist Lydia Maria Childs, was merged with Shellbanks. This farm, Canebreaks, was also intended for Indian education, although Hampton graduates soon operated both of these former slave plantations and black students alone largely worked the farm.[81] No whites lived there. When in 1879 the outing system became the primary means of teaching white farming methods to the Indian, Armstrong apparently felt that land originally designated for Indian use could serve Hampton's black students: after all, Hampton's Indians also benefited from facilities constructed for them.

Commitment to an Indian education that included mechanical arts led to further enlargement of the school. Here again a project started for Indians soon opened to blacks. The original Indian training shop in the basement of Marquand Cottage, a black boys' dormitory, was described by the white foreman, J. D. McDowell, as a dilapidated structure with a dirt floor and very dirty windows. Armstrong asked Mc-Dowell if he objected to instructing blacks along with Indians, because several had asked to share mechanical instruction with Indians. (Hampton never seemed able to accommodate all of its black students who desired to learn a trade.) McDowell reported that "the admission of colored students to the [Indian] shops gave me increased confidence to start a quiet drive for better quarters." J. C. Robbins, Hampton's first black teacher of Indians, secured $7,500 from his friend Miss Catherine Wolfe of New York to build the "Indian Training Shops."[82] Completed in 1883, the $9,000 building contained separate shops equipped for instruction in wheelwrighting, harness and shoemaking, tinsmithing, and blacksmithing—skills Indians were thought to need on the reservations.

While Hampton's work for Native Americans would never match its work as the premier industrial school for blacks, the coming of Indian students generated wider public exposure and stronger financial support than any event since the founding of the institute. Thousands of people, some nationally important, and many sizable donations came to the school only because of the Indian program, which linked Hampton with the work of the AMA, the Episcopal church, and the several Indian reform organizations. By adding consideration of a western problem of dispossessed Indians to the sectional problem of newly freed blacks, Armstrong gained a broader nationally focused platform. This helped inaugurate the federal government's effort at Indian assimilation and brought the American military into Hampton's orbit of influence. The Indian program allowed Hampton to unite the two most important racial minorities in the country, in what was seen by Armstrong as a prophetic mission to work out their destinies at the very location where red, black, and white had first met in English North America.

Notes

1. SCA, "Hampton and Its Surroundings," *SW* 1 (Jan. 1872): 1.

2. SCA to Emma Walker Armstrong, Apr. 11, 1878, Armstrong Family Papers, Williamsiana Collection, Williams College. *ARCIA* 1900, p. 54, credits Carlisle and Hampton for "an inaugural and sustaining part" in the development of government Indian education.

3. SCA to Edward Parmelee Smith, Sept. 5 and 9, 1870, Va files, frames HI-12807 and HI-12811, AMA MSS. The AMA collection is located at the Amistad Research Center, New Orleans.

4. Samuel S. Ross, Superintendent of Washington Territory, to Commissioner Ely S. Parker, July 13, 1871, RG75, M234, roll 798, frame 392, NARA;

Oliver Otis Howard to Commissioner Walker, Jan. 19, 1872, RG75, M234, roll 999, frames 073 and 281, NARA; Samuel F. Tappan to Commissioner Francis A. Walker, Aug. 6, 1872, RG75, M234, roll 999, frame 93, NARA. Rayford W. Logan, *Howard University: The First Hundred Years, 1867–1967* (New York, 1969), p. 56.

5. Tappan to Walker, Aug. 6, 1872, RG75, M234, roll 799, frame 593, NARA. Born in Manchester, Massachusetts, Samuel Forster Tappan (1832–1913) was one of the free state founders of Lawrence, Kansas (1854), and would ride against the Confederacy with Kit Carson. He later served as the superintendent of the Indian industrial school at Genoa, Nebraska (1883–85). SCA to Emma Walker Armstrong, June 5, 1872, Armstrong Family Papers, Williamsiana Collection, Williams College.

6. SCA, editorial, *SW* 2 (May 1873): 2.

7. Richard D. Komas to Quincy C. Smith and I. W. Randall to Q. C. Smith, both Mar. 17, 1876, RG75, M234, roll 905, Utah Superintendency, NARA. Dodge had broad interests: he was a vice president of the American Colonization Society before the Civil War, and after it served as a member of the Slater Fund, vice president of the ABCFM and as an original member of the Board of Indian Commissioners.

8. Ezra A. Hayt to Peter Johnson and SCA to Hayt, both Dec. 17, 1877, RG75, M21, roll 138, NARA.

9. SCA to Carl Schurz, Oct. 29, 1877, RG75, M234, roll 347, Idaho Superintendency, NARA.

10. SCA to Oliver Otis Howard, Nov. 1, 1877, HUA. The General also corresponded about his Nez Perce scheme with Eliphalet Whittlesey of the Board of Indian Commissioners, Representative William Goode of Virginia, Adjutant General E. D. Townsend, and Lucy Ware Webb Hayes. Ryan, "The Carlisle Indian Industrial School," p. 26.

11. RHP, *Battlefield and Classroom,* pp. xi, 7. See also William B. White, "The Military and the Melting Pot: The American Army and Minority Groups, 1865–1924" (Ph.D. diss., University of Wisconsin, 1968), p. 116.

12. RHP, "Equality for Minorities," (n.d.), folder 671, Pratt Papers, Beinecke Library, Yale University.

13. RHP to Anna Pratt, Dec. 7, 1868, Pratt Collection, Manuscript Archives, U.S. Army Military History Institute, Carlisle, Pa. Everette A. Gilcreast, "Richard Henry Pratt and American Indian Policy, 1877–1906: A Study of the Assimilation Movement" (Ph.D. diss., Yale University, 1967), p. 19. Pratt's decision was overturned, but the white orderly was so embarrassed at being bested by a Negro that he deserted.

14. RHP, "What Is the Matter with Our Indians?," *Quarterly Journal of the Society of American Indians* 3 (Apr. 1915): 130; RHP, "Report of the Carlisle School," *ARCIA* 1890, p. 308; RHP, "Address of Capt. Pratt before the National Educational Convention at Ocean Grove, New Jersey," *The Morning Star* 3 (Aug. 1883): 2.

15. RHP, "Colonel Pratt's Answer to Rev. Sanford's Letter," *Red Man and Helper* 11 (Oct. 8, 1892): 4. A good example of Pratt's reliance on muscle to

destroy tribal identity was his plan forceably to redistribute the 260,000 Indians of the country among its 2,600 counties. He also pushed compulsory school attendance, the exclusive use of English, and corporal punishment of students.

16. RHP, editorial, *The Morning Star* 3 (Aug. 1883): 2.

17. RHP, "The Advantages of Mingling Indians with Whites," *Proceedings of the Nineteenth Annual Conference on Charities and Corrections at the Nineteenth Annual Session Held in Denver, CO., June 23–29, 1892* (Boston, 1892), p. 52; RHP, "Captain Pratt's Answer," *The Red Man, His Present and Future* 13 (Jan. 1896): 2; Hertzberg, *The Search for an American Indian Identity,* p. 17.

18. RHP, "Our Sixteenth Anniversary and Seventh Graduating Exercises," *The Red Man, His Present and Future* 12 (Feb. 1895): 2.

19. RHP, no title, *The Missionary Review of the World* 33 (1910): 852; RHP, editorial, *Red Man and Helper* 19 (July 1, 1904): 1.

20. RHP, *Negroes and Indians: An Address before the Pennsylvania Commandery, Military Order of Foreign Wars of the United States, Bellevue-Stratford Hotel, Philadelphia, January 14, 1915,* Pamphlet A 258, IRA Papers. See also the letter to Pratt from black Principal William H. Council of the Agricultural and Mechanical School in Normal, Alabama, of Apr. 23, 1901, Pratt Papers, box 3, folder 65, Yale University.

21. RHP, "The Solution to the Indian Problem," *Quarterly Journal of the Society of American Indians* 1 (Jan.-Apr. 1913): 197. Pratt often indicated that he wanted to close Carlisle, as an Indian school, just as soon as Indians could be merged into the public schools. Indeed, he believed that association in everyday life was more important than schools in the assimilation process, pointing out that blacks had become civilized without them. Comment made in "The Advantages of Mingling."

22. RHP, "Colonel Pratt's Talk to the Students," *Red Man and Helper* 17 (Oct. 1902): 1; RHP, *SW* 13 (Sept. 1884): 99.

23. RHP, *Negroes and Indians;* Pratt's racial views were more in line with those expressed in the NAACP publication *Crisis* than those of the accommodationist *SW.* He once wrote W. E. B. Du Bois that segregation is "repugnant to Christian principles, to American principles, to true manhood and breeds war." See Pratt to Du Bois, Nov. 3, 1914, Du Bois Papers, Library of Congress. For Pratt's comparisons of immigrants and Indians see "The Advantages of Mingling": "Easy for a Nation to Be Inconsistent" in *Red Man and Helper* 17 (May 8, 1903), and "The Place and Destiny of the Indian in the Nation's Life," 1916, Pratt Papers, folder 666, p. 4, Yale University.

24. Pratt cited Thomas J. Morgan's "Carlisle Indian Industrial School," May 26, 1886, Pratt Collection, Military History Institute, Carlisle, Pa. RHP, *Negroes and Indians,* p. 3. Again expressing his preference for Indians over blacks, Pratt said "the Indian rather beats [the black] in natural gifts." See RHP, "A New Era for the Indians," (n.d.), clippings file, Peabody Collection, Hampton University Library.

25. RHP, *American Indians, Chained and Unchained: Being an Address before the Pennsylvania Commandery of the Military Order of the Royal Legion,*

at the Union League, Philadelphia, Oct. 23, 1912, p. 4, Library of Congress, Class E Misc. MSS, microform 41000–41046. This is Pratt's fullest personal account of the events leading to the establishment of Carlisle.

26. RHP, "Our Forlorn Indians," *LMC* 1916, p. 101. Like many reformers, Pratt ignored the fact that the Constitution treated Indian tribes as separate nations (inasmuch as the United States was compelled to negotiate formal treaties with them) arguing instead that Article 14, Section 1 granted citizenship to Indians because they had been born in the United States. Elaine Goodale Eastman, *Pratt: The Red Man's Moses,* p. 51.

27. RHP, *American Indians, Chained,* p. 6.

28. James F. B. Marshall, "Reminiscences," in *Twenty-Two Years' Work,* p. 16. Yet Marshall would later become director of the Negro and Indian Department of the American Unitarian Association.

29. The pertinent letters are published in RHP, *Battlefield and Classroom,* p. 172.

30. Graham, "Tender Violence: Old Hampton, the Indian Question, and the New South," p. 7.

31. Henry B. Whipple, "A Letter from Bishop Whipple," New York *Daily Tribune,* Apr. 1, 1876; Ludlow, "Personal Memories," p. 785; RHP to Rev. Thomas S. Childs, May 27, 1889, Pratt Papers, box 15, p. 159, Yale University.

32. Harriet Beecher Stowe, "The Indians at St. Augustine," *Christian Union* 15 (Apr. 18, 1877): 345. Spencer Baird of the Smithsonian Institute, Senator George Pendleton of Ohio, and Episcopal Bishop J. B. Wicks of New York had also shown interest.

33. RHP in "An Indian Raid on Hampton," *SW* 7 (May 1878), p. 36. For books about these Indian artists see Burton Supress and Ann Ross, *Bear's Heart: Scenes from the Life of a Cheyenne Artist* (New York, 1877); Karen Daniels Petersen, *Plains Indian Art from Fort Marion* (Norman, 1971), and Cohoe, with commentary by E. Adamson Hoebel and K. D. Petersen, *A Cheyenne Sketchbook* (Norman, 1964).

34. Charles Lenox Hall, *Forty Years in the Wilderness* (New York, 1916), p. 260.

35. Joseph Willard Tingey, "Blacks and Indians Together: An Experiment in Biracial Education at Hampton Institute (1878–1923)" (Ph.D. diss., Columbia Teacher's College, 1978), pp. 97–104; RHP to Hayt, Aug. 23, 1878, RG75, M234, roll 478, frame 212, NARA; *SW* 7 (May 1878): 36.

36. SCA to Robert C. Ogden, Mar. 8, 1878, Ogden Papers, box 6, Library of Congress; Cora M. Folsom, "Indian Days at Hampton" (Manuscript), p. 26, HUA.

37. H. I. Fontellio-Nanton, "Indian Education at Hampton Institute, 1878 1923" (Report), p. 4, HUA; John Wesley Cromwell, "The Indians at the Normal Institute," *Virginia Star,* Richmond, Va., Dec. 14, 1878; Folsom, "Indian Days," p. 6. Lieutenant Henry Romeyn was commandant of Hampton cadets from 1878 to 1881. He had been a corporal in the Fourteenth U.S. Colored Infantry during the Civil War and had fought against the Nez Perce at Bear Paw Mountain, Montana, in 1877.

38. Editorial remarks, *SW* 8 (Oct. 1879): 99.
39. Richmond *Daily Dispatch,* Apr. 9, 1878; Richard B. Sherman, "The 'Teachings at the Hampton Institute': Social Equality, Race Integrity, and the Virginia Public Assemblage Act of 1926," *The Virginia Magazine of History and Biography* 95 (July 1987): 275–300.
40. *SW* 7 (May 1878): 36, reported from *Virginia Star,* incorrectly referred to as the *Southern Star.*
41. Booker T. Washington, *The Story of the Negro, The Rise of the Race From Slavery* (New York, 1909), p. 138. Booker's brother, John H. Washington, asked Armstrong, "if you had not brought the Indians here could you have admitted as many more colored students?" See John Washington to SCA, (n.d.), Armstrong Family Papers, Hampton Institute Misc. Files, Williamsiana Collection, Williams College.
42. James C. Robbins to SCA, Sept. 11, 1878, Mary Armstrong to SCA, (?) 1881, HUA, J. D. W. Giles to SCA, Dec. 9, 1881, all HUA.
43. Robbins to SCA, Sept. 11, 1878, HUA.
44. Thomas K. Fessenden to SCA, Oct. 26, 1882, and Dec. 3, 1880, HUA; Romeyn to Fessenden, Nov. 12, 1880, Mont. files, frame 74574, AMA MSS.
45. Graham, "Tender Violence: Age of Fable," pp. 6–10; SCA in *Twenty-Two Years' Work,* p. 3.
46. SCA to General E. D. Townsend, May 20, 1878, Pratt MS, Yale University.
47. RHP, *American Indians, Chained,* p. 7.
48. SCA in *Twenty-Two Years' Work,* p. 3.
49. George E. Hyde, *A Sioux Chronicle* (Norman, 1956), p. 10; RHP, *LMC* 1913, p. 201.
50. See Szasz, *Indian Education in the American Colonies,* pp. 218–22; SCA to Schurz, Aug. 5, 1878, RG75, M234, roll 477, NARA; William Anthony Aery, "The Hampton Idea of Education, 1868–1893, with Special Reference to the Contributions of Samuel Chapman Armstrong" (Manuscript, n.d.), chap. "Benefactor of American Indians," HUA. Citations below denote Aery paginated each chapter separately.
51. Fontellio-Nanton, "Indian Education," p. 6; SCA in *Twenty-Two Years' Work,* p. 314.
52. RHP, "Report of Lieutenant R. H. Pratt, Special Agent to Collect Indian Youth to be Educated at Hampton Institute, Va.," Nov. 22, 1878, *ARCIA* 1878, p. 175; "Statement of Appeal on Behalf of Hampton Institute," (n.d.), HUA.
53. SCA to RHP, Aug. 26 and Sept. 2, 1878, Pratt Papers, Yale University.
54. RHP, "Report of Lieutenant R. H. Pratt, Special Agent," p. 173. For discussion of the Hidatsa' complex and meticulous horticultural methods see Gilbert L. Wilson, *Buffalo Bird Woman's Garden: Agriculture of the Hidatsa Indians* (1917; reprint, St. Paul, 1987). James C. Robbins to SCA, Sept. 11, 1879, HUA.
55. Fontellio-Nanton, "Indian Education," p. 4, 8.

56. RHP to Annie Beecher Scoville, Oct. 1, 1895, Pratt Papers, Yale University; Folsom, "Indian Days," p. 31 credits Armstrong's "stupendous ability at accomplishment" in originating the plan; see also Scoville, in *SW 24* (Sept. 1895): 157.

57. Tomlinson and Tomlinson, *A Leader of the Freedmen*, p. 53.

58. RHP to Scoville, Oct. 1, 1895, Pratt Papers, Yale University; "History of the Outing," (n.a., n.d.), typed article, Pratt Papers, box 43, folder 814, Yale University.

59. RHP to Scoville, Oct. 1, 1895, Pratt Papers, Yale University.

60. HBF, "To Be Typed," second box, (n.d.), p. 4, HUA.

61. Gilcreast, "Pratt," p. 28; SCA to RHP, Aug. 17, 1878, Pratt Papers, Yale University.

62. RHP, *American Indians, Chained*, p. 8.

63. In SCA to Hayt, Jan. 21, 1879, RG75, M234, roll 480, frame 7, NARA.

64. RHP, *American Indians, Chained*, p. 8.

65. RHP, *Battlefield and Classroom*, p. 214.

66. SCA wrote to RHP in Apr. 1880, Pratt Papers, Yale University, "Lots of 'Carlisle' in 'Workman.' Hope this will help you." On January 9, 1883, Armstrong offered to lobby for Pratt in Washington whenever that was needed. Moreover, Gilcreast, "Pratt," shows that Armstrong opened official and charitable channels for Pratt, and kept him assigned to educational work at Hampton, when returning to his regiment might have cut short his career in Indian education.

67. RHP, *ARCIA* 1890, p. 309; John G. Fee to Schurz, Feb. 20, 1880, Schurz Papers, Library of Congress.

68. RHP, *Battlefield and Classroom*, p. 214; RHP, "Why Most of Our Indians are Dependent and Non-citizen," p. 2, Pratt Papers, Yale University, 1915; RHP, "Catalogue of the Indian Industrial School," 1902, Pratt Papers, Military History Institute, Carlisle, Pa.

69. For references about Hampton made by Presidents Hayes and Arthur, see James D. Richardson, comp., *A Compilation of the Messages and Papers of the President's, 1789–1897*, 20 vols. (New York, 1897), 10:4455–56, 4529, 4575, 4644; SCA to Baxter Armstrong, May 6, 1871, HUA.

70. Ludlow, "Personal Memories," p. 774; (n.a.), Dec. 26, 1878, Pratt Box, Indian Collection, HUA.

71. SCA to Baxter Armstrong, May 6, 1871, HUA. The general said in the 1870s, "There never was a time when the colored race needed friends more than now. General sympathy is exhausted. The tide of enthusiasm which sustained their schools for the first ten years is now ebbing." See also SCA, *The Ideas on Education Expressed by Samuel Chapman Armstrong*, (Hampton, 1909), p. 8.

72. SCA to Henry L. Dawes, Sept. 24, 1881, Dawes Papers, box 25, General Correspondence, Library of Congress; SCA, *ARCIA* 1881, p. 196; Aery, "The Hampton Idea: Creator of Public Opinion," pp. 89–90. Hampton's general donations, annual scholarships, and income from endowments

steadily increased after the Indians arrived, as the nation also recovered from the 1870's depression. Income from these categories totaled $107,654 from 1876 to 1879, $120,911 from 1879 to 1882, and $135,761 from 1881 to 1884. Charitable gifts increased more sharply after the arrival of Indians—from $11,344 between 1876 and 1878 to $100,524 over the next three years. The following two years yielded $73,000 more.

73. RHP, *The Red Man, His Present and Future,* 10 (Jan. 1890): 1.

74. Although Armstrong repeatedly foresaw no need for additional large buildings—note his annual reports for 1876 and 1885—twelve were constructed from 1876 to 1890. Ludlow, "Personal Memories," pp. 776–77, gives dates and costs of Hampton's new buildings.

75. SCA, "Annual Report," *SW* 8 (June 1879): 63.

76. Ludlow, "Personal Memories," p. 591. Lincoln broke ground for Stone Building, costing $28,000.

77. Boston *Daily Advertiser,* May 24, 1880. Through an oversight the Poncas lost their land to the Sioux, and were forceably removed to Indian Territory. In December 1878 a portion of the tribe led by Chief Standing Bear fled Indian Territory for its home in Dakota. While these Poncas rested at the Omaha Reservation in Nebraska early the next year, Tibbles and his Omaha Committee secured a writ of habeas corpus for Standing Bear, reversing a judicial tradition that had indicated an Indian was not a person under law. Reform-minded Bostonians including Governor John D. Long, Mayor Frederick Prince, Oliver Wendell Holmes, and Wendell Phillips formed the Boston Indian Citizenship Committee. In the end, however, by refusing to hear the Ponca's case, the Supreme Court left the legal status of Indians unchanged. See Priest, *Uncle Sam's Stepchildren,* pp. 76–81; Mardock, *The Reformers,* pp. 168–91.

78. Henry B. Teller to SCA, Apr. 27, 1883, RG75, NARA; HBF, *Annual Report,* 1915, p. 30.

79. Minutes of the Indian Faculty Meeting, Nov. 5, 1913, HUA; SCA to Henry Foote, May 1, 1885, SCA papers in possession of Arthur Howe, Jr.

80. Mary Tileston Hemenway (1793–1894), whose reform interests included blacks, Indians, and poor whites, was the daughter of Thomas Tileston and the wife of Augustus Hemenway, both of whom made fortunes in shipping. Her contributions to Hampton of over $35,000 enabled Armstrong to launch the *Southern Workman* and the Hampton singers. Among Hemenway's other philanthropic concerns were archaeological and ethnological research into southwestern American Indian cultures, and the founding of Tileston Normal School for poor whites, in Wilmington, North Carolina. See *Lend a Hand,* 12 (Apr. 1894): 245.

81. SCA, "The Hemenway Farm," *American Missionary Magazine* 6 (Feb. 1883): 49; SCA, "The Indian Work at Hampton," *Wowapi* 1 (Nov. 7, 1883): 63.

82. J. D. McDowell, "Organization of the Indian Training Shop," box 21, Indian Affairs, Misc. Reports by Various Staff Members, HUA.

3

Armstrong's Influence on National Indian Policy

The "reformist" Vanishing Policy designed to dissolve Indian cultures into the national life of the 1880s could not have proceeded without the sympathetic participation of mainstream whites. Armstrong saw himself as the educator of this necessary white opinion. Considering how many more blacks there were than Indians, Armstrong asserted that "the Negro creates public sentiment, but it makes the Indian." He said the Negro question no longer required legislation for freedom or civil rights, but dealt with the blacks themselves—that is, with teaching them the means of self-help. He also believed "The Indian question is one of honor and of justice. The Negro question involves the salvation of the nation. The former touches the nation at no vital point." Armstrong viewed the Indian question as the only remaining "distinctly moral question before the government."[1]

However "incidental" to the major educational work being done in the West, eastern schools like Hampton were needed, Armstrong thought, to exert influence in the centers of power affecting public policy. He blamed Washington's indifference to Indian affairs on public ignorance, but hoped that Hampton and Carlisle would have "the effect of building up that public sentiment which is at the bottom of any political . . . or social movement." Through extensive northern campaigns, commencement exercises, and the *Southern Workman*, Armstrong reached a large and influential audience with a vigorous missionary message.[2] Talking about immaterial things to materialistic people, the man whom John Greenleaf Whittier called the "chief of the Christ-like school" sanctified Hampton in the eyes of rich and powerful whites; he enlisted them in a "Grand Army of God's Workers."[3]

Armstrong nevertheless saw the achievements of railroad, trade, and business magnates as more important in "civilizing" minority races than the efforts of all the missionaries and philanthropists. A proponent of the "great man" theory of history, he observed that "the intelligent selfishness of corporations has been on the side of schools and churches." He said, "We [missionaries] think we are the educators, nonsense, we are only doing a small part of it." The builders of the nation's railroads "have done ten times as much for civilization as any common charity—all in the way of business."[4]

Potential benefactors in a generation that admired the "lofty character" that wealth made possible were lured to perform "works of miraculous grace" by Armstrong's biblical imagery. He proclaimed that persons, races, and nations acquired spiritual power in proportion to the difficulties overcome. His inspirational epigrams taught that "to be helpful is the luxury of life," indeed the "elixer of life," and found "life would not be worth living if there were no Negro and Indian problems."[5] With collective redemption as well as national security in mind, the *Workman* quoted Whittier: "Everything we do for them we are really doing for our own benefit and safety." To the charge that blacks and Indians could not be "elevated" Armstrong replied, "Only what the world calls folly is worth the moral energies of man. Doing what 'can't be done' is the glory of living." Christians were placed on earth "to do the impossible."[6]

In short, Armstrong saw himself as more than an apostle to blacks and Indians. He helped to create a missionary climate among the "best" white men of the North and South, showing them how problems of racial adjustment could be interpreted and resolved. He enlisted their support by identifying his system of racial advancement with key American values—national honor, the capitalist ethic, and missionary Christianity—and by handling any prejudicial attitudes against blacks or Indians with discretion.

Nothing in Armstrong's characterization of "lower races" threatened whites. Assuming that blacks during antebellum times were on a "dead level," he saw himself as "creating" freedmen who were responding well, because they came with "tabula rasa, so far as real culture is concerned." In his famous rationalization for giving blacks (and later Indians) a different kind of education than whites received, Armstrong justified a system "constructive of mental and moral worth and destructive of the vices of the slave. What are these vices? They are improvidence, low ideas of honor and morality, and a general lack of directive energy, judgment and foresight."[7] Armstrong viewed the freedmens' overriding problem as "not ignorance, but deficiency of character; his grievances occupy him more than his deepest needs."[8]

Despite such public appeals, however, the general himself was ambivalent about the desirability of total acculturation. He wrote to his wife, Emma, that "natural Negro eloquence is a wonderful thing. I respect it. It makes the matter of civilization a puzzle. Should we educate them out of all this?" After witnessing the "strained, intense, and brilliant" Grass Dance of the Hunkpapa Sioux, Armstrong felt regret that "civilization will conquer all this. . . . One's mystic instincts are singularly awakened in the remote West [where] nature and her spirit is felt . . . as nowhere else."[9] Thus Armstrong's almost involuntary appreciation of certain aspects of black and Indian culture coexisted with his unremitting assumption of Anglo supremacy.

Attempting to reconcile his perceptions, Armstrong argued that the "Negro and the Indian are low but not degraded. They are not a moral ruin, like reprobates from a high civilization, whose fall is into a bottomless pit. The reprobate who lives on their plane is far lower than they. He is demoralized, they are not. They are not conscious of being debauched; he is."[10] These races, then, were "not immoral, but unmoral—the reason for morality had never been made clear to them." Armstrong saw great hope in the Negro and Indian races "who never fell because they had no place to fall from." There is "a pathos about these people, whose ignorance is not their fault. God seems nearer to them." Armstrong loved them for their imagined helplessness, and challenged whites by asking, "is it not for us, who have a better inheritance, to help these weaker ones who have not sinned against much light?"[11]

Armstrong as Catalyst for Introducing Indian Concerns into the Arena of Negro Reform and Founding the Indian Rights Association

From late 1879 to early 1883 Armstrong's labor at inducing the AMA to establish Indian programs in its various schools and at promoting passage of what would become the Blair Bill produced an unexpected offspring, the founding of the Indian Rights Association. In October 1879 Armstrong wrote to Michael Strieby, corresponding secretary of the AMA and one of the general's strongest supporters, that "the co-education of the red and black is an assured success. There is no better way to elevate the Indians than in Negro industrial schools. This is sound doctrine: push it."[12] In December 1880 Strieby told Armstrong that the AMA was doing "relatively much more" for Indian education at Hampton than in its own missionary schools in the West. AMA support for Hampton was an indirect acknowledgment that its black schools were acceptable for Indian education.[13]

Armstrong's plan to use black schools for Indian education probably appealed to the AMA for several reasons. Even as white students were increasingly boycotting AMA schools, the association could still support integration by opening them to Indians. "The AMA aims to destroy caste," Armstrong told readers of the *American Missionary Magazine;* educating Indians with blacks "is our way of doing it [at Hampton]. . . . Have faith and go in for Indians."[14]It could bring the association some of the federal dollars earmarked for Indian education as well as open new channels of popular support without any deviation from its original mission, since the AMA had always given some recognition to the needs of Indians. One of the organizations that had merged to form the AMA in 1846 was the Western Evangelical Missionary Society, centered in Ohio's Western Reserve and organized to oppose what its members believed was an attempt by southern whites to enslave Indians. The AMA had consistently maintained missionary fields among Indians until the Civil War, when it concentrated its resources on the crisis engendered by black emancipation. Then in 1868 the AMA was the first religious organization to respond to Grant's Peace Policy for Indians by nominating agents; by 1872 it had seven Indian missions.[15] The association, which also had small missions to the Chinese and white Appalachians, spent almost a quarter of its income on Indians, although it cared for twenty-five times more black than Indian students.

Armstrong certainly had a vested interest in seeing the AMA adopt his ideas. Opposition to biracial education could not be focused on Hampton if such programs were more common. And if AMA schools decided to educate frontier Indians, they would almost certainly have to become more like Hampton by expanding their industrial departments and reducing their emphasis on classical and higher education. This would validate the general's practice of limiting the curriculum for all nonwhites to rudimentary subjects laying the groundwork for membership in "civilization."

The executive committee of the AMA voted in December 1880 to seek government aid in sending about forty Indians to Fisk or Atlanta Universities, or to Berea College. But just one month later a combination of economic factors—the failure to raise funds for new school buildings for Indians, the overcrowding of existing facilities, the unlikelihood of a congressional appropriation for that fiscal year, and the meager funds remaining in the association's treasury for Indian education—led the AMA to withdraw its memorial.[16]

Yet the AMA's memorial rekindled the interest in Indians shown at Howard University during the 1870s. Also in December 1880, Howard's president, William W. Patton, made a more concrete proposal to educate Indians than had any of the AMA schools. He wrote Secretary Schurz offering to educate, clothe, and board sixty Indian girls in Minor Hall, pointing to the advantages of his school's location in Washington, which was under the eye of the Interior Department and accessible to Congress and public leaders, while offering the students the incidental educational influences of the nation's capital. He added that Howard already had the necessary buildings. In a sense Howard was already a government school, receiving $10,000 annually under the Sundry Civil Service Act.[17]

In May 1882 Congress provided for the education of Indian students at white industrial, mechanical, or agricultural schools. This revived the AMA's interest in Indian education, for in general, the instruction given in schools for blacks fit the guidelines of the act better than did the more classical offerings of white schools.[18] In addition, few white schools expressed interest in educating Indians. Clinton B. Fisk of the Board of Indian Commissioners and the AMA wrote Strieby that if the bill passed Congress, "we must arrange for our quota at Fisk, and maybe some at Atlanta [University]."[19] One month later, Patton also wrote Strieby saying that Howard University was "thinking quite seriously once more of securing twenty or twenty-five Indian girls," if the AMA would subsidize two teachers of Indians. But when the Interior Department told Patton that it would pay only $170 per Indian student, including transportation, and the AMA made no commitment to staffing, the plan was abandoned.[20]

Thus, after several years of discussion, Armstrong's scheme to get Indians placed in AMA schools bore no fruit, but the association was finding other ways to "socialize" Indians. In 1883 the AMA exchanged its Mendi mission in Africa (the original mission of the Amistad prisoners) for the ABCFM's Indian missions in Nebraska and Dakota. Having acquired Reverend Alfred L. Rigg's Santee Indian Training School as part of the Nebraska mission, the AMA decided to make of it another Hampton.[21] With this institution providing a focal point, the association had another reason to prefer schools among the Indians to eastern or southern schools.

Yet Armstrong's unsuccessful attempt to place Indians in AMA schools contributed to a larger networking effort at inducing government to fund educational programs profitable to missionary organizations devoted to blacks and Indians. In January 1880 Armstrong and Strieby began sharing the cost of a lobbyist; Armstrong's $500 was paid through a silent benefactor, Mary Hemenway.[22] The lobbyist was the Reverend Charles Cornelius Coffin Painter, the son of a Virginia slaveholder and, like Armstrong, a graduate of Williams College; after becoming a professor of theology at Fisk in 1878, he was also appointed editor of the *American Missionary Magazine* in 1880. Painter's lobbying efforts soon focused on passing a bill like the one made famous by Senator Henry P. Blair, which provided for federal aid to public education by allocating revenues obtained from land sales and liquor taxes to states in proportion to their rate of illiteracy. Although blacks in southern states were supposed to be the primary recipients of the fund, Painter sought to have Indians included, probably at Armstrong and Strieby's urging.

In January 1882 Painter wrote Strieby that he had discussed national aid to Indians with Eliphalet Whittlesey, a trustee of Howard University and member of the Board of Indian Commissioners, and with Indian Commissioner Hiram Price (1881–85).[23] These reformers were dismayed that Indians had to be made citizens before they could qualify for aid under the proposed bills. As a step toward citizenship for Indians and thus toward their eligibility for national educational programs, Painter lobbied for Secretary of Interior Samuel J. Kirkwood's proposal to replace communal landholding by Indians with individual patents in fee (a plan popularized in 1881 as the Coke land in severalty bill). After the Senate passed Kirkwood's severalty scheme for the Crow reservation in Montana, Painter urged the AMA to open a mission there. In the same month, February 1882, he asked Congress to aid the "Deep Creek" band of Spokane Indians, who although already cultivating and improving individual plots of land in the public domain, were in danger of losing them for lack of formal titles.[24]

Aided by Armstrong and Strieby, Painter's larger efforts on behalf of the AMA for national aid to education led to his appointment as the Washington agent and corresponding secretary of the National Education Committee (NEC). This committee was organized in August 1882 at the annual meeting of the National Education Convention at Ocean Grove, New Jersey, and included representatives of most of the major missionary boards for blacks. While the NEC primarily lobbied for national aid to education, the committee also sought to create a legislative framework that would include Indians. The NEC's manifesto declared its fear for the safety of the Republic should Congress permit Indians to continue in ignorance and listed as members prominent reformers for Indians and blacks—Sheldon Jackson (superintendent of Presbyterian missions in Alaska), Pratt, Armstrong, and Strieby. Painter had Armstrong and Strieby to thank for his NEC appointment: the general was "very urgent" that the lobbyist attend the meeting at Ocean Grove.[25]

Painter had essentially become Hampton's personal liaison to congressional Indian committees and the Indian Office. He brought congressmen to visit the institute and worked for increased appropriations for Indians at Hampton. Yet Armstrong was becoming disillusioned with the NEC's work for blacks. In November 1882 Painter, who could "only guess" at Armstrong's "laconics," complained to Strieby that the general had caused an "upheaval": he falsely "thinks we shall push also the idea of industrial education as part of the scheme [for national aid] which wd justify him in his expenditures."[26]

When in early 1883 the legislative fight for the Blair Bill stalled, Armstrong secured Painter as the Washington lobbyist for the recently formed Indian Rights Association (IRA). Thus the legislative work for Indians done by the AMA and NEC made them forerunners of the IRA. (Indeed Painter's efforts for black and Indian reform were so intertwined that the letterhead of his stationery contained the logos of both the NEC and the IRA). Herbert Welsh, the organizer and driving force behind the IRA, had become interested in Indians after he toured western reservations in May and June of 1882, under the guidance of Bishop William H. Hare.[27] Six months later, on December 15, the IRA was born at a meeting in Philadelphia held at the home of Herbert's father, John Welsh, former ambassador to England. A week later, Quaker philanthropist James E. Rhoads told Herbert Welsh that "the Am. Missy Soc, by advice and aid of Gen'l A, have a representative in Wash, a Mr. Painter, to look after the interests of the Negro and Indian work."[28] Lacking experience in Indian affairs, Welsh relied heavily on the advice of James Rhoads and Samuel Armstrong.[29]

Armstrong's Expanding Involvement with Indian Reform Organizations and the Indian Agent

Armstrong replied eagerly to Welsh's call for advice. The two men corresponded and met at Hampton. As a result, Armstrong charted the course for the newly conceived IRA. Welsh declared that "with largeness of spirit and nobility . . . (Armstrong) called the new work into existence," and that "the association's line of action was formulated by no less a man than Gen. Armstrong." The general saw the IRA as a force that could defeat legislative projects injurious to the Indians. The IRA was to become a clearing house for accurate information on Indian affairs; its being guided by facts and not sentiment would remove a major objection held against "friends of the Indian." Armstrong told Welsh to "go into the Indian field, and find out the true situation, send out agents to these different points and find out the facts, then present those facts to the public thereby working up a sentiment which would be operative" in redressing injustices to Indians.[30]

In a first such effort, Armstrong secured the necessary funds to send Painter to western Indian reservations in the summer of 1883. This fact-finding expedition was intended to prepare him for his work in the IRA.[31] As he had done when Painter lobbied for both the AMA and NEC, Armstrong contributed $500 to his yearly salary through Hemenway, whose annual donation continued until at least 1886.[32] Morris K. Jesup, another benefactor of Hampton and other endeavors in black education, pledged $1,000, a third of the budget for the new organization, and promised to raise the remaining $2,000 at a parlor meeting in his home or to make up the difference from his own pocket. In the fall of 1883 Armstrong himself spent seven weeks in the Southwest under the auspices of the IRA, putting together his pamphlet *The Indian Question* for the association. He later procured J. B. Harrison as the IRA's field representative to investigate conditions in the West.[33]

Thus Armstrong helped to organize the nineteenth century's most powerful legislative pressure group for setting Indian policy. According to Welsh, Armstrong was largely responsible for the IRA's strategy of stepping up political pressure for Indian citizenship through lobbying, civil suits, and public agitation just when political action by black organizations was waning; after all, Negro citizenship had already been legally achieved. The general also financed many of the IRA's endeavors, receiving in return open support for Hampton's Indian policies and behind-the-scenes manipulation of public officials.

Armstrong became a moving force in other Indian reform organizations as well. He served on the advisory board of the Women's National Indian Association headed by Sarah Kinney, was influential in the Boston Indian Citizenship Committee, and had close associates—Eliphalet Whittlesey, Clinton Fisk, and Albert Smiley—on the Board of Indian Commissioners. Richard Pratt believed that Armstrong, Welsh, and a few others helped direct the operations of the Lake Mohonk conferences for the Indian, which Smiley, a reform-minded Quaker, organized in 1883 at his scenic mountaintop retreat near New Paltz, New York.[34] The participants, both in and out of government, at these annual forums on Indian affairs (1883 to 1914) drafted much of the legislation for the Vanishing Policy. The general was chairman of the all-important Business Committee in 1884 and participated in conferences every year before 1893, except 1886 and 1891, when he was seriously ill. Pushed by Armstrong and his successor Hollis Frissell's linking of Indian and black reform, the Mohonk Indian Conference would be the catalyst for numerous important efforts for blacks, including the Mohonk Negro Conferences of 1890–91, the Tuskegee Negro Conferences begun in 1892, the 1897 Capon Springs Negro Conference, and the formation in 1901 of the Southern Education and in 1902 of the General Education Boards.[35]

Unlike both his own effort for blacks and the activities of most Indian reformers, Armstrong's work for Indians was subject to official regulations that shaped policy on a daily basis. The president, secretary of interior, commissioner of Indian Affairs, and the House Appropriations Committee set guidelines for Hampton's Indian program through the power of appropriation. While Armstrong had no official channels to contend with in influencing black education, neither did he have the advantage of permanent congressional committees and a government bureau for assistance in passing legislation or implementing his policies.

Although over the years Armstrong proposed many modifications to government Indian policy, he often found himself treated as just another contractor by the Indian Office. Robert Ogden referred to this as "bureau interference with school management," the placing of the "pioneer thinkers and educators under inexperienced officers—politicians." Armstrong was always able to maintain a working relationship with government oversight agencies, but he nevertheless resented his subordinate status. He declined any official position himself, however, arguing that "office really weakens men. How they sink out of sight when they are out! I will take no office under government. I wish to build that which shall stand."[36]

Yet in standing aside from government, Armstrong was only able to influence Indian policy substantially when he collaborated with other reform organizations. These interlocking groups of reformers agreed on the general themes of Indian reform—land, law, Christianity, and education—but targeted their efforts differently. For example, the missionaries were primarily concerned with converting Indians to Christianity, the Boston Indian Citizenship Committee with changing the Indians' legal status. Of particular concern to Armstrong was the fact that students returning to the reservations from schools hoping to change Indian life, were at the mercy of the ideas of the Indian agents.

———

Thus the appointment of good agents, especially at agencies from which Hampton drew its students, became a special concern of Armstrong's. Calling this issue "the Alpha and Omega of the Indian question," he asserted that "the strong conviction from the first has been that this [upholding of Anglo values on reservations] is the vital point of the Indian work." Hampton's educational success proved that "the question is no longer can the Indian be civilized, but what becomes of the civilized Indian?"[37]

To provide an object lesson illustrating what could be done for Indian communities, Armstrong decided to concentrate Hampton's effort at one agency, choosing the Lower Brule Sioux at Crow Creek as his showcase. In 1881 Armstrong accompanied the returning Sioux students so that he could personally place them into positions and discover the specific needs for which to train the new students he recruited at this agency. He obtained lodging away from the encampments for the returning students. Lower Brule agent William H. Parkhurst came to view this missionary extension effort as interference in agency business. Parkhurst reported in the *ARCIA* for 1882 that students returning from Hampton "had learned just sufficient of the vices of the whites to make them worse than at the beginning." Charging that his "official report was a slander," Armstrong, supported by Whittlesey and Hare, obtained Parkhurst's dismissal.[38]

The controversy flared in the *Council Fire,* the Indian reform monthly of Dr. Thomas A. Bland, maverick critic of forced acculturation. Parkhurst, backed by Chief Clerk William S. Dyer's sworn affidavit and by the agency master carpenter's unofficial statement, charged that the former students were incompetent. General laborer Joseph Winnebago and agency blacksmith Henry Rencontre were alleged to be "utterly worthless." Parkhurst said that George Bushotter, trained by Armstrong as an interpreter and teacher, failed at both positions: his interpreting was "almost as bad as his original Sioux." All three returned students allegedly quit their positions against the expressed wishes of Parkhurst, who had hoped to hold them up as exemplars. Parkhurst charged them with attempting to instigate a "general strike" over wages by native labor—a subversion of agency discipline. The agent claimed that the students refused orders given by anyone except himself and demanded the dismissal of white employees, so they could take their jobs.

Parkhurst accused Armstrong of "*whitewashing* operations" in defending his "special pets" by blaming the agent for the failures of Hampton's Indian program. Attacking biracial education directly, Parkhurst argued that Indians and blacks should be educated separately because their cases were opposite: blacks had to unlearn nothing but merely be pushed in the right direction, while Indians had to make a new beginning. He further charged that before his own dismissal Armstrong had offered his agency to a Dr. Bergen, post surgeon at Fort Hall agency. The ex-agent asked the commissioner whether Armstrong was "empowered to grant positions at his own sweet will in the Indian service?"[39]

Indeed Armstrong seemed to work on the premise of President Grant's Quaker Policy, in which the major religious denominations nominated agents within specific jurisdictions. This meant that advocates of Indian education Hampton style—Armstrong, for example—should name the head of certain Indian agencies. Although historians have thought this policy had been largely abandoned during the Hayes administration, important aspects survived throughout the 1880s: religious boards, missionary organizations, and the principals of eastern schools retained appointive and legislative influence. Firm in the belief that his work on behalf of certain agencies entitled him to sympathetic management, Armstrong sought the appointment of James McLaughlin, then at Standing Rock, as agent at Lower Brule. But Bishop Hare refused to accept a Roman Catholic agent at an Episcopal agency. As his third choice, Armstrong successfully pursued the appointment of Major John G. Gasmann.[40]

To Armstrong the Parkhurst controversy illustrated the personnel problems at Indian agencies. The incompetent agent, he said, was the destructive result of a search for "cheap men, cheap beef, cheap everything." Only four of sixty agents in the Indian Service received $2,200 per year in 1883, and twenty-one got $1,200 or less. In an effort to prevent good agents from leaving the service because of inadequate salaries, Armstrong privately boosted the salaries of some Indian agents during the 1880s, with funds donated by sympathetic friends. In 1883 Armstrong increased Gasmann's salary by $200 and McLaughlin's salary by $500, in protest against the false economy of Congress.[41] Critics viewed such payments as bribery—inducements to supply the agency's most promising youth as pupils and, more importantly, to report favorably on returning Hampton students.[42] With agents receiving bonuses, charged Pratt, Armstrong "draws a long bow and their support or silence is assumed." Parkhurst opined that inasmuch as his replacement at Lower Brule was employed to support Hampton, the man's name—Gasmann—symbolized his actions.[43]

By 1883 Armstrong's disgust with the general quality of Indian agents brought him to an even more controversial solution: outgoing civilian agents should be replaced at half the agencies with carefully selected army officers. Voicing the sentiment of the majority of the Indians' friends, Sarah Winnemuca, the famous Pauite, reminded Armstrong of the fable of the man who befriended the viper, since officers had in the past been responsible for the massacre of Indians. Armstrong countered that some of the best agents in the service—men like Valentine McGillycuddy, McLaughlin, and Pratt—were army officers.[44] Somewhat paradoxically, however, Armstrong opposed the transfer of the Indian Office from the Interior to the War Department.

Armstrong proposed army officers as agents because they "have had more practical experience with Indians than any other class of men;

because their training in many ways adapts them remarkably well to govern Indians; because they are, by their permanent commissions and salaries, protected against temptation and stimulated to make a good record; because they command the confidence of the country as a class; and because they are non-political, and being already in the public pay, would make their service an economy." He pointed out that army officers, unlike civilian agents, were subject to court-martial for misconduct in office. In addition, they were already conveniently stationed near Indian agencies to protect railroads and white settlements, and many were already detailed in not dissimilar if less important service as officers at agricultural schools—including Hampton.[45] Perhaps Armstrong also believed that he could have more influence on officer than in civilian appointments, through his friendship with Congressman Byron Cutcheon (R. Michigan), chairman of the House Committee on Military Affairs.

After ten solitary years of calling for army officers as Indian agents, Armstrong acquired a powerful ally in Herbert Welsh. At last, in 1893, during Armstrong's final illness, the IRA successfully pushed through a short-lived experiment of appointing twenty-seven army officers as Indian agents. Welsh secured its adoption by arguing that army appointments were more stable than political patronage. The *Southern Workman* reported that only Hampton and the IRA supported the plan while the president, the Interior Department, the Board of Indian Commissioners, and Senator Henry Dawes opposed the change, as did Commissioner Morgan and Superintendent of Indian Education William Dorchester. Considering such powerful opposition, the only reasonable explanation of the bill's passage would seem to be that the high rate of attrition required the discharge of no civilians to make room for army agents, and that the experiment could be repealed simply by deleting it from the next appropriation bill. The annual Indian Appropriation Act of 1892 included some of the same provisions as Armstrong's original proposal. In the end, however, this unpopular experiment failed because few army officers desired the burdensome and essentially unmilitary duty of running an Indian agency, and in some cases plainly would have preferred a more viperous disposition for the killers of Custer. Almost none of these Indian agents served willingly.[46]

Hampton's Abortive Apache Plan

Even as Armstrong continued his efforts to control policies on western reservations, he tried to establish an Indian reservation at Hampton. On the first of January in 1888 Armstrong proposed to

Secretary of War William C. Endicott that he permanently settle the entire tribe of nearly four hundred of Geronimo's Chiricahua Apaches at Sherwood Farm, adjoining Shellbanks. In the summer of 1887, these ill-treated Apaches whom the newspapers called "notorious" had been moved from their original confinement at St. Augustine, Florida, to Mount Vernon, Alabama; but within a year reformers headed by Welsh became convinced that nonarable land and the threat of smallpox made that locale unsatisfactory. The former head of Hampton's Indian Department, Isabel Eustis, was unimpressed by her inspection of Mount Vernon and likely influenced Armstrong's decision to offer Sherwood as an alternative.[47]

Armstrong suggested that philanthropists or preferably the government should purchase this eight-hundred-acre tract from Mary Hemenway for $20,000. He advised that it not only had fertile soil for crops but was well placed to market agricultural products in northeastern cities; Sherwood also possessed a healthy climate and was situated adjacent to a supportive and influential "civilized" community. Armstrong anticipated any local fear of "savage" Apaches by pointing not only to the proximity of Fort Monroe but also to geography: the farm was separated from the town of Hampton and its environs by the Back Bay River and by a buffer zone of school property. Although the Apaches would remain under the temporary control of the War Department, Hampton would train the coming generation and oversee the entire educational process. J. F. B. Marshall backed Armstrong but could not help observing that "it would be strange indeed if after all our bloody wars resulting in driving all our Indians away from the seaboard, we should now plant a flourishing colony in the tidewater region of Virginia of Indians brought from Arizona."[48]

Armstrong believed "Florida is the gateway of bad Indians. Send all the wicked ones there! Then the good earth will take them in her bosom & wash and civilize them." Armstrong indeed preferred to receive captive Indians at Hampton, sermonizing that "a wild Indian is never so near the kingdom of heaven as when a prisoner of war for then he is closer . . . to civilization and Christian truth." He believed that warfare culminating in complete surrender, forfeiture of treaty rights, and incarceration had produced the most successful attempts at "saving" Indians. Armstrong interpreted the nadir of each Indian tribe—the Santee Sioux after the mass hangings at Mankato prison; the Modocs subsequent to Captain Jack's imprisonment; the Dull Knife Comanches after surrender; and the Kiowa, Comanches, and Arapahos at St. Augustine under Pratt—as the necessary precondition for effective missionary work and "redemption from barbarism."[49]

Nevertheless, at the same time that Armstrong expressed interest in acquiring the captive and therefore manageable Apaches, he repeated expressions of outrage at the gross violations of their human rights voiced by the IRA, the Boston Citizenship Committee, and the Massachusetts Indian Association. An investigation by Welsh revealed that the overwhelming majority had remained on their reservation during the outbreak. Only twenty of eighty warriors had been belligerent, and many of the remainder had been regularly commissioned scouts for the U.S. Army, some employed chasing Geronimo.[50]

Secretary of War Endicott, unhappy with Welsh and his Boston supporters for publicly criticizing his Apache policy, turned to Armstrong and Pratt in January 1888 for advice on the disposition of the tribe.[51] As someone who had no desire to move the Apaches in the first place, Endicott could not have devised a better strategy to divide the reformers. Pratt, who thought the Apaches should be settled on his old stomping ground at Fort Sill, fought Armstrong's "back bay plan," claiming the tidewater was unhealthy for Indians and the woods near the farm were filled with a "low Negro population." Pratt feared Chiricahuas at Sherwood would cause more instability than there had been at either St. Augustine or Mount Vernon. Endicott, believing Negroes innately inferior to Indians, now joined Pratt in strongly opposing Armstrong, and together they influenced President Cleveland against the Sherwood plan.[52]

In February Armstrong, supported by Welsh, Smiley, and Eustis, countered Pratt's objections by emphasizing to the president the friendly white population and healthful situation of Sherwood. To remove the administration's excuse for inaction—the fact that reformers could not agree on a solution—Welsh sought compromise between Armstrong and Pratt. He suggested the Apaches be brought to Hampton for initial training and then sent to Fort Sill for final settlement.[53]

Little progress was made on this plan until August, when Welsh, Painter, and General Crook inspected Sherwood and advocated preliminary relocation of the Apaches there. Welsh reported that the president at last seemed interested, for Cleveland had asked Welsh to submit a written report to Endicott. According to Endicott, however, the report languished in the hands of a minor clerk until November. The next month, the president made his position clear in his annual message, smearing Welsh by falsely stating that the IRA advocated sending the Apaches back to their homeland in Arizona.[54]

In these discouraging circumstances, Armstrong had little chance to accomplish his Apache scheme. Although the general occasionally repeated his offer, it was only during the rare times when Welsh had softened an obdurate administration that Armstrong's plan received serious consideration.[55] On such occasions, however, other reformers offered plausible competing plans. The qualification "in case no better place can be found" was therefore appended to the Sherwood proposal. In July 1889 the new secretary of war, Redfield Procter, sent Captain George Bourke, long interested in the Apaches' plight, to investigate Hampton and another location in North Carolina. The Boston Citizenship Committee had offered to purchase either place. Although he liked Sherwood, Bourke preferred the tract in North Carolina.[56] However, Governor Daniel G. Fowle had his own plan, impressed by the advantages of Procter's home state of Vermont for the object he had in view. Throughout the debate, little attention was paid to the Apaches' desire to be settled in terrain similar to home, a mountainous area with plenty of snow and no large bodies of water. This did not describe Sherwood.[57] Although the back bay plan periodically re-emerged, none of these Apaches came to Hampton during Armstrong's lifetime. In 1894, after Armstrong's death, the *Workman* reported the arrival of a small contingent—eight Apache children, one of whom was thought to be a niece of Geronimo.[58]

That same year, after Bourke recommended against merging the Apaches with North Carolina's Eastern Band of Cherokees, Pratt finally managed to get adult Apaches sent to Fort Sill. This location was less unpopular with the Indians, as it was closer to their homeland and a place where they could hear real coyotes howl. Victory in the quest for newsworthy students was celebrated in the *Red Man:* "If we can here at Carlisle inside of four years take 60 of the much despised Chiricahua Apache youth as we have done here [and 'civilize' them] we say this should be done with all Indians."[59] But the controversy was resolved in Pratt's favor largely because Carlisle was a government school.

Armstrong's Ambivalent Attitude toward Civil Service

That Carlisle was a government school could prove to be a liability; the introduction of civil service meant that Pratt could no longer appoint his own employees, while a private school like Hampton remained unaffected. Not surprisingly, then, as civil service reform became the primary focus of the IRA's efforts at solving the Indian question, Armstrong generally supported it. Claiming that "political partisanship is the deadly foe of civilization of the Indian," he argued that because "neither party will march squarely to the [Indian] work," civil service offered an impartial remedy: "equal mourning in both parties." Armstrong wholeheartedly supported efforts to include under civil service regulations all agency personnel below the position of agent. As early as 1882 Armstrong had called for the creation of a

nonpartisan and independent Indian Department, with an educational bureau to oversee and manage all the agencies.[60]

In practice, however, Armstrong did not always uphold his own
nonpartisan principles. When the Republicans, with whom Armstrong
had greater influence, returned to power in 1889, they fully intended
to end the brief tenure of John Oberly as commissioner of Indian
Affairs. The IRA, however, convinced many of them to support Oberly's retention, on the principle that officials in the Indian Service should
not be removed except for incompetence or unfaithfulness to the Indian. But Welsh was disappointed in his expectation that Armstrong
would endorse Oberly.

The general had personal reasons for seeking the removal of Oberly, who as superintendent of Indian Schools in 1885 had shown the
temerity to state in the widely circulated *ARCIA* that Indian training
schools such as Hampton and Carlisle "have not yet commenced to
justify . . . the high expectations of their usefulness . . . entertained by
the philanthropic people who suggested them." Armstrong and Robert Ogden believed Oberly had hoped to influence the fiscally conservative Democrats to abolish the expensive system of eastern education.
Welsh concluded that the IRA's views on nonpartisanship "differ ma-
terially from General Armstrong's," fearing that the loss of Armstrong's
endorsement would mean defection by Ogden and his partner, John
Wanamaker in Philadelphia, as well as by much of Boston. Armstrong's
defection was a "serious loss" to Welsh because only a united front of
Indian reformers could prevent the Republicans from appointing a
home rule commissioner.[61]

In short, Armstrong's ambivalence about the spoils system reflected a concern that application of civil service principles to higher levels of the Indian Service would deprive men like him of exerting influence through extrapolitical channels. Armstrong thought men
more important than measures and viewed Indian "uplift" as the work
of missionaries rather than government. He was more comfortable
with the existing system, in which patrician Indian reformers brokered
the appointment of administrators who would implement their Indian legislation.

Indian Hampton in Jeopardy: Anti-Catholic Sentiment in Indian Reform and the Movement toward National Education for Indians and Blacks

The other reformers quickly forgot Oberly in their pleasure at Pres-
ident-elect Benjamin Harrison's nomination of Thomas Jefferson Mor-

gan, whose career before and after his term as Indian commissioner (1889–93) was closely tied to black causes.[62] Lacking a comprehensive school system for Indians, previous commissioners had relied so heavily on schools conducted by the various Protestant missionary societies that by the 1870s the federal government had even begun granting these mission schools an annual amount for each student enrolled. Under the Cleveland Democrats from 1885 to 1889, however, an increasing number of jobs in the Indian Service went to Catholics, whose schools now received the bulk of such government contracts, in part because Catholics made greater and more consistent efforts for Indians.[63] Although he was the most able commissioner Armstrong would deal with, Morgan's anti-Catholic stance (shared by most Protestant Indian reformers) prevented a good working relationship.

Morgan acted on behalf of anti-Catholic reformers in seeking to dismantle the contract system and replace it with a coordinated and graduated national school system, one that emphasized patriotic American values in a Protestant atmosphere. Instead of working harder for Indians and receiving more money for doing so, these reformers rather perversely refused what money the government had already appropriated to them. As a result, Protestant missionary work atrophied. The sectarian issue led to a split between Armstrong, fearing the consequences of a national school system on Hampton Institute, and his usual allies.

Armstrong "very strongly opposed" Morgan's educational schemes, and asked Senator Dawes whether Morgan would "ever produce a single valuable idea on the Indian question." At the 1888 Mohonk Conference, before Morgan became commissioner, Armstrong had already criticized the growing trend toward federal assumption of responsibility for Indian schools. In an unprecedented breach of etiquette, and against the advice of Lyman Abbott, editor of the *Christian Union,* Armstrong offered a resolution at Mohonk after the platform had already been arrived at: "government continue its aid to the various missionary societies and boards with prompt and generous support." He flatly told his auditors that contract schools "have always done the best work, and always will; let us have more of them."[64]

When at the next Mohonk Conference Morgan announced his plans to centralize Indian schools, Armstrong bluntly told the audience that Indian work was primarily the responsibility of churches. He called the contract system "an ideal one; because it insures a Christian and non-political management, while it secures government aid in the heavy and hard task to raise current expenses." Given the high turnover of school employees under patronage, Armstrong argued that contract schools were "the only permanent force in Indian education"; and in his view, the cardinal requirement for a successful educational system was stability.[65] As early as 1881 Armstrong had contrasted the "steady, persistent and increasingly effective" missionary activity to the erratic effort of government schools: unlike the pattern of more secular New England schools, missionary education supplied a solid Christian influence to Indian homes.[66]

After Morgan's announcement, the general nevertheless tried to refute the opposition's argument that government financing of missionary schools violated the concept of separation of church and state. Both sides conveniently overlooked the Protestant cast of public education in America. Indeed Armstrong denied that the government was spending public funds at all. Instead, he asserted, Washington was spending the Indians' own money, tribal funds held in trust that had been gained as compensation for land cessions. Thus by supporting contract schools, the government was merely acting properly as trustee in striking the best bargain for the Indians' money.[67]

Dividing himself even further from most Indian reformers, Armstrong argued that Catholic schools did the best work for Indians because of the centrally organized effort and perseverance of the Board of Catholic Missions. Since Protestants had not pushed the work, he said, reformers should at least be thankful that Catholics had. Further, Armstrong claimed to desire more schools of all kinds, since no serious effort at Indian education should be deprecated so long as half of all Indian children remained out of school.[68]

High-minded though Armstrong's pronouncements may have appeared, he was fully aware of Hampton's status as a missionary school receiving government contracts for Indian education. Threats to the contract system placed Indian Hampton in jeopardy, although the general did not mention this in his defense of Catholic efforts. Consistent with his earlier attempt to bolster this system by inducing the AMA to educate Indians in its black schools, Armstrong's view of the proper relation between government and missionary philanthrophy for Indians was grounded in his observation of post–Civil War black reform. At Mohonk in 1886 Armstrong had pointed out that between 1866 and 1870, through General O. O. Howard of the Freedmen's Bureau, the national government had helped to build the Hampton complex. In addition, government aid had been used to construct the leading southern institutions for blacks, with private charity responsible for the remainder.[69]

Citing this precedent, Armstrong had argued that for Indians "the very best possible relation between public and private work is that

Government shall supply the buildings and current expenses, and the churches the teachers and such supplemental aid as may be needed." Desiring a system of schools ultimately under private control, Armstrong asserted "the free Negro schools in the South are vitalized by a number of strong central institutions under Northern men that train the picked youth of the race as teachers. This is, I think, the true relation of Eastern charity to the Indian."[70]

Consequently, when the Blair Bill providing national aid to education had gained enough support to pass the Senate in 1887 and 1888, Armstrong withdrew his earlier support, citing that government work for Indians was undermining the private philanthropic sentiment necessary to their advancement. The long history of special treatment embraced in treaties, subsidies, and the like, had developed a tradition of Indian education conducted by the federal government which lacked the life-giving spirit of local sacrifice that was elsewhere creating universal education. The Indian lacked "a faithful constituency of friends because National aid has weakened the work for the Indians, as the lack of it has strengthened that for the Negro."[71]

Armstrong's attack on the Blair Bill was not limited to philosophical issues. He also pointed to the ineptitude of earlier government Indian schools. Although the "use of funds from local taxation is carefully watched and abuses are fought with vigor," Armstrong felt "less confident that Government bounty to Southern schools could be applied to the best advantage." Fearing that nationally aided Negro education would replicate the inadequacies of government Indian schools, he argued, "Take out the self-help, and the rest is not worth much." In 1907 Frissell agreed that government Indian schools do "not create any very great enthusiasm."[72]

Despite all of Armstrong's objections to such schools and despite his success in helping to block national aid to education, in 1891, just a few years after the Blair Bill had been rejected by the House, Morgan indeed established a national Indian school system. This sounded the knell for contract missionary schools, which, in turn, represented a loss of influence for Armstrong regarding Indians, just as the passage of the Blair Bill would have done regarding blacks. Armstrong's latitudinarian view of parochial schools and endorsement of many kinds of Indian work had enabled him to exert influence over personnel as well as policy. The consolidation of Indian schools under government control meant a loss of power both for individual reformers and for private endeavors such as Hampton. From the government point of view, however, consolidation meant more consistent centralized direction and implementation of Indian Bureau policy. No longer would individual Indian agencies be subject to the whims of outsiders. Of course, as trustee for the Indians, the government had always had potential power to control Indian education. The new national Indian school system made that power actual.

Although missionaries had continued to place their stamp on posts and policies during the 1880s, a decade in which Grant's policy was presumed to be resting in peace, their power diminished after 1891, along with Armstrong's hope that the effort to "civilize" Indians would carry the same missionary thrust as had Reconstruction. Leaving aside the government's special commitment to Indian education, the Catholic issue provided a central reason that Indian reform was developing differently than Negro reform. Indian reform increasingly became a government affair, which proved to be of vital importance to the fortunes of Hampton Institute. A larger measure of Catholic support for black education was just what the Blair Bill needed to rally a substantial number of Protestants for "nonsectarian" southern schools. As events evolved, however, while existing government schools for Indians made Armstrong oppose increased national aid to education, their example had given him a means to defeat the Blair Bill.

Indian Hampton's Role in Sectional Reconciliation

The presence of Indians at Hampton prompted a subtle shift in the alignment of the school's traditional constituents—southern whites, northern whites, and blacks. These constituents had conflicting interests that Armstrong, like the nation at large, had never united successfully. Under such difficult circumstances, Armstrong worked the limbs of his racial policy like those of a marionette: each string he pulled affected the overall balance of forces required for a reconciliation of sections after the Civil War. He never forgot Hampton's southern setting or expressed a commitment to higher education for blacks that would have offended popular southern sentiment generally opposed to any education for them. He joined southerners in criticizing the North for leaving the postwar South in the "depths of distress," calling Radical Reconstruction "a bridge of wood over a river of fire," and typically seated three southern whites on Hampton's board of trustees.[73]

In spite of these attempts, however, Armstrong had not always been successful in distancing Hampton from other northern efforts to educate the black; thus, the arrival of Indians at Hampton helped to change its image in southern eyes. "The coming of the Indians," said the general's daughter, Edith Armstrong Talbot, "brought the institute into closer relations with its southern neighbors, who had sympathy with the Indian which they could not summon for the Negro. From this time General Armstrong was able to rely confidently upon his neighbors for support in his work."[74] The *Workman* said that the Indians' arrival aroused sympathetic interest in the school not only in the Hampton area but throughout the South. In 1900 Frissell cultivated southern support at the NEA meeting in Charleston, South Carolina, informing the audience that the location of Pratt's St. Augustine experiment and Hampton meant that "Indian education had its birth in the South."[75]

Of course Hampton also needed to draw support from the North. Continuing northern contempt for the South—based partly on the inhumanity of slavery—needed to be overcome before the wounds of war could be healed. And here, once again Hampton's new arrivals provided a means. Armstrong tried to achieve sectional reconciliation in part by arguing that slavery had resulted in a positive good. In 1898, at the first Conference for Education in the South, while conceding one should not overlook the "villainies" of slavery, Frissell expounded Armstrong's view: "When the children of these two races are placed side by side as they are in the school rooms and work-shops and on the farms at Hampton, it is not difficult to perceive that the training which the blacks had under slavery was a much better training-school for life alongside the white man than was the reservation."[76]

Indeed, Armstrong called slavery "the greatest missionary enterprise of the century." The black in Africa and the Indian before Columbus had been isolated from the "civilizing" influences of commerce that were "uplifting" the various peoples of Europe. Speaking to the NEA in 1884, Armstrong contrasted the divergent histories of 250 years of black and Indian contact with the English: association versus separation, eventual emancipation versus continued guardianship, and great proliferation in numbers versus possible extinction. These differences convinced Armstrong that "there was no grander move, morally, in the history of man than that of American slavery. . . . We have not yet learned to look at the thing rightly. . . . The Indian [unlike the black] has neither our language, nor our labor habits, nor our industry, nor our religion." Bondage even taught blacks skills that promised the "ultimate redemption of Africa, which was, under God, the moral objective of American slavery." By counting their advantages over Indians, Negroes, Armstrong rejoiced, were overcoming "bitterness" by "accepting the thought of slavery as a providential fact all in the line of the development of the race." As if anticipating the rise to prominence of a Booker T. Washington, he predicted in 1889 that the "Ne-

gro will accept the large and just view of slavery sooner than the majority of northern whites."[77]

In his appeals to northerners, Armstrong contrasted the diverse
"benefits" achieved by blacks under bondage to the deprivation of the
Indian: "For the Indian there were no clearly marked lines of development, no rigorous pressure of circumstances, no inherited habit of
doing right in any direction, and from the first the advantage of the
Negro in all these points has been evident."[78] He repeatedly claimed
that the "severe discipline of slavery strengthened a weak race," and
argued that "professed friendship for a strong one [the Indian] has
weakened it."[79] He emphasized to largely northern audiences that the
"tender mercies of the government to the Indians are cruel; the much
talked of treatment of the slaveowners was tender by comparison."[80]
Thus by blaming the Indians' condition on the government's special
treatment of them through treaties, Armstrong sought to place southerners in a morally ascendant position. As a result of the disfranchisement and political impotence of the South after the Civil War, the
Indian Office, the military, and the powers that be in Congress were
dominated by northerners, as was the majority party, the Republicans.
But there would be no ground for northerners to denigrate the South,
once it was seen to be the only section of the nation to have "civilized"
a racial minority.

Besides interesting southerners in Hampton and partially neutral-
izing the moral argument underpinning northern hostility to the
South, Armstrong's strategy of contrasting blacks with Indians com-
plimented Hampton Negroes. When, as shown earlier, blacks had
objected to the admission of Indians to Hampton, Armstrong sought
to sooth them by ranking black achievements above those of Indians,
a race that even southerners admired as the original Americans. Black
superiority to Indians in the skills and behavior valued by whites was
implicit if not explicit in nearly all of Armstrong's racial comparisons.
The general congratulated Negro students for helping to raise the
"savage" Indian from "barbarism," finding their philanthropy a "feath-
er in the colored man's cap he was not expected to wear."[81]

Recognition of this opportunity and capacity for philanthropy dis-
tracted blacks and their northern friends from dissatisfaction with the
nonacademic emphasis of Hampton's curriculum. Biracially educating
Indians with blacks justified Hampton's industrial focus, inasmuch as
Indians presumably had not been exposed to European forms of manual labor or domestic skills, neither rules of etiquette nor habits of
personal hygiene. Armstrong promised not to "spoil" Indians with too
much education: "Sending Indians East for a college education is a

blunder unless there is a place for one with such an education." And even northern liberals could agree with Armstrong's statement that "over-education may break the [Indians'] race tie and sympathy, and make him a man without a country." Indeed Armstrong encouraged ex-Confederates and northern liberals to believe that a "brain full of book knowledge, whose physical basis is the product of centuries of barbarism, is an absurdity we do not half realize from our excessive traditional reverence for school and college training."[82]

Yet at the same time, no matter how ready they were to move beyond the rudimentary skills in which Hampton specialized, blacks were no longer alone in being singled out on racial grounds, once Indians were understood as being peculiarly needful of industrial education. But as Indian education and industrial education became synonymous at Hampton, the actual effect was to hold the school back from becoming a college until the Indian program was terminated in the 1920s.

While an Indian presence at Hampton helped Armstrong reconcile his various constituencies and justify the emphasis on industrial education, it may also have helped him defend the school's military discipline. Rigid separation of the sexes and the organization of the students into military companies—intended to teach lessons of promptness, deportment, and obedience to authority, that is, lessons of social control—had long given Hampton a reputation for strict discipline. When reference was made to the blacks' passionate nature, Armstrong replied, "There is little mischief done when there is not time for it. . . . My boys are rung up at 5 o'clock . . . kept busy all day until 8 P.M., always under military discipline, and after that hour I will risk all the harm they will do to anybody."[83] When adult blacks chafed under such severe restraints on their personal time and behavior, Armstrong could now point to the presence of "wild" Indians of diverse tribes as requiring stringent regulations.

Thus Armstrong placed his model for racial advancement in a strong position. Through the accommodationist implications of industrial education, the American Indian at Hampton became pivotal to uniting whites of the North, whites of the South, and the cause of much of their contention—the black. Educating both races in this manner disarmed his critics by illustrating the universality of Hampton's methods and the breadth of Armstrong's commitment to minorities. Criticism of Hampton's emphasis on manual training and social control was bound to appear unrealistic, while criticism of biracial education was made to appear prejudiced against either blacks or Indians. And the mere placing of reservation Indians beside southern blacks suggested that blacks had been saved from savagery by slavery.

The Impact of Emancipation on the Theory and Reality of Indian Reform

Armstrong believed the future of the Indian race, its progress to "civilization," needed to follow steps parallel to those taken as a consequence of the emancipation of the black. Although both groups suffered cataclysmic changes transforming their place in American life during the second half of the nineteenth century, Armstrong advanced the proposition that "the destruction of the buffalo has been more trying to the Indian than was the sudden emancipation of the Negro. The latter changed the relations rather than the realities of life; the former the realities rather than the relations."[84] Despite the end of slavery, the lifeways of the South continued to revolve around cotton, land, and the subordination of black labor, but the extinction of the Plains Indians' major source for food, clothing, and shelter precipitated the collapse of an entire way of life. The military defeat of many western tribes, the surrounding of Indian reservations by white settlers, and the extermination of the bison occurred at the same time in the late 1870s. When the white man replaced the buffalo as reality in the everyday life of nomadic Plains Indians, conditions were ripe for the emergence of Hampton's Indian program. For the first time negative comparisons of Indians with blacks could indeed be translated into bases for policy.

In Armstrong's view, the white man's practice of issuing "free" rations to able-bodied Indians as partial fulfillment of treaty promises undermined Indian self-reliance and eventual "civilization." In 1866, as district superintendent of the Freedmen's Bureau, he had withdrawn rations to freedmen because he held dependence on free food responsible for much of their poverty. The "surprising" resourcefulness of blacks convinced him that "the Negro in a tight space is a genius." A private letter written in 1868 reveals that, instead of returning those rations to the government, the equally resourceful general had made the freedmen pay for them in work, "like men." Recalling these events in an 1882 editorial, Armstrong revived the bad memory: "Feeding Indians at agencies is the old 'Contraband' system perpetuated, with the same wretched results—breeding beggars."[85]

Armstrong argued that the "submissive" Negro was stronger than the proud Indian because the former was forced to labor while the latter was not. Such statements tacitly endorsed the results of the southern labor system and rebuked northern Republicans who countenanced special treatment or reparations for past injustices to racial minorities. Armstrong said that if the operation of natural causes, that is, self-help, "could be applied to the Indian as it is to the Negro it would go far towards making men of them. The wisest thing in Reconstruction was the refusal, at the end of two and a half centuries of unpaid labor, to give the Negro the coveted 'forty acres and a mule.' The Indian endowment of land and his right to rations is like a millstone around his neck, for only when it is work or starve will the average man work."[86] He claimed the Indian would make no material progress until the reservation system had been abolished and all tribal monies had been distributed and spent. In Armstrong's "survival of the fittest" policy, "Many Indians might die, but the severe training of real life . . . would probably result in creating out of the residue a people who would assimilate with us, like the Negro and the Irishman." In saying this the general dismissed questions about the realities of Indian life; as one contemporary author, William Barrows, countered, "The effrontery of this [work or die] proposition would be ludicrous if it were not cruel. . . . [whites] have taken every cornfield between Plymouth and the Rocky Mountains."[87]

Pointing again to the paradox of black servitude forcing the adoption of the values of the white owners, Armstrong wanted to push Indians even nearer the bottom of society as a means for developing the "character" needed to reach the top. Discounting all pre-existing Indian achievements, the *Workman* editorialized that the Indian "must build his own civilization, beginning where the white man began and where Booker T. Washington is trying to make the Negro begin—at the ground, and he cannot begin until he is freed from the pauperizing influence of too much coddling." In reform circles, Armstrong was known for his unflinching pronouncements that Indians who would not "work" should be permitted to starve in spite of the treaties. He argued that rations were a "stupendous wholesale charity to a warlike people."[88] Even as warlike whites were killing off and moving the Indians away from all forms of sustenance, he reasoned that because the implicit aim of the treaties was Indian self-support, withholding rations for idleness was within the spirit of compliance. Armstrong lamented that the most "warlike" tribes, whose members predominated in Hampton's early Indian student body, received the most money, and thereby were confirmed in their belligerence as a way to gain still greater benefits.[89]

In a practical attempt to influence agency policy, Armstrong asked Commissioner Price to deny food to any returned student from Hampton who refused to apply Hampton training. For the rest of the able-bodied Indians living at agencies from which Hampton drew its students, Armstrong asked Price to use "luxury items"—sugar, coffee, and tobacco—as leverage to create a taste for a European style of work. Sometimes Armstrong sought to use the ration system to force compulsory education of Indians, or in the case of the Sac and Fox Tribe, whose members received a yearly annuity of $90 each, to deny schooling for the children if elders refused to pay the cost of transportation.[90]

In Armstrong's detailed blueprint for aligning the Indian with the goal of "independent" manhood, citizenship and the accompanying franchise would follow directly upon his acceptance of the necessity for steady work—acceptance itself induced by the withdrawal of "free" food. This was seen as the proper sequence for the advancement of Indians as it had been for blacks. Armstrong regarded the "Negro vote as the greatest factor in the settlement of the Negro problem, and it will be that too in the Indian problem." He supported general and immediate rather than selective and gradual citizenship for Indians, and believed that the abrupt change in status that blacks had experienced with freedom evidenced not only the strength of American institutions but also the capacity of racial minorities to adjust to them.[91]

Although objecting to the abuses of state governments under Radical Reconstruction, Armstrong called Negro voting the "chief developing force in the progress of the race." However, he did not see Negro voting as an expression of rightful group interest, but rather as a tremendous stimulus toward getting white southerners to educate these new voters. Arguing that granting blacks the vote did not signify the end but the means toward "fitness," Armstrong claimed that the "recognition of the Negroes' manhood has done much to create it."[92] While supporting the same wholesale enfranchisement as did the Garrisonian Boston Citizenship Committee and Massachusetts Indian Association, Armstrong's reasoning to that end seems more consistent with the views of conservative southern—and northern—businessmen. Far from interpreting the vote as an egalitarian gesture or mandate for equal participation, he felt that minority races were unfit to use political power, counseling black leaders that "no sensible colored man could wish to have his race take a leading part in government" until an informed electorate had been created. As late as 1887 on a visit South, Armstrong referred to the Sea Islands as a "most complete bit of unmitigated Negrodom": black rule in South Carolina was "unspeakably bad; civilization could hardly stand before it."[93]

Armstrong asserted that blacks were better off during the period of Redemption after 1877 than they had been while "holding power" during Radical Reconstruction. He regretted the disfranchisement of blacks only out of fear that the principles of popular government were imperiled through the undermining of constitutional guidelines.[94]

Thus, reversing the prevailing conservative notion that fitness should precede citizenship, Armstrong argued—perhaps perversely but certainly in the interest of Hampton—that citizenship for Indians should precede education. He declared, "Give him [the Indian] the vote as it was given to the blacks. This would force things, as it did in the South. The Indian is not fit for it; neither was the Negro; but it compelled the South to educate him. [Once Indians become voters] delegation after delegation from the West would stay in Washington, and demand education as protection from these wild voters, until they got it." Using this analogy with blacks, he asserted that to "enfranchise the ignorant, then disfranchise ignorance, is the order of progress today." Later Armstrong cautioned, "the man who does not vote is even more dangerous than the man who does, for little or nothing will be done to improve him." Without the vote, there was no basis on which to build constructive public sentiment. Armstrong viewed the efforts of neighboring whites to educate ignorant black voters from motives of self preservation, as probably more important than the racial minorities' own fight for educational opportunities. He warned those having power, "When nothing else will, danger drives us to fulfill our duty to the ignorant and lowly."

Frissell supported and further clarified Armstrong's unusual stance in 1895:

> Those of us who labor in the South feel that the common school, now as firmly established in Virginia as in Massachusetts, would never have been possible except for the fact that the negro was given the privilege of voting; and although he has at times been deprived of this privilege, the knowledge on his part, and on the part of the white man, that he has the right to vote, has made legislation possible in the South, which would otherwise have been utterly impossible. I think that some of the Western politicians pay more attention to the Indian question today than they would do if it were not understood that in a little while the Indians will become voters.

As early as 1882, Armstrong thought Indians should be made voters in some states, believing that Oregon, California, and Colorado could take better care of their Indians than the federal government. Most interested because they would be most affected by Indian voters, these states would be compelled to attend to Indian education and welfare just as southerners were supposed to be taking care of the needs of Negroes. Armstrong predicted that Indian "homesteading, education and legal rights would fall into line naturally and not have to be forced upon an unwieldy, indifferent Congress."[95]

Although many reformers believed that Indians had already been made citizens by the Fourteenth Amendment, the Supreme Court ruled in *Elk v. Wilkins* (1884) that an Indian could only be made a citizen through an act of Congress.[96] Thus Armstrong and other reformers fought (unsuccessfully) to include absolute Indian citizenship in the Dawes General Allotment Act of 1887. Instead the act granted only conditional and gradual citizenship, enfranchising those Indians who would receive an allotment or who had already received one through previous treaty, and those who had separated from their tribes and lived as whites. To Armstrong this act fell far short of pushing Indians toward independent living.

The general accepted granting land in severalty as the only possible rather than as the most desirable solution to the Indian question. The Dawes Act empowered the president to select reservations for allotment. Each Indian on these reservations was to receive 160 acres of land, which was to be inalienable for a period of twenty-five years, at which time a title in fee would be granted, and the Indian would become subject to state law and local taxation. Although Armstrong preferred the land provisions of the Dawes Bill to those of the 1881 Coke Bill, which allowed a tribe to choose for itself whether to be allotted, he really desired that Indians, like blacks, begin the "march to civilization" without land. He found it "a bad thing the Indian was given 300 [or however many] acres," since this, too, would supposedly retard the Indian from taking full responsibility for advancing himself within white society.[97]

Armstrong's preference for the utmost submission of Indians as a means to establish the optimum conditions for their eventual elevation made him an adherent of what one historian called "coercive benevolence." The highest moral position, Armstrong insisted, was to act in the best interest of the Indians without their consent. Thus he was in favor of abrogating treaty promises about rations, titles to land, and tribal affiliations, replacing all of them with American citizenship and voting rights. Such an extreme course of action he paradoxically saw as justified by his respect for the Indian: "To fight the Indian is to know his manly and heroic qualities, just as to educate him is to know his mental and moral capabilities."[98]

Second only to Lyman Abbott, editor of the *Christian Union,* Armstrong took a leading role in pushing public sentiment to embrace the aggressive change in land policy from the Coke Bill to the Dawes Act, once he understood that his position against Indians receiving any land at all was not tenable. Although not an entirely neutral observer, Frissell called Armstrong "instrumental" in the passage of the act. To set policy for the upcoming Mohonk Conference, Armstrong wrote the position paper for a meeting held in the New York offices of the *Christian Union* on July 7, 1885. He mailed a copy of this paper to each of the seven participants before the meeting as a basis for discussion, which, Abbott pointed out, aimed to promote a policy whereby the best men of the West and East could work in harmony.[99] Conferees at this meeting first articulated the momentous change in focus from voluntary consent to enforced compliance and from gradual to prompt allotment. The new policy was a frank admission that the federal government was powerless to stop white encroachment on Indian land.[100]

Indian reformers had long debated the whole question of treaties. According to Helen Hunt Jackson the traditional assumption of reformers during the "century of dishonor" was that the violation of solemn treaties prevented the solution of the Indian question. But Welsh, "feeling quite alone" after the *Christian Union* meeting, wrote Dawes that the Abbott and Armstrong view—that the treaties themselves prevented the progress of Indians—had prevailed.[101] Thus at the October Mohonk Conference itself, Armstrong attempted to convince a surprised audience that the morally ascendant position for Christians was to violate treaties with "a feeling that we must save them from themselves."[102] The treaty itself, Armstrong later said, was a "compromise with barbarism"; it stood in the way of abolishing the reservation system, which segregated Indians from whites.[103]

Either Armstrong overlooked the fact that violating treaties would often destroy self-sufficient indigenous communities or he felt that ignoring treaties was unimportant; after all, uprootedness had preceded the cultural assimilation of blacks. Speaking as if Indians, like blacks, had been "imported" to American soil, he asked, "if the Anti-Slavery Society had set before itself the goal of establishing sixty independent Negro states in South Carolina and Texas, with self government according to the ideas of Ashanti and Uganda, instead of American citizenship and civil rights, would it be a sin and a shame to reconsider?" Not surprisingly, these justifications for violating Indian treaties were so successful that the *Workman* found no opposition to the idea at the next Mohonk Conference in 1886. In fact the only Indian reform organization that opposed the Dawes Act was the National Indian Defense Association headed by Thomas Bland, who called the act one of "despotism and robbery."[104]

In sum, Armstrong's influence on Indian affairs was considerable, because as a charismatic principal of a school devoted to both blacks and Indians, he was in a uniquely persuasive position to suggest shaping a future for Indians on the model of the recent history of blacks during freedom. The analogy made sense to a generation of reformers whose pride at having freed the slaves did not diminish their ignorance of Indians. Twenty-five years earlier some of them as abolitionists had been called "fanatics," yet twenty-five times as many Africans as Indians in the total population had already been made citizens. In 1887 the *Workman* proclaimed that both the South's past and the West's present economic backwardness resulted from distorted social arrangements: "The Indians under the agency system were kept within the reservation which corresponded in many respects to the slave plantations of the South. The Indian, like the Negro, was made accountable to an agent at all times. He could not go off the agency without permission. Like the slave, he was provided with food and clothes, and his mental, moral, and physical condition depended upon the will of one man."[105]

Armstrong reminded those who feared allotment would proceed recklessly that the "success of emancipation was largely due to its suddenness and completeness. . . . men adjust themselves to the inevitable." Citizenship, the vote, and education would follow Dawes by necessity.[106] Thoroughly optimistic about the nation's capacity for eventually absorbing Indians, Armstrong commonly referred to the Dawes Act as the Indian Emancipation Act; he expected Indians to divide along lines based on ability and "refinement," to acquire property, and to influence policy, as part of a "New West" similar to the New South "freedom" for blacks had made.[107] Several years of deliberation on Indian reform had made Armstrong and other reformers even more enthusiastic about their own society's heritage and mission, leading in turn to their abrupt shift from gradual and voluntary to immediate and compulsory acculturation.

In reality, however, at this point in Native American history, the "black man's road" to Indian reform offered solutions only for whites. The premise behind the Dawes Act—arming Indians with citizenship to justify withdrawing federal protection and expanding the area of state control—was similar to the reasoning behind the termination of military Reconstruction in the South. Western settlers fought government regulation just as persistently as southerners resisted radical rule. By ending Reconstruction and dismantling the reservation system, the government hoped to discard its official responsibility for the welfare of minority races. The overthrow of the Indian agency brought the West into alignment with the social arrangements of the East as a basis for national growth, while sectional peace between the North and South was encouraged by recounting the advantages a history of slavery gave blacks over Indians. By 1887 the Northeast was achieving unity with the South and West at the cost of racial minorities. The New

West did not take care of its new citizens any better than did the New South, but it did take their land.

While Armstrong may have been correct in believing that a push for Indian citizenship, voting, and individual landholding created greater pressure on white society to educate Indians, he nevertheless did not fully appreciate that, lacking the "advantage" of acculturation through slavery, Indians would not embrace white culture until they respected it. Consequently, the principal was able to mold the opinion of only some of his own Indian students. While rejoicing in the passage of the Dawes Act, Armstrong himself sounded an ominous note: "There is a great difference between the new Indian citizens and the Negro freedmen; that, while the gift of citizenship was received by the emancipated slaves with universal, ecstatic joy and thanksgiving, great masses of the Indians are unconscious of the benefits of the Act or are suspicious of its intentions."[108] His urging of policies toward Indians like those adopted toward blacks moved whites to support the Indian "assimilation" movement, but by most indications Native Americans wanted the opposite of what Armstrong and the reformers forced on them.

Notes

1. SCA, *Annual Report,* 1885 (Hampton, 1885), p. 10. Yale University has the most complete run of the printed reports of Hampton's early principals. SCA, "Educational Work among the Freedmen," *American Missionary Magazine* 1 (Dec. 1877): 29; SCA, "Annual Report," *SW* 12 (June 1883): 63; SCA to Henry Dawes, Mar. 6, 1889, Dawes Papers, Library of Congress.

2. SCA, "Education of the Indian," *NEA* 1884, p. 178. When Armstrong returned from the "warpath," as he called his northern campaigns, the bells tolled at Memorial Church, and students were awakened to form a torchlight parade to welcome him at the dock. Interview with Fritz J. Malval, Apr. 1, 1983.

3. Peabody, *Education for Life,* p. 220.

4. SCA, "The Indian and His Future," 1890, p. 9, box 21, Armstrong, Indians, Indian Collection, HUA; SCA, "Education of the Indian," p. 180; SCA, *Proceedings of the First Lake Mohonk Conference for the Negro* (New Paltz, N.Y.: 1890), p. 84.

5. Comments appended to Ludlow, "Personal Memories," dated Mar. 7, 1892. Copy in possession of Arthur Howe, Jr.; quoted in HBF, *The Work and Influence of Hampton* (New York, 1904), p. 16.

6. John Greenleaf Whittier in *SW* 18 (Dec. 1889): 129; SCA to *SW* Dec. (?), 1880, cited in Ludlow, "Personal Memories," p. 857.

7. SCA, "The Indian and His Future," p. 7; SCA, *The Ideas on Education,* p. 8; SCA, "Annual Report," *SW* 19 (June 1890): 64. Armstrong quoted from his first report and found the inclusion of Indians made him hardly have to

change a word of it. See also SCA, "Lessons from the Hawaiian Islands," *Journal of Christian Philosophy* 3 (Jan. 1884): 216.

8. SCA, "Educational Work among the Freedmen," p. 29.

9. SCA to Emma Armstrong, Jan. (?), 1878, Armstrong Family Papers, Williamsiana Collection, Williams College; Aery, "The Hampton Idea: Education," p. 39. Indian delegations to the capital, lacking white political know-how, "are often morally above the statesmen whom they meet. 'They learn to lie at Washington.'" Armstrong said he believed that "noble savages [had] splendid largeness and force." See SCA "Lessons from the Hawaiian Islands," p. 205.

10. SCA, "Annual Report," 1891, p. 6. A "loose" black woman, Armstrong theorized, "may have sinned without being demoralized by it. Her moral sense was too weak to be shocked." See SCA, "Educational Work," p. 2

11. J. W. Church, *The Regeneration of Sam Jackson* (Hampton, 1911), p. 8; SCA, "Education of the Indian," p. 177; comments appended to Ludlow, "Personal Memories," dated Oct. 15, 1882, copy in possession of Howe.

12. SCA to Michael Strieby, Oct. 10, 1879, HUA. In 1881, when AMA schools were considering emulating Hampton's biracial example, Emelen Institute, near Johnstown, Pennsylvania, brought six Quapaws from Indian Territory to be educated with its fifteen black scholars. Emelen had been established in 1838 for the education of Negroes and Indians from the bequest of Samuel Emelen, although no Indians attended until 1881. After six months Principal Israel Johnson said that the Indians were "seriously demoralizing the African boys." The difficulties were racial; Quapaw W. D. Perry complained about being educated with blacks. The Indians had been under the impression that they were on their way to Carlisle, where, in fact, they were then sent. See I. Johnson to Commissioner Hiram Price, May 9, 1881; Price to C. Schurz, May 27, 1881; W. Perry to Price, Oct. 28, 1881; Johnson to RHP, Nov. 1, 1881; and Johnson to Price, Nov. 8, 1881, in RG75, NARA.

13. Strieby to SCA, Dec. 7, 1881, box 1, Armstrong Papers, Indian Collection, HUA.

14. SCA, "The Indian Problem," *American Missionary Magazine* 4 (Mar. 1881): 72.

15. These agencies included Red Lake in Minnesota, Lake Superior and Green Bay in Wisconsin, Fort Berthold and Sisseton in Dakota, Skokomish in Washington Territory, and one among the Mission Indians in California.

16. AMA Executive Committee Minutes, Dec. 13, 1880, Amistad Research Center, New Orleans, LA; Strieby to SCA, Jan. 14, 1881, Dec. 20, 1880, box 1, Armstrong Papers, Indian Collection, HUA.

17. Patton to Schurz, Dec. 20, 1880, RG75, NARA.

18. *ARCIA* 1883, p. xxxiv. Besides the AMA schools and Howard University, only one black school, Cookman Institute (later Bethune-Cookman) in Daytona Beach, Florida, showed interest in Price's offer. Principal S. B. Darnell asked to educate twenty Seminoles, in view of the fact that this tribe had no schools whatever. But he was turned down because the government did not recognize the Seminoles as a tribe. See Darnell to Price, Aug. 10, 1882;

Price to Edward Teller, Secretary of the Interior, Aug. 16, 1882; Price to Darnell, Sept. 19, 1882, all in RG75, NARA.

19. Clinton Bowen Fisk to Strieby, May 8, 1882, N.Y. files, frame 99300, AMA Papers. A close associate of Armstrong, Fisk had strong interests in both blacks and Indians. As assistant commissioner in the Freedmen's Bureau, Fisk wrote two important manuals outlining freedmen's rights ("Rules for the Government of the Freedmens' Courts," and "Plain Counsel For Freedmen"), was president of the board of trustees at his namesake, Fisk University, president of the Board of Indian Commissioners, a trustee of Carlisle Indian School, and often presided at the Lake Mohonk Conferences for the Indian. Fisk's wife, Janetta Crippen Fisk, was president of the Women's Home Missionary Society and honorary vice president of the Women's National Indian Association, where he was on the advisory board. Alphonso A. Hopkins, *The Life of Clinton Bowen Fisk* (New York, 1910); *The Red Man* 9 (July 1890): 1; and the *Annual Reports of the Women's National Indian Association*, 1901.

20. Patton to Strieby, June 23 and July 14, 1882, Washingon, D.C., files, frame 18604, AMA MSS. Howard University maintained its interest in Indians. Between 1885 and 1887, Tuscarora Lansing Jack attended Howard; he had transferred from Hampton because it had no college preparatory department. In January 1891, Howard President J. E. Rankin wrote Commissioner T. J. Morgan that the trustees had instructed him to offer the facilities of the university to any Indians who desired to come.

21. Strieby to Schurz, Feb. 23, 1883, RG75, item 17151, NARA.

22. Minutes of Executive Committee, Jan. 5, 1880, AMA Papers.

23. Painter to Strieby, Jan. 22, 1882, Washington, D.C. files, AMA MSS. Eliphalet Whittlesey (1816–89) attended Williams College and spent ten years as an ABCFM missionary in Hawaii (1844–54) where he first met Armstrong. A reformer interested in both blacks and Indians, Whittlesey was an assistant commissioner of the Freedmen's Bureau, held numerous positions at Howard University, served on the Board of Indian Commissioners, and participated regularly at the Mohonk Indian Conferences. John H. Hewitt, *Williams College and Foreign Missions* (Boston, 1914); Walter Dyson, *Howard University: The Capstone of Negro Education* (Washington, D.C., 1941).

24. Painter to Strieby, Jan. 22, 1882, Washington, D.C. files, AMA MSS; Painter to SCA, Feb. 13, 1882, HUA; Painter to Strieby, Feb. 15, 1882, Washington, D.C. files, frame 18575, AMA MSS; Price to Strieby, Feb. 18, 1882, Washington, D.C. files, frame 18578, AMA MSS.

25. National Education Committee brochure, pamphlet A 247, IRA Papers. The Executive Committee of the NEC included Armstrong, Strieby, J. M. L. Curry, Atticus Haygood, J. C. Hartzell, and Rev. Robert Collyer. Painter to Strieby, July 21, 1882, Mass. files, frame 66868, AMA MSS; Minutes of Executive Committee, Feb. 9, 1882, AMA Papers.

26. See box on NEC at HUA for about forty letters concerning Painter's work on behalf of Hampton under both the AMA and NEC, especially Jan. 24, 27, and 30, 1882. Painter to Strieby, Nov. 20, 1882, Mass. files, frame 66888, AMA MSS.

27. Herbert Welsh, "Abstract of Welsh's Address," *SW* 26 (Mar. 1897): 50. Welsh pushed reforms concerning blacks, civil service, international peace, and municipal government. He aided the work of the Institute for Colored Youth at Cheney, Pennsylvania, spoke at the Capon Springs Conference on the Negro in 1900, and regularly wrote articles on Indians for the *SW*. An outspoken advocate of industrial education for blacks and national aid to education, he saw similarities between the Indian and Negro problems in that both races constituted a formidable domestic peril. For this information, see Matthew Sniffen to Mary L. Carter, Feb. 12, 1912, IRA Papers; Welsh in *Proceedings of the Capon Springs Conference for Education in the South* 1900; Welsh, "Some Present Aspects of the Negro Problem," an address delivered at the Coulter Street Meeting House, Germantown, Pa, Mar. 18, 1907 (copy in possession of author). For a comprehensive study of the IRA, see William T. Hagan, *The Indian Rights Association: The Herbert Welsh Years, 1882–1904* (Tucson, 1985).

28. James E. Rhoads to Herbert Welsh, Dec. 22, 1882, IRA Papers. Editor of the *Friends Review* and leader of the Associated Executive Committee of Orthodox Quakers, Rhoads would soon serve on the executive committee of the IRA and become president of Bryn Mawr College. It was on Rhoad's advice that Welsh first corresponded with Armstrong about Painter. See Welsh to SCA, Jan. 5, 1883, box on NEC, HUA; Painter to SCA, Mar. 19, 1883, box on NEC, HUA.

29. Hagan, *Indian Rights Association,* pp. 16–19, and especially p. 21. Rhoads implied that he and Armstrong viewed Welsh as a beginner in Indian reform, although "he will *grow* and become well informed and practically useful as he goes on." See Rhoads to SCA, Jan. 13, 1883, HUA.

30. Welsh, "Abstract," p. 50; Welsh, "Reform Work in Indian Affairs," *LMC* 1913, pp. 194–95. Also see, *SW* 50 (Mar. 1921): 112; *Eleventh Annual Report of the IRA* 1894, p. 53. Unlike Welsh, Hagan fails to credit Armstrong for originating the IRA mandate and overlooks the IRA's beginnings in the primarily Negro concerns of the AMA and NEC. See Hagan, *Indian Rights Association,* especially p. 21.

31. J. W. Davis to Welsh, July, 1883, IRA Papers; Painter to SCA, Jan. 24, 1882, box on NEC, HUA.

32. Welsh to SCA, Apr. 7, 1885, HUA; Welsh to A. M. Homans, June 3, 1886, IRA Papers.

33. Welsh to SCA, May 1, 1883, IRA Papers. Morris Jesup, known to historians of blacks as treasurer of the John F. Slater Fund, friend of Hampton and Tuskegee Institutes, and founder of the Jesup Agricultural Wagons (which did demonstrations for Negro farmers), was also involved in Indian work as president of the American Museum of Natural History and as contributor to the IRA (as mentioned here). Welsh to Mrs. Russell, Nov. 19, 1886 and to SCA, Jan. 8, 1887, both in IRA Papers.

34. RHP to T. S. Childs, Oct. 12, 1889, Pratt Papers, Yale University.

35. Wilma King Hunter, "Coming of Age: Hollis B. Frissell and the Emergence of Hampton Institute, 1893–1917" (Ph.D. diss., Indiana University,

1982), pp. 269–72. See *LMC,* 1900, p. 175; *SW* 32 (Mar. 1903), p. 133. Frissell built black organizations much like Armstrong built Indian ones. Dr. Edward Abbott of Cambridge, Massachusetts (a brother of Lyman Abbott of the *Outlook),* suggested to William H. Sale, an ex-confederate officer who owned a resort hotel at Capon Springs, West Virginia, that he hold a conference on blacks similar to those that Smiley had been holding for Indians at Lake Mohonk. See *SW* 27 (Aug. 1898), p. 154; Hunter, "Coming of Age: Frissell," p. 270.

36. For example, Armstrong was never satisfied with the annual appropriation of $167 for each Indian student. This sum was arrived at arbitrarily when the Sioux came to Hampton in 1879. The question of proper compensation consumed more of Armstrong's correspondence than any other issue. Ogden to SCA, Oct. 24, 1885, Ogden Papers, Library of Congress; SCA to Welsh, July 19, 1886, IRA Papers. Welsh nominated Armstrong for superintendent of Indian Schools; in 1880 James Rhoads had nominated him for commissioner.

37. SCA in *SW* 11 (Feb. 1882): 27; SCA, "The Indian Work at Hampton," *Wowapi* 1 (Nov. 7 1883): 63; SCA, "Report of Hampton School," *ARCIA* 1883, p. 178.

38. SCA, "Annual Report," *SW* 13 (June 1884): 63; W. H. Parkhurst, "Report of Lower Brule," *ARCIA* 1882, p. 30; SCA, "A Letter From General Armstrong," *Council Fire and Arbitrator* 8 (Jan. 1884): 9.

39. SCA, "A Letter From General Armstrong," p. 9; Parkhurst, "General A Reviewed," *Council Fire* 9 (June 1885): 99–100; Parkhurst, "Part Two, General A Reviewed," *Council Fire* 9 (July 1885): 111–13.

40. SCA to Price, Feb. 23, and Mar. 1, 1883, HUA.

41. SCA, "Education of the Indian," *NEA* 1884, p. 178; Editorial remarks, *SW* 12 (July 1883): 78; SCA to Price, May 7, 1883, HUA. Armstrong augmented the salaries of agents throughout the 1880s, except during the 1885 recession.

42. W. J. Wicks to Welsh, Mar. 29, 1889, IRA Papers.

43. RHP to Childs, July 10, 1889, Pratt Papers, Yale University; Parkhurst, "Part Two, General A. Reviewed," *Council Fire* 9 (July 1885): 113.

44. SCA, "Annual Report," *SW* 12 (June 1883): 63; Sarah Winnemuca, "Letter to Senator Logan," *Council Fire* 7 (Feb. 1883): 18; SCA, *LMC* 1889, p. 31.

45. SCA, "Letter of General Armstrong," *LMC* 1886, p. 22; Talbot, *Samuel Chapman Armstrong,* p. 76.

46. Editorial remarks, *SW* 21 (May 1892): 68; *ARCIA* 1893, pp. 5–6. Part of Armstrong's original proposal was incorporated in the clause providing for army officers to be placed at half the agencies but not to replace existing agents; Painter to Sniffen, Nov. 4, 1893, IRA Papers.

47. SCA to William C. Endicott, Jan. 1, 1888, HUA. Isabel Eustis visited the Apaches in May 1866, only one month after their incarceration at Fort Marion. Armstrong immediately offered to educate between twelve and fifteen Apaches. In February 1887 Armstrong himself visited Fort Marion and proposed that fifteen married couples be housed on school grounds in cottages.

48. SCA to Endicott, Jan. 1, 1888, HUA; *Sixth Annual Report of the IRA* 1888, p. 56; Capt. George Bourke, "From the Report of Captain Bourke," *Seventh Annual Report of the IRA* 1889, pp. 37–38; Marshall to SCA, Jan. 26, 1888, HUA.

49. SCA to Sarah Mather, June 14, 188?, Pratt Papers, box 18, folder 439, Yale University; SCA, Feb. 9, 1887, Armstrong Biographical Boxes, HUA; SCA, *Annual Report,* 1889, p. 19; SCA, "General Armstrong Tells How a Slaughter Led to Civilization," Philadelphia *Inquirer,* Jan. 15, 1890; SCA, "Concerning Indians," *SW* 10 (Dec. 1881): 120.

50. SCA, *LMC* 1888, p. 100, for Armstrong's depiction of the injustices publicized by Welsh in Mar. 1887. In fact one of these friendly Indians, Chato, was taken to Fort Marion directly from a conference in Washington, having gone there under federal protection. No distinction had been made between innocent and guilty Apaches, and both General Crook, who had long chased Geronimo, and General Nelson A. Miles, who arrived in time to exact a surrender, denounced the government's actions.

51. David M. Goodman, "The Apache Prisoners of War, 1886–1894" (Ph.D. diss., Texas Christian University, 1969), especially pp. 124–25, best describes the relations between various groups of reformers seeking to settle the Apache question.

52. Albert Smiley to SCA, Feb. 11, 1888, HUA; RHP to SCA, Jan. 19, 1888, Pratt Papers, box 13, p. 474, Yale University.

53. Smiley to SCA, Feb. 11, 1888, HUA; Eustis to Endicott, Feb. 15, 1888, M689, roll 191, p. 442, NARA; Welsh to SCA, June 26, 1888, IRA Papers.

54. Crook to Welsh, Aug. 22, 1888 and SCA to Welsh, Aug. 29, 1888, IRA Papers; Welsh, "The Chiricahua Apaches," New York *Evening Post,* submitted Dec. 14, 1888; Grover Cleveland, "Annual Message," Dec. 3, 1888, in James D. Richardson, *A Compilation of the Messages and Papers of the President's, 1789–1897,* 20 vols. (New York), p. 790. Typically cautious, the IRA never ventured beyond the recommendations of Generals Crook or Miles, not even to advocate that the innocent Apaches be returned to Arizona.

55. SCA, *LMC,* 1888, p. 100. Marion Stephens of Hampton and Vincentine Booth of Carlisle were sent to Fort Marion as teachers.

56. Welsh to W. F. Vilas, Secretary of Interior, Nov. 27, 1888, IRA Papers; Welsh to the Editor of the Boston *Journal,* Dec. 5, 1888, IRA Papers; "Geronimo and His Apaches," Washington *Evening Star,* Aug. 14, 1889; Bourke, "Report," p. 38.

57. Goodman, "Apache Prisoners," p. 164; Bourke, "Report," pp. 33–34.

58. Josephine Richards, "The Arrival of the Apaches," p. 1, box 14, entitled Cora M. Folsom MS, HUA. The Massachusetts Indian Association paid their scholarships. See *Twelfth Annual Report of the Massachusetts Indian Association* (Boston, 1894), p. 4.

59. Walter L. Williams, "The Merger of the Apaches with Eastern Cherokees: Qualla in 1893," *Journal of Cherokee Studies* 2 (Spring 1977): 240–45; Editorial remarks, *The Red Man, His Present and Future* 10 (Dec.-Jan. 1891): 4.

60. SCA, *SW* 14 (Dec. 1885): 27; SCA to Welsh, July 19, 1886, IRA Papers; SCA, "Report of Hampton School," *ARCIA* 1883, p. 166.

61. John Oberly, "Report of the Indian School Superintendent," *ARCIA* 1885, p. cxv; Ogden to SCA, Oct. 24, and 30, 1885, Ogden Papers, Library of Congress; Welsh to J. E. R., Nov. (?), 1888, p. 806, and to Painter, Feb. 7, and Mar. 26, 1889, all IRA Papers. For further information on the Oberly controversy, see HUA letterbooks: Welsh to SCA, Nov. 28, 1888, and Feb. 5, 1889, to Henry Bowditch, Feb. 15, 1889, to W. W. Frazier, Feb. 27 and Mar. 9, and 18, 1889, to Teller, Mar. 8, 1889, to Oberly, Mar. 8, 1889, to Mrs. Brinton Coxe, Mar. 21, 1889, and to Chas. Briggs, Mar. 27, 1889.

62. Thomas J. Morgan (1839–1902) had long-standing family interests in blacks and Indians. His father, Lewis, had been both an abolitionist and a missionary among Indians. As colonel in the Fourteenth Infantry and as a member of O. O. Howard's staff during the Civil War, Thomas organized and commanded four Negro regiments. Catholics opposed Morgan's confirmation and stressed his court-martial for falsifying muster rolls. Before his appointment as commissioner, Morgan had been principal of the state normal school in Connecticut and secretary of the Providence, Rhode Island, branch of the IRA. He is perhaps best known for his later post as executive secretary of the Baptist Home Missionary Society (1893–1902). See Morgan, *The Negro in the Ideal American Republic* (Philadelphia, 1898); and Morgan, *Reminiscences of Service with Colored Troops in the Army of the Cumberland* (Providence, 1885). He also published numerous articles on Indians.

63. Francis Paul Prucha, *The Churches and the Indian Schools, 1888–1912* (Lincoln, 1979), especially pp. 1–9.

64. SCA to Sen. John W. David, Dec. 18, 1889, HUA; SCA to Dawes, Sept. 7, 1889, Dawes Papers, box 28, Library of Congress; SCA, *LMC* 1888, pp. 100–101.

65. SCA, *LMC* 1889, p. 35; *SW* 18 (Oct. 1889): 104. Because Armstrong opposed his views at Mohonk, Morgan had intended to expose the practice of Hampton teachers raiding pupils from government schools and publicly claiming that Hampton was superior to Carlisle. But Morgan "fully felt the force" of Welsh's warning that he needed Armstrong during confirmation hearings. See Welsh to SCA, Nov. 7, 1889, IRA Papers.

66. SCA, *SW* 10 (Nov. 1881): 109.

67. SCA, *LMC* 1888, p. 101, and *LMC* 1890, p. 58.

68. SCA, *LMC* 1890, p. 58; SCA, *SW* 20 (Apr. 1891): 169.

69. SCA, *LMC* 1886, p. 27.

70. Ibid.; SCA, "Work and Duty in the East," *American Missionary Magazine* 4 (Dec. 1881): 380.

71. SCA, "Report of Hampton School," *ARCIA* 1893, p. 166.

72. SCA in *A Bill To Promote Mendicancy, Further Exposition of Its Demoralizing Tendencies* (New York, 1889), pp. 14, 85; HBF, commentary on Welsh, "Present Aspects of the Negro Problem," p. 15. Welsh advocated national aid to education to combat the continuing illiteracy in the South.

73. SCA to Secretary of Class at Williams College, Sept. 30, 1874, cited

in Ludlow, "Personal Memories," p. 753. For example, Hampton's Indians regularly attended local churches; St. John's Episcopal Church was closely involved with the Indian program.

Armstrong generally believed that white southerners exaggerated the danger of miscegenation and unnecessarily used it as a reason to oppose the elevation of blacks. Attempting to convince southerners that their defeat during the Civil War was for their own good, he argued in 1874 that a Confederate victory would have resulted in "Africanization." Thus the North had saved the South by preventing new importations of Africans, opening the South to white immigration, and eliminating the main source of interracial sex, the slave concubine. In effect deflating the blacks' antipathy toward white southerners for their crimes against slave women, the general noted that the offspring of such illicit unions had given the Negro race some of its greatest leaders. See Editorial remarks, *SW* 3 (Nov. 1874): 82; HBF, "Speech," Apr. 6, 1900, box 83, HBF Speeches, HUA.

74. Talbot, *Samuel Chapman Armstrong*, p. 215.

75. In Tomlinson and Tomlinson, *A Leader of the Freedmen*, p. 65. The Tomlinsons quote Armstrong: "Southerners who would not have anything to do with the negroes were only too glad to assist the Indians"; HBF, *SW* 29 (Aug. 1900): 455.

76. HBF, "A Survey of the Field," *Proceedings of the First Capon Springs Conference* 1898, p. 4.

77. Ibid. SCA's original quote comes from *The Red Man, His Past, Present, and Future* 9 (Jan. 1890): 1; SCA, "Education of the Indian," *NEA* 1884, p. 179; SCA to Elbert Monroe, Mar. 1, 1889, HUA.

78. SCA, "Industrial Education," *SW* 15 (Apr. 1886): 46.

79. Talbot, *Samuel Chapman Armstrong*, p. 278.

80. SCA, *The Indian Question* (Hampton, 1883), p. 7.

81. SCA, *SW* 10 (Feb. 1881): 11.

82. SCA, "Indian Education at the East," 1881, pp. 5, 3, 9, in *Pamphlets in American History*, fiche 1014, item 674, Library of Congress.

83. Peabody, *Education for Life*, p. 135.

84. SCA, *The Indian Question*, p. 5.

85. SCA, *SW* 11 (Feb. 1882): 27; SCA to E. P. Smith, Aug. 21, 1868, Va files, roll 10, frame 11376, AMA MSS.

86. SCA, *SW* 10 (June 1881): 63 and *SW* 17 (June 1888): 61; David Wallace Adams, "Education in Hues: Red and Black at Hampton Institute, 1878–1893," *South Atlantic Quarterly*, 76 (Spring 1977): 164.

87. SCA, *SW* 11 (Apr. 1882): 39; William Barrows, *The Indians' Side of the Indian Question* (Boston, 1887), p. 134.

88. Editorial remarks, *SW* 33 (Mar. 1904): 135; SCA, *SW* 11 (Feb. 1882): 27.

89. SCA to Price, May 7, 1883, RG75, item 8339, NARA; SCA, *The Indian Question*, p. 6.

90. SCA to Price, May 7, 1883, RG75, item 8339, NARA; SCA, "Annual Report," *SW* 14 (June 1885): 64.

91. SCA to Price, Dec. 6, 1882, RG75, item 22053, NARA; SCA, *SW* 18 (Jan. 1889): 14; Armstrong claimed that "we should probably be safe enough in making *all* the Indians citizens of the United States without further ceremony." See *SW* 15 (Apr. 1886): 43.

92. SCA, "The Future of the American Negro," *Proceedings of the Fourteenth Annual Conference on Charities and Corrections* in Omaha, Nebr., 1887, session on the African and Indian races, p. 1698. Armstrong advocated that Negroes split their votes. Instead of crediting blacks with seeking their own best interests, he argued that a solid party vote made each man a machine, deepened interracial hostility, separated the "similar interests" of labor and capital, hindered immigration, and prevented the best men from rising to power. See *SW* 5 (Dec. 1876): 90.

93. SCA, *SW* 3 (Dec. 1874): 90; Ludlow, "Personal Memories," p. 1041; SCA, *SW* 16 (Jan. 1887), in Ludlow, "Personal Memories," p. 1034.

94. Ibid.; SCA, Springfield (Mass.) *Republican*, Mar. 4, 1887, Peabody Collection, HUA. But see *SW* 16 (Feb. 1887) for a softening of Armstrong's views on black voting.

95. SCA, *SW* 11 (Feb. 1882): 27 and 11 (Apr. 1882): 29; SCA, "Jubilee Address," delivered at Kawaiahao Church, Honolulu, on the Fiftieth Anniversary of Oahu College, June 25, 1891, in *SW* 20 (Sept. 1891): 226; HBF, "Land in Severalty," *ARCIA* 1895, p. 1021; SCA in Ludlow, "Personal Memories," p. 885.

96. In *Elk v. Wilkins*, the Supreme Court took up the question of the Indians' legal status in a way that it had refused to do with the Poncas. The case arose from an effort by John Elk, a "civilized" Indian, to vote in an Omaha election. The local registrar, Wilkins, had denied Elk the vote on the grounds that he was not a citizen. The court upheld Wilkins.

97. SCA, *SW* 20 (May 1891): 209.

98. Wilcomb Washburn, *Assault On American Tribalism: The Dawes Act* (New York, 1975), p. 18; SCA, *SW* 11 (Oct. 1882): 100.

99. HBF, *SW* 22 (Mar. 1893): 45; Washburn, *Assault on American Tribalism*, pp. 53–54, has the best discussion of the meeting in the Christian Union offices. The other participants were Pratt, Smiley, Whittlesey, James E. Rhoads, Lyman Abbott, and Alice C. Fletcher, the first woman anthropologist and prime mover behind the Omaha allotments, which set a precedent for the Dawes Severalty Act. Welsh to Dawes, July 25, 1885, has appended to it the "Proceedings of An Informal Meeting Held by Request of Dr. Lyman Abbott," Dawes Papers, Library of Congress.

100. In contrast to the sudden grant of black citizenship, Indians gained this right in increments: Indians who married white men were made citizens in 1891, Indian veterans after World War I, and all remaining Indians in 1924.

101. Welsh to Dawes, July 25, 1885, Dawes Papers, box 27, Library of Congress. At first a proponent of gradualism, Dawes came to believe that the pressure of western settlers was inevitable and Indians must, in justice, obtain some compensation for their dispossession. See Washburn, *Assault on American Tribalism*, pp. 21–22.

102. SCA, *LMC* 1886, p. 25. Abbott shocked the audience even more than Armstrong, questioning not only whether the Indians efficiently "utilized" their land, but whether their "residency" implied ownership, saying, "The Indians can scarcely be said to have occupied this country any more than the buffalo they hunted."

103. SCA, *SW* 15 (Nov. 1886): 115. In September 1888 Armstrong advocated violating the Sioux Treaty to obtain a further reduction of Sioux land. He said that backing the Pratt Commission with force was "justifiable and inevitable in case of prolonged obdurancy on their [Sioux] part." See SCA to Commissioner Alexander B. Upshaw, Sept. 6, 1888, RG75, item 23158, NARA.

104. SCA, *SW* 15 (Nov. 1886): 115; "The Lake Mohonk Conference," *SW* 15 (Nov. 1886): 115. In *ARCIA* 1887, p. 53, Commissioner Price said that "there would never have been such a law [as Dawes] had it not been for the Mohonk Conference." *Council Fire* 13 (Apr.-May 1887): 57. For Bland see Thomas W. Cowger, "Dr. Thomas A. Bland, Critic of Forced Assimilation," *American Indian Culture and Research Journal* 16 (Fall 1992): 77–97.

105. HBF, "A Visit Among the Omahas," *SW* 16 (Nov. 1887): 117.

106. SCA, "Annual Report," *SW* 19 (June 1890): 64. Like Armstrong, Abbott used the example of black emancipation to encourage Indian reformers: "If a little handful of abolitionists . . . could start a revival . . . which ended in the emancipation of the Negro race, in spite of all the financial interests linked together to keep the whole race in bondage, it is not hopeless for this body to inaugurate" a successful Indian policy. See *LMC* 1893, p. 76.

107. Harris Barrett, a Hampton graduate and local business leader, said on Indian Emancipation Day, "Let us hope that this great emancipation will be the means of making a 'New West' for the Indians as emancipation has made a 'New South,' for the Negro." See Barrett, "A Welcome to Our New Fellow Citizens," *SW* 16 (Apr. 1887): 43.

108. SCA, SW 16 (Mar. 1887): 25.

Samuel Chapman Armstrong, founder and principal (1868–93): "Simply to Thy Cross I cling." (Courtesy of Hampton University Archives)

Rev. Hollis Burke Frissell, principal and corporate philanthropist of black education (1893–1917). (Courtesy of Hampton University Archives)

Robert Russa Moton, synthesizer of racial discord on campus (1889–1915). (Courtesy of Hampton University Archives)

Cora Mae Folsom (1855–1943) of Clarendon Springs, Vt., came to Hampton as a nurse in 1880 but soon assumed other roles. She founded the Diet Kitchen for ill Indians and the Indian Records Office and made eleven recruiting trips to the West learning Lakota. She also became the *Workman's* Indian editor and organized fundraising pageants whose exhibits led her to become curator of Hampton's museum. She retired in 1922. (Courtesy of Hampton University Archives)

Caroline Andrus (1875–1961) of Saratoga Springs, N.Y., succeeded Folsom as Indian correspondent in 1911. Andrus had begun working in the Indian Records Office while still a girl, having come to Hampton at the age of ten to assist in caring for her elder sister, a teacher of Hampton's Indians who fell ill with malaria. (Courtesy of Hampton University Archives)

Helen W. Ludlow (1840–1924) of New Haven, Conn., became the *Workman's* first managing editor in 1872 and continued as editor of writing on both races several years after her retirement in 1910. She also taught advanced English, coauthored *Hampton and Its Students,* and helped to found the Armstrong League of Hampton Workers. (Courtesy of Hampton University Archives)

The Wigwam, the Indian boys' dormitory. (Courtesy of Hampton University Archives)

Winona Hall, the Indian girls' dormitory. (Courtesy of Hampton University Archives)

The first Indian workshop was in the cellar of Marquand Cottage. (Courtesy of Hampton University Archives)

The new quarters of the Wolfe Indian Training Shop. (Courtesy of Hampton University Archives)

Indians exhibiting the wares of civilization. (Courtesy of Hampton University Archives)

Indians and blacks in a senior class picture, 1887. (Courtesy of Hampton University Archives)

4

Teaching through the Power of Example: Shaping Indian "Freedom" by Defusing Black Citizenship

If one half of Armstrong's problem was inducing more whites to accept and push for the Vanishing Policy, the other half was persuading Indians to disappear into white society. Like most American institutions before the lessons of modern anthropology, Hampton failed to address Indian reform within the context of Indian culture. Contemporary social scientists and missionaries attributed strong prejudice to nonwhites, who were seen as afflicted by a combination of ignorance, uncleanliness, vice, and distrust. Thus, ethnocentric Hamptonians felt that effective education of the Indian should address the "wrongness" of his antiwhite feelings. Similarly, in black education Hampton policy held that making first-class workers of freedmen willing "in all fairness" to accept second-class citizenship in real, if not legal terms, was essential to the economic and political reconstruction of the South.

The *Southern Workman* said that the relations of blacks and Indians to whites as well as to each other are peculiar: "Neither has the faculty or the inclination to put themselves in the other's place. Ignorant people are apt to be narrow and jealous, and on the alert for grievances. Disinterestedness is not innate, it is the product of Christian civilization." This mechanism of projection obscured Hampton's institutionalized prejudice. Voicing Armstrong's opinions as he often did, Hollis Frissell advised that "to wipe out the false and fancied antagonism between white and black and to heal the alienation, false, but not fancied, between the native and the later American, must be the foundation of [understanding] the tremendous problem which has been faced and handled here for all these years."[1] The juxtaposition of Indians and blacks was seen as offering a way to address the specific "problems" of each race.

Armstrong had complained to reformers that the central focus of the Indian "assimilation" movement "points to us rather than to them," that is, rather than to the real obstacle—Indian nonacceptance of whites and their culture. As IRA President Philip Garrett told the Mohonk Indian Conference of 1892, an Indian with the ways of whites was regarded by other Indians much as early Puritans regarded a "witch."[2] From infancy, Frissell observed, Indian children were bred to hate whites, who represented to them "all that was bad." He told introspective whites, "We sometimes think of race prejudice as belonging to the whites alone. It is quite as much a characteristic of the black and red races." He argued that Indians believed themselves to be "natural aristocrats," superior beings, "like men who came to England with [William] the Conqueror, whose names were written in the Domesday Book entitling them to land and to lives of luxury while others labored."[3] Of blacks, he said that slavery had produced "a belief in the injustice of the ruling race which makes it well-nigh impossible for the average Negro to express his real thoughts to a white man." While conceding that race prejudice was somewhat less pronounced among blacks than among whites, Frissell thought it "vastly stronger" among Indians, for behind Indian prejudice stood "the sanctions of religion . . . bound up with all the tribal customs of the people."[4]

Of course what Hampton regarded as Indian prejudgment arose naturally from defensive anger at the militarily successful, but in Indian eyes morally hypocritical white invasion. This anger colored Indian perceptions and interpretations of events. Traditional Indians often blamed deaths and misfortunes befalling their children at school or soon after their return home on insults to the Great Mystery. Likewise they blamed trachoma, a virus spread through the sharing of towels at school, on book reading. When Tony Blackbird suffered "great pain" while going blind in one eye and nearly so in the other, he told a Hampton correspondent that his fellow Sioux called it a "judgment on Tony." When Joshua Givens "ruined his eyes with hard study," and had to wear spectacles, he was called the "dangerous . . . Kiowa white man [with] glass eyes," and a "turkey buzzard" because of his short hair. When drought took the crops of a former student, other Indians would "jeeringly remind the plodder, 'I told you so. That's what you get for trying to be a white man.'"[5]

But what whites called prejudice was just as likely to be a rejection of white ways based on sound observation of white behavior. Countering the case for white education made by Sioux physician Charles Eastman, an elderly chief declared, "The white man has shown neither respect for nature nor reverence towards God. If you live long, and some day the Great Spirit will permit you to visit us again, you will find us still Indians, eating with wooden spoons out of bowls of wood." The Anglos failed to distribute wealth evenly and honor the spiritual and ecological "biology" of America because they do "not know any better."[6] When Washichus (a Lakota term for whites meaning "takes the fat") and their government issued wagons to the Sioux, they used them as serving trays to "feed their ponies; stoves, they knocked off the tops and used them over the camp fires; and the cows the Indians saw in them what they had in the buffalo—meat—and ate them up." A Sioux student took advantage of his role as Iagoo in Hampton's production of *Hiawatha* to tell his white audience what a white teacher termed "truths not at all flattering." In Lakota, he laughingly called them "witkokoka" (fools) who "only sit there and smile."[7]

Hampton officials saw this Indian "prejudice" against whites as a major reason black schools were the best place to educate Indians. The *Workman* said that whites "agreed that the policy of having Indians on reservations and in schools alone by themselves is not altogether desirable." Separate schools could not effectively transmit Anglo values, although the institute also maintained at least until 1900 that educating Indians in white schools was never successful.[8] Despite the Indian Office's policy after 1891 of educating Indians in local white public schools, by the end of the century only 359 Indian pupils were attending these schools; even the high of 558 students in 1896 was unimpressive. Furthermore, the daily attendance averaged only half the enrollment, and according to Commissioner William A. Jones nearly all of those enrolled were mixed bloods.[9] And historical precedent suggested that educating Indians in eastern white schools would also fail. Frissell argued, "William and Mary, Dartmouth, and Harvard were started with the thought of educating red men as well as white. The white man was too far ahead in the race for civilization. His brother in red could not keep up with him."[10]

An opponent of placing Indians in white schools, J. J. Gravatt, rector of the local St. John's Episcopal Church, described Indians brought from the Quaker White's Institute in Wabash, Indiana, as "very much demoralized"; but after coming among blacks at Hampton, these same students "improved in every respect," because Indians would not imitate the vices of Negroes. Instead, the Indian, "with his innate feelings crushed by the white man, unable to compete with him, finds his ambitions stirred, hope awakened and energies aroused when brought in connection with ⌊another⌋ people in a lower condition."[11]

The *Southern Workman* would later say, "our colored students, selected as they are from a wide range, furnished the best practicable conditions for building up wild Indians in ideas, decency and manhood." This statement also expressed the effort by Hampton staff to foster, through pride in "achievements" the Indian had yet to realize, acceptance in blacks of their own subordinate position in the South. Thus, bringing Indians into association with blacks initially served to bypass Indian hostility toward whites, and ultimately attempted to eliminate such hostility through the power of example, with the hope that the comparison might reduce black demands for equality as well. After all, almost no whites took seriously the equality implied in an off-the-cuff remark of Bishop Charles Cardwell McCabe at the 1900 Hampton commencement: "If you can Christianize and civilize the Anglo-Saxon, you can Christianize and civilize any race on the face of the earth."[12]

Hampton's Approach to Early Racial Adjustment: The Black Philanthropist

Armstrong confronted the common fear that trouble might erupt from racial prejudice between blacks and Indians by systematically fostering association. Apparently unconcerned with the opposition of southern whites to racial mingling, Armstrong asked blacks to share rooms with the first group of Indians. Although initially no black student volunteered for the duty, one finally took the hint and soon all of the Indians had black roommates.[13] A structure was being set for race relations: Armstrong placed blacks over Indians as "civilizers," hoping to make Indians more "teachable" by exposing them to a race praised as sunny and demonstrative.

Consequently, blacks at Hampton as much as the white staff taught the first and least adapted groups of Indians isolated among the white enemy how to dress, walk, talk, eat, and sleep like white men. One black head teacher formed them into a line, "grinned" and demonstrated the skill of brushing one's teeth, and the next prompted a once leery Indian to state that the Negroes' "happy faces and cheery words of welcome immediately banished all thought of care, and through the personality of the Major [Moton] I was forced to believe that the Negro was the kindest and jolliest man on earth." Of course, any comedy in the Indians' first use of shoes, stairs, and forks was balanced by sorrow, as in Kiowa Chief Koba's lament that he "prayed all day and hoed onions" upon becoming "righteous." But the effect of Hampton's approach was to disarm most of the Indians through exposure to friendly Negroes. *Ten Years' Work* likened the impact of blacks on Indians at Hampton to the practice of the old fur traders, who were said to have brought a Negro along to negotiations for his "pacifying effects" on Indians.[14]

Armstrong called his Indian program the first instance of black philanthropy and placed his best talent in the Indian Department. James C. Robbins, a Hampton graduate in 1876, became the first "House Father" to some seventy-five Indian boys in the Wigwam, who may not have known he was considered black since Robbins had no "visible trace of Negro blood." He had served as Armstrong's personal clerk until assigned to accompany Indian boys to Shellbanks farm in the summer of 1878. At the same time Amelia Perry, who would graduate the next year, cared for the Indian girls on campus while black janitors, the most "trustworthy" of the original Negro roommates, were already supervising and submitting daily written reports on how male Indians cared for their persons, rooms, and building. When school opened that autumn Robbins moved into the Wigwam, and he and Helen W. Ludlow, the managing editor of the *Workman*, began the column "Incidents of Indian Life at Hampton," which soon proved very popular. In what became a dominant Hampton theme, Robbins told Indians "not to think of wrongs but of blessings. All the tools you have are made by the thinking of the white man. Now what have you done?" Although Robbins liked working with Indians, he resigned in July 1880 because he did not receive the full authority over them on school grounds that he understood Armstrong to have promised. (Robbins remained an educator of Indians, however, becoming a teacher at the ABCFM's Santee Indian School.)[15]

Upon Robbin's departure, Booker T. Washington became the leading black in Hampton's Indian program: the success or failure of racial association at Hampton rested on his shoulders. Taking what would become an important step in his rise to eminence, Washington left a teaching post in West Virginia to assume charge of the Wigwam in September 1880. Discounting Robbins, Armstrong long recalled Washington's impact: "When Indians were first brought to this school in 1878, there was a difficult and delicate race question to settle. Could the black and red races be educated together without too much friction? I selected Mr. Washington as house father of the Indian boys . . . he settled the whole question most satisfactorily, and, chiefly through his wise initiative, we have for nearly fourteen years educated the two races together."[16]

In search of black support for Hampton's Indian program, Washington wrote "The Magnanimity of the Negro towards the Indian," which appeared in the first *Workman* after his appointment. He described black Hampton as aspiring to a morally superior position, rebuking the "many white institutions both North and South, especially such veneered institutions as West Point, where the sons of the so-called civilized parents refuse to associate with a colored boy." Black benevolence at Hampton would be an object lesson, encouraging whites to meet the obligation for Negro education incurred by the act of emancipation. Thus Washington put moral pressure on Hampton blacks to accept the Indian by suggesting refusal would parallel the segregation whites imposed upon them, while fair treatment of Indians would show "that though he himself was oppressed, [the Negro has] become enough enlightened to rise above mere race prejudice [and] has learned enough to know that it is his duty to help the unfortunate wherever he finds them."[17]

Although Washington believed his views were influencing blacks, he doubted his ability to reach Indians. Contrary to the stated beliefs of Hampton whites, he was convinced that the task of civilizing Indians would be more difficult for a black than for a white man. He knew that the "average Indian felt himself above the white man and, of course, he felt himself far above the Negro."[18] He wondered whether a race thought to cherish freedom even more than the white would obey a former slave. Given the Indians' openly superior attitude, it seemed to Washington fair to say in his "Incidents" column that he came to Indian work "with no little prejudice against the race," since blacks were waging an epic struggle to attain status in a society that Indians spurned.

Washington came to define the Indian question as a challenge to discover "whether interest in and application to education, agriculture and mechanical pursuits can be created and fostered in the race . . . [as] the first step in the white man's ways which . . . inevitably must lead to the rights and privileges of white men." He argued that Indian education should proceed along lines of proven success: national progress was impossible without interracial cooperation, which was incompatible with the claim that any minority had opposing interests or cultures. An Indian who internalized this argument was believed to have insured his future at Hampton, and indeed in America. It was a platform on which Hampton hoped to unite northern and southern whites, and blacks and Indians. In a column entitled "Bear's Heart Returns to the West," Washington heralded the transformation of one of the St. Augustine prisoners thus: "instead of the weak, dirty, ignorant piece of humanity that he was, with no correct ideas of this life or the next, [Bear's Heart] goes back a strong, decent, Christian *man,* with the rudiments of an English education, and hands trained to earn himself a living at the carpenter's bench or on the farm."[19]

Other columns by Washington suggest he felt that maximum progress toward racial conciliation lay in minimizing differences. For example, Washington claimed even of Indians who had come straight from the reservation that "two years schooling makes [them] so much like other people it is hard to find anything interesting to write." Another time he asked, "Will another two years produce as great a change in as many more Indians? We hope so. Will another two years cause as many whites to change their minds in regards to the Indian? . . . The future will tell which will have the honor of changing the other." Aware of the potential obstacle posed by differences among Indians, he said on still another occasion that students from different tribes mingled as pleasantly as so many young whites from different states: "The children of the sly and quarrelsome Sioux, live peacefully in the same room with the children of the fierce and warlike Apache."[20]

But Washington's stay as graduate teacher at Hampton lasted less than a year; his work for Indians and as the head of Hampton's new night school program led to his appointment as principal of Tuskegee Institute. Washington's duties with Indians were assumed by Orpheus E. McAdoo and Alexander McNeil, both new graduates of the institute. Olivia Davidson, later to become Washington's second wife, spent the summer of 1882 working with Indian girls as preparation for her move to Tuskegee that autumn. Although not from choice, Washington quickly lost touch with Hampton's Indian program. One year after his departure he complained, "About all I hear of the Indian Department is through the *Workman* and then I can not make out who writes the 'incidents.'"[21]

While the Hampton administration saw itself as deliberately intensifying association between Indians and blacks to reduce potential racial tension, the extent of the contact was partly a matter of convenience. The small number of blacks who worked for Hampton in official capacities was concentrated in areas of service least desired by whites but consistent with Hampton training. Rarely included in academic and administrative positions, blacks typically taught trades, agriculture, and domestic science, and acted in disciplinary capacities as assistants, or what the general termed "old recruits in a raw unit."[22] Thus, blacks usually met Indians at the most elemental levels—in face to face encounters between bosses and workers, day to day enforcement of school regulations, and informal shop talk and gossip.

About six blacks instructed Indian boys. William H. Gaddis and J. E. Smith, both former students at Hampton, taught Indians harnessmaking and shoemaking during the early 1880s, while George W. Brandon (1882) taught "ciphering." After teaching black children at Hampton's Butler School (later renamed Whittier), George W. Davis (1874), a future farm demonstration agent for Virginia (1914–23), served as the Indian boys' instructor of agriculture from 1880 to 1887.[23] Practical experience in farming was provided at Shellbanks, where Indians were placed under Charles H. Vanison, a Hampton graduate of 1877 who ran year-round operations from 1881 to 1891, when another alumnus, Captain Henry B. Jordan, took over until at least 1905. No whites worked on this stock and grain farm, which school authorities often also used as a reformatory or penal colony for refractory Indians.[24] Indians sent there dreaded its stricter discipline and the exile from friends, and some may also have felt shame, because their tribes viewed farming as women's work. Since Plains Indians had land but typically no inclination to farm while blacks confronted the opposite reality, the latter took charge of agriculture during the summer months, when few northern white staff were present because there were fewer nonwhites to administer.

The Indian girls also had some black teachers. Georgia Washington (1882) spent ten years at Winona (1881–91) teaching domestic science—another position unattractive to the white teachers at Hampton. Primarily training students in housekeeping, laundry, ironing and cooking, she took her duties seriously, asserting of blacks and Indians that "two people down can't help each other, but two people rising together can." Although she liked her work with Indians at Hampton, Washington really wanted to found a black school in a "primitive rural area." Thus in 1892 she established Mount Meigs Institute in Waugh, Alabama, which became an important source of Hampton student recruits.[25] Her future colleague, Lovey A. Mayo (1880), taught elementary English to Indians before joining the faculty at Mount Meigs.

By the mid-1880s blacks began gaining more official positions at Hampton, largely by default. Discipline at the school had long been organized in military fashion, with a United States Army officer detailed as Hampton's commandant through a provision of the land grant fund. In 1884 when Hampton lost its land grant funds to the Virginia Polytechnic Institute at Blacksburg, Commandant George LeRoy Brown was restationed, and his place was taken by a civilian, George L. Curtis. Since blacks knew the drills, in November 1884 Arthur T. Boykin (1883) became the first black drillmaster, then the highest position of a black on campus.[26]

Robert Russa Moton would become the school's first black commandant. He was appointed acting commandant in May 1889, when the civilian commandant, Charles W. Freeland, ventured west to recruit Indians (a practice begun under Pratt, whereby army men used their commissions as leverage to gain students). Moton apparently had gained Armstrong's attention several months earlier by helping to avert a general strike at Hampton (see chap. 6), and upon Freeland's return, moved into the Wigwam and retained charge of the Indian boys. Moton became commandant in June 1891, when Freeland resigned. Allen Wadsworth Washington, just graduated, became Moton's assistant and honorary captain, and he would replace Moton in 1915 when Moton succeeded Booker Washington at Tuskegee.

Moton's appointment as commandant surprised him. When summoned before the general, Moton thought the close questioning implied that he had failed at his central task of containing differences between the races and sections at Hampton. Although it was widely believed that blacks usually refused to follow one of their own number, Moton's friends later told him he might succeed as commandant with blacks but would surely fail with Indians. Moton himself believed "the Indians would naturally expect me to be partial to the Negroes, while the Negroes, on the other hand, would suspect that, to escape criticism, I would very likely be partial to the Indians."[27]

Thus Moton tried to settle interracial disputes in a manner intended "to win favor with both parties." He eliminated confrontational situations between races or tribes by helping contestants to understand each other's viewpoints so well that they would apologize to one another. Moton came to believe that "much of the friction between races, as well as between nations and individuals, is due to misunderstanding." His experience with Indians taught him that "the ground for racial adjustment lies, not in the emphasis of faults and of (jarring) differences between races, but rather in the discovery of likenesses and of virtues which make possible their mutual understanding and cooperation."[28] Overall, black teachers were expected to neutralize the potential for racial discord among students on campus in order to defend and maintain the biracial program. Hampton needed such defense as a prerequisite for its offensive thrust against the "prejudice" that blacks and Indians held toward whites.

The Politics of Comparative Example

In declaring that ignorance, lack of skills, low living conditions, a sense of grievance, and protest among blacks and Indians combined to perpetuate prejudice and inferior rights on both races, Hampton did not distinguish between results and social causes of their subordinate positions. Since dwelling on white supremacy would deprive students of incentive for self-improvement, Hampton argued that the abolition of slavery and the passing of the reservation system had recently created conditions for racial advancement: now it was up to racial minorities to quit blaming whites and to help each other and themselves, gaining rights "naturally" in proportion to their dedication to self-help.

The institute's policy of constructive engagement between minorities "brought mutual benefit, the traits of one race supplementing those of the other," said Hampton's Susan M. Giles. While educators like Booker Washington called positive attention to racial similarities, Hampton also stressed positive differences, finding them to be "helps instead of hindrances to their mutual development. Each becomes in many ways a daily lesson to the other in the meaning and use of life."[29] By manipulating the races' interaction, Armstrong's biracial program aimed to create both a reconstructed, politically contented Negro work force in the South and an Indian people who believed the ways of whites superior to their own. Encouraging blacks and Indians to teach each other the lessons of white civilization became a central tool of Hampton's strategy of accommodation, and the views of students who rejected this approach rarely got heard, translated, or printed.

The dialectical power of minority example was most evident at celebrations held to commemorate Indian "Emancipation" Day on February 8 and black Emancipation Day on January 1. Indians and blacks exchanged keynote speakers at both Hampton and Tuskegee. Government Indian schools also adopted Hampton's practice of commemorating the Dawes Act of 1887. Because of the "very mixed audiences" at Hampton's major celebrations, some "changes and omissions" were made to students' speeches. In 1896, after having admitted that emancipation day was a "spectacular arranged for them as an object lesson," the *Workman* reported that the festivities had been organized "for impressing upon the Indian students the importance of this day to them." The white staff looked for Negro speakers who would help soften Indian resistance to white civilization, although as historian George Hyde has pointed out, "Indian emancipation" was a strange name for a coercive law which violated treaties and took the Indians' land without their consent.[30]

At the first Indian day in 1887, Harris Barrett, future president of the local black People's Building and Loan Association, explained why it was appropriate for a Negro to open the ceremonies. He said the Dawes Act placed the Indian where the Emancipation Proclamation had placed blacks twenty-five years earlier. Being black made him more able than a white to "sympathize" with Indians and "rejoice with them in their turn of fortune." Barrett told his audience that freedom had endowed blacks with benefits such as the ability to satisfy individual and race ambition by accumulating wealth and property, as well as respect for the name of their people. Barrett desired to enlighten Indians on the meaning of their new freedom, "to give you a glimpse of the good that citizenship will do for the Indian if he will but accept it." Barrett suggested that no purpose was served for either race by recounting the wrongs inflicted by whites during the past three hundred years.[31]

Hampton officials seem to have followed the dictum of Commissioner T. J. Morgan that red students "should hear little or nothing of the wrongs of the Indian, and of the injustice of the white race. If their unhappy history is alluded to it should be to contrast it with the better future that is within their grasp." Thus Sioux Edward Ukipata on the anniversary of the Emancipation Proclamation in 1904 told a black student body that both races should "meditate over the past history in a way that will inspire us to future improvement." Tuscarora Reuben Williams advised a black audience that his race "will in time forget the injustice of the white man in robbing him of his land . . . it is useless to brood over past grievances."[32]

Suggesting that both black and Indian history had evolved providentially, Moton declared on Indian day in 1900 that God no more intended Indians to roam over "undeveloped" land than he desired "the Negro to bathe beneath the tropical sun of Africa." "Indian and Negro Traits," an article attributed in the *Workman* to Moton but actually plagiarized from an article by an earlier white commandant, George Curtis, attempted to quiet Indian resentment: "the question to be solved by the Indian is simple and easy compared with that of the Negro." That is, the Indian had only to forget grievances and choose assimilation, while Negro adjustment to white society was more difficult because "the factors of race hatred, social prejudice and political inequality . . . cast over its ultimate solution a shadow of uncertainty which only succeeding generations can remove."[33]

This perceived imbalance was countered on another occasion by Reuben Williams. "The Negro of America had some advantages over the Indian: He has always mingled with the white man, while the Indian has been apart on the reservations. He early accepted the white man's customs of living, while the Indian remained uncivilized. The Negro, even before his emancipation, knew the value of education and strove to attain it." It was presumably encouraging for blacks to hear an Indian commend the "southern workman" for his economic contribution to the nation, comparing him favorably to "the uneducated Indian [who] has no special occupations, and [whose] labor is of little or no value." Similarly, Sac and Fox tribesman Walter Battice told his black auditors of a bright future in which they could expect to make more rapid progress than Indians, because the government had not forced blacks into habits of idleness; indeed slavery had taught them to work.[34]

Nevertheless, no matter how dismal the prospects for Indian advancement seemed, the example of blacks also suggested that great progress was possible. Sioux Ben Brave told a Hampton camp meeting, "Today as I look back in history and see the Negro race, that was crushed and degraded . . . take its place among the people of the world, I feel hopeful for the future of my own race." In February 1914 Anishinabe Fred Bender even proclaimed, "I am proud of the fact that I am an Indian, and glad . . . we have been handicapped by unearned prejudice, because . . . [this has] tended to make our march to civilization a hard one."[35]

Always the institute spurred and steered both blacks and Indians toward behavior acceptable to whites and away from protest for civil or treaty rights. Thus in apparent identification with the assumptions of white paternalism, Moton was quoted as having written, "The Negro learns that he has not a monopoly of grievances and that he is not the only one on the foot of the ladder, and comes gradually into sympathy with the universal problem of life other than his own personal interests. The Indian sees the teachings of the superior intelligence put into practice by one nearer his own plane, like himself struggling to rise to the full stature of civilized manhood. From the Negroes he learns the habits of industry, thrift and inquisitiveness, and these lead to character and competency."[36] In this case, differences between black and Indian were de-emphasized in favor of mechanisms for acculturation, basic factors that united black and white, such as language, religion, customs, and general concern for economic development.

It was popularly believed that the demise of the Indian would follow not from his "dark" color but from his refusal to adopt white culture. For the Indian who clung to his old way of life, Armstrong said the "locomotive screams his fate." Moton warned his student audience on Indian day in 1900 that the more the "precious treasures" of civilization were shared with blacks and Indians, the more whites had a right to expect minorities to measure up to their duties. He said that "the Red man and Black man are on trial. They are constantly under examination, and the question as to whether they pass must be decided in this generation. Upon the evidence of progress that you and I must give, the court's decision will be rendered."[37]

Thus only blacks and Indians themselves could overcome the grim possibility of extinction. Sioux David Simmons told his fellow Indians, "As with the Negro, so with the Red man. For the former enslavement or extinction, for the latter extermination, has been said to be the only destiny, but General Armstrong [has proved] self-help could be a better solution."[38] The February 1877 *Workman* pointed out that history offered only two ways by which a minority could gain civil power, and the example of Indians showed blacks that the military option was suicidal. The second method, perfected at Hampton, was for a minority itself to prove that the "ill-opinions of the majority were undeserved, not so much by argument as by the demonstration of good works."[39]

Booker T. Washington had earlier summed up his lessons as Hampton's house father to the Indians by writing in "The Negro and the Indian" that he and other blacks became broader men as they came to extend their sympathies: "Just so far as we, as a race, learn that our trials and our difficulties are not wholly exceptional and peculiar to ourselves; that, on the contrary, other peoples have passed through the same periods of trial and have had to stand the same tests, *we shall cease to feel discouraged and embittered* [emphasis added]." He had learned from the Indian that "if I permitted myself to hate a man because of his race I was doing a greater wrong to myself than I could possibly do to him." Thus in the midst of deteriorated conditions for blacks during the early twentieth century, Frissell would argue that Hampton's multiracial climate helped produce a Negro who understood "restraint, self-control, cooperation, and the ability to see things from another's point of view."[40]

The Application of Comparative Example on Campus

Black Hampton did offer Plains Indians a genuine addition to native strategies for survival, a means toward accommodation with whites just when violent resistance had proved futile. Hampton's white staff had undertaken a difficult task: to convince Indians to accept not only white standards of civilization in the abstract, but concrete obligations and duties, within a society attempting to destroy their own. Members of the Hampton hierarchy tried to allay the effrontery of such a suggestion by employing blacks to do it for them. The black experience spoke to the Indian through a history of capture, enslavement, torture, and shattered families. Despite all the injustice they had suffered, most blacks seemed to have rejected retribution or repatriation in favor of mainstream culture and American citizenship.

White Hamptonians believed that by directing the Indians' attention to the misery of blacks at the bottom of Virginia society, they could inculcate a sense of missionary obligation in the Indian, *and* thus counteract the debilitating effects of the reservation system. Frissell said that "the pauperizing, hardening influences on the reservation which cause the Indians to be thoroughly self-centered can be overcome only as they are thoroughly imbued with the Christian idea of service for others."[41] Whites not only imagined themselves too advanced to elicit philanthropic impulses from Indians, but recognized Indian animosity toward them. Because of their destitution, blacks, on the other hand, seemed obvious recipients of Indian charity.

Thus Hampton organized small groups of Indians for missionary excursions to the poor house and the cabins of a nearby Negro neighborhood, where the Indians read the Bible to elderly blacks and fed them leftovers from the school cafeteria. Charity was also extended to black inmates of the Hampton jail.[42] On at least two occasions, Indians donated some of the proceeds from Hampton events—an ice cream social and later a "food and fancy art sale"—toward a scholarship for Georgia Washington's Mount Meigs Institute. Indians assisted in sewing classes at nearby Buckroe, taught Sunday school at a black Baptist church, and gave more formal instruction to black children at Whittier School, where student teachers of both races spent a month or two while preparing for their senior year at Hampton, and where Indian graduates were sometimes given regular employment.[43] As if compensating Indians for consistently appointing a black commandant, Hampton appointed an Indian drill master of the children at Whittier.[44]

In 1880 well-known educator Anna C. Brackett described as "exact opposites" the children of slaves and warriors in Hampton classrooms. It was a common assessment. More overtly patronizing than Hampton's own writers, Brackett said the Negro "comes to us trustfully and unconsciously to be petted" and is "only stimulated to more activity" by being viewed in class. In contrast, watching made the Indian "shy and distrustful." When the Indian had difficulty following the "clear utterances of his teacher, and she only a young girl, his sense of mortification and humiliation makes him sullen." Since whites often wished the black were more like the Indian, and the Indian more like the black, the optimistic statements of the Reverend Addison P. Foster must have held special interest for them. This Congregational minister from Boston told those at Hampton's commencement in 1880 that the two races' "dispositions supplement each other. The Negro is enthusiastic, demonstrative and dependent, the Indian reserved, bashful and self contained. Each finds in the other, qualities that he needs and that attract him."[45]

Armstrong himself declared contact with blacks to be of "the greatest benefit to the Indians in [teaching] vivacity of character and cheerfulness of manner." Frissell also saw the psychodynamics of classroom association as helpful in modifying personality. In a statement careful not to give either minority the impression it was any better than the other, he said that "the colored student is ready to ask questions, to discuss freely the topics under consideration, and to join heartily in a laugh, even at his own expense. This has often a stimulating and helpful effect upon the more reserved, sensitive, and self-conscious Indian, even though at times it may grate upon his native ideas of dignity and decorum."[46] Since many whites felt blacks took these characteristics to an undesirable extreme, the last part of Frissell's statement may have implied a hope that blacks would gain a greater sense of reserve and sensitivity through their association with Indians.

Indeed the *Southern Workman* asserted that the effect of civilization and education was to eliminate or reduce distinguishing race characteristics and powers. In the case of the Indian, "the caution and reticence . . . so general and marked among the newcomers . . . diminish in three years very noticeably. . . . they grow much more spontaneous and demonstrative." Certainly in Hampton classes the outspokenness of blacks contradicted the Plains Indian belief that it was bad manners to presume to know more than another by correcting an erroneous response. Francis G. Peabody, vice president of the Hampton Board of Trustees, claimed that "the mind of the Negro is not hampered by tradition or by self-esteem [i.e., the sin of pride]; but is impressionable and imitative. A most plastic material for education." For the sake of Indian survival, it was thought that his proud but inflexible nature had to be made more "teachable." On visiting Hampton, Elsie Eaton Newton, a United States Indian school inspector, asked how many teachers of Indians comprehended that "to bring out *initiative* in the Indian child is the greatest task before him."[47]

Frissell too believed about Indians that "perhaps among no other untaught people do the educated children find quite so much difficulty in introducing new customs; certainly not among the Negroes where old folks are generally quite as anxious to learn as the children to teach." He told the story of a traditional Indian chief who declined the offer of a white man to send his son to college on the grounds that such training would never fit his son to hunt deer, kill an enemy, make a tent, or endure cold or heat. As a counterproposal, the chief offered to educate the sons of the white man in the woods and make men of them. The sharply contrasting thirst of black Americans for a general European education, so apparent to white educators of the period—and sometimes criticized by them as imitativeness or dependence—was seen at Hampton as the essential model for the cultural assimilation of Indians. None of Hampton's administrators anticipated future Commissioner John Collier's view that "Indian education was as old as Indian life," nor questioned whether white education would solve the "Indian problem," or had created it in the first place.[48]

Thus blacks at Hampton more than the white staff were primary role models for Indians on campus. Hampton frequently touted its superiority over purely Indian schools even by pointing out the benefit for Indians in learning English from blacks, whose natural "talkativeness" would provide Indians with constant exposure. Armstrong called the blacks' knowledge of English an "advantage without parallel in the history of any race in a similar condition." Yet one contributor to the *Workman* feared that "the Negro dialect was almost an additional language for [Indians] to learn." But the magazine had formulated an answer to this criticism years earlier, remarking that Indians could not learn a "bad accent or low dialect" from blacks because "Negroisms" were not permitted at Hampton.[49] Indeed Hampton gave daily exercises in phonetics to prevent "careless enunciation."

In fact, although Hampton credited blacks with teaching English to Indians, Helen Ludlow occasionally looked to Indians to help blacks use the language "properly." While she reported that blacks in her senior English class "have a passion for oratory, and their musical ear tempts them to prefer a large, sonorous, and unusual word to a short and common one," she also claimed that with equivalent knowledge of English Indians held "some advantage over the colored in the power of using it. . . . Indians are not tempted to its misuse by a sense of musical certainty, and the love of display would be more restrained by self-consciousness, and a sense of the ludicrous with a consequent fear of ridicule." On another occasion, Ludlow complained that "even with the printed page before them, some [blacks] who have gone through the whole course cannot be relied on to make a copy without blunders." Nonstandard enunciation and spelling were attributed not to African dialect, but to "carelessness and long habits of inaccuracy." She said that Indians, on the other hand, "learn to spell quickly and more accurately," and credited not only the better initial training at Hampton, but as more important, an inherited habit of close observation.[50]

Books are "essential to knowledge," Armstrong once said, "but not to wisdom and manly force. The taboo of books [during slavery] was the greatest stimulus the [Negro] race ever had. . . . Restricting knowledge gave it a charm; it was the white man's source of power; with it he would be like him; to possess its secret became a passion, and this passion . . . is the hope of the race in its sudden emancipation." Booker Washington suggests Armstrong copied this slave code to make Indians hunger for education. At least during the early years of Hampton's Indian program, Armstrong greatly restricted the Indians' reading, except, of course, for the *Southern Workman*. Washington said, "to attend study hour like the colored students, and have a big pile of school books, has been one of the greatest desires of the Indians. This they have not been permitted to do," in order to make Indians resent being treated "as little children, both as to studies and to discipline, and from this comes their desire to be placed on a footing with others [i.e., blacks] as soon as possible."[51]

The Hampton philosophy described both Indians and blacks as having deficient notions of work: Armstrong said that before emancipation the Negro had worked only through being worked and the Indian had never worked at all. A reporter found Indians in the shops labored erratically because of "the inherited habits of the hunter, the fitfulness bred by the alternation of violent exertion with lethargic repose." Indolence had once also been ingrained in blacks, said Frissell, since labor in Africa was "obviated because [it was a] tropical country where nature does everything for man and where habits of work are not acquired." Slavery later taught blacks in America to work but had not endowed their work with dignity; it brought too little of the character building mental and moral effects to the Negroes that work ought to bring. It was understandable then, he argued, that blacks thought freedom meant freedom from manual labor and that their energies became directed toward intellectual pursuits without their having acquired the work ethic upon which higher callings were built. Unless Negroes gained the work habit and performed "from the love of it rather than compulsion," Frissell claimed, "there is no hope for them" advancing through the stages of civilization. On the foundation of work, Armstrong said, "ideal character is built, men are made, and the [race] problem is solved."[52] Of course all of this rhetoric ignored the fact that even as tribal peoples blacks and Indians worked, especially the women, who gathered foodstuff, cultivated fields, and provided clothing and materials for shelter, while the men hunted, fished, and defended the community if needed.

Yet even in dealing with the perceived need to teach the work ethic to both groups, which in varying degrees did not "understand it" as whites defined it, Hampton emphasized the differences between them to reap the benefit of interracial examples. Hampton dignified labor by contrasting the work habits of Indians and blacks, using the strengths of each to reveal the weaknesses of the other. Thus when Indians were placed in the school's shops alongside blacks, Charles McDowell, the manager, argued that the interaction was instructional for both:

The average Indian [at Hampton] had seen but little skilled labor done, but when shown how his task should be done, took
the information seriously. . . . If it took his entire work period to
make a piece of work right, he would devote that much time to
it, however small the job. On the other hand, the average negro
boy had all his life seen mechanical operations going on . . . naturally assumed that he knew quite a little about them, and did
not seem to realize the importance of giving serious attention to
his instructor, and he sought quantity instead of quality as the
result of the day's work. . . . The bringing of these two opposite
characters into the same shop proved helpful to each. The Negro, seeing the carefully prepared piece of work of the Indian,
became ashamed of his carelessness, while the Indian was not
willing that the other should finish his task so far ahead of him
every time, and was induced to put more "ginger" in his work,
but would not slight it for anybody.[53]

Even as black students were thus encouraged to appreciate native
craftmanship, Ludlow posed the question: "Can [Indians] be broken
in [to] civilized pursuits?" She replied that Hampton answers with
"farms, and work rooms, and training shops, where Indian apprentices are working under white masters side by side with a race long trained
to labor." Moreover, Robert S. Abbott, a black Hampton graduate of
1896 and editor of the Chicago *Defender,* argued that placing Indians among selected members of his race gave the Indians "a stability
and strength quite remarkable."[54] The belief of some Plains tribes that
warriors were "too good to work" elicited only ridicule at an industrial school for blacks. It must have been chastening for Indians to hear
Albert Howe, the white farm manager, describe the plight of an Indian among a seasoned squad of Negroes hoeing potatoes. Howe told
visitors, "See that tired Indian sitting down? . . . he will not get up until
he is rested. It is not shirking either; but a genuine backache, for which
indulgence is allowed for these Indians." School officials and the
Hampton physician depicted Indians as possessing softer muscles than
blacks, with weakness in the arms and chest and more width at the
hips.[55]

As the the Indian was made to feel ignoble, black students were
made proud not only of the amount of work performed but of their
mechanical skills (a contrast it was hoped would also give them confidence to improve conditions at home). When a white reporter asked
how Indians got on with the Negroes, his guide "smiled as if this were
the usual 'chestnut' [and replied] they get along right well, sir,

because . . . copying all our ways . . . they are always learning something." The reporter, "taken aback," as were many who were unfamiliar with the Hampton project, had "never been accustomed to regard the noble red man as inferior to the negro."[56] Armstrong asserted that unrestrained freedom had given the Indian "finer mental and moral fiber than the negro—it is the prairie pony and the work horse." But as if finishing this common analogy, Ludlow said that the Indians' advantage was "more than offset by the Negroes' sturdier qualities— of patience, perseverance, disposition to labor [and] greater physical stamina—which makes their prospects more hopeful at the present than the Indians'." Hampton staff believed that the survival of Negroes and Indians in America depended not on superior mental qualities but on their ability to earn a living, and that the very freedom-loving qualities that distinguished the warrior would, until the dignity of work was understood, retard any advancement in civilization. Paradoxically Armstrong admired the clarity of thought of great Indian chiefs, lamenting, "The Negro race can produce nothing like his type. It must disappear from the land.—too bad."[57]

But, as Commissioner Francis Ellington Leupp complained, there was no example of self-support in government schools where treaties provided for free board, clothing, and tuition, unlike Hampton, where "all the black students worked their way through school [and] Indians were brought under an influence which stimulates a wholesome pride in *earning their way*." Witnessing the relentless struggle there of blacks for education, "occasionally an Indian student has his self-respect stirred by this example and shows a disposition to do something of the same sort. [By law] the only way in which we can improve upon them is by bringing a little moral influence to bear here and there, either by example or by personal appeal, and this is where I think a finishing course at Hampton would be of the greatest advantage."[58]

Although *Ten Years' Work* had much earlier found that the government's "head right" policy of paying the Indians' expenses to get them to come to school might be a necessary act of "justice and mercy" for the present, it argued that such support came at a "loss [of] true education and progress." Hampton officials believed that Indians were clearly at a disadvantage beside unsubsidized Negro classmates who could more easily learn self-help; without self-help Indians were prone to view privileges as rights. Susan H. Showers, a Hampton teacher, asserted Indians were "inclined to get the wrong notions and to think that everything is done for the others rather than with reference to them." Like others who primarily taught blacks at Hampton, she wanted to incorporate Indians into the self-help system of education.[59]

Such critics of the Indian program's funding either knew little about how Indian education had developed, or were so committed to the individualism of their own culture that concessions made to Indians collectively were dismissed as abstract rather than real. Government schools begun among Indians as a "concession" made to their tribes in treaties came "freely" because Indians refused to pay for them. Armstrong inverted this reasoning by maintaining that those Indian schools that did exist did not develop character because Indians had not paid for them. He conveniently forgot that Indian tribes had paid for their education as compensation for land cessions (a point he did remember when urging the continuation of the contract school system). If Indians supported themselves in school as did blacks, they would in fact be paying for their education twice. And if assessed taxes for neighborhood schools, as Armstrong desired, Indians would be paying for their schooling three ways: by land, by work, and by local taxation. Nonetheless, six years before the government's withdrawal of funding for Indian students made self-support a fact, Hamptonians wanted to place Indians on a more equal footing with blacks. In January 1906 George Phenix, Hampton's vice principal in charge of the Academic Department, asked the commissioner whether Hampton was honoring the spirit of the contract or the wishes of the department when it matriculated Indian students who paid no personal contributions. Phenix protested that the Indian "had no incentives to prudence or economy at all comparable to what the colored student enjoys and which constitute a valuable part of his training." In response, the commissioner approved "in a general way" of having Indians do more manual labor to earn money for such items as clothes, laundry, and stationery.[60]

The example of blacks itself put pressure on Indians to pull their own load. When Cherokee Eli Bird asked to return to Hampton after the school year had already begun, Caroline Andrus, the institute's second correspondent to Indian students, expressed unhappiness with making an exception for an Indian: "you boys often say yourselves that you aren't held up as strictly as the colored boys are, and sometimes say it would be better for you if you were." Andrus used similar comparisons to embarrass two Indian girls into saving money to replace government funds lost after 1912, saying, "I hate to have the colored girls so much better about that sort of thing." These Indians girls, who already owed the school $50 each, had returned home for vacation instead of accepting jobs in the North. Andrus believed such Indians, who thought they were doing well just to arrive at Hampton, needed "hard knocks," since black girls came to school with money for the entire year. Of course the point was most potent when made by black students themselves. When Daniel Thomas, a Pima, told a black classmate that without funding he lacked the money to continue at Hampton, his classmate asked him "rather emphatically, 'Aren't you man enough to stay and work your way?'" Thomas remained at Hampton to "show that particular boy that I was a man," and felt he owed a "great deal" to that Negro who "made me stay."[61]

Not fathoming the sophisticated world views and viable political economies of traditional Indian cultures, Hampton authorities believed the dominant failing of *Indians* to be an excessive and largely unwarranted amount of racial pride. Alice M. Bacon, a pioneer Hampton teacher, claimed that Indians possessed pride to such an extent that they regarded favors as rights, making them contemptuous of efforts toward their advancement. Whites easily accepted this explanation, especially when Moton compared Indians with his fellow blacks, saying the one had too much pride and the other too little: "The Indian considers himself superior to every people; the Negro has a confident sense of his superiority to the Indian. While dealing with two such peoples, great care must be exercised that the pride of the one is not too highly appreciated, and with the other, that his pride is not unduly deprecated."[62]

Thus, since all races were givers and takers in Frissell's "great law of complement," Hamptonians found desirable and undesirable traits and suppositions of one minority useful in promoting a "wholesome discontent" in the other.[63] By having a black teach an Indian to use a hammer, the lesson of charity and the pride of possessing a valuable skill were brought home. The recognition that blacks were more acculturated than Indians set the conceptual world of Hampton somewhat apart from most contemporary white reformist ideas, but as blacks were to Indians, whites were to blacks. The Hampton formula of race relations infused the racial hierarchy of white over black with a sense of "balance"; it attempted to ease the disappointment of blacks at the retreat from the constitutional guarantees of Reconstruction. By teaching another race new skills, blacks were made to feel proud of what they had and less resentful of what was denied them, thereby promoting contentment without social change. Whenever Hampton equated technical advantage with cultural superiority, black pride was raised and Indian lowered. There was always a shaming aspect connected to competition with blacks, whereby Indian resentment might lose focus toward whites, who seemingly stood above the racial competition. Armstrong called his system a "tender violence" and exclaimed to his friend Archibald Hopkins, "You see I've only done something as a beggar, boosted darkies a bit, and so to speak, lassoed wild Indians all to be cleaned and tamed by a simple process I have invented known as the 'Hampton method.'"[64]

Notes

1. Editorial, "The Co-education of Negroes and Indians at Hampton," *SW* 8 (Mar. 1879): 79; HBF (Speech, n.d.), box 3, unsorted Frissell speeches, HUA.

2. SCA, *Indian Education at the Hampton Normal and Agricultural Institute* (New York, 1881), p. 6; Philip C. Garrett, "On the Influence of Returned Scholars upon their Tribe," *LMC* 1892, p. 45. A graduate of Quaker Haverford College, Garrett was on the Pennsylvania Board of Charities and Correction, and headed the Committee of One Hundred, a group of Philadelphia's most prominent municipal reformers. His power as president of the IRA, however, was inferior to that of Corresponding Secretary Welsh.

3. HBF, "The Attitude of the Indian towards White Civilization," box on HBF printed reports, HUA; HBF, "Hampton Institute," (n.d.), box 3, unsorted Frissell speeches, p. 139, HUA. In "Attitude," he said that the Indians who remembered Custer's massacre of Indians on the Washita River had believed that whites were "children unfit to bear arms." In fact, Indians, Frissell said, did not initially believe that whites were really human beings because they had hair on their faces. This article gives the fullest version of Frissell's viewpoint; he expressed similar ideas in "The Indian Problem," *NEA* 1900, p. 624, reprinted in *ARCIA* 1900, p. 445.

4. HBF, "Work among Exceptional Home Populations," Mar. 8, 1912, box on HBF printed reports, HUA.

5. Charles Eastman, *From Deep Woods to Civilization: Chapters in the Autobiography of an Indian* (Boston, 1916), p. 24; Tony Blackbird to Folsom on her 1909 trip west, Blackbird's student file, HUA (all of the Indian student files are also in Hampton's Indian Collection); Joshua Givens to Commissioner, Sept. 9, 1890, item 28577, RG75, NARA; Cora M. Folsom in "Report of Hampton School," *ARCIA* 1891, p. 606.

6. Charles Eastman, *From Deep Woods to Civilization*, p. 149; remarks of Rev. Thomas L. Riggs, *LMC* 1914, p. 88.

7. Annie Beecher Scoville, "Field Work among the Indians," *SW* 30 (Nov. 1901): 573; Folsom, "Indian Days," p. 24.

8. Editorial, "The Co-education of Races," *SW* 28 (Jan. 1899): 2; HBF, "Annual Report," *SW* 24 (June 1895): 88.

9. *ARCIA* 1899, p. 15; Commissioner William A. Jones to Elaine Goodale Eastman, Nov. 23, 1899, RG75, NARA. Laurence Schmeckebier, *The Office of Indian Affairs* (Baltimore, 1927), shows that the movement to place In-

dians in public schools gained momentum only after 1900. Only then did Hampton support it. See "Consolidation of Indian and White Schools," *SW* 39 (Mar. 1910): 131, and in the final chap. here.

10. HBF, box 50, Indian Affairs, Christian Endeavor, and the YMCA, Indian Collection, HUA. See also "The Co-education," p. 2.

11. J. J. Gravatt in *Ten Years' Work for Indians at Hampton, Virginia, 1878–1888* (Hampton, 1888), p. 69; Gravatt, report dated Dec. 24, 1887, box 21, Indian Affairs, Reports of Various Staff Members, Indian Collection, HUA. Gravatt served as rector of St. John's from 1878 to 1893, when he became minister of a church in Richmond.

12. *SW* 8 (Sept. 1879): 90; Address of Bishop Charles Cardwell McCabe at the Hampton Commencement, 1903, p. 2, HUA.

13. Folsom, "Activities of the Boys," p. 3, box on "Indian Days," Indian Collection, HUA; "General Armstrong and His Indian Pupils," June 25, 1889, Boston *Evening Transcript.*

14. BTW, "Incidents," *SW* 10 (Apr. 1881): 121; Daniel Thomas, "Indian School Life at Hampton," p. 278, in Andrus Box, Indian Collection, HUA; *Twenty-Two Years' Work,* p. 313; *Ten Years' Work,* p. 14.

15. SCA, *Indian Education,* p. 1; Folsom, "Indian Days," p. 29; Robbins to SCA, Feb. 28, 1880, HUA; Robbins in *Word Carrier* 9 (Oct. 1880). This monthly was the organ of the Santee Indian School. Robbins later studied medicine, before becoming a divinity student.

16. SCA quoted in "General S. C. Armstrong on the Tuskegee School," New York *Post,* Dec. 14, 1892, in Peabody Collection, HUA; BTW, *Up from Slavery* (New York, 1901), p. 101. For a discussion of Washington's experience at Hampton and Armstrong's impact on his life and thought, see Louis R. Harlan, *Booker T. Washington: The Making of a Black Leader, 1856–1901* (New York, 1972), especially chap. 3; Harlan, "Booker T. Washington in Biographical Perspective," *American Historical Review* 75 (Oct. 1970): 1590.

17. BTW, "The Magnanimity of the Negro towards the Indian," *SW* 9 (Oct. 1880): 103. BTW, *Up from Slavery,* p. 103, said that both the white and black races "lift themselves up in proportion that they help to lift others, and the more unfortunate the race, the lower in the scale of civilization, the more does one raise one's self by giving the assistance."

18. BTW, *Up from Slavery,* p. 101.

19. BTW, "Incidents," *SW* 10 (Jan. 1881): 7, and *SW* 10 (May 1881): 55.

20. BTW, "Incidents," *SW* 10 (Feb. 1881): 19; *SW* 10 (Sept. 1881): 93; BTW, "Incidents," *SW* 9 (Dec. 1880): 94, and SW 10 (Apr. 1881): 12.

21. BTW to Folsom, Mar. 31, 1883, box 27, Folsom, Indian Collection, HUA; Editorial remarks, *SW* 10 (July 1881): 76.

22. HBF, "Industrial Training," typed undated speech, box on HBF printed reports, HUA.

23. SCA, "Indian Work," *Wowapi* 1 (Nov. 7, 1883): 65; SCA, "Annual Report," *SW* 21 (June 1892): 85; SCA, "Report of Hampton School," *ARCIA* 1883, p. 167; Louis R. Harlan, ed., *The Booker T. Washington Papers,* 13 vols. (Urbana, 1972), 2: 45; George Davis in *ARCIA* 1888, p. 92.

24. "List of Hampton Employees, 1868–1883," HUA; Ludlow, "The Shellbanks Farm," *SW* 34 (Oct. 1905): 533; SCA, "The Hemenway Farm," *American Missionary Magazine* 6 (Feb. 1883): 49; George Davis, in *ARCIA* 1888, p. 45; SCA, "Report of Hampton School," *ARCIA* 1885, p. 241. The school was renamed Whittier so as to not offend southerners by honoring the man who had taken their slaves as "contraband" of war.

25. Ludlow, "Georgia's Investment," *SW* 36 (Apr. 1907): 228; Georgia Washington, "A Resident Graduate's Fifteen Years at Hampton," *SW* 21 (July 1892): 116.

26. Robert Russa Moton, "Report of Discipline and Military Instruction," *ARCIA* 1892 and 1893, p. 703, 464 respectively.

27. Moton, *Finding a Way Out* (College Park, 1920), pp. 123, 130, 142; Aery, "The Hampton Idea: Friend of the Students," p. 23, HUA.

28. Editorial, "Captain R. R. Moton," *T&T* 11 (Jan. 1897): 1; Moton, *Finding a Way Out*, pp. 143, 146. After Armstrong's death, Frissell persuaded Moton to remain permanently at Hampton because the delicate relations between the white in the North and South, and the black and red were of the "utmost importance to the Institute."

29. Susan M. Giles, "May Day at Hampton," *Lend a Hand* 5 (Sept. 1890): 642; Moton, "Indian and Negro Traits," quoted in *SW* 32 (July 1903): 311, plagiarized from an article by Commandant George L. Curtis, "Race Contact at Hampton," the Chicago *Interior,* Jan. 10, 1889.

30. Andrus to Joseph Estes, Apr. 2, 1916, box on Indian Letters, HUA; Editorial remarks, *SW* 25 (Mar. 1896): 51. Not until 1896 did school authorities believe that Indians were advanced enough to present chiefly original contributions. See also Editorial, "Indian Citizenship Day," *SW* 25 (Mar. 1896): 44 and George E. Hyde, *A Sioux Chronicle* (Norman, 1956), p. 185.

31. Harris Barrett, "Welcome to Our New Fellow Citizens," *SW* 16 (Apr. 1887): 43. For a similar view on Indian Day and "one of the best speeches of its kind," see James Hilton in *SW* 25 (Mar., 1896): 51.

32. U.S. House, untitled text of Commissioner T. J. Morgan, House Ex. Doc. 51-1 (Washington D. C, 1891), Serial Set 2725, 11: 104; Edward Ukipata, "The Negro and the Indian," a speech given on Indian Emancipation Day, Feb. 8, 1904, *SW* 33 (Mar. 1904): 4; Reuben Williams, (n.d.), speech given on Negro Emancipation Day, Williams's student file, HUA.

33. Moton, speech given on Indian Emancipation Day, Feb. 8, 1900, box on Indian Emancipation Day, Indian Collection, HUA; Moton, "Indian and Negro Traits," p. 311. W. T. B. Williams made this same point on Indian Emancipation Day in 1889, *SW* 18 (Feb. 1889): 32.

34. Williams, (n.d.), speech given on Negro Emancipation Day, Williams's student file, HUA; Walter Battice, paper read at Hampton Commencement in July 1888, Battice's student file, HUA. For a similar comment, see the Indian Emancipation Day speech of Arthur Harris, box on Pratt and Indian Testimonials, Indian Collection, HUA.

35. Benjamin Brave, "Speech of Benjamin Brave," *SW* 25 (May 1896): 99; Fred Bender, speech given on Indian Emancipation Day, Feb. 8, 1914, box on Indian testimonials, Indian Collection, HUA.

36. Moton, "Indian and Negro Traits," p. 311. For another speech on how an Indian's contact with blacks taught "respect for others and sympathy for mankind," see Daniel Thomas, box on Indian Testimonials, Indian Collection, HUA.

37. Moton, "Indian Day Speech," 1900, box on Indian Emancipation Day, Indian Collection, HUA.

38. SCA, "Indian Education at the East," p. 2; David Simmons, "Indian Citizenship Day," *SW* 23 (Mar. 1894): 44; SCA, *SW* 12 (Sept. 1883): 95. For blacks also fearing the alternative of extinction, see J. M. Ricks, "Letters From Graduates," *SW* 4 (Mar. 1875): 30. Considering their depopulation from disease and warfare, Indians must have found the occasional mentions of extermination threatening.

39. Editorial remarks, *SW* 6 (Feb. 1877): 27.

40. BTW, *The Story of the Negro,* p. 139; HBF, "Annual Report," *SW* 45 (June 1916): 63.

41. HBF, "Learning By Doing," President's Address, *NEA* 1901, p. 895.

42. Folsom, "Indians as Missionaries," *SW* 18 (Jan. 1889): 12; Editorial remarks, *T&T* 20 (July 1904): 3; "The Indian Sale," *SW* 49 (Jan. 1920): 90.

43. *SW* 22 (Apr. 1893): 62; Rebecca Mazakute to Helen Hilts, Feb. 7, 1932, Mazakute's student file, HUA; *SW* 23 (Apr. 1894): 62 and 20 (Mar. 1891): 166.

44. Editorial remarks, *SW* 6 (Feb. 1877): 27; Ludlow, "The Evolution of the Whittier School," *SW* 35 (June 1906): 340.

45. Anna C. Brackett, "Indian and Negro," *Harper's New Monthly Magazine* 61 (Sept. 1880): 627; Addison P. Foster, "The Hampton Anniversary," *American Missionary Magazine* 3 (July 1880): 207.

46. SCA, *Annual Report,* 1883, p. 34; HBF, "Indian Education at Hampton," (n.d.), p. 6, Yale University Library.

47. Editorial, "Civilization Versus Nature," *SW* 14 (Mar. 1885): 26. The article maintained that the craftsmanship and originality of native pottery and painting declined with the advent of "civilization." Peabody, *Education for Life,* p. 274; Elsie Eaton Newton, "Some Observations of Indian Education," *The Native American* (Phoenix Indian School) 11 (June 25, 1910).

48. HBF, "The American Indian in Old and New Environments," p. 2, box 3, unsorted Frissell speeches, HUA; HBF, *Annual Report,* 1912, p. 7; HBF, "The Attitude," p. 1; John Collier in Evelyn C. Adams, *American Indian Education,* p. vi.

49. Ludlow in SCA, *Annual Report,* 1883, p. 13; SCA, "Annual Report," *SW* 9 (June 1880): 63; Edmund Thickstun, "Indian Humor," *SW* 45 (Sept. 1916): 529; *SW* 8 (Oct. 1879): 99.

50. Ludlow, "Results of English Teaching at Hampton," *SW* 11 (June 1882): 64; Ludlow in SCA, *Annual Report,* 1883, p 14

51. SCA, "Paper Read at the Annual Meeting of the AMA," *American Missionary Magazine* ns 1 (Dec. 1877): 29; BTW, "Incidents," *SW* 9 (Dec. 1880): 125; Harlan, ed., *BTW Papers* 2: 96. In 1883 Armstrong said, "Knowing the reaction sure to follow gratifying a childish desire for school books, we kept them back, to their discontent, gradually allowing their use." See SCA, "Indian Education," p. 4.

52. SCA, "Industrial Work," *Proceedings of the Lake Mohonk Conferences on the Negro,* June 1890, p. 13, 15; New York *Independent,* Apr. 26, 1888, clippings file, Peabody Collection, HUA; HBF, "Annual Report," *SW* 28 (July 1899): 249; HBF, "Negro Education," *The New World* 9 (Dec. 1900): 630.

53. Charles McDowell, "Organization of the Indian Training Shop," (n.d.), box 21, Indian Collection, HUA. p. 12.

54. Ludlow in *Hampton Institute: Its Work For Two Races* (Hampton, 1885), p. 10; Ludlow, "Hampton's Indian Students at Home," (n.d.), typed, publications box, HUA; "Many Indians at Hampton," Chicago *Defender,* July 15, 1916.

55. "Hampton Normal and Agricultural School," Springfield (Mass.) *Republican,* May 22, 1879, and Editorial remarks in same May 26, 1887, clippings file, Peabody Collection, HUA; SCA, "Indian Education at the East," p. 5; Martha M. Waldron to SCA, Jan. 1, 1890, HUA; "Red Youth at School," New York *Sun,* June 9, 1895, clippings file, Peabody Collection, HUA.

56. H. L. (not Helen Ludlow), "General Armstrong and His School," The New York *Evening Post,* Jan. 4, 1892, clippings file, Peabody Collection, HUA.

57. M. J., "Good Indian Work," Nov. 4, 1889, Boston *Evening Transcript,* quoting from a recent address by Armstrong in Boston; Ludlow to Mr. E. da Silva, Mar. 12, 1883, HUA, telling him "the Indians have the finer quality of mind; greater mental strength and quickness." SCA to RHP, Mar. 11, 1880, Pratt Papers, box 1, folder 13, Yale University.

58. Commissioner Francis E. Leupp to Elsie Eaton Newton, Feb. 10, 1909, RG75, file 820, item 15709, NARA.

59. Ludlow in *Ten Years' Work,* p. 25; Susan H. Showers to HBF, Mar. 5, 1909, HUA.

60. George P. Phenix to Leupp, Jan. 26, 1906, RG75, item 9599, NARA; Minutes of Faculty Meetings, Jan. 31, 1909, HUA.

61. Andrus to Eli Bird, Sept 12, 1917. Bird's "good reason"—building a house—was granted anyway. Andrus to Irene Halfton, Sept. 21, 1916, and to Irene Trippe, Sept. 20, 1916; Daniel Thomas, "Easter Meeting at Chamberland," 1915, typed MS. All in respective student files, HUA.

62. Alice Bacon, "Hampton Indians," Denver *Republican,* Aug. 20, 1893, clippings file, Peabody Collection, HUA. Three-year old Alice Bacon, the daughter of New Haven's Rev. Dr. Leonard Bacon, came to Hampton in 1871 with her elder sister, Rebecca. She later taught classes for fifteen years and wrote a series of articles in the *Workman* entitled "Silhouettes," before assisting Helen Ludlow in editing that paper. She established the Hampton Folk-lore Society in 1893 and founded the Dixie Hospital, one of the first schools to train black nurses. Moton, "Indian and Negro Traits," p. 311.

63. HBF, (n.d.), p. 3, box 3 on HBF speeches, HUA; HBF, "The Indian Problem," *NEA* 1900, p. 449.

64. SCA to Archibald Hopkins, June 30, 1888(?), Misc. MSS, v. 33, Armstrong Family Papers, Williamsiana Collection, Williams College.

5

The False Faces of Segregation

Historians have correctly emphasized the high degree of segregation between whites and blacks at Hampton, while incorrectly assuming that this separation held true for black and Indian students as well. What they have failed to note is that, by the ongoing use of comparative example, the school thoroughly and consciously manipulated its racial policy to shape both red and black attitudes. In light of this reality, the prevailing view of how much and to what purpose Hampton was segregated demands review.

When Elaine Goodale Eastman, a teacher of Hampton Indians from 1883 to 1885, wrote a biography of Richard Pratt, she claimed that blacks and Indians there had been segregated on "social grounds." It is not clear whether her view was influenced by Pratt's own desire to disassociate Indians from Negroes, or whether she just did not look deeply enough, after a lapse of fifty years, into an issue peripheral to her larger study. As a consequence of Indians coming to Hampton, Eastman recalled, "new dormitories were built, and a new force of teachers given special training for their exacting task. Negroes and Indians . . . had little direct contact. They were organized into separate companies, ate in different dining rooms, took their recreation separately, and the racial blocs were maintained even in the seating at chapel." Following Eastman's assessment, one recent study said blacks and Indians lived under a policy of "social separatism" that hardened over time; another saw at Hampton not one but two student bodies, while a third, taking what had become the dominant interpretation of its policy to a logical conclusion, found "not a school for two races but rather two distinct schools."[1]

This inaccurate portrait leaves the impression that Hampton completely accepted southern segregationist convention, as if only the forces of the South were responsible for the school's racial policies. Such analyses, even while illustrating points of racial contact, argue that Hampton authorities separated the races to keep Indians from associating with the "inferior" Negro race, as if the impact of 400 blacks on every facet of school life could be discounted. Although when writing about the exotic Indians to a trustee, Armstrong added "no end to darkies," this slur only negatively reflected what he acknowledged positively elsewhere: "the simple, orderly, industrious life of our three hundred colored students is a current that carries our Indian students along in spite of the barriers of heredity."[2]

Actually, in line with his early policy of making blacks and Indians roommates, Armstrong told a northern audience in 1883 that "as far as practicable, the colored and Indian students are mingled in classes and work, at the table, in military organization, and social intercourse." Race was not the main reason he sanctioned some segregation of blacks and Indians on campus: the "necessity [in order to honor the intent of benefactors] of supplying new buildings given especially for the Indians, the convenience of caring for health and habits, and the necessity of different methods of instruction for the majority who do not understand English, compel a certain amount of separation but only to this extent is it allowed."[3] As shown in chapter four, he believed frequent contact between blacks and Indians promoted conciliatory approaches to race relations in general. Although at odds with preferred southern practice, he felt the integration of Indians and blacks in such areas of student life as the classroom, work, and for a time, living arrangements ultimately encouraged both groups to accept segregation between whites and nonwhites. Not surprisingly, there was far more integration on campus between blacks and Indians on all levels than between blacks and whites: since Hampton rarely admitted white students, almost all whites on campus were in positions of authority. The complex and shifting kaleidoscope of racial contact and separation blacks and Indians experienced at Hampton cannot be ignored, however nonegalitarian the administration's goal of accommodating students to a larger white society outside. Relations between the races at Hampton presented fluid, ever changing "false faces."[4]

In the Classrooms

From the moment Indians arrived at Hampton, some adjustment to their level of familiarity with white culture had to be made. Generally this meant recognizing the problem of language. Indian children who were too young to have learned their own language were often immediately integrated into the Whittier School, bypassing the Indian Department completely.[5] Since Indians had to know English before any formal education could be provided, those versed only in their tribal languages were taught by methods of instruction then being developed to assist the deaf; thus they demanded too much personal attention for placement in regular Hampton classes.[6] This reality, more than ideology, led to isolating Indians in a separate department, one needing more staff than any other in the school. As Armstrong stated, "Hampton has a large corp of teachers with small Indian classes averaging fifteen, much smaller than those of the colored students." As Frissell later explained of the early years of the school, "There were always exceptionally bright Indians, [but] it was quite impossible to hold the mass of Indian pupils to the same standards as the colored students either in work or study."[7] At one point, the Indian Department contained seven divisions of developmental classes, the lowest of which, according to one teacher, was "always known for its proverbial stupidity."[8]

Thus the Indian Department served not a racial agenda but those students least familiar with the amalgam of white/black culture shared by most Hampton students.[9] The few blacks coming to Hampton from Cuba, Latin America, or Africa, who like most of the Indians brought their own culture and language with them, were placed in the Indian Department. Since Indian entrants with part white or part black ancestry were often already somewhat acculturated, they usually moved quickly "out" of the Indian Department. Thus only four of twenty Indians who reached the Normal School level in 1885 were full-bloods.[10] Conversely, full-blooded Indians reared in tribal surroundings stayed longest in the Indian Department. Paradoxically, therefore, the department intended to lay the foundation for assimilation also served as a reservoir of tribal culture.

Integration occurred as advancing Indians reached the lower grades for blacks. In 1881, when the Indian program was only three years old, Armstrong described the regimen as placing "the negro in advanced, the Indian in primary classes, mixing [them] in the intermediate, the former by influence and example pushing the latter along."[11] Already by the next year, however, three Indians had advanced through the Normal School program: members of three different tribes, Thomas Wildcat Alford (Absentee Shawnee), John Downing (Eastern Cherokee), and Michael Oshkeneny (Menominee), became Hampton's first Indian graduates.[12]

The principal's annual reports to the trustees and to the commissioner of Indian Affairs show a steadily increasing number of Indians entering regular classes.[13] In 1886 Armstrong reported eight Indians in the Night School and twenty-five in the Normal, although the remedial Indian Department had eighty-seven. Five years later fifty-seven Indians were in the Normal School, while seventy-seven Indians still required separate classes.[14] Coursework for the most advanced class in the Indian Department was designed to prepare students for the first year of Normal. In her review of industries for 1891, teacher Susan de Lancey Van Rensselaer called the Indian Department "the antechamber of the Normal School where students of both races are educated together." By then, Indians were found in all grades, including eight seniors, sixteen middlers, twenty-two juniors, and eleven intermediates. But between 1893 and 1901 students and faculty of the two schools were gradually merged. Until then each department had even had a separate administration. Frissell explained in 1901 that "as western schools have improved we have been able to secure more advanced students . . . thus doing away with a separate Indian department."[15]

After 1898 Indians, like other students, were required to pass entrance examinations. Those Indians not sufficiently prepared to enter classes with blacks were now only rarely admitted. Although a discouraging backlog of Indians remained in preparatory classes, Hampton was achieving its aim of unified classes. Lady Principal Elizabeth Hyde said, "Many of the difficulties with the Indian are over when we get him into the regular academic classes, and he feels the dignity of being able to recite and do the regular work of the School." Once the so-called post graduate courses became available in 1898, Indians also moved into these normal, trade and agricultural courses, roughly equivalent to the first or second year of high school. For example, in 1904 three Indians took the "graduate" course in agriculture.[16]

In the Productive Industries: The Shops and Farms

Since most Indians received "free" schooling, they were exempted from Hampton industries where gainful production was the foremost concern. However, those few Indians who came every year from tribes lacking treaty provisions for education were placed in the Night School with blacks, and worked all day without segregation.[17] While allowing students to be self-supporting, the Night School run by Booker Washington served black students whose academic preparation was inadequate for entering the Day School. But Indian students who attended the Night School during the early years of government funding were among Hampton's best Indian scholars (and certainly, in Washington's terms, among its most "plucky").

For the average Indian, freed from (or from Hampton's point of view, denied) the requirement of self-support, manual labor was purely instructional—for the head, hand, and heart rather than the pocket. Indeed, on an occasion when he was charged with preferring blacks over Indians, Armstrong defended himself by saying that Hampton's offerings for Indians were primarily educational, while education for Negroes was largely incidental to production.[18] The school could not rely on production from Indians largely unfamiliar with European tools and methods. "The work of the colored students is steady and profitable," Armstrong said in 1879; "that of the Indians has almost no value the first year and little afterwards."[19]

Given Armstrong's firm belief in the primary educational value of work itself and given Hampton's small proportion of graduates, it seems likely that some of the poorest blacks at Hampton in the 1880s were relegated to campus maintenance and may have returned home without learning a trade or having taken classes even in the Night School. William M. Reid, an 1877 Hampton graduate, stated that "if a boy came to Hampton and could do a given piece of work, he was allowed to do it and thereby earn some money, but he could not really learn a trade. . . . No definite effort was made to teach [these] boys what are now known as trades."[20] Such students—more properly employees of the school who labored in productive agriculture, and in the greenhouse, the oystering plant, and the lumber mills—would have had little opportunity for extensive interaction with the main body of Indians or indeed with members of their own race who had brought enough money to attend Normal or to learn trades.

The status of Indians at Hampton differed from that of most blacks not only in their home conditions and financial needs and opportunities but in the type and range of skills whites demanded they learn. This resulted initially and again later on in different methods of instruction for Indians and blacks and consequently in some separation of the races. In 1890 Alice Bacon said, "the fact that many Negroes come with industrialized habits of mind and merely need one more specialized trade, makes their requirements markedly different than Indians where a generalized knowledge of the many branches of industry . . . is needed."[21] Hampton was always a place where some blacks, primarily males, could learn a trade, despite southern segregation and the exclusionary practices of northern trade unions. But Hampton's stance on providing Indians with specialized trade training changed over time.

———

George B. Starkweather, who established the first Indian workshop in Marquand Cottage, argued that specialized training was unsuited for the work done on Indian reservations. He doubted that Indians needed skills as exacting and perfect as those demanded for working in a European watch factory, "where life is devoted to tempering or

adjusting hairsprings." Thus in the first two years of the Indian program, he instituted the jack-of-all trades, or "house and farm approach"
of New England pioneers. Under this system, four groups of about a
dozen Indians each rotated between carpentry, tinning, blacksmithing,
cartwrighting, and leatherworking. In substituting brief but frequent
periods of instruction for concentrated work at a single activity, Starkweather's Marquand Indian Shop adopted a different approach than
the larger school.[22]

However, in October 1880 J. D. McDowell replaced Starkweather
and reversed the philosophy governing the industrial training of Indians to align it with the Negro curriculum.[23] It became an economic
advantage for the school to organize the training shops so that Indian
apprentices could be taught specific trades for which a market was
available to Hampton. In 1880 the Indian Office promised Hampton
and Carlisle that it would purchase student-made goods if the schools
could match the price of the lowest bidder.[24] Thus the Marquand Shop
was no longer operated for educational purposes alone; its output
augmented the school's income, while providing some spending money
for the Indians. In 1883 Armstrong sold two thousand pairs of brogan shoes, five hundred dozen articles of tinware, and seventy-five sets
of double plow harnesses for distribution on reservations. Inconsistent
not only with Starkweather's approach but with his own stance on
blacks, of only training them for positions already open to them at
home, Armstrong now claimed that "nothing is more important than
to establish a force of Indian mechanics at once, in advance, if possible, of this radical change," that is, the coming of "civilization" to the
reservations. Indian artisans making marketable goods at the agencies
would demonstrate to critics of Indian education their capacity for
mastering new skills.[25]

Thus while the integrated classroom was a stated goal of Hampton's
educational policy, the integrated shop was an eventual outcome of the
institute's economic self-interest. Although blacks do not seem to have
participated in the pre-1880 Marquand Shop system of handyman
training devised for the Indian, under the later apprentice system they
were barred from contracts with the Interior Department by its stipu-
lation that all goods were to be Indian made. However, Armstrong
duly reported to the commissioner the presence of blacks in the Indian Shops after three of them entered in 1881, and it seems likely that
blacks did in fact help to fill the government contracts. For example,
in 1886 the principal reported that his harness shop of three Indians
and two blacks made 165 sets of harnesses for the government and only
seventeen sets for school use.[26] After 1883, when Negro funds were

used to complete the new Wolfe Indian Training Shop, blacks had implicitly been given as much right to the building as Indians and were present in increasing numbers alongside Indians.[27]

Once the Wolfe Shops were built, blacks were needed more than ever to boost production and instruct Indians, since different trades were now being conducted simultaneously in separate facilities. By 1885 there were thirty-one Indians and thirteen blacks learning trades in the Indian Training Shops; in 1887 there were fourteen black apprentices and four of the seven shops had black instructors. Together the biracial apprentices of the Indian carpentry shop built not only six cottages as model homes for Indians during the mid-1880s but also the King's Chapel Hospital in 1886 and the Holly Tree Inn in 1889. Upon completion, these structures were painted by the racially mixed crew from the "Indian" paint shop.[28] Indians generally outnumbered blacks about three to one in the Wolfe Shops. On rare occasions, however, a training shop listed as being for Indians might contain more blacks, who also often worked more total hours. In 1889 the shoe shop, under J. E. Smith, a black instructor, had five blacks working full time, one black and four Indians on half time, and one black and two Indians working two days a week. (In 1887 the shoe shop even included a black girl and two white inmates of the "Old Soldiers' Home"—the Southern Branch of the National Asylum for Disabled Volunteers).[29]

Once again, however, the relation of blacks and Indians at Hampton would change for nonracial reasons. In 1886 the Indian Office had restricted noncompetitive bidding for government schools, leaving Hampton without contracts and with surplus goods. Hampton responded by cutting back Indian apprenticeship and reinstituting a separate unspecialized Indian program called the "technical round": forty-one Indians divided into groups of seven spent nine months moving through carpentry and wheelwrighting to blacksmithing. In addition weekly technical classes to meet the "minor emergencies" of home ownership, such as making a good plain box, replacing a windowpane, or repairing a wagon, were organized for both faculty and students. Their teacher, F. W. Colcord, indicated how classes were grouped: separate classes were "made up of the smaller Indian boys [later including Negro boys from the Whittier Elementary School], Indian and colored girls, the senior boys who have not learned a trade, and . . . also a class for the lady teachers."[30]

To learn agriculture, both separate and mixed groups of blacks and Indians labored productively at each of the two school farms. Farming at Shellbanks "was done by a force of from nine to eighteen Negro or Indian boys—either or both."[31] Individual Indians were sent to Shellbanks for disciplinary reasons; groups went as trainees under black overseers. However, most Indians took lessons in agriculture not at Shellbanks, but at Whipple, the "Home Farm," a spread of some 150 acres near campus. The largest group of students, those from Indian Preparatory, worked in all-Indian groups and were dismissed from classes to farm half a day and then later for one day a week.[32] The problem of keeping track of preparatory boys going to and from the farm, the logistics of scheduling, the need to assemble squads based on grade level, and the general unfamiliarity of Indians with European agricultural methods all encouraged segregation in the Day School's agricultural program. (Indians were under a black supervisor, George Davis, while the Negro units reported to Albert Howe, the white manager.) On the other hand, Indians in the Night School were placed in common squads with blacks. In 1885 six such Indians and nine blacks worked full time at the Whipple Farm; thirty-four blacks from the Normal School and sixteen Indians from the Indian classes worked alternate half days.[33]

Since work done in the wheelwright and blacksmith shops was centered on repair of farm equipment rather than money-producing output, these two shops were more integrated than the other shops at Hampton. Here, Indians and blacks were united or divided to satisfy the whim of the instructor, efficiency, or convenience of size. Whenever about the same number of blacks and Indians were available for instruction in these trades, Howe organized them into separate wheelwrighting or blacksmithing classes, each for one half day. But when he had unequal numbers from each race, he formed one segregated and one biracial class. In 1888 Howe divided nine black and five Indian apprentices between blacksmiths and wheelwrights and then placed a white foreman in each shop.[34]

The Negro shops were open to Indians whenever they had reason to learn trades not offered by the Indian Training Shops. For example, C. W. Betts, the white manager of the print shop, reported that he had five Indians and eight blacks in 1885, three Indians and nine blacks in 1886, and six Indians and sixteen blacks in 1893. The print shop was responsible for two monthlies, the *Workman* and the *Alumni Journal;* for the quarterly *African Repository* of the American Colonization Society, and for *Twenty-Two Years' Work.* Hampton's best known Indian printer, Pawnee James Murie, later set type on the Pawnee Agency's newspaper, the *New Era.* In 1886 the Hampton print shop's adjoining bindery even took two white apprentices, an ex-soldier and a young woman. In 1887 there were three Indians and four blacks in tailoring; in 1890 the Pierce Machine Shop trained twenty boys: twelve blacks, five Indians, one Chinese, one Japanese, and one Cuban.[35]

When the $114,500 Armstrong-Slater Memorial Trade School opened in 1896, Hampton's industrial activity no longer focused solely on an academic diploma, with teacher-training at the apex of the curriculum. Now, as Frissell's report for 1897 stated, academic instruction and shop production could be stepping stones into the Trade School. This effort to raise the standards of the new school's industrial work through a combined academic and vocational prerequisite served to limit dramatically Indian participation in its training programs for specialized trades.[36] By 1905 the director of the Trade School, Frank Rogers, reported 202 Negroes and only nine Indians taking full trades. Thus most of Hampton's Indians were excluded from one of the best equipped facilities in the nation. In fact the opportunity for Indians to participate in Hampton's industrial complex was one of the main reasons Congress continued to send them there after the government built large nonreservation boarding schools in the West. Presumably in an attempt to compensate for this new imbalance, thirty-nine Indians and four blacks were given "special work" in the Trade School, one or two days a week.[37]

In short, despite the lip service to segregation paid in the very nomenclature of "Indian" and "Negro" shops, the practicality of organizing the school as an industrial village was apparently a more important determinant of racial balance within a shop or farm than was any racial ideology. Indeed, it would appear that the profit motive and a willingness to formulate whatever racial policies promoted efficiency, were the dominant forces in Hampton's management of the shops and farms—and even in the shifting relative emphasis placed on educational versus productive objectives.

In the Disciplinary Structure and Housing: Contrasting Aims, Similar Results

Disciplinary and housing practices at Hampton also formed a complex and shifting pattern of interracial contact and separation. Hampton's largely military style of discipline was considered especially useful in regulating student behavior in the housing or "barracks" assigned to males, where no teachers resided. Female students, of course, were free of such traditionally male hierarchies, although they could not aspire to positions of power vis à vis other students of either race. But this did not leave female Indians without discipline since their teachers lived with them. For male Indian students, however, an exception to the military pattern of discipline was created to allow something more compatible with their cultural patterns, when that seemed workable.

At the top of the undergraduate military organization of the school was the biracial male Officers' Court begun in 1880. This formal court-martial was composed of six officers drawn from Hampton's three departments, the Normal, Indian, and Night schools. The court sat on cases involving both blacks and Indians. Two Indian representatives—one third of the court—typically overrepresented the percentage of Indians at Hampton. The postgraduate commandant was the real power, however. He appointed the court and reviewed its decisions. Panel members could not amass much influence because the term of appointment was only a month.[38]

In April 1887 a five-man Wigwam Council was created to deal with a rash of disciplinary problems involving Indians. Armstrong gave all the Indian boys a "fatherly talk" about their behavior, and Walter Battice asked them to do all in their power to support the authority of the school. Forty-eight residents of the Wigwam pledged to "abstain from using tobacco, drinking liquor, leaving the school grounds after taps, using profane words and swearing that we will exert our influence by example, and reporting all cases of disorder and breaking of the school rules, for the purpose of bringing up the moral standard of the Indian students to what it should be." Armstrong then invited them to form a council, thereby bringing male but not female Indians more fully into the power structure of the school.[39]

Whereas the Officers' Court generally heard cases referred to it by the administration, the council used Indian informants to initiate proceedings against those breaking school rules in the Wigwam. As in the Officers' Court, the scales of justice were weighted in the administration's favor, with the commandant empowered to revise the council's findings. Although Commandant Freeland found that in general this "experiment in partial self government carried public sentiment in the Wigwam and produced better results than any previous method of discipline," in December 1889 he determined the council was "not doing its work as expected," and the faculty "decided to dissolve the present council and [have the students] elect a new one."[40]

The school battalion was integrated for the first twelve years of the Indian program. Officials drew four mixed companies from the Normal and Indian Departments, and two companies of work students from the Night School, all officered from their own number. Companies from the Night School appeared segregated only because so few Indians attended. Commandant Curtis stated that "no distinction upon race grounds is made. . . . Separate organization would tend to produce a feeling of rivalry, jealousy and friction not now observed, and contrary to the aims and policy of the school [under whose] authority . . . colored and Indian officers receive equal respect and obedience" from the ranks.[41]

Segregated companies arose in 1890 not by the wishes of the white staff but by those of the red students. Indian objections to mixed companies were first publicized during Reverend Thomas S. Childs's investigation of Hampton in December 1887 (see chap. 8). Childs noted a "very general complaint on the part of the Indian students that they were compelled, once a day, and when their time was limited, to repair to the negro quarters to 'fall in' to the companies of the colored students. Their claim was that they should be allowed to form a company of their own, with their own officers, and 'fall in' at their own quarters, at least for this daily exercise, which is simply for the purpose of marching to the dining room." Three years later an Indian students' petition brought results. Armstrong wrote only that, "after some deliberation" by the staff, Indians had been formed into a company by themselves at their own request.[42]

This separate organization prevailed until Hampton no longer enrolled a sufficient number of Indians to form a company. In 1909 Indians consented to admit blacks into their company provided that the unit remain intact. Thereafter, Company C became the integrated unit.[43] Thus, despite the administration's favoring an integrated military corps, Indian student preferences imposed a more segregated one.

Hampton's housing policy ultimately satisfied segregationists by housing Indians separately, although here again practicality rather than principle played a large part. For over a year, the St. Augustine prisoners lodged with blacks even as roommates until their own dorm was completed. Furthermore, the Wigwam was originally planned as an interracial structure of sorts, albeit housing Indians in its large central portion, black students in its west wing, and a white family who would serve as chaperones and counselors in its smaller east wing.[44] But Indian students had soon entirely filled the Wigwam, ending not only the early experiment of Negro and Indian roommates but even the sharing of one structure.

The policy of encouraging biracial roommates gave way in 1878 to one of forced association between very different intraracial groups, when as house father in the Wigwam Booker Washington employed a missionary solution to the problem of older and more acculturated Indian students making fun of newcomers: "I had to turn the joke on the old boys by making them take the new for roommates and teach them how to keep house." *Ten Years' Work* said that the second party of Indians, Dakotas, arriving that November, "petitioned to have colored room-mates in order to get along faster in English and civilized customs," but gave broader reasons for Hampton's refusing their request: "The growth of numbers and the necessity of special instruction and management have made [biracial roommates] no longer possible, and have tended to a degree towards separation."[45] The Wigwam did, however, retain a black presence with Washington as house father until 1880 and with black janitors, whose supervisory role at Hampton "dignified" the job as nowhere else, remaining until at least the mid-1880s.

Any vision of an integrated campus tacitly subordinated Indians to their more numerous and acculturated black classmates, and as Indians from different tribes settled in and came to know one another, they increasingly resented black disciplinary power over them and called for Indian self-government. This movement, in turn, as had the formation of the Wigwam Council and separate military companies, increased Indian separation from blacks. Indian officers were first given disciplinary control over other Indians on a temporary basis during the summer of 1884, when the white commandant was away from school. By 1887 Indians chosen from the emerging Indian leadership in the Wigwam Council, and later also from the officers of the Indian Company, were replacing blacks as janitors of the Wigwam.[46]

However, in 1889, when Robert Moton became acting commandant and moved into the Wigwam, the Indian boys viewed this as a repudiation of their recent gains. For the previous two years, an Indian had been given general oversight of the Wigwam, first Sac and Fox tribesman Walter Battice and then Omaha Thomas Sloan.[47] Under the auspices of the council, eighty-six residents of the Wigwam drafted a petition in late 1890 or early 1891 asking Armstrong to remove Moton as house father. Their statement shows obvious dissatisfaction with Moton's veto power over every avenue of Indian self-government. Defending their concern for equal treatment with cogent arguments, the petition read in part,

> We, the members of the Council, do respectfully ask to have Capt. Moton removed from the Wigwam . . . not because [the boys] have any feelings against him personally, but because they do not like to have a Colored person over them.
> There used to be White men from the North stay in the Wigwam and look after the boys. As we understand, this Council was

established, that in some measure, it might take the place of this officer, and enable the boys to take care of themselves more, and also learn to govern themselves. When we asked for our Indian company it was with a view that we might have officers among ourselves, who could take care of the boys in the Wigwam, and so not need any school officer in the building besides them. Keeping Capt. Moton in the Wigwam shows very plainly that you do not trust the Indian officers. . . . If our own officers are not able to take care of the boys, and can't be trusted to look after their own people in the Wigwam, where, when necessary, they have the school authorities to fall back upon, surely you won't trust them when they go out West to lead their own people, where they must stand alone and fight it out by themselves.

The Colored boys have no school officers in their buildings. You trust the Colored boys who are officers, and their janitors to take care of the rest. Why can't you trust us?

Signators from four tribes, writing as representatives of the Indians from the many other tribes of the Wigwam as well, displayed an intertribal unity that challenged any notion that divisions between tribes went deeper than those of race. The second paragraph of the petition, asserting that the Wigwam Council was established in part to bypass the need for a white officer in the Wigwam, shows that the issue was less Indian versus Negro than Indian versus non-Indian.[48] Indian students had become accustomed to monitoring their own behavior in the Wigwam.

Although it would seem difficult to ignore a petition endorsed by an overwhelming majority of the male Indian students, apparently Armstrong did just that, because Moton retained custody of the Wigwam. Nothing more was said in any of the school records. Indian arguments, coming only a couple years after the Childs investigation, when Indian students had spoken freely to outsiders against school policy, evidently did nothing to change Armstrong's conviction that Indians were not responsible enough to be house fathers. He had said then that "Indians are fickle, readily magnify a grievance or make imaginary ones when opportunity occurs. . . . Their childish nature is always to be taken into account in their statements."[49] Given such an attitude, the mere presentation of the petition may have been taken as evidence that Moton was needed in the Wigwam. Moton's appointment and retention by the Hampton administration did not, then, imply a concern for integration, so much as a low opinion of Indian self-government.

Nevertheless the degree of segregation in the dormitories was based less on color prejudice than once again on practical grounds. For without the construction of special facilities, there would have been no assurance that the Indian program would become permanent, there would have been less new money, and there would perhaps have been no federal commitment. Much later, in 1910, Hampton considered reintroducing black lodgers into the Wigwam because the efficiency study of Vice Principal George P. Phenix had found that "of all the boys' dormitories, the Wigwam is the most expensive to maintain. This is due to the small number of Indian boys. Many of the Indian boys occupy single rooms, thus doubling the per capita cost for light, heat, and janitor service." His committee recommended that all the Indian boys be placed into Division B and that Division A be used for single black male employees. The faculty approved, although there is no indication that the plan went into operation.[50]

And it should not be assumed that the above plan segregating the two races even within the Wigwam was prompted by the administration's own desire. At that time Indian students themselves were believed to desire segregated housing. During World War I, when black recruits were sent to Hampton for the purpose of learning trades useful to the military, fifty were placed in the Wigwam as an "emergency measure" during the summer of 1918, while most of the Indians were on outing. Incoming principal James Edgar Gregg evidently feared that Indians would leave the school if the practice continued. He assured Hampton's representative for Indians, Caroline Andrus, that he would deal fairly with them and provide separate quarters, "if that is understood to be their right and privilege." Gregg claimed that Captain Allen Washington, the black commandant, had decided to use the Wigwam for Negro troops, believing that there would not be enough Indians returning to Hampton to fill the Wigwam.[51]

In 1922, during the last year of the Indian program, the faculty decided that the small number of Indian boys who might return to Hampton would have rooms in the Wigwam, but that for economic reasons the rest of the building would be given to blacks. Black male teachers were to occupy Division A and small Indian children were to reside in Division C. This decision to bring blacks into the Wigwam was not an assault on segregation; the black and Indian students of the same age would still be kept apart.[52] Ironically, however, greater interracial proximity was becoming a practical necessity at the same time that the attitudes of white society were drawing ever sharper boundaries between the races, boundaries that would eventually influence crucial members of the white Hampton staff to oppose the Indian program altogether.

Housing for Indian girls underwent a somewhat different series of changes. From 1879 to 1881, Indian girls were housed in Virginia Hall with black girls, before spending the next two years in their own quarters at Lexington Cottage, while Winona Lodge was being completed. The $30,000 Winona project resulted from another of those opportunities that the tradition of segregation gave Armstrong: to ask for two of everything—one for blacks and one for Indians. But even before the lodge was built, it was common knowledge that few Indian girls—thirteen—would be immediately available as occupants. By a sort of manifest destiny Winona was taken over by Hampton's white lady teachers. No doubt outsiders would have been critical if black girls had filled the large number of empty rooms that philanthrophy erected for Indians. As it was, housing patterns at Winona jived with southern convention because they not only reduced the chances for improper contact between Indian females and all males, especially black males, but they also separated white teachers in Winona Hall from the black girls. White women visiting Hampton also stayed in Winona: in 1912 Helen Townsend, the Indian girls' house mother, reported that "the Farmers Conference is in full swing and [we] have some 25 lady guests lodging in Winona."[53]

Nevertheless, in at least one instance, necessity drove Hampton to disregard tradition and open Winona to black girls. In 1909 Dean of Women Elizabeth Hyde remarked matter of factly, "Colored girls' dorms overcrowded, placed some in Winona." However, unlike the other "Indian" buildings that became "black" after the Indian program ended in 1923, Winona Lodge became fully white, as an elementary school for the children of white teachers.[54]

In short, although Hampton officials desired an integrated military disciplinary structure, the difficulty of managing male Indian students as well as the Indians' own demands gradually prompted considerable segregation. At the same time, Hampton needed separate dormitories to maintain credibility as well as to establish an economic foundation for its Indian program, so a policy of housing segregation for both sexes was set early in the program. In spite of this, the need to fill empty rooms on an overcrowded campus sometimes opened both the Wigwam and Winona to blacks, especially after the government stopped funding the Indian program in 1912. Clearly the degree of segregation between blacks and Indians at Hampton was not consistent, but at times shifted according to practical concerns or even student pressures. Both Hampton's disciplinary structure and its housing were most segregated during the middle years when the Indian program was at its height, and more integrated both when the program was getting off the ground, and again later, coming down to earth.

In Extracurricular Activities: Religious, Social, and Athletic

Hampton designed its "extracurricular" activities to teach its students, both black and Indian, the religious, moral, and competitive values of white society. This was done in ways that carefully avoided confronting the racial prejudices pervading that society.

On Sundays worship took up much of the day, as students attended integrated, segregated and semisegregated religious observances. The day began with a voluntary early morning prayer meeting, where a black or an Indian student introduced a biblical passage as the theme for the week.[55]

For the main service of the morning Indian students were grouped according to the denomination that held jurisdiction over their tribe in the West. Nearly half of Hampton's Indians attended the historic St. John's Episcopal Church (in town). Its ties to Hampton's Indian program were more important than was any expression of sympathy with southern racist views. St. John's rector, J. J. Gravatt, linked Hampton to Episcopal Indian agencies. Gravatt made eight recruiting trips for Hampton, providing the most reliable supply of promising Indian students; he assisted Hampton's shift of recruiting efforts from the "camps" to the missionary schools. Gravatt assured western ministers that Hampton's Indian students would study the Bible under his personal care. Thus Episcopal Indians did not attend the nondenominational mid-day service on campus, and St. John's sometimes admitted the Episcopal Negroes of the school as well. *Talks and Thoughts,* the monthly journal of Hampton's Indian students, reported that in 1903, as for the past several years, black and Indian students attended Holy Communion at St. John's the third Sunday of every month.[56]

Hampton sent its few Catholic Indians to mass at the Old Soldiers' Home.[57] It is not unlikely that mass there also ministered to the spiritual needs of a few Hampton blacks, inasmuch as one-seventh of its inmates were black and some were probably Catholic. The record shows that in at least one instance the faculty gave two black girls permission to attend mass with the handful of Indian parishioners and army veterans.[58]

Those Indians—a slim majority—who were neither Episcopal nor Catholic attended morning worship services at an Indian Sunday School in Winona's chapel, where Gravatt's Indians joined them later in the day. The Indian Sunday School was segregated but pointedly nonsectarian: Hampton did not want to offend any denomination. Teachers of five different denominations led the service and homage was paid to others, as illustrated by observing a "Quaker" moment of silence. While Frissell coordinated Bible classes for blacks, Gravatt, accompanying his Indian Episcopalians back to campus, assumed oversight of the regular session of the Indian Sunday School.[59] Instead of being grouped according to their Protestant denominations, however, students attending the Indian or black Bible schools retained the same teachers as they had during weekday classes.

The Indian Sunday School was said to be segregated from the black for the same reasons as the Indian Preparatory classes. Frissell said that Sunday school "classes are graded according to their knowledge of English . . . [so] the lesson can be suited to the capacity of each class. The beginners from Dakota are taught in their own language by a teacher who understands it." This bilingual instructor, translating from Lakota to English, also taught an advanced class of Sioux catechists on Saturday afternoons.[60]

After these classes ended, the main on-campus service was held at Bethesda Chapel until Memorial Church was completed in 1886. This service united the entire school into one assembly but divided it into racial blocs, a quasi-integrated seating arrangement least offensive to the white dignitaries who sat in front. An unnamed Indian girl reported that blacks were given preference to Indians in seating, placed "first up in the chapel" before the Indians were seated on a platform. Such group seating lasted until the very end of the Indian program; in 1922 the faculty decided that any Indians coming to Hampton in the future would sit with blacks.[61]

Yet even with the "congregation's" racial grouping the extent of integration at Memorial Church was celebrated by the *Workman,* when it described a New Year's Day baptism in 1911. "Three [new communicants] were children of Hampton officers—Ogden-Purves, Julia Turner, and Mary Roger; nine were Indians and four, colored students . . . among those standing together before the altar were young people of both sexes and from three races—white, Negro, and Indian."[62]

———

Hampton-sponsored extracurricular activities were of course not limited to largely mandatory religious services; by 1917 it also sponsored numerous more voluntary social clubs and organizations, some integrated, some segregated, depending on their purpose and often on gender as well as race. Both those for special interests (such as the Old

Dominion Debating Society) and those with broader appeal (such as the Chesterfield Club for promoting gentlemanly behavior, the Temperance Committee, and the Committee on Prayer Meetings), were usually integrated, if closely supervised. In 1894 Hampton organized the Self-Control Alliance for male Indians; its initials were meant to remind potentially unruly Indians of the self-control Samuel Chapman Armstrong had recently exercised during his final illness. The Minnehaha Glee Club accepted only Indian women, as did the Lend a Hand Club, begun in 1885 to assemble Christmas packages for the schools of Hampton alumni. Since a larger black girls' society formed in 1890, the King's Daughters Society, did similar work, the Lend a Hand Club merged with it in 1896. A black, Fanny McKenney, became president, and an Indian, Inez Splitlog, became vice president of the newly integrated club. *Talks and Thoughts* boasted that the "organization is strewn plentiful with Indian girls as officers."[63]

The coeducational Christian Endeavor Society (CES), begun in April 1882, was the one instance of a campus organization segregated by race but not by gender. The Indian CES was segregated from its black counterpart by Ludlow and by Hampton treasurer F. D. Gleason, who believed that "because of [the Indians'] imperfect English and their natural timidity in expressing themselves, few would ever take an active part in a voluntary meeting of the two races." Hampton staff also hoped the Indian CES would promote racial over tribal identity among Indians. Andrus said that, besides teaching the Christian life, the CES "has brought together the boys and girls of different tribes who did not understand each others language and ways any better than they understand English." In 1893 pan-Indian leadership was clearly fostered when a Sac and Fox boy became president, a Winnebago girl vice president, an Omaha boy treasurer, and a Sioux girl secretary.[64]

———

Like so many other activities at Hampton, sports included both integrated and segregated efforts going on simultaneously. Segregated intramural teams fostered a sense of racial self-awareness while an integrated intercollegiate program aroused a common black and Indian competitive school spirit. The *Workman* reported as early as 1892 that intramural baseball teams were wholly Indian or Negro, while the intercollegiate Normal School Nine had seven blacks and two Indians. One faculty member asserted that an Indian was already half civilized when he learned to play baseball.[65]

These baseball contests were among the first occasions in America of Indians engaging in the organized sports of the white nation, and of blacks and Indians joining the same team or playing one another. Especially unusual, Indian girls vied against black girls in intramural basketball, and in 1905 the *Workman* reported that the "Winona team had to pass the championship flag to Virginia Hall's Negro girls' team, having lost to them."[66] Although banned by the larger community from competing with white teams, blacks at Hampton did gain the opportunity to compete with another race and to disprove the then popular assumption of white fans that Negroes lacked athletic talent.

Unlike black units, segregated Indian units did get a short-lived chance to compete directly with white teams. In 1913 the faculty ended Indian-YMCA games, even those held on school grounds. They decided Indians were exceeding the limits of proper conduct for a Negro school, and were learning too much about town through their association with streetwise white teenagers. Thus the faculty itself segregated Indians from whites and placed them on the Negro side of the color line. In 1915 Frissell took a different approach when disallowing a request made by Indians to compete against local whites: he asked them to put themselves in the Negroes' position. Requesting Indians to take a stronger stand for black rights than he generally found appropriate to ask of whites, Frissell exhorted Indians to "be more loyal to their co-students, the colored boys, to refuse to play with these white teams who would not play with our colored team."[67]

In February 1916 the Indian athletes of Hampton's integrated basketball team were expected to make an even greater gesture: to assist black teammates in defeating the all-Indian team from Carlisle. On Indian Emancipation Day Hampton Indians were asked to emphasize school spirit over racial solidarity. Hampton's best ever Indian forward, Anishinabe George Gurnoe, was slated to join in this contest with its premier Negro forward, James "Pop" Gayle. When asked by some fellow Hampton Indians not to forsake his race by playing Carlisle, Gurnoe refused. He told his coach, Charles H. Williams, Hampton's second athletic director (1910–51), "I started with basketball, playing with these [black] boys, and I don't care what they [the Indian Boys] say. I'm going to play with the team. This is one team against another . . . it's not Indians against Negroes . . . it's Hampton playing Carlisle."[68] In a blow-out with possible implications for the old Pratt Armstrong debate about whether all-Indian or mixed black and Indian schools produced better results, Hampton won thirty-seven to twenty-three, with Gayle and Gunroe scoring thirteen and twelve points respectively. Not a white but an Indian school thus became the first nonblack school to compete against blacks at Hampton.[69]

As the showdown with Carlisle demonstrated, the integrated male teams representing Hampton were usually recruited from the best athletes regardless of race, a competitive philosophy that eventually proved stronger than racial prejudice in integrating black and white athletes elsewhere in the nation.[70] Three Indians played on Hampton's first intercollegiate championships in both football and basketball.

Yet even as intramural sports stimulated racial pride, and intercollegiate sports, on competitive values, athletic activity at Hampton also discouraged individual protest. Charles Williams argued that while releasing surplus energy and teaching both teamwork and adherence to laws, a sports program "brings out any underlying faults [the player] may have and then aids him to control them. It teaches him not to sulk when displeased, not to strike back when hurt by mistake, and to meet roughness with determination and without resentment."[71] In providing such preparation for enduring the virulent racism prevailing at the turn of the century, "contact sports" at Hampton were used to promote not only school spirit but the spirit of the school.

In the Student and Faculty Dining Rooms: Student Interests, Faculty Bias

Hampton's dining room arrangements exhibited elements of segregation on both student and faculty levels, but only the latter caused major tension on campus. The former can be dealt with more briefly as it was regulated in response to essentially practical considerations, with emphasis on student needs and often on their preferences.

————

From 1878 to 1886, black and Indian students shared the same dining room, albeit with tables divided by race and seating divided by sex. But in 1886 Indians were assigned a separate dining room, as part of a larger attempt to improve their health. Hampton Indians had an alarmingly high death rate: one in fifteen, or thirty-one of 467 Indians, had died at school since 1878. To meet this crisis, Hampton provided Indians with a special diet and engaged Dr. Anna Johnson to monitor their eating habits. Armstrong said, "Negro and Indian pupils, hitherto eating together, were separated at meals, because the salt food [mostly bacon] and pork, which the former delight in, was injurious to the latter."[72] Boiled or stewed beef was substituted, he added, and proved to be "more satisfying [for Indians] as it is undoubtedly more wholesome."[73]

In 1898, after a decade of segregation, the dining rooms were re-united but still not fully integrated, and remained so until the Indian program ended in 1923. No reason for remerging the dining rooms was given, but in fact a more careful selection of students and the avoidance of agencies whose students had proven sickly, had effectively eliminated the Indian health problem. Although Frissell said that separate tables were still "desirable" because the races "naturally" prefer to socialize among themselves, Indians were seated with blacks whenever there were not enough of them for a separate table. In June 1907 the faculty minutes read, "Six Indian boys left in the Boarding Department [over the summer]. They ask to have a table by themselves in the dining room. The last two years, this has not been allowed." Frissell also denied this Indian request. Even while school was in session, in February 1910, an Indian girl was assigned to sit with black girls because the two Indian girls' tables were full. She refused to go.[74] In short, it appears that some Indians, at least, did indeed prefer to sit among themselves.

———————

While the seating arrangements of black and Indian students at meals did not usually affect whites, all three races were at times represented on Hampton's faculty, thus raising the issue in faculty dining facilities. Armstrong himself touched off a controversy in the spring of 1889 that laid bare the racial opinions of Hampton's staff more thoroughly than any other issue during his years as principal. Only whites and blacks could debate the issue since there were no Indians on the staff that year, but when there were, they had always been seated in a segregated dining room along with the blacks. As Cora Folsom, the white teacher most involved with Indians, pointed out, "the individual Indian is quite as much affected by [the issue of segregated dining rooms] as the colored graduate."[75]

The original decision in the early 1870s to segregate nonwhite from white teachers by having "graduates'" and teachers' dining rooms had not been made by Armstrong, but like many of Hampton's household arrangements, by a woman—in this case, Vice Principal Rebecca T. Bacon. Although the food and table settings in both dining rooms were identical, the rooms themselves were unequal. The Graduates' Dining Room, Folsom said, was "small and close; the other was cool and spacious." On April 13, 1889, Armstrong asked the resident graduates for letters expressing their feelings about this separate dining room, and whether they would prefer to come into the Teachers' Dining

Room as a table, or even be scattered among the white teachers. After a private conversation, Armstrong transmitted his request by letter through Harris Barrett (1885), a future cashier at Hampton. Armstrong brought up the issue as follows: "Now that all seems pleasant [on campus]—not a word of complaint having come to me for a long time and feeling that there is a highly commendable spirit among you all, I think it a good time to ask these questions and invite your answer." Although he told his "dear friends" that he believed "frank discussions between us by creating a better understanding will do good," Armstrong was clearly unprepared for the degree of frankness and vehemence that his questions evoked.[76]

The black graduates unanimously agreed not to discuss the matter among themselves before writing their opinions. In fact their individual letters display remarkable consensus: they all protested any degree of segregated dining and requested to be scattered among the white teachers, arguing that coming in as a table would not erase the color line but make it more visible.[77] In rejecting what Armstrong had seen as a compromise solution, Sara F. Peake (1885) said, "It is not necessary that we should be 'grouped according to color.' There can be no mistaking that we are *'graduates'* (and I almost hate the term). We carry our diplomas on our faces." The graduates opposed separation of any sort on principle, because segregation imposed a stigma of inferiority. Peake, whose condemnation carries the tone of one having to reveal the obvious, told Armstrong that "it impresses me as a very peculiar kind of Christianity which enables folks to leave their homes, relatives and friends to come and labor for and with the Negro and yet makes it an impossibility for them to summon up enough respect and unprejudiced friendship to eat at the same table with him."[78]

Barrett himself felt that graduates, "who are counted among the most level headed of the school's sons and daughters," had had "a great deal of their love and regard for their *Alma Mater* taken away." He said that segregated dining induced "white employees to look upon us with somewhat of contemptuous condescension, and [other alumni] to look upon us with something akin to scorn because of . . . our quiet acceptance of the 'sitting of us aside' by the authorities. It has given to many people the idea . . . that a graduate is kept here more for effect than for the value of his services." Teaching graduates had been placed in a position of "continual defense" of Hampton, he said, for black leaders asked them why such a division persisted "here in an Institution that they seemed to think should take the lead in wiping out just such differences." Barrett said that it was "humiliating" for him to escort prominent blacks around campus and then have these men "wonder why we do not appear among the other employees in the dining room."

Barrett said that unlike Hampton, Fisk, Oberlin, Berea, and Howard Universities had no segregation, and white and black "fared alike in every respect." Even Hampton's "best wishers," he lamented, "believe that you favor the drawing of the color line; they [have said] your Principal has become thoroughly Southernized; they have led persons to accuse the school of adopting in the North a policy that it does not sustain in the South." Assuring Armstrong that none of the graduates believed that Hampton stood for segregation, Barrett nevertheless found it, suggesting that if separation in the dining room was based on color, it was a "grievous wrong; if the difference is made because of [the black graduate's] lack of refinement . . . would it not help him greatly . . . to place him among people who have had such advantages?"[79]

Since the graduates' letters disapproving segregated dining were not marked "confidential," Armstrong read them to a predominantly white staff meeting on April 24. He asked the white faculty members for their written opinions, "within the logic of the position." Upon receiving this second round of letters, the principal asked the school's teacher of advanced English, Helen Ludlow, to analyze their contents objectively. She reported that of thirty-seven replies, thirteen advised granting the graduates' requests in full and eighteen advised against it. Six more expressed no preference, with five of these stating that they would abide by any decision.[80]

Eight of the teachers who supported the graduates' request saw no difficulty or danger in "scattering" [integrating] the employees at the same tables. Not unlike the black graduates, these teachers typically cited as their reasons equity, fair play, the Good Book and the Golden Rule, kindness, "living up to our principles," and bettering blacks through association with the white staff. This group apparently all believed, as George W. Andrews phrased it, that "this is a question of color and engrained race prejudice." Regarding the present policy as a "drag on our usefulness," he saw the graduates' stand as motivated by their "growing self-respect as individuals and as representatives of their race, together with a desire for [further] improvement." Dora Freeman thought it revealing that among this group of Hampton's graduates—which included Barrett and W. T. B. Williams, the future field agent for the Slater Fund—"the most loyal feel the most bitter." Because such Negroes should be taught to respect their color, Anna L. Bellows told Armstrong that he should "throw expediency to the winds and act on principle."[81]

Ludlow found five teachers more ambivalent. For example, Mary

R. Hamlin desired the change to integrated dining out of fear that Hampton was promoting bitter racial tension through exclusion, although she warned that "closer intimacy would only make the real differences and distinctions more evident," and ultimately increase the graduates' unhappiness.[82] Like Hamlin, four of the white teachers who supported the graduates saw dangers in mixed seating, but felt that the dangers were outweighed by either principled or expedient grounds for change.

Fifteen of the eighteen teachers who opposed integrated tables cited various present and future difficulties. Ludlow's analysis of the teachers' viewpoints produced a concise list of the objections put forth by this group, among whom she numbered herself:

> The difficulties that would arise on the question of admitting not only the graduates but friends who would visit them.
>
> The discomfort to teachers some of whom have no other leisure moments during the day for restful social enjoyment.
>
> Indiscretions to be looked for on the part of some of the white people who may be here, in the opposite directions of prejudice against the race and Quixotic sympathy for it [in other words that it would increase friction either between the races or among whites].
>
> The fostering of false views in graduates as to their real social status, leading to disappointment and bitterness after leaving here. . . . Spoiling them for their real work among their people.
>
> The suspicious, jealous and morbidly sensitive character of the race would lead to friction, misunderstandings and new unhappiness or offensive self-assertion.
>
> The impossibility of ever satisfying them. The certainty that new demands would follow and new miseries result.
>
> Injury to the school in loss of approval of both Southern and Northern people who approve its common sense views and methods.
>
> The falseness or unnaturalness of the position and its artificial and strained relations.
>
> The irrevocableness of such a radical change.[83]

Some of these conservative teachers simply defended the status quo, arguing, as Hampton's business agent F. C. Briggs put it, "the policy of the school has long been decided—why change it?" This group of teachers voiced most vigorously a complaint heard generally on this side of the issue, against the "harsh and ill feeling" tone of the graduates' letters. Mary M. Gordon, for example, believed that their demands could infringe upon the teachers' right to sit where they wanted. As Hampton treasurer F. N. Gilman understood etiquette, "No gentleman ever wished to enter any society without first observing to himself that his presence there is desired." Similarly, Commandant Curtis found "the demand to be seated among the teachers as evidence of the lack of delicacy of feeling which would qualify them for it." He claimed that pride and not principle motivated the graduates' letters. Elizabeth Hyde agreed, arguing that the graduates could not have been merely attempting to establish the precedent of admitting Negroes to the white dining room because visiting black dignitaries had already dined there on occasion. Hyde, whose extreme opposition to eating with blacks did not prevent her from being placed in charge of the Academic Department in 1890, flatly stated that if the present graduates did not like the arrangements they should leave.[84]

Two teachers articulated their sense of superiority over and separation from their black co-workers in terms of social class. In defense of her belief that white New Englanders like herself deserved a social status at Hampton superior to that of black employees, Mary F. Mackie said, "Many of these ladies come from families who represent many, many years of culture and refinement and all the advantages which good family gives and they *honor* the positions which they hold in the school. On the contrary, our graduates in accepting a position among the workers of this school have stepped up and are honored by the positions they hold." She claimed the graduates were inferior not racially but because of "*previous condition* [and] the *present* condition of the families from which our students come." One of the white teachers—unnamed—went so far as to use this controversy as an occasion for disapproving of the employment of graduates at Hampton in any capacity, because they were "swallowed up by the largeness of the institution, have no position here, and are doing work white people could do while they are needed among their people."[85]

According to Ludlow's analysis, eight of the fifteen teachers opposing scattered seating proposed some sort of compromise. Four white teachers sought compromise, with graduates and perhaps with their own consciences, by advancing novel "solutions." The least liberal of the proposals mentioned by Ludlow was for an annual "Negro holiday," when blacks would be invited to a tea party or dinner, individually or even with their spouses. Ludlow herself desired a more frequent but informal exchange of teachers and graduates to each other's dining rooms and tables. The beauty of her plan, she argued, was that it would remove the grievance of exclusion, deal with individuals rather than race, retain (in some beautifully unspecified manner) the independence of one's own table, and place the whole matter on a natural and spontaneous rather than an artificial basis. Another four teachers believed that blacks should be admitted to the dining room but be placed at separate tables, and one of them, Gilman, was willing to leave any further mixing to "natural selection."[86]

Finally, Ludlow reported that three teachers "strongly and absolutely" opposed any change of seating on the explicit grounds of what she herself called their color prejudice against blacks. Irene H. Stansbury, a kindergarten teacher whose response was particularly irate, "would not submit to such a *condition* of things."[87]

Of all the white teachers, only Cora Folsom looked beyond the immediate question of black and white faculty to consider the place of the Indian in the dining hall controversy. Calling Armstrong's attention to the impropriety of extending the color line to include Indian graduates, Folsom said, "the taking of an Indian *graduate* even from his own race [in the Indian dining room for students] and promoting him [as a graduate] to a table with colored people only, is a phase of the question that has so far escaped general notice and comment." She claimed that this issue had not yet come to a head because the four Indians who had dined in the Graduate Dining Room in 1887 had been members of small tribes. If, on the other hand, these Indians had been members of a more powerful tribe, like the Sioux, there would have been "trouble at once," which would have caused "bad feeling all along the line in the West." Avoiding direct reference to the blacks' reaction to the dining room issue, Folsom continued by saying that all of the Indian graduates who returned to teach had attended white schools after Hampton

> where their social treatment has been very different from anything they can expect here under the existing system. They may not be any more fit to associate with the white teachers than are the colored graduates, yet their previous training and circumstances make the change so marked that friction and hard feeling is the result. Some have felt what they consider the injustice of the graduate system quite as keenly for their colored friends as for themselves, and I have to confess that I have been unable to . . . sweeten the atom of bitterness. . . . [If the sentiment of those grieved] is wounded pride, it is in the best and strongest of them and *has* to be considered.
>
> Every one of these four graduates has spent two years in white schools . . . where they are treated in every way as social equals, and we cannot now ask them to return here under the present system.

Anna Dawson was, even before she left here, one of our best teachers—the greatest attraction to visitors we had and a girl whose influence among the Indian girls especially was of the greatest value. Her two years at Framingham Normal School expires this spring and Miss Richards has invited her to return here as teacher next year; but with all her love for her Hampton home, which I know is sincere, she is not willing to come . . . her experience before as a "graduate" has much to do with her decision. . . . In this case *we* are the sufferers, not the graduates.

In the light of these and similar facts . . . Hampton's Indian graduates should be treated as they would be in any other school, and if they, then the colored graduate whose social level is the same when the color line is withdrawn and the same test of intelligence, education, and refinement applied to him, should be treated in the same generous manner or kept away [from Hampton] as the Indian is [on reservations].[88]

As Folsom indicated, far from presenting a "false face" to Indians suggesting that they would be accorded equal rights in white society, Hampton's dining room policies assigned them a social status below what they had become accustomed to elsewhere. Not surprisingly, Hampton never had many Indian teachers. By emphasizing how educated Indians were treated among educated whites outside the institute, Folsom's argument put fellow staff members on the defensive about their refusal to eat with blacks. She concluded her letter by pointing out that Hampton's students did not attend school for the benefit of white teachers, but that the teachers were there to serve the students: "I do not see that I have any right to consider my personal preferences where their welfare is concerned."[89]

After amassing letters from both graduates and staff, the principal did nothing to resolve the conflict. Nor did he further explain why he had raised the issue. Clearly, however, it would not have furthered Armstrong's proposed solutions to the racial problems of the nation to admit he could not resolve difficulties in his own dining room. But as Edward Graham suggests, the general surely would not have raised the issue unless it was simmering nor ask the graduates' opinions without being willing to change the dining arrangements.[90]

Armstrong apparently felt that the then prevailing calm among graduates would facilitate a peaceful transition to separate tables in the Teachers' Dining Room. He may even have wanted to encourage this form of resolution to the conflict in his original letter to the graduates which said that he would not object to "changing tables" with them, but disliked scattering.[91] Since Barrett—presumably having learned Armstrong's true feelings through their private meeting—wrote him that "to a plain point . . . scattering . . . would seem to you to break down all other social barriers and pave the way towards intermarriage," the principal must have seen separate seating in one dining room as the compromise that would free the institute from the charge of segregation without raising one of amalgamation. Indeed, although several white teachers had expressed similar fears about miscegenation, Ludlow's statistics indicate that most of the white staff would have accepted a biracial dining room with separate tables.[92]

However, upon discovering that black graduates' viewed such bloc seating as the most embarrassing form of segregation, Armstrong expediently passed the buck to the white staff. A statement by Barrett appears to have made this course of inaction easier. Despite Barrett's fairly strong critique of segregated dining quoted earlier, he had shown the very delicacy the graduates were accused of lacking, when he said he would "earnestly beg, that if in the future—no matter how far distant—any such change is contemplated, before it is made that you would if possible ascertain if there is a single objection on the part of the [white] teachers . . . it would be infinitely more humiliating for us to feel that we are . . . being forced upon people and in places where we are not wanted."[93]

If indeed Armstrong was taking cover behind Barrett's tact by asking for white input, once the white teachers gave it, the issue became a standoff, as they opposed the only option acceptable to the graduates—scattered seating. Their opposition must have come as no surprise to Armstrong, since even among themselves the white teachers had traditionally sat in cliques based on rank and seniority. As Briggs said, "Teachers do not gather at the tables haphazard. The society at some of them have been years in forming."[94] For Armstrong to inquire whether teachers desired to mix by color when they did not by class was to answer the question by asking it.

Moreover, Armstrong may have felt that leaving things alone would rid him of the controversy, because on an emotional level, neither party was really eager to sit with the other. Alongside their passionate appeals to principle, the graduates' letters rarely failed to mention their lack of any personal desire to eat with whites. Indeed the letters all indicated some reluctance to forsake the freer intercourse and camaraderie their own dining room provided. F. D. Wheelock (1883), for example, wrote that "there was a congenial spirit existing among us which I can never hope to experience should I become separated from them." The graduates' own ambivalence was best expressed by Peake:

"The knowledge of being where we are so emphatically not wanted will not be very flattering to say the least—but that is only of secondary importance. Believing as I do such proceedings to be wrong—unfair—unjust, I am willing to sacrifice my own personal feelings that we may obtain what is justly ours. . . . we'd much rather remain where we are but in my estimation the question has assumed quite a different aspect."[95]

With greater acknowledgment of the attachment that both white and black teachers held toward their own tables and present company than of the principles involved, Armstrong simply concluded that scattering would prove to be the "least comfortable and pleasant" arrangement for his employees.[96] Thus the Teachers' and Graduates' Dining Rooms remained segregated well into the twentieth century.

Conclusion

As the dining room controversy demonstrates, Hampton devised a more flexible and varied racial policy for relations between blacks and Indians than between either and whites. After all, popular concern did not focus on the former policy as it did on the latter. Inferentially, however, when Hampton mixed Indians with blacks, the color line was widened to include Indians, but when these races were divided, caste was tightened around blacks. Unable to improve the public image of both races at once, Hampton was also unable or unwilling to address immediate campus realities by consistently integrating or segregating its students.

The gradual integration of Indians into predominantly black classes became a measure of Indian progress, showing that Indians were capable of the same scholarship as African Americans. By creating a distinct department with free schooling and intensive care for Indians, Hampton was not acting primarily on racial bias, as has too readily been assumed, but from practical considerations. For economic and cultural reasons Indians could not originally have been admitted to the school had integration been required, and Hampton would have remained for blacks only. As it was, initial segregation in the Indian Department was culturally based, marking Indian and not Negro "inferiority." Armstrong believed that making the proud Indian feel the stigma of being set aside and discriminated against would help develop his character as he felt the Negro did when being forced to rely upon himself. School officials argued partially segregating Indians from blacks created new positions of leadership and promoted new concepts of racial self-awareness, self-reliance, self-control, and self-government.[97]

In short, the racial policies Hampton adopted for blacks and Indians were not a simple matter of abject submission to the traditions of the South. Building separate facilities for Indians enabled the school to enlarge its plant, even as blacks and Indians were put to work in shops created for only one of them. But the motives for integrating Indians and blacks went beyond the transmission of cultural values to encourage both minorities to accommodate to whatever fate whites prescribed. While specific racial policies at Hampton were often determined by factors other than race prejudice, those factors themselves held latent implications for evolving racial policy. By arguing that exclusion had some motivational benefits, Hampton made the practice of segregation seem a viable alternative even to those who believed they had the best interests of the black at heart. Conversely, when applied strictly between blacks and Indians, the concept of integration was shown able to survive outside of a liberal context, unavoidably providing validation to white supremacy. Lacking an egalitarian commitment to integration, Hampton, as the dining room controversy illustrated, seemed concerned with what racial pattern prevailed not on principle but mostly as it affected the internal harmony of the school and of the nation.[98] Interpreting human nature as evolving from chaos upward rather than as a fall from grace, Armstrong made no call to arms like that of William Lloyd Garrison, the moral abolitionist. Hampton's avowed aim was not to liberate the races but rather to create more Indian farmers in the West and better black workers in the South. Hampton's stance was that good citizens and devoted workers who owned clean, comfortable homes, and contributed toward building safer and more cohesive European-style communities, could be created by focusing on the "faults" of racial minorities, and not those of the society they were to join. These goals were pursued without much regard to the racial patterns of segregation or integration in particular educational contexts.

It will be seen, however, that this flexibility was largely absent in areas of student life where staff members were unable directly to monitor and structure the interaction, especially between the sexes.

Notes

1. Elaine Goodale Eastman, *Pratt: The Red Man's Moses*, p. 65; Margaret Rosten Muir, "Indian Education at Hampton Institute and Federal Indian Policy: Solutions to the Indian Problem" (Master's thesis, Brown University, 1970), p. 87; Graham, "Tender Violence: The Black and the White," p. 4; Robert F. Engs, "Red, Black, and White: A Study of Intellectual Inequality," in James M. McPherson and J. Morgan Kouss, eds., *Region, Race and Reconstruction: Essays in Honor of C. Vann Woodward* (New York, 1982), p. 250.

2. SCA to H. W. Foote, Oct. 18, 1881, Howe Papers; SCA, "Indian Education," p. 15.

3. SCA, "The Indian Work at Hampton," *Wowapi* 1 (Nov. 7, 1883): 64.

4. The term "false face" refers to the Iroquois society whose practitioners were transfigured into the wolf, bear, or eagle by wearing masks resembling them. Likewise, segregation at Hampton had changing faces.

5. Ludlow, "The Evolution of the Whittier School," *SW* 35 (June 1906): 340. In October 1914 John Hunter attended Hampton while his eight-year-old son attended Whittier. See Minutes of Faculty Meetings, Oct. 3, 1914, HUA. At other times or perhaps in addition to placing some of the Indian children in Whittier, small Indian boys, "sadly in need of mothering," were taught by Irene H. Stansbury in the home-like atmosphere of Division A of the Wigwam. See Stansbury, "The Little Boys," *ARCIA* 1884, p. 195.

6. HBF, "Annual Report," *SW* 27 (May 1898): 24. For example, J. D. McDowell, the manager of the Indian Training Shops, was drawn to Hampton by Armstrong's enticing letter to Professor Chickering of the National Deaf and Dumb Institute in Washington, D. C. See box 21, Indian Affairs, Misc. Reports of Staff Members, HUA. Moreover, one of the two texts used for first year Indian students was Isaac L. Peet, *Language Lessons: Designed to Introduce Young Learners, Deaf Mutes and Foreigners to a Correct Understanding of the English Language* (New York, 1875).

7. SCA to Gen. E. Whittlesey and A. K. Smiley of the Board of Indian Commissioners, Mar. 15, 1888, p. 7, box on Childs Report, HUA; SCA, "Report of Hampton School," *ARCIA* 1881, p. 196; HBF, "Annual Report," *SW* 30 (May 1901): 291.

8. Cited by HBF, "Annual Report," *SW* 30 (May 1901): 301.

9. SCA in *Twenty-Two Years' Work*, p. 114. In 1883 Armstrong said that there was a Zulu student, Balany Selon, and a South African in the Indian Department. The two most noteworthy foreign blacks who attended Indian classes were Madikane Cele, a Zulu from Natal, and Kamba Simango, a Bantu from Portuguese South Africa; they helped provide African materials for folklorist Natalie Curtis Burlin's *Songs and Tales from the Dark Continent* (New York, 1920). See SCA in *ARCIA* 1883, p. 168; HBF, "Annual Report," *SW* 33 (May 1904): 291.

10. Ludlow in *ARCIA* 1885, p. 241.

11. SCA, "Report of Hampton School," *ARCIA* 1881, p. 196. In 1881 there was one Indian senior in Normal, two in the middle class, and nineteen juniors.

12. Folsom, "Indian Days," p. 40. Alford became principal of the tribal school and later taught at the Chilocco Indian School. He was the first Absentee Shawnee to take land in severalty and assisted Special Agent N. S. Porter in surveying and allotting tribal land. Downing, a half blood Cherokee who was adopted into the Wichita tribe, worked as an agency policeman upon his return from Hampton before becoming a cattle rancher. Oshkeneny studied medicine with the agency physician before returning to Hampton as a bookkeeper; he was generally regarded as working below his potential. See Thomas Wildcat Alford, *Civilization, and the Story of the Absentee Shawnee*, as told

to Florence Drake (Norman, 1936); *Twenty-Two Years' Work*, pp. 179, 329, 349.

13. Unfortunately, neither of these sources kept track of blacks and Indians attending classes or shops together in a regular or systematic manner.

14. SCA, "Report of Hampton School," ARCIA 1886, p. 23; SW, 12 (Nov. 1883): 114; SCA, "Report of Hampton School," *ARCIA* 1891, p. 602.

15. Susan de Lancey Van Rensselaer, "General Review of Industries," in "Annual Report," *SW* 20 (June 1891): 94; SCA, "Report of Hampton School," *ARCIA* 1891, p. 602; Peabody, *Education for Life*, p. 366; HBF, "Annual Report," *SW* 30 (May 1901): 288. He repeated these comments in nearly all of his reports to the trustees and to the commissioner from 1897 to 1901.

16. Elizabeth Hyde, "Academic Work," *SW* 27 (May 1898): 93, 98; W. S. Sweeter to HBF, Jan. (?), 1904, HUA.

17. See SCA, "Report of Hampton School," *ARCIA* 1881, p. 166. Twelve boys had voluntarily become work students. See Natalie Curtis Burlin, *Negro Folk Songs* (New York, 1919), p. 4.

18. SCA to T. S. Childs, Dec. (?), 1887, in Childs to Commissioner J. T. B. Atkins, Jan. 11, 1888, RG75, item 1014, NARA. Armstrong contradicted this statement to Childs (who opposed the Indian program) when accused of sacrificing Negro education for the sake of production. He argued that if production alone was its goal, Hampton would have employed skilled workers, and would not have continually trained new student workers: industries were often maintained at a loss because of this concern for education. But Graham shows that the treasurer's reports indicate that student labor was indeed profitable, because students were not paid in cash but on account in the school's books to defray their expenses. Credits were forfeited when a student left school. Indeed, apprentices sometimes complained that they had no chance to learn the more specialized skills of a trade. See Graham, "Tender Violence: Old Hampton, the Indian Question, and the New South," p. 52; J. L. Crispin (a black student) to SCA, Jan. 6, 1888, HUA; "Academic Work, 1897–1898," *SW* 27 (May 1898): 93. Alice Bacon, "General Review of Industries," *SW* 19 (May 1890): 71, classified the offerings of the Indian Department as mainly educational while those for blacks as largely productive.

19. SCA to Dorman Steele, June 13, 1879, HUA.

20. Peabody, *Education for Life*, pp. 372–73. Alice Bacon reported in 1894 that 223 of 319 black industrial students were not learning trades but "had employment viewed mainly for support of the student and carrying forward the work of the school." Most of these students attended Night School. See Bacon, "General Review of Industries," *SW* 23 (July 1894): 99. See note 37 below for an expanded discussion. Reid's statement is in Publicity Director William A. Aery's "The Hampton Idea: Organizer of Industries," p. 36.

21. Bacon, "General Review of Industries," *SW* 19 (June 1890): 71.

22. George B. Starkweather to SCA, Feb. 10, 1879, HUA; SCA, "Annual Report," *SW* 8 (June 1879): 63 shows that the principal indeed instituted Starkweather's model for the Indian shops.

23. SCA, "Annual Report," *SW* 10 (June 1881): 63. See Muir, "Indian Education at Hampton," p. 35.

24. SCA to Commissioner Roland E. Trowbridge, Sept. 21, 1880, RG75, roll 484, frame 253, NARA.

25. SCA, "The Indian," *Wowapi* 1 (Nov. 7, 1883): 65; SCA, "Concerning Educating Indians," *SW* 13 (Apr. 1884): 44.

26. SCA, "Annual Report," *SW* 10 (June 1881): 63; SCA, "Report of Hampton School," *ARCIA* 1881, p. 27.

27. J. D. McDowell, "Organization of the Indian Training Shop," 14 pages, box 21, Indian Affairs, Misc. Reports by Various Staff Members, Indian Collection, HUA.

28. McDowell, "Indian Training Shops," *ARCIA* 1889, 1885 and 1887, pp. 371, 248 and 263 respectively.

29. E. F. Coolidge, "The Shoe Shop," *ARCIA* 1884, p. 191; McDowell, "Indian Training Shops," *ARCIA* 1886 and 1889, pp. 27 and 371. In 1887 blacks were instructors in the woodcarving, carpentry, harnessmaking, and woodworking shops, while whites taught in the tin, paint, and shoe shops (later under J. E. Smith, a Hampton graduate). See McDowell, "Indian Training Shops," *ARCIA* 1887, p. 263.

30. The decline of contracts did not increase the number of blacks in Indian shops. See *ARCIA* 1885, p. 248. McDowell, "Indian Training Shops," *ARCIA* 1889, p. 370. F. W. Colcord, "The Technical Class," *ARCIA* 1886, p. 29. Colcord's students' basic ignorance of tools made these classes the most purely educational on campus.

31. Ludlow, "The Shellbanks Farm School," *SW* 34 (Oct. 1905): 533. For example, in 1891 a group of five Indian boys was sent to Shellbanks to further their skill, gained either at Hampton itself or on outing, with European farming tools and methods. Although most of Hampton's Indians would eventually become herdsmen or farmers, no formal courses in agriculture were offered until 1892. William Robinson and Edward Graham suggest that Armstrong's reports stressed agriculture only to insure funding under the Morrill Act, but abandoned formal offerings when authorities ruled that any manual labor performed on the farms would satisfy them. See William Robinson, "The History of Hampton Institute" (Ph.D. dissertation, New York University, 1959), pp. 274–75; and Graham, "Tender Violence: Old Hampton, the Indian Question, and the New South," p. 53.

32. George Davis, "Indian Boys on the Farm," *ARCIA* 1884, p. 192; Albert Howe, "Agricultural Division," *ARCIA* 1885, p. 248 and "Agricultural Department," *ARCIA* 1886, p. 29.

33. Howe, "Agricultural Division," *ARCIA* 1885, p. 248. Howe says he had nine blacks and six Indians working "in daily detail."

34. McDowell, "Indian Training Shops," *ARCIA* 1885 and 1887, pp. 248 and 264 respectively; SCA, "Report of Hampton School," *ARCIA* 1888, p. 282.

35. C. W. Betts, "Printing Office and Bindery," *ARCIA* 1885 and 1886, pp. 248 and 28 respectively; SCA, "Report of Hampton School," *ARCIA*

1893, p. 466; McDowell, "Indian Training Shops," *ARCIA* 1887, p. 264; SCA, "Report of Hampton School," *ARCIA* 1890, p. 318.

36. HBF, "Annual Report," *SW* 26 (May 1897): 93; Editorial, "On the Opening at Hampton Institute of the Armstrong-Slater Memorial Trades School," *SW* 25 (Dec. 1896): 233. Justifying the need for the building in his annual report for 1897, Frissell said, "by thus separating the trade training school from the productive industries . . . our sixteen shops will be helped to a more business basis, thus avoiding the heavy debtor balance which has hitherto been unavoidable."

37. Frank Rogers in "Annual Report," *SW* 34 (May 1905): 291. Robinson and Graham argue that Armstrong's Hampton was primarily concerned with teacher training, while Frissell's shifted towards industrial education, with all of its connotations of second-class education. Graham claims that Armstrong did not speak favorably until the early 1890s about a class of students who came to learn trades instead of teaching. By then enrollment in the Night School had increased by 455 percent while that of the Normal School had fallen from 67 to 37 percent of Hampton's student body. See Robinson, "The History," pp. 294–97; Graham, "Tender Violence: Old Hampton," pp. 225–37. Other observers dismiss any sharp break between the principals and point to the pre-existence of the Night School and manual training as proof of continuity at Hampton. See James D. Anderson, "The Hampton Model of Normal School Industrial Education, 1868–1900," in Anderson and Vincent P. Franklin, eds., *New Perspectives on Black Educational History* (Boston, 1978), pp. 61–96; James D. Anderson, *The Education of Blacks in the South, 1860–1935* (Chapel Hill, 1988), pp. 33–78.

38. SCA, *ARCIA* 1889, p. 374; George Curtis in "Annual Report," *SW* 17 (June 1888): 95; Curtis to SCA, "Statement of the Commandant's Office," Dec. 6, 1887, RG75, item 1014, enclosure 24, NARA.

39. Proceedings of the Wigwam Council, HUA; SCA, "Report of Hampton School," *ARCIA* 1888, p. 285; "Report of Indian Teachers Faculty," Apr. 13, 1887, HUA. The original Wigwam Council included Omaha Thomas Sloan as president, Omaha Eugene Fontenelle, Sioux Charles T. Picotte, Sioux Baptiste P. Lambert, and Sioux Claymore P. Arphan; Onondaga Charles Doxon and Oneida Richard S. Powless were alternates.

40. Moton, "Report of Department of Discipline and Military Instruction," in *ARCIA* 1893, p. 464; Charles W. Freeland, "Report of Department of Discipline and Military Instruction," in *ARCIA* 1889, p. 374; Minutes of the Indian Faculty, Dec. 17, 1889, HUA.

41. SCA, "Annual Report," *SW* 14 (June 1885): 74; Curtis to SCA, "Statement," Dec. 7, 1887, in Childs to Atkins, Jan. 11, 1888, RG75, item 1014, enclosure 24, NARA; Freeland, "Report of Commandant of the Hampton School," in *ARCIA* 1888, p. 284.

42. Childs to Atkins, Jan. 11, 1888, RG75, item 1014, p. 16, NARA. The companies were also put through their paces marching to dinner, weekly drills after school, battalion drills on Wednesdays (supervised by a white officer from Fortress Monroe), and at formal inspections on Sunday. SCA, *Annual Report,*

1891, p. 30; Moton, "Report on Department of Discipline and Military Instruction," *SW* 20 (May 1891): 206; *T&T* 5 (Nov. 1890): 3.

43. Moton in Minutes of Faculty Meetings, Oct. 9 and Nov. 15, 1909, HUA.

44. Graham, "Tender Violence: And the Red," p. 14; *SW* 7 (Oct. 1878): 73.

45. BTW in Harlan, ed., *BTW Papers*, 2: 83; *Ten Years' Work*, p. 13.

46. Josephine Richards in "Report of Hampton School," *ARCIA* 1884, p. 196; Curtis to SCA, "Statement," Dec. 6, 1887, enclosure 24, in Childs to Atkins, Jan. 11, 1888, RG75, item 1014, NARA.

47. Moton, "Report of Discipline and Military Instruction," *ARCIA* 1892 and 1893, pp. 703 and 464 respectively; Proceedings of the Wigwam Council, June 15, 1888, HUA; Minutes of Faculty Meetings, June 15, 1888, HUA.

48. Proceedings of the Wigwam Council, 1890–1891, HUA. The council's petition was signed by President Jas. P. Pattee (Sioux), Secretary J. S. Whistler (Sac and Fox), A. Johnson (Pottawattomie), N. W. Robertson (Sioux), and Chas. Rulo (Ponca); Tingey, "Blacks and Indians Together," p. 198.

49. SCA to Atkins, Jan. 11, 1888, RG75, item 1014, enclosure 33, NARA.

50. Phenix to HBF, May 11, 1910, HUA.

51. James E. Gregg to Andrus, Aug. 9, 1918, box 6, Indian Affairs, Correspondence to Andrus, 1900–1959, HUA. Although this allowed Hampton to accommodate 300 instead of 250 black recruits, with over 1000 expected, Hampton would have had to make new arrangements anyway.

52. Minutes of Faculty Meetings, May 29, 1922, HUA.

53. Folsom, "Indian Days," typewritten material excluded from Folsom's final draft, HUA; *Ten Years' Work*, p. 31; Minutes of Faculty Meetings, Oct. 2, 1909, HUA; Helen Townsend to Andrus, Nov. 20, 1912, last student box in Indian Collection, HUA.

54. Elizabeth Hyde, "Report of Dean of Women, 1909–1910," box on Biographies of Early Hampton Teachers, HUA; "Hampton Incidents," *SW* 51 (Nov. 1922): 533.

55. SCA, "Report of Hampton School," in *ARCIA* 1891, p. 605.

56. HBF, "Religious Work," in *ARCIA* 1887, p. 265 and 1889, p. 375; *T&T* 18 (Mar. 1903): 2.

57. HBF, *LMC* 1906, pp. 198–99. Hampton refused to permit either a Catholic or Protestant Indian from changing faiths, but whenever one's creed was unclear that Indian was pressured into becoming an Episcopalian. After it was discovered that James All Yellow had not been married in a Christian manner, he claimed his right to be wed as a Roman Catholic, inasmuch as he came from a Catholic Agency, Standing Rock. But after "arguing" with Gravatt, All Yellow consented to be married at St. John's. See Discipline File, 1887/88, HUA.

58. "Hampton and Its Surroundings," *SW* 1 (Jan. 1872): 1. The article said, "No distinction is made on account of color or race [at the asylum]. All eat at the same table, and as far as they are competent, are employed in the same duties." Minutes of Faculty Meetings, Nov. 4, 1903, HUA.

59. HBF, "Christian Work For Indians," in *ARCIA* 1884, p. 199 and "Moral and Religious," in *ARCIA* 1894, p. 418; SCA, "Annual Report," *SW* 13 (June 1884): 63 and *SW* 20 (May 1891): 207.

60. SCA, "Report of Hampton School," in *ARCIA* 1891, p. 604.

61. Caroline K. Knowles, "Social Life at Winona," in *ARCIA* 1885, p. 246. An Indian girl's letter in "The Indian's Emancipation Day," *SW* 16 (Apr. 1887): 56; Minutes of Faculty Meetings, May 29, 1922, HUA.

62. "Hampton Incidents," *SW* 40 (Feb. 1911): 120.

63. *T&T* 3 (Oct. 1888): 1; HBF, "Religious Work," in *ARCIA* 1889, p. 375; *T&T* 12 (Dec. 1897): 2 and 10 (Apr. 1895): 5; Editorial remarks, *SW* 24 (Dec. 1895): 204.

64. Helen Townsend, "The Indian Christian Endeavor Society," box 28, Indian Affairs, HI Staff, Indian Collection, HUA; Caroline Andrus, "Notes by Miss Andrus for an Address to the Christian Endeavor Society," 1915, box 50, "Christian Endeavor and YMCA," HUA; SCA, "Report of the Hampton School," *ARCIA* 1893, p. 697.

65. "Incidents," *SW* 21 (Sept. 1892): 143; Folsom in "Incidents," *SW* 18 (Oct. 1889): 106.

66. "Incidents," *SW* 34 (Jan. 1905): 58.

67. HBF in Minutes of Faculty Meetings, Dec. 9, 1914 and Oct. 21, 1915, HUA.

68. Charles H. Williams, interview at Huntington Library, Aug. 27, 1974, conducted by Eleanor Gilman and William Tingey, in Tingey, "Blacks and Indians Together," p. 259. Williams, who later became Hampton's fifth black trustee (1954–69), had come to Hampton from Berea College in 1905, when the Day Act segregated Kentucky schools and ended Berea's position as one of the last integrated southern colleges. While at Hampton, Williams had been assisted by trustee Francis G. Peabody in gaining his M.A. (from Harvard); as athletic director he solicited funds for Armstrong Field, introduced basketball, and played a leading role in the organization of the black Central Inter-Collegiate Athletic Association. See Tingey, "Blacks and Indians Together," pp. 255–57.

69. "Incidents," *SW* 45 (Feb. 1916): 195.

70. *SW* 23 (Dec. 1894): 206; *T&T* 17 (Jan. 1903): 3; Daniel Thomas, "Indian School Life at Hampton," 1914, Andrus Box, p. 277, Indian Collection, HUA; Tingey, "Blacks and Indians Together," p. 259.

71. Thomas, "Indian School Life," p. 277; Tingey, "Blacks and Indians Together," p. 258. Blacks first played basketball at Howard University. Williams, "Hampton Incidents," *SW* 40 (Jan. 1911): 59.

72. SCA to Gen. E. Whittlesey and A. K. Smiley, Mar. 15, 1888, box on Childs Report, HUA; SCA in *SW* 18 (July 1889): 77. In addition to the main dining rooms, there was a special diet kitchen where about forty students could, if needed, receive what Armstrong called a "milk and farinaceous or fresh beef and vegetable diet." For example, in 1885 there were 633 meals served to blacks and 376 served to Indians in the diet kitchen. See SCA to Whittlesey and Smiley, Mar. 15, 1888, box on Childs Report, HUA; E. F. Patterson, "The Diet Kitchen," in *ARCIA* 1885, p. 244.

73. SCA to Childs, Dec. 23, 1887, in Childs to Atkins, Jan. 11, 1888, RG75, item 1014, NARA.

74. HBF, "Annual Report," *SW* 27 (May 1898): 92; Minutes of Faculty Meetings, May 26, 1906, June 5, 1907 and Feb. 2, 1910, HUA. The consequences of the Indian girl's refusal were not recorded.

75. Jane E. Davis to SCA, May 2, 1889, box on Dining Room Controversy (hereafter cited as DRC), HUA. Davis said that "the line that separates the two dining rooms is certainly not one of difference in official position, for there are several [teachers] at least in the large dining room who hold positions that correspond exactly with those held by some of the graduates." Folsom to SCA, May 3, 1889, DRC, HUA.

76. Aery, "The Hampton Idea: Founder of Hampton Institute," p. 62; Folsom to SCA, May 3, 1889, DRC, HUA; Harris Barrett to SCA, Apr. 20, 1889, Va. files, frame HI-13341, AMA Papers; SCA to the Graduate Teachers, Apr. 13, 1889, Va. files, frame HI-33410, AMA Papers.

77. SCA received responses from all the resident graduates: Harris Barrett (1885), Georgia Washington (1882), Sara F. Peake (1885), Arthur T. Boykin (1884), W. T. B. Williams (1889), Fred D. Wheelock (1888), and John H. Evans (1887). See Apr. 1889, Va. files, AMA Papers.

78. Peake to SCA, Apr. 18, 1889, Va. files, frame HI-13341, AMA Papers.

79. Barrett to SCA, Apr. 20, 1889, Va. files, frame HI-13341, AMA Papers.

80. Mary R. Hamlin to SCA, Apr. 28, 1889, DRC, HUA; Ludlow to SCA, May 29, 1889, DRC, HUA. The discussion in the text uses Ludlow's analysis of the responses of teachers, supplemented by materials from the letters themselves.

81. George W. Andrews to SCA, May 4, 1889, DRC, HUA; Dora Freeman to SCA, May 1, 1889, DRC, HUA. Making comments similar to Barrett, Williams had said integrated dining "would do a great deal to heighten the respect for the school at least among those [for whom] you are working." See Williams to SCA, Apr. 18, 1889, Va. files, frame HI-13341, AMA Papers. Anna L. Bellows to SCA, May 2, 1889, DRC, HUA.

82. Hamlin to SCA, Apr. 28, 1889, DRC, HUA.

83. Ludlow to SCA, May 29, 1889, DRC, HUA.

84. Francis C. Briggs to SCA, May 4, 1889, Mary M. Gordon to SCA, May 1, 1889, F. N. Gilman to SCA, May 3, 1889, George L. Curtis to SCA, May 4, 1889, Elizabeth Hyde to SCA, May 2, 1889, all in DRC, HUA.

85. Mary F. Mackie to SCA, May 3, 1889, Ludlow to SCA, May 29, 1889, both in DRC, HUA.

86. Ludlow to SCA, May 29, 1889; Gilman to SCA, May 3, 1889, both in DRC, HUA.

87. Irene H. Stansbury in Ludlow to SCA, May 29, 1889, DRC, HUA.

88. Folsom to SCA, May 3, 1889, DRC, HUA. Soon after coming to Hampton from Dakota in 1878 as part of Pratt's first party, nine-year-old Arickara Anna Dawson was left an orphan. Consequently, she was virtually raised by the Indian Department's staff; she was graduated from Hampton in 1885. In effect, Folsom asked the staff members what justice they found

in a system that would place their own foster daughter in a segregated dining room. Indeed Dawson did return to teach at Hampton, but only for a few months before staff members secured a post for her at the Santee Indian School. See *Twenty-Two Years' Work,* p. 330.

89. Hampton's placement of Indians in the segregated graduate dining room (like its prohibition against Indians playing white teams) throws into question Engs' conclusion that Hampton Indians were falsely led to believe that they would be treated as equals of whites whereas blacks experienced nothing at Hampton to create such illusions. In truth, neither of Hampton's nonwhite races was led to expect the privileges of whites. See Engs, "Intellectual Inequality," in McPherson, *Race,* p. 261. Folsom to SCA, May 3, 1889, DRC, HUA.

90. Graham, "Tender Violence: The Black and The White," p. 31.

91. SCA to the Graduate Teachers, Apr. 13, 1889, Va. files, frame HI-33410, AMA Papers. Armstrong could not have said this earlier. In late August 1885 there had been a petition by eight graduates against a takeover of their kitchen for use in preparing meals for the acting faculty. See Graham, "Tender Violence: The Black and the White," pp. 17–18.

92. Barrett to SCA, Apr. 20, 1889, Va. files, frame HI-13341, AMA Papers. Although Barrett assured Armstrong that both whites and blacks felt "mutual adversion" to miscegenation, two letters by younger white teachers, one who described herself as a "foolish virgin," revealed indiscretions "almost from within the confessional booth." See Graham, "Tender Violence: The Black and the White," p. 26. Ludlow to SCA, May 19, 1889, DRC, HUA. According to Ludlow's tabulations, the issue would have passed seventeen to fourteen.

93. Graham, "Tender Violence: The Black and the White," p. 24; Barrett to SCA, Apr. 20, 1889, Va. files, frame HI-13341, AMA Papers.

94. F. C. Briggs to SCA, May 4, 1889, DRC, HUA.

95. F. D. Wheelock to SCA, Apr. 20, 1889, Va. files, frame HI-13341, AMA Papers; Peake to SCA, Apr. 18, 1889, Va. files, frame HI-13341, AMA Papers.

96. SCA to Graduate Teachers, Apr. 13, 1889, Va. files, frame HI-33410, AMA Papers. It was not until 1927 that a black was appointed to the regular teaching staff and the 1930s that one was lodged in the Trustees' House.

97. Hampton authorities argued that neither Negro education in the South nor the black economic community could have occurred without segregation. Armstrong stated that "the aggressive, tyrannical manifestation of this prejudice among the whites that we so much deplore, is driving the Negro into a race assertiveness which is just what he needs." In a statement which also had implications for Indians, Frissell explained that for a race whose members "had been treated like children . . . the separation which race-prejudice brought was absolutely necessary to the formation of character and of self-reliance . . . the patronage of the superior [race] has a tendency to downgrade character." See SCA quoted in HBF, "A History of the Education of the Negro," 1900,

p. 11, box 83 on HBF, HUA, and HBF, "Negro Education," *The New World* 9 (Dec. 1900): 632.

98. In 1875 the *Workman* said of mixed schools, "the whites won't have them and the blacks don't want them. The march of education should not be stopped for a useless, hopeless battle on that line, because it can go on without it, and can go on in no other way." Twelve years later the paper repeated that "co-education of the races in the South was as yet impracticable." See *SW* 4 (Feb. 1875): 10, 16 (Sept. 1887): 91 and 30 (May 1901): 233. For the *Workman's* acceptance of residential segregation, see *SW* 33 (Apr. 1904): 199 and 43 (July 1914): 377.

6

Friction and Fraternity on a Biracial Campus

Perhaps the most common question outsiders asked about Hampton's biracial program was "How do the races actually get along?" Looking for new ways to confirm old bias, they usually expected "uncivilized" races to treat each other in a "primitive" manner. Many were unsure whether disaffection or affection between the races posed a greater danger. According to an early white teacher at Hampton, such inquirers were concerned that "there might be fights, and there might be love affairs, both of which were regarded as undesirable."[1]

Consequently, only one public view of Hampton's racial interaction could serve the interests of the school and its black and Indian students. Hampton officials maintained throughout the biracial years what Armstrong asserted in 1888, that race relations have "proven pleasant and profitable; yet there is little intimacy . . . in ten years not a serious fracas has occurred, not a single case of immorality, between the students of both races and of both sexes."[2] This declaration implicitly credited both the students' complaisance and the school's internal security measures with this happy situation. Indeed, school records—the discipline logs, Moton's papers as commandant, and faculty meetings—reveal relatively few instances of racial conflict between blacks and Indians, perhaps fewer than a dozen in total.

Indian life at Hampton was not quite as officials described, however. Hampton's records show considerably more friction than its officials admitted, much of it generated or aggravated by the school's own policies. Hampton staff also denied the reality of sexual interest that crossed racial lines. Despite the strictest sanctions, there was kissing, though Hampton was not telling. And in addition to the occasional extremes of hostility and attraction that outsiders expected to hear about, Hampton experienced a full range of human reactions and interaction in between.

Both General Armstrong and Richard Pratt of Carlisle claimed Indians held no natural animosity toward blacks.[3] In fact most Indians had had no direct opportunity to have formed opinions about blacks at all. The common racial slur among traditional Indians was not "nigger" but "white man." Yet, picking up whites' prejudice against blacks was an early sign of an Indian's "civilizing." At the beginning of the first school year that Indians attended Hampton, in October 1878, the *Workman* reported that when asked what English he knew, an Indian "with a roguish twinkle in his eye, went to the blackboard and wrote 'sambo.'"[4]

Such potential threats to the harmony of biracial interaction could sometimes be positively transformed. In January 1885 Hampton was visited by Sioux Chief White Ghost. Cora Folsom, the most active member of Hampton's Indian Department, said that the chief entertained "strong feelings" against blacks, and "found it very difficult to believe that the photograph I showed him of the Senior Class was made up almost entirely of Negroes. He looked at it long and earnestly and then, pointing to a particularly fine looking fellow, said, as one having authority, 'That Indian.'" Although some of the blacks pictured may have had Indian ancestry, White Ghost's repeated mistaking of blacks for Indians eventually disarmed him and made the chief more willing to listen to "the similar needs of the red and black races." Recognizing that occasional prejudice toward blacks was unavoidable even among chiefs, Folsom acknowledged that some bridge had to be built "if one schoolmate called another 'nigger,' and he retaliated with 'savage.'" She believed that "generally the natural method recommended itself." Thus, authorities attempted to resolve such matters by asking each student to imagine how he would feel if he were burdened by the hardships of the other race. In minor altercations, such as the school boy fracus that occurred between Cherokee Allen Sawyer and John Deveaux of Savannah, Georgia, and particularly when racial slurs were not involved, authorities encouraged the contestants to shake hands and part as friends.[5]

Yet at the same time, according to Commandant Curtis, each race "possesses a confident sense of superiority to the other, that of itself prevents friction." As Reverend J. J. Gravatt pointed out, the Indian felt that he had never been a slave while the Negro had never been a "savage . . . at least in this country."[6] Such mutual disparagement, so much of it clearly the product of white society's treatment of each group, made it possible for one to shore up its self-respect by seeing the other as even lower in the social pecking order.

In any event, the potential for interracial trouble was minimal, since those Indians who had already acquired white prejudices avoided Hampton. Sioux Joseph Estes, for instance, was unable to induce his son Leonard to attend his Alma Mater, because Leonard had acquired prejudice against blacks after the family moved to Orlando, Florida. Hampton did not even recruit from those tribes who had held slaves, and this was only partly because the Five Civilized Tribes had their own school systems.[7]

Moreover, individual Indian students from any tribe who harbored enough racial hostility to become disruptive were encouraged to stay away from Hampton. In April 1911, when Joseph Metoxen asked Vice Principal George Phenix for permission to return to Hampton from his home in Oneida, Wisconsin, he nevertheless took the occasion to remind Phenix that he had refused to play basketball with blacks because "they have a distinct fragrance of their own" that nearly caused him to "throw up all my dinner." He asked Phenix how he would like Negroes to "rut against your body." Phenix replied to Metoxen, "There are plenty of schools where there are no colored people in attendance and if you feel this way it seems to us that you ought to go to this kind of school. . . . it is very unfortunate for an Indian to come to a school like Hampton and feel and express his feelings as you felt and expressed your feelings. The influence of such a student is not good; it is not good for him to be here."[8]

Indian or black students who committed racially motivated violence on campus were sent home. During the 1890–91 school year, John Block, a Caddo from Indian Territory (where prejudice against blacks prevailed), was expelled for throwing two bricks at Charles H. Stokes of Gloucester, Virginia, "without provocation, so as to endanger his life." While awaiting his exit west, Block was quarantined from other students by confinement in the industrial room during the day and the Marquand guard room at night. Conversely, in September 1893 a black student, Charles A. Parker, was dismissed for starting a fight with an Indian in which he "struck the boy with some weapon which cut a gash in his head about 1½" long and about a ¼ of an inch deep."[9]

Although Hampton's administration had flatly denied any instances of collective violence between blacks and Indians, there were snowball fights that reflected intergroup tensions. The only one to be publicized, the celebrated "Rouge et Noir," occurred in the winter of 1879 and included about fifty antagonists of each race. Folsom described the contest in "Indian Days at Hampton": "The colored troops inclined to union for strength, always advancing in close formation. The Indians, on the other hand, scattered out for surprises. Another racial difference was shown in the red man's conservation of ammunition, the black man lavishly expending his [snowballs], only laying himself open to attack by his more frugal foe." Managing Editor Helen Ludlow's account in the *Workman* described even more stereotypically how "above the din of battle, was heard the genuine war whoop, and a frightful song it is, even without the scalping knife accompaniment. Not to be outdone in din making, the colored boys procured a drummer and a drum . . . [but as he continually had to dodge snowballs] there was a melancholy uncertainty about the drumbeats that reminded one of the 'tom tom' described by jungle travelers." Folsom reported that the skirmish concluded "with the repulse of the red men," when an Indian was backed into the pond at Marquand Hall. This "diversion" was said to end the affair with each side gaining "mutual respect and pleasure."[10]

The motives of everyone except the commentators on this incident may have been pure as new snow, but two later contests occurred that were neither innocent nor written up by school officials for public consumption. During the winter of 1887 Sidney Smith was suspended for "wounding" an Indian with a brick thrown in "snowball combat." Smith then wrote a letter to the Boston *Advocate* in which, according to Commandant Curtis, the black student "represented himself as the object of persecution by the school's authorities for defending himself against being 'mobbed by savages.'" Curtis reported Smith was readmitted in October 1887, after "publicly retracting his libel and being thoroughly put to shame before the school." In another more serious instance in December 1891 Moton reported to the faculty that a snowball fight between the residents of Stone Building and the Wigwam resulted in "bricks [being] thrown by both colored and Indian boys."[11]

Much of the racial tension was caused by the methods of control the school deemed necessary to carry out federal regulations. Like government policies regulating the activities of Indians on reservations, Hampton's version of the red code reflected, though it did not always enforce, their distinct legal status. Low as the Negro's place was in the nation, he was an American citizen and a free agent who could leave school if he chose, either permanently or for summers, the holiday season, or family emergency. In contrast, Indians, even adult Indians, were wards of the government assigned by contract to Armstrong's custody. In April 1885 Commissioner John Atkins told the general, "Indian pupils are placed under your charge . . . by authority of this department and with the consent of their parents, and acting 'in loco parentis' you are authorized to exercise your rights and prerogatives . . . as the parent, or guardian, can exercise his authority over his minor children." Accordingly, only Indians underwent such indignities as having the staff open their mail or being compelled to open it in the presence of a teacher, and being refused railway tickets without Armstrong's permission.[12] Former Indian students, some of them over fifty years old, were greeted as "Dear Children" by the Alumni Office. Virtually captives during the program's early years, Hampton's Indian students came and went under military escort and were returned by the sheriff if they ran away.

An underground guard house was established as the ultimate punishment for Indians. Ludlow explained why Indians but not blacks were singled out for confinement: "With the colored student, the strongest possible influence that can be brought to bear is suspension or expulsion from the advantages for which his chances are so few and so highly prized. A refractory Indian, on the contrary, cannot be sent a thousand miles home to his woods nor be turned adrift" in a white community. Some homesick Indians longed for expulsion. Josephine Richards of the Indian Department said that one Indian girl, on hearing black students warned that fifteen zeros would send them home, eagerly added up the number of zeros she had received. Similarly, Sioux Robert Goodwind complained to Moton that since he had done an unspecified "very wrong thing [he] ought to be sent home" like an unruly Negro, not sentenced to the guard house.[13]

Since Indians also chafed at being under Negroes as the military muscle of the school, black officers felt they needed Hampton's authority to perform their duties. Superintendent Thomas D. McAlpine of the Old Soldiers' Home next door to Hampton argued that his black residents could not be used in security assignments there because "a 'Sioux Indian' of the Normal School will not allow himself to be spoken to by a negro guard." Discipline files at Hampton suggest that Indians sometimes recreated conditions on the reservations by looking toward white soldiers for access to alcohol and prostitution, and thus may have resented blacks acting as military police who interfered. In July 1887 a "serious fight" ensued when a black, Major Arthur Boykin, attempted to escort James Garfield to the guard house. The Sioux hit Boykin with a stick, whereupon the incensed major struck the Indian at least five times with his nightstick. Since Garfield had previously warned Boykin that the Negro had better not attempt to place him in the guard house, Hampton prosecuted the act as premeditated assault against a school officer representing the state; Garfield pulled thirty days in the city jail.[14]

Blacks viewed their exemption from Hampton's code for Indians as evidence of their superior status and as their reward for accepting and helping to "tame" Indians. On the single occasion when Hampton violated this tacit understanding a major dispute ensued. In November 1884 Thomas Hebron was placed in the guard house following a fist fight with another black. A "mob" of Negro students threatened to release Hebron, arguing that "school authorities had no right to put a colored boy in the guard house, that the guard house was for Indians." The protesters failed to affect Hebron's escape despite arming him with an axe and stealing the bar that locked the cell. Eleven blacks, most of them officers in the school battalion, faced various charges. First Sergeant Henry Harris and Second Sergeant Mordecai Park were each suspended one year for "mutinous and exciting language, and rendering no assistance to confiscate the axe." Even the officer in charge, Second Lieutenant Thomas Langon, was court-martialed for joining the mob. Five blacks, all officers with good records, left school rather than receive punishment for upholding the tradition that the guard house was reserved for Indians, and it does not appear that blacks were placed in the guard house again.[15]

The Indian code at Hampton prescribed other discriminatory punishments that probably also produced racial tension, although corroborating evidence is unavailable. Contrary to Armstrong's claim that physical force was unnecessary for managing Indians, teacher Jacobina Koch was authorized, "in view of her motherly offices to the little [Indian] boys to inflict corporal punishment . . . treating them thus not as a Hampton student, but as a naughty child." After the faculty empowered her to call on some "strong man" either to hold the offender or to administer the punishment, Koch employed black officers to beat Indian children. Although the use of physical punishment was not frequent, the discipline files reported, for example, that Omaha Garry Myers was "whipped"—on November 3, 1884, by Major Gibson, and again on January 12, 1885, by Major Boykin (both blacks)—in front of other small Indian boys.[16] This very public beating must have been a highly intimidating experience for all of them, since in most Indian tribes parents never struck their children.

If considered intractable, even adult Indians at Hampton sometimes received punishments difficult to imagine being inflicted on Hampton's black freemen, punishments that implied no future life of equality in white society. Sioux Sam Four Stars, for example, was taken from the Hampton jail by black guards and "placed at Shellbanks to work under ball and chain." Similarly, Cassie McCoy, a Sac and Fox who had lost her temper after being locked in her room for "impudence," was handcuffed and shackled while "quieting medicines" were administered.[17]

The very harshness of Hampton's Indian code, however, apparently mitigated against its consistent enforcement. No evidence suggests that anyone at Hampton liked having to resort to extreme measures in dealing with fractious Indians. Folsom reported that some teachers got very nervous when they had a refractory Indian to deal with. In classrooms where lone white women, sometimes younger than their charges, were expected to manage warriors, an Indian sometimes got away with conduct for which blacks would be expelled. For example, teacher Myrtilla Sherman, outraged to learn that one Indian was not banished for attacking a faculty member, asked if such inequality will not "create ill-feeling among the [Negro] students." Another teacher, Carrie Erskine, "secretly rebelled" at the leniency accorded Indian malefactors and had not been at Hampton a month before a number of teachers told her that since Indians "could be sent away only for very grave offenses, one must avoid issue with them."[18] Indians were so hard to recruit that the school was reluctant to part with them without first trying methods that were by turns both more severe and more forgiving than those applied to black students, of whom there was never a shortage.

Therefore, although blacks felt affirmed as superior to the Indians by a less demeaning code of discipline, they must have resented individual Indians going unpunished for offenses that teachers themselves believed would have sent blacks packing. At the same time, Indians saw themselves treated both as chattels and as special people. The ambiguous multileveled status of each group—the constant shifting of their relative positions on a racial ladder—could not help but cause tension. Far from being the "natural" racism assumed by many to exist between Indians and blacks, prejudice between these groups at Hampton arose or increased in response to racial distinctions made by the white staff even though the teachers were constantly reminded not to show partiality to either race.

In addition to its disciplinary practices, the school's uneven student wage policies were bound to cause racial friction. During an audience with Hampton's Indians in December 1887, Inspector Thomas S. Childs received complaints of "unjust discrimination" against them in wages, which represented an "element of discontent . . . a constantly rasping force between the races." An earlier letter by Winnebago Julia St. Cyr to Commissioner Atkins had placed the wage question on Childs's agenda; in it she not only complained that she was paid less than blacks, but also that she could not collect what was owed her, although "if it were a negro, they would pay her every cent. I told you negroes were over us Indians here."[19] *Ten Years' Work* openly admitted that blacks received higher wages than Indians, and tabulated (unfortunately using dissimilar indices) that Indians made from $.01 to $.05 per hour—with small boys and new hands at the lower rates—while blacks earned from $4.00 to $10.00 per month. In E. F. Coolidge's shoe shop, where there was an especially wide disparity in wages, Indians were paid from $.25 to $4.00 per month while blacks received up to $26.00.[20]

Ten Years' Work maintained that blacks merited higher wages because their "skill, endurance and reliability" made their work more valuable to the school. Also, as discussed in chapter five, blacks could not have afforded school without wages, whereas Indians' education was paid for by treaty, making renumeration largely a "gratuity" or allowance. Work was often assigned to Indians more for instruction than for the economic needs of the school. Although Armstrong maintained "care has been taken to explain our methods to Indians," he observed that "all are not satisfied with it, for it is based on facts they dislike to accept." Believing Indians "do not realize their physical inferiority to Negroes as workmen," the general was clearly irritated that the Indians had complained to Childs. Armstrong told the inspector that despite earning less, the "Indians have an easier time and more money. They could not endure the struggle of the Negroes who are more strong and more manly and more self-reliant for it, and their example is good for these red fellow citizens, whose earnings are a surplus. They have not like the Negro a struggle for life, and most of them could not bear it."[21] In short, never pleased that Indians received their education for free, Armstrong compensated by paying them lower wages.

What angered Indians even more than wage discrimination was the fact that half the money they did earn was withheld as a so-called "tool fund," supposedly to equip them after they returned home. But school officials also believed that too much spending money would "demoralize them."[22] Whatever the merit of Hampton's stance, Indians resented being treated differently than blacks not only in earning a smaller loaf to begin with, but in getting only half of that; furthermore, even the tool funds were sometimes withheld for delinquent accounts or forfeited because of poor school records. Moreover, Indians believed the tool fund was administered unfairly. For in a kind of circular chicken and egg dilemma, Hampton required the returned Indians to document their employment before agreeing to release tool funds, while employers often required Indians to possess tools before hiring them.[23]

Even former students with good records occasionally had problems collecting their money from the tool fund. In September 1909 Seneca Benjamin F. Bishop complained to the commissioner about having to go to "humiliating extremes" in getting his $32 tool fund. He asked why Hampton still treated him as a minor if it was "willing to grant me not only a trade certificate but an Academic Diploma." In another incident, in December 1909 the agent at Oneida informed the faculty that former student Duncan Powless had died, and requested his tool fund money to help his father pay for the funeral. The faculty refused without giving any reason. In an earlier, 1904 case, Seneca Spencer F. Williams refused to fuss with Hampton Treasurer F. D. Gleason over his tool fund money, telling him that "if the school needs it more than I do I am willing to let it go for a good cause," but that otherwise, "I plan to buy me a slide trombone."[24]

Of course black students must have known that Hampton's preferential treatment would not follow them into the larger society. For once freed from Bureau and school regulations, the Indian ward was more highly regarded than the Negro citizen. Unlike blacks, Indians were often treated (especially when among easterners) as the equals of whites in regard to public accommodations, schools, employment, wages, union affiliation, and even marriage. When Booker Washington escorted a consumptive Indian from Hampton to Washington D.C., the headwaiter aboard one of the Old Dominion steamships agreed to serve the Indian but not Washington. And upon reaching the capital, the clerk in the hotel at which they had reservations admitted the Indian but not the Negro. Generally, red but not black students were permitted to board with whites on northern fundraising campaigns, and only Indians were invited to march in Garfield's inaugural. White outsiders typically assumed a "harmful" influence of Hampton blacks on Indians, rather than the other way around.[25]

Even at Hampton itself officials sometimes worked at cross purposes to the school's program of "racial elevation," by reflecting popular prejudices against blacks, and for Indians. Such lapses flew in the face of the school's mainstream of thought and policy, which placed Negroes in positions of authority over the Indian, in recognition of their acculturation and "civilizing" during slavery. When Armstrong himself predicted that "the Indian would eventually merge with the white race while the Negro would not," blacks were being told that color prejudice rather than "fitness" would determine their future as Americans.[26] Paradoxically, at the same time Indians at a school for Negroes saw their claims to nationhood undermined by associating with blacks, whose ambitions for integration were assumed to be true of Indians also. Thus the inconsistencies of Hampton's racial policies encouraged alienation among its students. By succumbing to the wishful thinking of most whites—who reversed the traditional goals of these groups by believing the Negro satisfied with separation and the Indian desirous of integration—the general provided both minorities with grounds for resentment.

On occasion Hampton staff went so far as to accept the intermarriage of Indians and whites (though without generally promoting it, as has been claimed).[27] Two of Hampton's white teachers married Indian men. In 1891, after moving on from Hampton, but before becoming the first woman supervisor of Indian schools, Elaine Goodale married the agency physician at Pine Ridge, Sioux Charles Eastman—who would become probably the most prominent Indian of the era.[28] In 1919 teacher Rebecca Pond wed a former Hampton student, Cherokee George Owl, who, long after her untimely death, would become tribal chairman of the Eastern Cherokees.[29] Moreover, a third white teacher at Hampton, head of the Indian Department Caroline Andrus, was engaged to her most accomplished graduate, Sac and Fox tribesman William A. Jones, who was the first Indian to graduate from Harvard in 250 years and the first to receive a Ph.D. (in 1904, from Columbia under Franz Boas). Before the marriage could take place, Jones went to the Philippines to conduct anthropological research and was killed there by Illgonot tribesmen in March 1909.[30] While these remarkable Indians had little in common with the vast majority of Hampton's Indian students, the school's teachers found no Negro light or bright enough to marry a white person.[31]

Although most blacks looked forward to their return home for the summer, Hampton's outing system offered only Indians the opportunity for closer contact with whites. The school selected northern homes where, instead of being treated as one of a large number of servants or field hands, the Indian would share the life of a white family. For those few Indians who remained North for a winter, outing also opened the door to white education, undermining Hampton's claim that white schools were unsuitable for Indians. Believing that one of the "strong inducements with the scholars to fall in so readily with the plan [for outing] . . . was the thought of attending school with white children," the Indian teachers faculty ignored a stronger inducement—the chance to ride horses.[32]

The black press reflected black student discontent, reacting vigorously against attitudes and practices at Hampton that appeared partial toward Indians. In an August 1879 issue of the *People's Advocate* of Washington and Alexandria, anti-Hampton black editor John W. Cromwell, objected to Armstrong's assertion that Indians were "decidedly stronger in intellect" than Negroes. Cromwell sarcastically rejoined, "no one would think that Gen. A. meant to degrade the Indians by giving them colored teachers. Yet such is the fact. What does Gen. A. mean by thus compelling the weaker to train the 'stronger in intellect'?" Renewing his charge that Hampton disparaged blacks, Cromwell reported in August 1887 that J. C. Reed, a recently deceased Negro student, had been buried wearing only his night shirt. Without denying that the deceased student was improperly attired for eternity, Armstrong said that his burial was dignified in all other respects. Indeed Armstrong contended that the school displayed partiality toward blacks on this issue, because "the funeral expenses of Indians [were] paid for by the government, those of Negroes by the school."[33]

Even a black paper far afield demonstrated concern about Hampton and its biracial program. In June 1892 the Indianapolis *Freeman* criticized a Chicago *Interocean* article's favorable account of Indian girls in Winona Hall playing the piano, while the only black who "must be noticed" was the cook, as a "pure type of the Negro." In response to the article's praise for the tidiness of the Indians' rooms, the *Freeman* asked, "What was the matter with the colored girls' rooms? I presume [the white reporter] would have them all in the laundry, washing the clothes of the Indian ladies, while they 'banged away' at the piano."[34]

———

While distinctions made between black and Indian students produced or intensified conflict at the institute, there were enough occasions when these races united against white presumptions to rule out the anticipated automatic, unremitting hostility. Booker Washington described an instance when a teacher of American history asked a black and an Indian classmate whether they could find any special contribution that the other race had made toward "civilization." The two students readily responded, the Indian referring to the Negroes' patience, musical aptitude, and desire to learn, the Negro to the Indians' courage, sense of honor, and racial pride. But when the teacher asked *anyone* of either race in what respects the white race was superior, "no member of the class rose." The teacher repeated the question, but "to his surprise, not one of the class had a word to say." For Washington, this "comparatively trivial incident . . . [illustrated] how all the darkcoloured people of this country, no matter how different . . . are being drawn together in sympathy and interest in the presence of the prejudice of the white man against all other people of a different colour from his own." Washington suggested that the pretensions of white superiority, threatening blacks and Indians alike, have "led them, perhaps, to have a special interest in one another."[35]

Robert Moton related another incident in which blacks and Indians together actually punished the faculty for disrespect. Male students of both races customarily escorted their dates back to the women's dormitories after the annual Christmas concert; however, in 1888 an assistant matron broke up the couples strolling from the gymnasium and made students of each sex walk home alone. A "protest meeting" was held the next day; those present drafted Moton, then a senior, as chairman. He was able to fend off a proposed general strike of Hampton's productive industries during the holiday season only by counterproposing a boycott of all social gatherings, for "insulting ladies and gentlemen without cause." The support of Indian students for this cause was assured when black protesters accepted the amendment offered by Sioux John Bruyier, to make the action come as a surprise. For Indians to have allied themselves with blacks at this time was remarkable because Indians had to snub not only Armstrong but his guests of honor, Commissioner of Indian Affairs Thomas J. Morgan and his wife. In the end, Moton said that "the teachers felt very badly; and we felt that the holidays had been very dull and dreary, [but] found ample compensation in the fact that we had 'disciplined' the officials of the Institute."[36]

The very next year Indians and blacks again joined together, this time challenging the moral consistency of Hampton officials on a serious nineteenth-century question for Christians, the morality of dancing. At Hampton dancing was forbidden among students, a ruling consistent with the teachings of most black churches and of missionary stations among Indians. However, as Folsom recalled, Armstrong himself was "very fond of dancing and often gave little hops in the two big parlors here, a student orchestra furnishing the music"—for the staff. Suggesting blacks accepted this double standard, Folsom maintained that Negro students realized the "downward path for one race need not be necessarily the same for all, and enjoyed watching these gaieties from outside," while the Indian students protested that "Christians should not dance." To Folsom's explanation about the difference between "Indian and other dances," the red students retorted, "Indian dance all alone, White man and woman dance together, no good." Although Folsom had claimed that blacks were not shocked by the behavior of their teachers at these southern balls, teacher Myrtilla Sherman would "not soon forget the expression on the faces of two of the [Negro] waiter boys that night, when I went to get my coat."[37]

In 1891 the moral disapproval of Indian and black students finally purged Hampton of all dancing. After two years of hesitation, in a statement indicating that the disapproval of blacks had preceded the disapproval of Indians, Armstrong decided that "to go against the prejudice of [Negroes] might be merely doubtful, [but] this added objection from [Indians] made it seem best to give it up altogether and this was done."[38] Moton put the larger issue in perspective when he asserted that blacks and Indians found common cause against white hypocrisy, although they reacted to it quite differently:

> I was surprised to find how hard it was for many Indians to adapt themselves to the customs of the white man, for they thought the old way, their way, better and in many cases found very good reasons to support their view. Their opinion, for example about the white man's religion was that he preached one thing and frequently practised another; that he preached human brotherhood, for instance, while very few whites, so far as Indians could observe, actually practised human brotherhood. . . . This was a new experience for a Negro, for while many of us shared this view about the inconsistencies of the white man and how far he actually was from practicing his religion, we had nevertheless adapted ourselves to the white man's ways.[39]

If for most blacks the inconsistencies of the white man's stance only intensified their demands for equality through integration as Americans, for most Indians they were reasons to live as Indians. Although blacks and Indians may sometimes have found each other's reasoning inexplicable, they learned from each other: between them they agreed that Christianity had not prevented whites from seizing a people from one continent to develop the continent stolen from another. Neither race could lay anything at the other's doorstep that compared to the injuries whites had done to each of them.

———

Finally, that most basic and most feared consequence of interracial contact—sexual attraction across racial lines—was a fact of life on campus, although it was given even less publicity than were incidents of biracial unity against whites. In 1888, at the same time that *Ten Years' Work* was saying of the potential for illicit sex between the minority races, that although "trouble might come of it . . . none ever has," three black men were dating Indian women. Typically, neither the faculty minutes nor the discipline files were detailed, merely noting that group "midnight strolls" had "frequently" taken place, pairing off W.

T. Penn and Sioux Josephine McCarthy, Fletcher Ricks and Assiniboine Jennie Ampetu, and James Atkinson and Ponca Cora Rulo. Yet it was charged that these couples had triple-dated for the purpose of engaging in "criminal conduct." The record shows that four of the students were severely punished: Penn and Ricks were dismissed, Atkinson was told not to return, and Ampetu was "sent away." The faculty minutes reported that the black student body, believing interracial dating a matter of personal preference, was disposed to "persecute" the informant, Sydney Williams, for having "betrayed Penn and Ricks." In another occurrence, after having been threatened with suspension if he continued to meet with an unnamed female Indian, Leroy Spriggs was dismissed by the commandant when the two were "caught in Cleveland Chapel alone." In 1902 still another biracial couple fell in love. James Garvin wrote to Sioux Winona Keith several times after he left school, but "his letters were opened and kept from her, so that no harm came of it."[40]

Although David Owl, a member of a prominent Cherokee family, recalled in 1960 that a few of the Indian women at Hampton married Negro men, developing "congenially integrated families of culture," and that no male Indian married a black female, sexual interest between Indian men and black women was not unknown. As early as July 1879 Ludlow reported that "Indian boys are looking favorably upon colored girls at the school." One Indian asked his father for six horses to give to the father of a Negro. In speaking of the proposed nuptials, the Indian told Ludlow that he would sleep and hunt buffalo while his wife worked. He told her he would give a black bride "one year try; if she can't work, I throw her away and get another wife." Moreover, the discipline files reported during the 1888–89 school year that Cheyenne James Paypay was returned to Shellbanks for attempting to "repeat his previous misconduct and establish improper intimacy" with a black female.[41]

Hampton's policies affected gender relations within the races as well as between them. Just as white men tried to emasculate black men during slavery, Hampton's emphasis on the greater "civilization" of blacks lowered the image of Indian men in the eyes of some Indian women, thereby inadvertently making black men seem more desirable. Dean of Women Elizabeth Hyde asserted that "the Indian boys do not seem equal to the girls. . . . Some of the boys are good enough boys perhaps, but have not shown much strength yet. This affects the social life of the girls, and tends to make the weaker ones seek the companionship of the colored boys rather than those of their own race, while the stronger girls feel the loss of proper male companionship."

In 1912 the resulting resentments flared into a war between the sexes. The boys requested a table in the dining room separate from the girls; the faculty minutes reported that "the Indian boys are jealous of the Indian girls having anything to do with the colored boys."[42] Indian males must have also felt hostility toward those black rivals who "stole" their women, as Indians were forced to adopt the traits and dating behavior of Negro gentlemen in order to attract their female counterparts. Once again hostility and discord, in this case dividing the sexes within one race as well as the males of both races, occurred largely because of the white staff, which in its zeal to "elevate" Indians by making them unhappy with themselves, succeeded in this instance in alienating them from each other.

In sum, in claiming that no noteworthy amount of friction existed between the student races and that no expressions of sexual interest occurred between them, Hampton officials served only their own interests. But the supposition of Hampton's white critics that disorder and "reversion to type" were the inevitable outcome of mixing "lower" races obscured the fact that the bringing together at one school of two different discriminatory traditions in law and custom was demonstrably the cause for most conflicts in the biracial program. Nevertheless, given the numerous opportunities for serious racial trouble to develop, the forty-five years of Hampton's Indian program were remarkably low in conflict.

For the most part this apparent lack of conflict was so because the different types of discrimination faced by blacks and Indians seemed largely to cancel each other out. Whenever the Hampton system pushed a black or Indian further than he could accommodate himself, some official of the institute could usually heal the fissure by pointing to the miseries of the other race. However, on those occasions when Hampton's accommodationist motive for teaching through the power of example became apparent to the student and resulted in his estrangement from the system, that student had to go. For example, John P. Johnson, a Winnebago student who could "never quite subscribe to, let alone accept, the vague principles so unceasingly preached at Hampton," found no alternative but to have himself expelled. He explained, "I am clearly out of sympathy with the falsity of ideals and practices that placed me, an innocent Indian, in Hampton, a Negro institution. 'Why are Indians necessary to Hampton?' I used to wonder until I saw the 'necessity' was the identical means to the identical ends of Parasitism."[43] Clearly, when a student's disaffection from Hampton had reached so advanced a stage, one way or another that student was on the outside looking in, and the juggling of Hampton's biracial program had no more relevance.

Notes

1. Elaine Goodale Eastman, *Pratt: The Red Man's Moses,* p. 65.

2. SCA in *Ten Years' Work,* p. 4; *ARCIA* 1880, p. 185.

3. Armstrong said in 1883 that "there is no caste feeling naturally between the races." Pratt had said in 1879 that he had "found no prejudice against the colored race existing naturally among the Indians anywhere." See SCA, "Indian Work," *Wowapi* 1 (Nov. 7, 1883): 64; Pratt in *SW* 8 (Feb. 1879): 93.

4. *SW* 7 (Oct. 1878): 73.

5. Folsom, "Indian Work at Hampton," (Manuscript, n.d.), HUA, p. 113; Folsom, *SW* 14 (Feb. 1885): 19; Folsom, "Indian Days," p. 6; Discipline Files, 1898/99, p. 91, HUA.

6. George L. Curtis, "Race Contact at Hampton," Chicago *Interior,* Jan. 10, 1889; J. J. Gravatt to SCA, Dec. 24, 1887, box 21, Indian Affairs, Misc. Reports by Various Staff Members, Indian Collection, HUA; Moton, "Indian and Negro Traits," *SW* 32 (July 1903): 311.

7. Ludlow to Andrus, May 10, 1918, Joseph Estes's student file, HUA; "Sixty-Five Tribes Represented at Hampton," Indian Collection, HUA; Kenneth Wiggins Porter, "Notes Supplementary to Relations between Negroes and Indians," *Journal of Negro History* 18 (July 1933): 292.

8. Joseph Metoxen to George Phenix, Apr. 9, 1911, and Phenix to Metoxen, Apr. 21, 1911, both in Metoxen's student file, HUA.

9. Discipline Files, 1890/91, p. 207, HUA; Moton to Miss Burke, Sept. 18, 1893, Moton Papers, HUA.

10. Folsom, "Indian Days," HUA, p. 22; David Wallace Adams, "Education in Hues," p. 170; Ludlow, *SW* 8 (Feb. 1879): 21; Folsom, "Indian Days," p. 91.

11. Minutes of Faculty Meetings, Oct. 6, 1887 and Dec. 5, 1891, HUA.

12. Commissioner J. T. B. Atkins to SCA, Apr. 18, 1885, box 70, Office of Indian Affairs, Indian Collection, HUA. In 1888 the Indian Office approved Hampton's practice of opening its Indian students' mail. Begun before 1883, this practice was intended to prevent Indians from spending their money on alcohol or other forms of vice, establishing improper intimacy with the opposite sex (and of a different race), and openly criticizing Hampton's policies. Teachers usually withheld money from home and doled it out to the student for meeting expenses. See Minutes of the Indian Teachers Faculty, May 21, 1883, and Dec. 21 and 30, 1886, Indian Collection, HUA; SCA to Atkins, May 16, 1888, RG75, item 13016, NARA; Atkins to SCA, May 18, 1888, box 70, Office of Indian Affairs, Indian Collection, HUA. In April

1888, after Sioux Edward Dupuis booked his own passage from Hampton to Pierre, South Dakota, Armstrong got local depots to refuse to sell railroad tickets to Indians. See H. E. W. Fuller, General Purchasing Agent for the Chesapeake and Ohio Railroad to SCA, Apr. 15, 1888, HUA; Minutes of the Indian Teachers Faculty, Apr. 22, 1885, Indian Collection, HUA.

13. Ludlow, "The Question of Discipline," *SW* 8 (June 1879): 67; Josephine Richards, "Report on Indian Department," *SW* 26 (May 1897): 100; Robert Goodwind to Moton, Jan. 8, 1892, Goodwind's student file, HUA.

14. Thomas D. McAlpine to Col. G. B. Dandy, Depot, Quartermaster, Washington D. C., Apr. 26, 1888, Indian Collection, box 80, Indian Affairs, Assistant Quartermaster's Office, War Department, HUA; Discipline Files, 1884–1903, HUA; Minutes of Faculty Meetings, July 15, 1887, HUA; Discipline Files, 1886/87, p. 303.

15. Minutes of Faculty Meetings, Nov. 28, 1884, and Dec. 2, 1884, HUA.

16. Minutes of the Indian Teachers Faculty, Mar. 3, 1883, HUA; Discipline Files, 1885, p. 143, HUA and p. 243 for another instance of corporal punishment.

17. Minutes of Faculty Meetings, Sept. 6, 1887, HUA. The previous January, Four Stars had been reduced in rank for contracting venereal disease. See Discipline Files, Jan. 3, 1887. Minutes of Faculty Meetings, Dec. 21, 1887, HUA.

18. Folsom, "Indian Days," p. 26; Myrtilla Sherman to SCA, Jan. 5, 1893, HUA; Carrie Erskine to HBF, May 16, 1895, HUA.

19. Minutes of Faculty Meetings, Oct. 21, 1885, and Oct. 8, 1894, HUA; "Synopsis of Report of Rev. T. S. Childs, D. D.," Dec. (?), 1887, in Childs to Atkins, Jan. 11, 1888, RG75, item 1014, NARA; Julia St. Cyr to Atkins, Oct. 14, 1887, RG75, item 27582, NARA. Chapter eight will show that St. Cyr was the Indian most responsible for igniting the important Childs controversy. See Josephine Richards to Atkins in Childs to Atkins, Jan. 11, 1888, RG75, item 1014, enclosure 27, NARA and Childs to Atkins, p. 21.

20. *Ten Years' Work*, p. 29; E. F. Coolidge, "The Shoe Shop," in *ARCIA* 1886, p. 28.

21. *Ten Years' Work*, p. 29; SCA to Atkins, Mar. 13, 1888, RG75, item 7344, NARA; SCA to Gen. E. Whittlesey and Mr. A. K. Smiley, Mar. 15, 1888, box on Childs Report, Indian Collection, HUA; SCA to Childs, Dec. 23, 1887, in Childs to Atkins, Jan. 11, 1888, RG75, item 1014, NARA.

22. SCA, "Report of Hampton School," *ARCIA* 1880, p. 184.

23. Phenix to Commissioner F. E. Leupp, Jan. 26, 1906, RG75, item 9599, NARA; Benjamin F. Bishop to the Commissioner of Indian Affairs, copy to HBF, Sept. 13, 1909, Bishop's student file, HUA; Andrus to Theodore Owl, Dec. 19, 1910, box on Caroline Andrus, Indian Collection, HUA; Superintendent Charles M. Buchanan to Commissioner, May 11, 1912, box 66, Correspondence from Commissioner of Indian Affairs, Indian Collection, HUA.

24. Benjamin Bishop to the Commissioner of Indian Affairs, copy to HBF, Sept. 13, 1909, Bishop's student file, HUA; Minutes of Faculty Meetings, Jan.

2, 1909, HUA; S. F. Williams to Frederick Gleason, Feb. 18, 1904, Williams's student file, HUA; Minutes of the Indian Teachers Faculty, Apr. 30, 1885, HUA.

25. BTW, *Up from Slavery*, p. 106. As an exception, Secretary of War Robert Lincoln told Armstrong's closest friend, Archibald Hopkins, "it was not fair on the negro to take him around & exhibit him with the Indian who was everywhere regarded as a sort of show." See Hopkins to SCA, Mar. 13, 1884, box 2, SCA Correspondence, Indian Collection, HUA.

26. John H. Wainwright, a Hampton student, 1888–90, "Impressions of General Armstrong," p. 8, Misc. Box on Hampton Institute, Williamsiana Collection, Williams College. Armstrong predicted, "an Indian problem without Indians," in which Indians would disappear through intermixture with whites, who themselves would carry on the special political status of Indians. See SCA, *Report of a Trip Made on Behalf of the IRA to Some Indian Reservations of the Southwest* (Philadelphia, 1883), p. 26, pamphlet A-4, roll 102, IRA Papers; also *LMC* 1887, p. 28.

27. Robert Francis Engs, "Red, Black, and White, p. 252. It should be noted that white males who married Indian women were commonly labeled "squaw men," and their offspring "half breeds." Especially when the white father was described as "low, married, whereabouts unknown," Hampton teachers highly disapproved. Folsom was shocked at the pregnancy of Addie Stevens, who had come to Hampton when she was ten years old in 1883. Like Annie Dawson, Stevens had largely been raised by the staff of Hampton's Indian Department. Of Stevens, someone given all the advantages and now bringing shame to Hampton, Folsom said, "It is *Indian* to want to lay the blame on someone else—its the curse of the race." She said that Stevens should be made to "feel the full burden of [the baby's] support—not only to realize it but *feel* it." Later a graduate of the Illinois Training School for Nurses, Stevens's career in maternal care made her one of the best known Indian women in the nation. In 1921 Indian Lousia Bissell was expelled for getting pregnant by an unmarried white private, Charles Cappizoli. Caroline Andrus of Hampton's Indian Department termed Bissell's attitude as "all in a day's work." See Folsom Letters, Mar. 12, 1894, p. 102, Indian Collection, HUA; *SW* 53 (July 1924): 427; Andrus to Miss Prophet, Dec. 6, 1921, in Stevens's student file, HUA.

28. Charles Eastman, a popular author and lecturer on Indian life, graduated from the Santee Indian School before going on to Dartmouth and Boston University Medical School. See Hertzberg, *The Search for an American Indian Identity*, pp. 38–41.

29. George Alan Owl, although remembering that Indians "weren't allowed to be socially mixed with female teachers," nevertheless found the opportunity through his work as the teachers' gardener to meet Rebecca Pond of the Heinz-Pond cosmetic family. Owl was the first Eastern Cherokee to serve in World War I, the first vice president of the Cherokee Chamber of Commerce, and a member of the executive council of the National Congress of American Indians (1944). See Tingey, "Blacks and Indians Together," pp. 235–42.

30. William Jones, a quarter Sac and Fox raised by his Indian grandmother, was the first Indian to graduate from Harvard since Caleb Cheeshahteamuck in 1665. Jones served as editor of the *Harvard Monthly*. Boas called his dissertation at Columbia, "Some Principles of Algonkin Word Formation," the "first considerable body of Algonkin lore published in accurate and reliable form in the native tongue." Jones wrote the "Fox Texts," volume 1 of the publications of the American Ethnological Society, before working among the Anishinabe in Canada. As a condition for Jones's employment at the Chicago Museum of Natural History Curator O. A. Dorsey required him to do fieldwork abroad; unfortunately he choose the Philippines. See Henry M. Rideout, *William Jones: Indian, Cowboy, Scholar, and Anthropologist in the Field* (New York, 1912); Tingey, "Blacks and Indians Together," pp. 216–20; Franz Boas, "William Jones," in *SW* 38 (June 1909): 338.

31. Engs, "Red, Black, and White," p. 252.

32. Caroline Andrus to Louise D. Amerman, May 31, 1911, p. 256, box on Indian Letters and Andrus, Indian Collection, HUA; Editorial, "Indian Outings," *SW* 23 (Dec. 1894): 207; Indian Teachers Faculty, May 7, 1883, HUA.

33. John W. Cromwell, "General Armstrong," *People's Advocate* (Alexandria and Washington, D.C.), Aug. 9, 1879; SCA to Michael Strieby, Oct. 7, 1887, HUA. Armstrong explained that it had been raining and Reed's coat had to be removed because it was too small, but that the funeral included a six-man corp of pallbearers, that it was conducted by the Rev. Gravatt, and that Reed's family had seen no reason to complain. See also *People's Advocate*, Aug. 13, 1887.

34. "Negro Students Misrepresented," Indianapolis *Freeman*, June 25, 1892; Chicago *Interocean*, May 29, 1892.

35. BTW, *The Story of the Negro*, pp. 127–28.

36. Moton, *Finding a Way Out*, pp. 111–19.

37. Folsom, "Random Recollections," (typed), box on Folsom separate from the Indian Collection, HUA; Myrtilla Sherman to SCA, May 28, 1891, HUA; SCA, "Memorandum," Oct., 1889, Hampton Institute—Misc. Papers, Armstrong Family Papers, Williamsiana Collection, Williams College.

38. Folsom, "Random Recollections," (typed), box on Folsom separate from the Indian Collection, HUA.

39. Moton, *Finding a Way Out*, p. 124; William Harden Hughes, *Robert Russa Moton of Hampton and Tuskegee* (Chapel Hill, 1956), p. 44.

40. *Ten Years' Work*, p. 50; Minutes of Faculty Meetings, Aug. 15, 1888, HUA; Discipline Files, 1887/88, pp. 214 and 310, and May 15, 1903, (frontispiece), HUA; Folsom to Mr. Keith, Feb. 17, 1902, Folsom Box, Indian Collection, HUA. Hampton's black athletic director, Charles Williams, did not marry his Indian friend, Irene Tabrachetti, because their "different [racial] problems" made it "unwise." See interview with Charles Williams, Aug. 27, 1974, in Tingey, "Blacks and Indians Together," p. 263.

41. David Owl to Mr. Frissell, Aug 1, 1960, box on Prominent Students, Indian Collection, HUA. Both Maude Abbie Goodwin and Elsie G. Doxsta-

der married black Hampton students. See these Indians' student files, HUA. Ludlow in *SW* 8 (July 1879): 77; Discipline Files, 1888/89, HUA.

42. Elizabeth Hyde to HBF, "Report of the Dean of Women," (n.d.), box on early Hampton teachers, HUA; Minutes of Faculty Meetings, Mar. 29, 1912, HUA. The boy's request was refused.

43. John Johnson to Records Department, Dec. 19, 1926, Johnson's student file, HUA.

7

Indians and Blacks at the Crossroads of Indigenous Culture and Social Adjustment

Observers have been sharply divided on whether Hampton respected the cultural diversity of its students, or only offered—even enforced—acculturation. Idealizing the institute for its multicultural missionary spirit would seem to preclude the pervasive accommodationism observed by others. In reality it was the interplay between these forces at Hampton that warrants scrutiny, as these seemingly incompatible themes did indeed come together through Armstrong's skillful reconciliation of divergent forces. How this was done can be shown most fully by juxtaposing Hampton's preservation of native cultures with its social studies curriculum.

"Ringing out the Old": The Question of Culture

No other school celebrated the cultural products of blacks and Indians as much as Hampton, although its appreciation of their cultures had limits consistent with an ethnocentric curriculum. In a typical statement, Armstrong called Negro spirituals a "priceless legacy." Declaring that the Negro had the only American music, the Indian the only American art, he believed it to be a "duty to preserve and in a wise and natural way to develop both." The principal later exclaimed, "These despised races [are] the rejected stones of our civilization, but they will yet have their places."[1]

What enabled Hampton to affirm Indian and black artistic achievements so boldly, however, was the perception that cultural exchange could further its program for sectional and racial harmony. Thus in an article on "Negro and Indian Folk-lore," Frissell would later lament that because of "caricature, rag-time and coon songs of the coarsest type," Negroes had come to "despise whatever is peculiarly their own," and that Indians concealed their traditions from outsiders. He told whites that Hampton aimed to "dignify" the folklore of both blacks

and Indians "in your eyes and theirs. . . . Ceremonials once sacred, once
the expression of some deep spiritual emotion, may seem absurd and
futile now, but to the thoughtful and enlightened mind, they demand
a certain reverence which scientific study only intensifies. Instead of
separating primitive and civilized man, such study seems to lessen the
gulf between them." Frissell also believed that an awareness of other
people's cultural traditions could prevent racial "misunderstanding."
Without advocating change in any of the nation's institutional inequal-
ities or acknowledging the substantive reasons behind black and Indian protest, he argued that an awareness which taught students to respect their own cultures was "closely related with the minimizing of
race prejudice."[2]

More specifically, during World War I Hampton implemented folklorist Natalie Curtis Burlin's suggestion that "in the music of the Negro
lay a possible bond between the races." Moton's half brother, J. E.
Blanton, taught Burlin's "The Hymn of Freedom" to black soldiers
in northern camps, an endeavor blessed by Secretary of War Newton
D. Baker and actively directed by his special assistant, Emmett J. Scott
of Tuskegee Institute. The *Workman* claimed that Negro spirituals sung
in the presence of white soldiers both at home and in France would
"keep down a number of unpleasant [racial] events that are constantly happening."[3] Of course, it was not difficult for whites to celebrate
an African American legacy that embraced Christianity.

––––––

This process of racial conciliation began fifty years earlier, when the
institute was less than a year old. With some Hawaiian relics, Armstrong
opened a museum that would become an important repository of both
the Indian and the black heritage, but that also served to further the
acculturation process through its "industrial" exhibits. Thirteen years
later, in 1881, Armstrong acquired his first Indian specimens, which
included several buckskin robes sent by James McLaughlin, the agent
at Crow Creek. The principal explained that "the Indian will not respect our civilization the more for being taught to despise his own."
Except for a few specimens from the South collected during the 1890s,
no attempt was made to procure Negro artifacts until after 1910, when
Hampton alumnus and Presbyterian minister William H. Sheppard
brought back a large collection of African rarities from his work in the
(then) Upper Congo.[4]

Numerous additions to the Indian collection were gathered on recruiting trips in the West, especially those taken by Cora Folsom, whose

specimens would later be supplemented by purchases of moundbuilder implements. In 1905 former Hampton teacher Whitney Blake bequeathed $5,000 to organize the Blake Indian Museum in the old library rooms. By 1919 the Indian collection contained 908 items, making it much larger than the African American collection of 328 items.[5]

Folsom gradually became the museum's first real curator and brought the repository to national prominence during the early twentieth century, for both its Indian and African collections. She argued that the museum served an especially valuable function because "no museum in the South is open to the Negro. Little curios familiar to every Northern child are unknown to him (and have therefore a peculiar value in his scheme of education). This is also true of the Indians. Our general plan made to fit existing conditions, is quite unlike that of the ordinary museum and to be of the greatest help requires the cooperation of the departments it is designed to help." This special museum for blacks and Indians also reinforced what was taught in the classrooms and shops by incorporating the larger "industrial" aims of the curriculum. African and Indian materials, serving Folsom's stated purpose of "stimulating race pride," were exhibited alongside some sixty-five hundred reflectoscopic slides and cards depicting rural conditions and practical applications for the trades and agricultural methods taught at Hampton.[6]

In December 1893, a quarter of a century after the museum's founding, Alice M. Bacon established a branch of the American Folklore Society at Hampton. Unlike the parent society, whose largely white and wealthy membership was more interested in Indians than in blacks, the Hampton Folk-lore Society consisted of the school's Negro graduates. Opening a Department of Folk-lore and Ethnology in the *Workman* at the same time, Bacon urgently sought to generate interest among black graduates: "The American negroes are rising so rapidly from the condition of ignorance and poverty in which slavery left them, to a position among the cultivated and civilized people of the earth, that the time seems not far distant when they shall have cast off their past entirely, and stand an anomaly among civilized races, as a people having no distinct traditions, beliefs, or ideas from which a history of their growth may be traced."[7]

Bacon's moving summons was aimed especially at those educated Negroes who had returned to their communities and were thus in the best position to explain the lifeways of black hamlets. She asked the *Workman*'s black readers to submit materials on all aspects of African American life: customs peculiar to blacks in matters of birth, marriage, and death, African survivals, proverbs and sayings, folk tales, ceremonies, and superstitions. She used their submissions as topics in the monthly meetings of the Hampton Folk-lore Society, and once the data were analyzed, the society published whatever it believed had never seen print. Over the next seven years, Hampton's Department of Folklore and Ethnology published articles on such diverse topics as plantation courtships, conjurers, the sermons and chants of backwoods preachers called "night-hawks," and stories of havoc wreaked by the nocturnal visits of "hags" (whom the society determined to be in fact African American vampires).[8] These reflections of the souls of black folk appeared not in the *Journal of American Folk-Lore* but in the *Workman,* which Bacon helped to edit. The former publication's Negro Department did not approach the standards of scholarship set by its Indian Department until the coming of Elsie Clews Parsons in 1910. But long before that time the Hampton Society and its column in the *Workman* provided a conduit for blacks to discover their past. Meanwhile the *Workman* also regularly published articles about Indian life, and in 1902 the school's Indian newspaper, *Talks and Thoughts,* issued a call of its own for Indian students to collect their tribal folklore. Respondents received the latter paper for three months free of charge.[9]

Hampton's contributions to the study of Indian and African American cultures were nevertheless made to reinforce both its stance on education and its training methods, fitting the student for a life of service to his community but not for advancement in a rapidly modernizing white nation. The extolling of their rural origins strengthened a sense of the "good life" in Hampton students that discouraged them from acquiring skills necessary to urban survival. "The Indian," Frissell maintained, "should learn to farm and till the soil. The Indian of the future is to live in the country, and he should find his comfort and happiness in the flowers, the trees, the rivers, and all nature." Similarly, building a stronger sense of race pride in blacks discouraged desire for interaction with whites and encouraged respect for racial purity, which was expected, in turn, to reduce racial tensions generally. As Ludlow said, Hampton's "effort is to build up self-respect and mutual respect. And we believe that education of the mind and heart tends to individual morality and race purity."[10] Thus there was no inconsistency in acknowledging Hampton's building of bridges for cultural understanding while recognizing that its philosophy buttressed a rurally oriented, largely manual training that suited white supremacy.

Consequently, not all those wanting equality for Indians admired Hampton's role as cultural ambassador. In 1901, twenty-two years after leaving Hampton because of his objections to Armstrong's racial policies, Carlisle's Richard Pratt, principal of the nation's most assimilationist school for nonwhites, claimed that he had "known for many years just where Hampton Institute stood on race elevation, but could not speak of it because it was not plainly declared."[11]

Although for the most part publicly quiet before 1901 about Carlisle's differences with Hampton, Pratt had long thought that its policies of tying the educated individuals back to the masses and of developing race pride by producing race leaders, envisioned Indians joining Negroes as another people separated from white society. If Indians were to be absorbed into the mainstream—and Pratt argued that there was no widespread opposition among whites to such integration—then to emphasize their ethnic culture would only reinforce separation. After Anna T. Dawes, the daughter of Senator Henry Dawes of Massachusetts, called in 1898 in the *Workman* for "RACE genius, RACE ideals and for a leader to raise up the Indian people," Pratt admonished her not to confuse the Indian problem with the Negro problem because the "vital difference" was the "SOCIAL ONE." He argued, "The negro may need race pride to sustain him in his forced separation; the Indian does not need it, since he is not forever set apart as a peculiar people."[12]

Thus, when in 1901 the *Workman* stated, "Civilization has never come and never will come to a people in a day or in a year or in a hundred years," Pratt responded in his school's *Red Man* that this was "the biggest plaster to cover and encourage failure coming within our knowledge." He termed the *Workman's* assertion that "there is no patent method of uplifting a race," the inevitable result of efforts to maintain Indians as a distinct people.[13] Certainly Armstrong's main rival for eastern opinion, Pratt opposed all forms of separation, however much integration ignored the Indians' own wishes.

The divergent attitudes toward Indian culture between Carlisle and Hampton produced conflicting plans for alumni and other ex-students. As an advocate of assimilation by individually "feeding the Indians to civilization," Pratt encouraged his students to remain among eastern whites and vanish into American life. He did not envision integration as a reciprocal process, and discounted the popular belief that separating Indians from their tribes caused them special hardship. After all, he argued, Americans were a mobile people, and a temporary sense of displacement, such as his own family had experienced, commonly accompanied relocation.[14]

In sharp contrast, Armstrong trained his Indian like his black students, as "cultural missionaries" expected to return home to "uplift" their people. How this was to be accomplished is unclear, considering his justification of a largely industrial education: "there must be a difference in the educational methods for the races in our country that are a thousand years behind the whites in the line of development."[15] Indeed, despite his admiration for the art and music of the nonwhite races, Armstrong claimed in 1881 that "inherited traits and ideas rather than mere ignorance is the difficulty with low or savage races. Heredity and not vice is the trouble." He believed that the mental development of different races was asymmetrical, that the retention of facts quickly surpasses the more slowly evolving faculties of comprehension, wisdom, morality, and self-control: "a well balanced mind is attained only after generations of improvement." Therefore, "We may hope for much more by the year 2000."[16] Based on the social evolutionary approach of early anthropologist Lewis Henry Morgan, Armstrong's schema ranked cultures in stages ascending from savagery to civilization.

Frissell wondered whether indigenous cultures had more than merely historical and transitional value, going so far as to question the ultimate mutability of racial traits. Assumed to be taking visible form in cultural products, racial traits seemed to mandate a different education for each race: "It is quite true, as a distinguished educator has remarked, that 'there is no color in education,' yet each race of men is a peculiar people, and for each God has his own plans. To try to make an Anglo-Saxon out of a Negro or an Indian is not only to try to perform the impossible, but it is an endeavor to thwart these plans."[17]

Charles Dyke, a Hampton teacher, most clearly coupled the study and preservation of "primitive" cultures with the successful re-education of the "primitive" races who created those cultures. He summarized his understanding of the school's views on culture for the NEA in 1900: "The races of men feel, think, and act differently not only because of environment, but also because of hereditary impulses. . . . Education does not eliminate these differences. [Without knowledge of race characteristics] the emotions will be improperly trained, the intellectual capacity will be misjudged, and the place that the child can best fill in the community will be misunderstood." Dyke linked the students' need for cultural preservation with the complementary need for industrial education: since the "emotions lie at the foundation of personal happiness and of all moral and social relations, [their] development can best be accomplished through folk-lore, art, music, and religion. But for economic reasons, primitive man must be trained in vocations that fit him for life in the white man's world."[18] In short, Hampton increasingly deemed much of the preservation of its students' cultures as vital to their long-term well-being, thereby moving further and further from the belief implemented at Carlisle that Indians at least could and should be instantly assimilated.

Hampton students should become "not routine teachers but civilizers" Armstrong had said, regarding the "idea of a *mission* in the mind of an Indian, Negro, or any other youth as a directive and helpful force of the greatest value in the formation of character."[19] This idea was, of course, rooted in Armstrong's own Hawaiian background, but in this case the missionary torch was being passed from Hampton's white faculty to the students they had "civilized," with the latter commissioned to impart a semblance of mainstream culture to their "primitive" fellows back home. However high-sounding this statement of Armstrong's motive, in effect if not intent, sending partially acculturated Indians back to their tribes was a policy of segregation; removing Indians from the centers of white population of course reduced opportunities for amalgamation. Indians thus would retain a racial identity, but at the cost of living perpetually under the external control of government agents and westerners. The great paradox of the Hampton position on the worth of indigenous cultures is that honoring the cultural histories and artifacts of racial minorities seemed perfectly compatible with white supremacy and paternalism.

Clearly, despite their contrasting natures, both Carlisle's and Hampton's cultural policies faced overwhelming practical problems. As a proponent of the essentially integrationist Gilded Age philosophy of laissez-faire individualism, Pratt believed that Armstrong's ideal of creating so many Moses-like figures to "redeem" their peoples discouraged talented individuals who desired to become "civilized and educated." Seemingly unaware that radical W. E. B. Du Bois was making similar criticisms of Hampton's model for educated blacks, Pratt said that the sacrifice demanded of the educated Indian for his community was unlike that demanded of any other American. Since whites were not expected to look after each other, Pratt asked why advancement for Indians must "always be in mass or not at all?" Moreover, after the mid-1880s, the number of unemployed returned students unable to put their training into practice greatly increased.[20]

For his part, pointing out the central flaw in Pratt's view, Armstrong observed that Indians who "have strong home and filial feeling would seldom consent to settle permanently among strangers." Going even further, an article in *The Indian School Journal* criticized Pratt's aim to "kill the Indian and save the man" as a policy of cultural genocide, whereby Indian values would be replaced by a veneer of white mannerisms and Indians made ashamed of both their race and their heritage. Moreover, Pratt's policy of divorcing "civilized" Indians from their own people left those behind without "desirable" models, easy prey to unscrupulous whites.[21] Of course, as the twentieth century progressed an increasing number of Indians have followed Pratt's model, and quietly integrated themselves into white society, marrying whites and remaining silent about native cultures to their children. But Hampton's approach rather than Carlisle's would have been chosen by the vast majority of Indians of the day, even though their preference for the reservation over white communities appeared to strengthen the argument that the Indian was not only unassimilable but also needed paternal care.

Those like Armstrong believing Indian students should return to the reservations generally looked to native industries to make this a viable option; Hampton itself profited from those industries. Hampton's marketing of Indian crafts honored the special talents of its students, as did the public performances of Negro spirituals, which the *Workman* noted were "peculiarly fitted to move the heart and open the pocket." Similarly, Bacon felt that the Folk-Lore Society made it "easier for us to push forward the philanthropic work that Hampton is doing."[22] The institute first introduced art instruction for Indians in 1883, employing at various times both white and native teachers of Indian pottery, woodcarving, and basketweaving.[23] In 1910 Indian-made articles were the only goods sold at the school store and visitors were regularly brought there to purchase souvenirs. But Indian students were pressured to spend so much of their spare time making handicrafts that the school doctor forbade the practice, and the faculty decided not to bring visitors to the store unless they specifically asked. Thereafter, the Hampton store received its stock—"all genuine Indian"—from the Mohonk Lodge in Colony, Oklahoma, a charitable endeavor of the Lake Mohonk Conferences. Reese Kincade, the proprietor, charged Hampton the same as regular dealers for goods the store then sold at catalog prices, making a 20 percent commission.[24]

Pratt argued that "remanding" Indians to work along race lines, whether in native handicrafts or even in government jobs at the agency, denied them wider opportunity. And far from valuing Hampton's northern campaigns as a way to educate the public about the needs of Indians, Pratt's private letters in the early 1880s described Armstrong's fundraising group of Indians in native dress as a "traveling circus," whose purpose, akin to wild west shows, was "bleeding" the public. As late as 1909 Pratt called such displays of cultural items "another insidious system of maintaining race differences by prejudicing our people against the Indians," and asked, "Where is the profit to [force] Indian youth during education to hold onto primitive ideas, conditions, and the peculiarities we must lift them from? . . . Why compel them to carry two loads, to become civilized and at the same time to remain uncivilized? I inherit the blood of several races, but the only thing of real value to me is my Americanism."[25] Nor was the captain the only one to regard Hampton's fascination with its students' indigenous cultural items as patronizing. Even a friend of the institute, Edward W. Blyden, the president of Liberia College, told Armstrong, "I have heard your operations cynically described as a sort of zoological-anthropological experiment, undertaken less in the interest of a genuine philanthropy, than to gratify a morbid curiosity as to the possibility of races essentially and permanently inferior."[26]

Certainly, collecting and publicizing its students' cultural items gave Hampton its surest, most popular means of generating the white interest in both blacks and Indians that was crucial to the school's success. For Hampton's historical collections increased knowledge of the cultures of these peoples, increased donations for their education, increased subscriptions to the *Workman*—and may have decreased racial tension as well. Instead of force-feeding white culture to its students as Carlisle advocated, Hampton made the entire "civilizing" process seem less one-sided: whites, too, were learning—about how blacks and Indians were unique and offered their own contributions to American culture.

But Hampton's promotion of cultural awareness and marketable native skills was not a serious effort at cultural retention, for the school's ultimate aim, while preserving a historical record in its publications and museum, was to eradicate much of what its students themselves valued about their cultures. Perhaps nothing more clearly illustrates this intended emphasis than the instruction of Indian students in skills peculiar to white society, skills too various to qualify for work in an urban setting, but assumed to be necessary and proper for life on the reservation. Frank K. Rogers, director of the Hampton Trade School, described his instructional objectives quite comprehensively in 1901:

> I have in mind a Cherokee boy who is about to go back to his reservation, who can do a very good job at house-building, and in addition some brick-laying, plastering, and tin-roofing. He can thoroughly paint a house, barn or wagon, and has lately added to his accomplishments some skill in harness-making and shoe-making. I have seen some straps which he has just made with the buckles neatly stitched on, also a complete bridle, all of which are very creditably done. He has also half-soled and heeled his own shoes for nearly a year.

The class of girls who will return this summer have added in the last few months to their general knowledge of household work a little skill in paper-hanging, mattress-making, painting and glazing.[27]

The *Workman* once reported that the Cleveland Hall bell tolled on Indian Day, "Ring out the Old, Ring in the New." On that day "the old customs and superstitions . . . and the multiplicity of languages, were described and deprecated—they are the old things to be rung out, while the new things to be rung in . . . are Christian homes, education, and citizenship."[28] Yet paradoxically, for blacks as well as Indians, Hampton's preserving of artifacts and skills unique to their cultures not only reflected its perception that a "school for civilization" should not move too far beyond its students' actual conditions and talents, but also assumed and implied a remoteness from contemporary white society, from its educational methods and widest range of employment. The school thus tied the students closely to their own pasts regardless of its overt efforts to transmit new values and skills.

"Ringing in the New": Social Sciences and Thomas Jesse Jones

However worthy of study and preservation, black and Indian cultures were still considered "primitive"; indeed all of the arguments that Hampton used to convince its students of the superiority of Anglo-Saxon culture were construed as "social studies." But only in 1902, when Thomas Jesse Jones (1873–1950) came to Hampton as associate chaplain and head of the Economics and Missionary Department, did this body of theory become systematically joined to "scientific" coursework.

Jones had been exposed to country living, rural trades, and the problems of community adjustment even before his 1884 immigration to the small town of Middleport, Ohio, from Llanfacthraeth, Wales. In this Welsh village of fewer than a thousand inhabitants, his father had been the saddler, his grandfather the blacksmith, and his mother the innkeeper of the local community center, the Mona Inn.

Despite having spent a year in the South at Washington and Lee University (1891–92), Jones's abiding interest in blacks and his lesser but still significant interest in Indians, began at Hampton. While there in 1904, Jones received his Ph.D. from Columbia University. His dissertation, "Sociology of a New York City Block," focused on the largely Italian and Jewish communities served by Columbia University's Social Settlement, and his mentor was Franklin H. Giddings, whose social evolutionary concepts on ethnicity of "consciousness of kind" and the "social mind" would remain at the core of Jones's own philosophy.[29]

Jones's professional activities would take him far beyond Hampton, although he would return as a trustee. Jones left the institute in 1909 to direct the collection of statistics on blacks for the 1910 census, moved to the Bureau of Education as a specialist in racial minorities in 1910, and in 1913 also became an agent for the Phelps-Stokes Fund. In 1916, under their combined auspices, he completed the first comprehensive federal study of black schools—a two-volume treatise, *Negro Education: A Study of the Private and Higher Schools for Colored People in the United States*.[30] In 1919 Jones served as chairman of the Committee on After-War Cooperation, which organized the Commission on Interracial Cooperation in Atlanta. As the first educational director of Phelps-Stokes (1917–46), Jones united American efforts with those of the British Colonial Office in the research and writing of *Education in East Africa* (1925), an examination of the educational methods there in light of the teachings of Hampton and Tuskegee.[31] He also found time to study the conditions of Indians in Oklahoma (a 1922 study financed by the state government and the United States Bureau of Agriculture); served as a trustee of the Indian Rights Association; assisted Lewis Meriam in the first comprehensive study of Indians in the United States, *The Problem of Indian Administration* (1928) and edited *The Navaho Problem* (1939).

While still at Hampton, in 1906 Jones was appointed director of research and organizer of the Hampton Negro Conferences, and wrote a revealing series of articles in the *Southern Workman* entitled "Social Studies in the Hampton Curriculum" (SSHC). Jones was one of the first to use the term "social studies," although he did not invent it as he claimed. Throughout this six-part series, Jones employed census data about blacks and Indians to address those "discrepancies" from the larger society that "admit to exact numerical description." The Hampton course of studies described in these articles may have been the first anywhere to unite such diverse disciplines as civics, political economy, history, and sociology, and certainly was the first to apply them to race.[32] It seems fitting that a school whose students differed culturally from the dominant society would pioneer a general course offering a selective introduction to American life.

Jones's justified the presentation of such "advanced" course work— usually reserved for high school and college—to students who "but three years earlier could scarcely read . . . from the fact that [blacks and Indians] have been suddenly transferred from an earlier form of society into a later one without the necessary time of preparation." Existing conditions required "some effort be made to supply these races with as many as possible of the habits and ideals of the social stage into which they have been forced," in lieu of the gradual, independent evolution races were believed to experience under natural conditions. Jones agreed with Frissell's contention that the enslavement of blacks and the communal life of Indians had not only made a "proper home life" among them impossible but continued to hinder it even when the primary causes themselves had been removed, and bolstered this claim with the example that in a class of fourteen blacks and four Indians all but one student agreed that a boarding school was a better place than one of their homes to raise an orphan under sixteen. Such empirical "evidence" provided by his black and Indian students made Jones's assessment of the process of Indian and black development seem more scientific.

Jones wanted students to see discrimination as justified by their own stage of evolution: "instead of regarding the difficulties of his race as the oppression of a weaker by the stronger, he interprets them as the natural difficulties that almost every race has been compelled to overcome in its upward movement." Upon reaching this understanding, the individual "becomes more hopeful. . . . Each social study contributes to this picture of the evolution of races."[33] Thus Jones apparently believed, for example, that a knowledge of social studies would provide some basis for compromise between "radical" blacks and white southerners—the one group believing that Negroes were already equal to whites, the other that they never would be—by making each group aware of the crucial element of change over time.

Jones's philosophical framework for the series encompassed much of his training under Giddings, especially the books *Elements of Sociology* and *Inductive Sociology*. Jones's called attention to a myriad of familiar and unfamiliar differences standing between racial minorities and equality with whites, divisions which could not be resolved by the "inflamed imagination of some 'social reform' novelist." He maintained that "differences or similarities in the physique, or in the economic standing, or in the literacy of individuals and of races are generally recognized and stated in measured terms; but differences in the dispositions, in the mental and moral characteristics, in the formation and efficiency of such organizations as the home, the church, the club, are noted by very few, and then only in very indefinite terms."

According to Jones, the differences in social organization between whites and the racial minorities Hampton served began with their differing "social minds," the study of which enabled the pupil to recognize the "various grades of mental and moral activities." From such study, Jones claimed, the minority student "can see that feeling, or emotion, prevails in one group, and that reason, or deliberation, is present in another; he realizes that tradition and custom bind one set of people, while another set combines tradition and reason into a progressive and helpful public opinion." Jones asserted that in class, both student races confessed to numerous examples of "impulsive motor" as opposed to "rational" public opinion.

Jones termed "'Negro independence' a shibboleth used by certain Negroes to persuade the race into their own power and away from the influence of the whites."[34] Social studies helped students to recognize and guard against such "impulsive motor" behavior. As Michael Lybarger pointed out in his brief and incomplete yet astute discussion of SSHC, the Du Bois style of protest, to which Jones seemed to be alluding, demonstrated "THE DANGER OF IMPULSIVE ACTION OR UNCONTROLLED EMOTION WHETHER IN RELIGIOUS OR POLITICAL MATTERS."[35]

Any such divisive behavior, Jones thought, violated the "law of sympathy" between individuals or races because "consciousness of kind is the basis of all truly social organizations." He argued that even with likenesses in literacy, language, economic standing, and physique, including color, if people "differ in mental and moral qualities they cannot permanently associate." Thus for Jones it was a "law of liberty" that "social organizations . . . are necessarily coercive if, in their membership, there is great diversity of kind and great inequality."[36]

Jones acknowledged that blacks and Indians saw an "arbitrary" power driving the history of American government, both in its machinery and in its relation to the public welfare. "For this reason legislation limiting their privileges is interpreted as a special attack upon their race, emanating entirely from the blind bigotry of the legislators." This view is a misconception, he argued: "knowledge of the evolution of government and of the forces that bring about legislation proves conclusively that prejudice alone has not usually been the basis of laws and that the existing prejudice, being subject to natural forces, will in the course of time disappear, leaving government to evolve into a true democracy."

Thus the historical part of Jones's civics course proffered Armstrong's position that enslaving blacks and dispossessing Indians had been justifiable: conquest, history showed, was "natural" because it had civilized new peoples. The selective comparison of early European history with the present condition of blacks and Indians in the United States assured students that their current status was only a temporary step in their "evolution." Blacks and Indians who understand the universal principles of social evolution gain a "more sympathetic view of the position of those who oppose them. Thus they become more intelligent in their work, more patient under oppression, more hopeful as to the future."

Jones devoted two-thirds of his civics course to government and the public welfare, because the "real meaning of government dawns upon the pupil when he learns of the government's study of foods, of soils, of vegetable life, of roads, of the weather, of mineral resources, of labor and commercial conditions, and of many other things too numerous to mention." He argued that these activities of the government influenced his students' lives "more frequently than those ordinarily classified under the legislative, executive and judicial functions of the state." Accordingly, the section on civics in SSHC devoted four pages to farming, centering on the efforts of the Bureau of Agriculture, but spent only seven lines on the other workings of the three main branches of government, because "this section of the course is the least important." Concentrating on the public welfare functions of government that related to the presumed "actual needs" of black and Indian students implied that agriculture was the main facet of government to concern them. Dispensing with any discussion of the rights of citizenship, or rather the lack of them, of blacks and by implication of Indians, Jones's civics course lacked civics.[37]

Jones's analysis of "Economics and Material Welfare" aimed to "impart a knowledge of the simple principles underlying the acquisition and use of wealth." These simple principles were verily ones of promoting frugal personal habits by correcting what he identified through class discussion as a disregard for the usefulness or worth of the items students purchased. For both blacks and Indians, "Present pleasures almost totally eclipsed the future pleasures. When the cotton is being sold [blacks purchase] all sorts of useless articles. . . . A little while afterwards these very Negroes are borrowing money at usurious rates of interest to buy the necessities of life. Similarly the Indian on ration day eats gluttonously . . . never thinking of the morrow." To remedy what he saw as wasteful spending, Jones emphasized minority-run savings associations and insurance or benefit societies. Apparently unaware of tribal communal practices, he reported that Indian students knew nothing of economics, while black students cited numerous unsound business practices in Negro mutual benefit societies. Jones pointed out that Negro self-help societies had arisen because the large white insurance companies charged blacks high premiums due to their high death rate, using this example as "one of the most convincing arguments presented to the colored people that some racial prejudice is based upon actual conditions rather than upon blind prejudice."

Having learned that good business practice sometimes justified dis-

crimination, students were to be praised for entertaining "no erroneous theories" of inherent conflict between capital and labor. Jones
rejoiced that "neither the South nor the western reservation has been
invaded by the socialistic notions." Since any study of capital "does not
require very much time," he dispensed with it by saying only that "the
principal facts impressed are the great power of capital and the self-
sacrificing efforts necessary to accumulate such power." In short, by
discounting impediments of both race and class in general, and of the
crop lien system of debt peonage and overall stagnation of the southern economy in particular, Jones's analysis of economics suggested that
thrifty blacks and Indians could become captains of industry.[38]

Finally, Jones examined black and Indian progress believing that
analysis of 1900 census returns on the demography, economic conditions, and education of blacks could "train" them to have an imper-
sonal and scientific attitude toward a problem "befogged by strong
prejudices." Perhaps because census data focused on the existing conditions that Hampton emphasized, his discussion was more neutral in
tone here than elsewhere. Indeed it seemed to follow from census
returns for blacks showing 90 percent to be southern, 80 percent rural, and 52 percent farmers, that blacks who were potential agents of
change—northerners, city-dwellers, or artisans—could be discounted
as numerically insignificant. Thus Jones claimed that "the large proportion of Negroes on farms" rendered owning one's own land the
"best test of economic progress."[39] Omitting all mention of lynching
or the multifarious intimidations of bulldozing, he went on to assert
that southern rural life offered the "freedom of activity necessary to
the development of a people in the process of assimilating the customs
of another people. The rural process is slower but is attended with less
irritation." As Kenneth James King has pointed out, Jones interpreted the census data to validate his own theory that the black farm owner
"suffers less from the prejudice of those who do not like him than [a
Negro] in any other occupation."[40] Such a narrow focus on "actual
conditions" implied blacks would perpetually do the same jobs and
hold the same economic status.

Where the "Progress of the Indians" was concerned, Jones's theme
was that the Indian reservation map reveals "an interesting picture of
some of the wonderful changes that have occurred in the condition
of the Indian during the last three hundred years." This must have been
difficult for Indians to swallow and is contradicted by his own evidence.
The conditions on reservations he described added up to the highest
rate of tuberculosis and infant mortality rates in the nation: Indians
died at the youngest age.

Jones's optimism rested on firmer ground when he compared the illiteracy rates of blacks and Indians. Census figures indicated that blacks faced greater educational disadvantages than Indians: 62 percent of blacks, but only 19 percent of Indians, had attended school for less than six months in 1900. Although the overall illiteracy rate was of course nevertheless greater among Indians than among blacks, census materials suggested to him that there was slightly less illiteracy among Indians in the specific age group of ten to seventeen years. Moreover, a greater percentage of Indians than blacks between the ages of five and twenty had attended school in 1900. Jones believed that the educational advantages of Indians over Negroes at the lower grades were "the results of the superior school system for Indians," unintentionally undermining Hampton's earlier argument against national aid to education.[41]

In sum, as a description of an academic course taught at Hampton, the SSHC revealed that academic classwork possessed no sacred power to free blacks or Indians even intellectually from the accommodationist bonds of industrial education. Indeed such a course could furnish a student with philosophical justification for disfranchisement, civil inequality, and occupational discrimination. SSHC provided an outline for white educators that rationalized which areas of "social studies" to pursue and which to avoid, in a curriculum designed to explain—in a manner seeming unbiased yet full of hope for the patient—why the racial minorities could not immediately expect equality to whites, all cloaked in the "scientific" authority of the Census Bureau.[42]

Moreover, scholars have argued that the theories expressed in SSHC had an impact that reached far beyond the students at Hampton Institute or educators directly aware of its methods. In 1912 Thomas Jesse Jones was appointed chairman of the Committee on Social Studies, under the NEA's Commission on the Reorganization of Secondary Education. Although observers disagree on the extent of Jones's impact on it, the committee's final 1916 document—*Social Studies in Secondary Education*—soon came to form the core of high school social studies classes in the United States.[43]

Whatever the ultimate scope of the SSHC's influence, *within* Hampton it clearly contributed greatly to the message implicit even in the school's concern with preserving black and Indian artifacts. Far from being truly anthropological in spirit, such preservation was largely historical. If Indians and blacks retained sufficient awareness of their roots, of where they had been, then they could more easily be shown how much further they had to travel before catching up to whites. The crossroads of ethnic culture and social studies confronting them at Hampton was essentially one of converging paths toward a single goal of accommodation, by leading the students of each race toward a certain detachment both from their own cultural heritage and from the traditions of white society to which they were humbly expected to aspire.

Notes

1. SCA, "Annual Report," *SW* 8 (June 1879): 63. Armstrong said of blacks, "music is the only adequate interpreter of the past and offers for the future a lifting, inspiring force not half appreciated." See *Armstrong's Ideas on Education for Life,* with an introduction by Francis G. Peabody (Hampton, 1926), p. 36. SCA, "Report of the Hampton School," in *ARCIA* 1882, p. 187.

2. HBF, "Negro and Indian Folklore" (Article, n.d.), pp. 2–5, box on HBF Speeches, HUA; Hunter, "Coming of Age: Frissell," pp. 188–89, 318; HBF, "Hampton Institute," in Kelly Miller, ed., *From Servitude to Service* (Boston, 1905), p. 139.

3. Editorial, "The Hymn in the Camps," *SW* 47 (Oct. 1918): 476–78.

4. In "American Indian Culture in Transition," exhibition script of the Hampton Museum, 1985, p. 1, Hampton University Museum. During its first thirteen years the museum contained neither black nor Indian artifacts, but rather housed relics from Hawaiian dynasties, which, upon Armstrong's request, were sent by his mother. Folsom, "Historical Notes on the Museum," circa 1920, p. 2, Museum files, Hampton Institute Museum. For further information on Sheppard, see William H. Sheppard, *Pioneers in Congo* (Louisville, 1923); Larryetta M. Schall, "William H. Sheppard: Fighter for African Rights," in Keith Schall, ed., *Stony the Road: Chapters in the History of Hampton Institute* (Charlottesville, 1977), pp. 105–24; Walter L. Williams, *Black Americans and the Evangelization of Africa, 1877–1900* (Madison, 1982).

5. Folsom, "The Museum," in Gregg, *Annual Report* 1919, p. 26. The museum also had a significant collection of 343 items (larger than the African American collection) of Japanese and Filipino materials, which were donated by Bacon and Miss Francis Curtis of Boston respectively. Folsom, "Historical Notes," p. 1.

6. Folsom, "Historical Notes," pp. 2, 3. I have inserted in parentheses a clause that Folsom had included in an earlier draft. See Folsom Box, the Museum, typed, Hampton Teacher's Section, box on Folsom, HUA.

7. Alice M. Bacon, "Folk-Lore and Ethnology," *SW* 22 (Dec. 1893): 180. Bacon's call was repeated in the New York *Age* 28, 1893.

8. Bacon, "Folk-Lore," p. 180; Bacon, "Work and Methods of the Hampton Folk-Lore Society," *Journal of American Folk-Lore* 11 (Jan.-Mar. 1898): 17–21. The best single description of Hampton's folklore materials can be found in A. M. Bacon and E. C. Parsons "Folk-Lore from Elizabeth City

County Virginia," *Journal of American Folk-Lore* 35 (Jan.-Mar. 1922): 250–327.

9. *T&T* 13 (Dec. 1902): Supplement.

10. HBF, "What is the Relation of the Indian of the Present Decade to the Indian of the Future?," *ARCIA* 1900, p. 470; Helen Ludlow in *Ten Years' Work,* p. 50.

11. RHP, "The Infirmity of the Situation," *The Red Man and Helper* 16 (May 1901): 2. Pratt asked Indians, with Hampton, the "great leader asserting on 'every hill-top' that you 'cannot be civilized in a hundred years.' What do you think of it?"

12. RHP, "Sense and Sentimentality," *The Red Man, His Present and Future* 14 (Dec. 1899): 1; Anna L. Dawes, "A Great Opportunity," *SW* 27 (Dec. 1898): 249. Pratt also criticized many other institutions for perpetuating the separation of Indians (as mentioned in chap. 2). When Pratt's daughter told him on his death bed that perhaps God had a better plan for the Indians, he replied, "There is no better plan."

13. RHP, "The Infirmity," p. 2.

14. RHP, "Helps and Hindrances," *The Morning Star* 4 (Jan. 1884): 2.

15. Ludlow, "Personal Memories," p. 888; SCA, "Annual Report," *SW* 22 (June 1893): 87; SCA, *Indian Education at the Hampton Normal and Agricultural Institute* (New York, 1881), p. 4; SCA, *SW* 9 (Nov. 1880): 114.

16. SCA, *Indian Education,* p. 4; SCA, "Lessons from the Hawaiian Islands," p. 216; Anderson, "The Hampton Model," in Franklin and Anderson, eds., *New Perspectives on Black Educational History,* pp. 65–66; Anderson, *The Education of Blacks in the South,* pp. 38–40; SCA, "Annual Report," *SW* 20 (Apr. 1891): 195.

17. HBF, "Work among Exceptional Home Populations," p. 6.

18. Charles B. Dyke, "The Essential Features in the Education of Child Races," *NEA* 1909, p. 932.

19. SCA, "Concerning Educated Indians," *SW* 13 (Apr. 1884): 44.

20. RHP, "Helps and Hindrances," p. 2. For a description of Hampton's view, see Ogden, "Address," *SW* 26 (May 1897): 83; RHP, "While Sentimentalists Dream," *The Red Man and Helper* 30 (July 1901): 2; J. B. Harrison, *The Latest Studies on Indian Reservations* (Philadelphia, 1886), p. 149.

21. SCA in *U.S. Bureau of Education,* "Circulars of Information for 1884," p. 40; "Training Primitive Peoples," n.a., *The Indian School Journal* 5 (Jan. 1905): 30–31. See also Elaine Goodale Eastman, *Pratt: The Red Man's Moses,* p. 237 and Goodale (Eastman), "Indian Education," Boston *Daily Advertiser,* Apr. 1886.

22. Editorial remarks, *SW* 12 (May 1883): 2; Bacon, "Works and Methods," p. 17.

23. Folsom, "Indian Days," p. 3. Miss Park, whom Indians nicknamed "the woodpecker," came to Hampton from New Haven to teach woodcarving during the Indian program's early years. Moreover, beginning in 1899 Indian girls were taught handweaving and basketry, and in 1902 teacher Cherokee Arizona Swayney spent several months on her reservation to revive the

then vanishing double weave method of older Indian women. See *SW* 29 (Dec. 1900): 729; "Hampton Incidents," *SW* 31 (Mar. 1902): 164.

24. Minutes of Faculty Meetings, Oct. 5, 1910, HUA; Folsom, "Indian Days," p. 3; Reese Kincade to Andrus, July 11, 1913, and June 25, 1914, box 7, Andrus Correspondence, Indian Collection, HUA. In 1940, long after the Indian program had ended, Folsom and Andrus were still marketing Indian crafts at their gift shop in town. See Eva Johnson to Andrus, Oct. 12, 1940, box 13, Andrus Correspondence, Indian Collection, HUA.

25. RHP, "Save Their Primitive Industries," *The Red Man and Helper* 17 (July 1902): 2; RHP to SCA, Jan. 12, 1880, box 72, U.S. Indian School, Carlisle, Indian Collection, HUA; RHP to A. J. Standing, Oct. 12, 1884, Pratt Papers, Yale University; RHP, "Address by Gen. R. H. Pratt, before Gen. Louis Wagner's Bible Class, Market Square Presbyterian Church," Germantown, Pa, Apr. 15, 1909, Pratt Papers, Yale University. Pratt opposed creating jobs for Indians on reservations, saying, "go where work is." There is plenty of work to do in Pennsylvania. See "Report of Rev. Cleveland for IRA," Mar. 31, 1891, IRA Papers.

26. Edward Blyden to SCA, Apr. 12, 1883, box 4, Indian Affairs, Additional Correspondence, SCA, Indian Collection, HUA.

27. Frank K. Rogers, "An All Around Mechanical Training for Indians," *NEA* 1901, p. 910.

28. Editorial remarks, *SW* 30 (Mar. 1901): 177.

29. For biographical information about Jones, see Stephen Correia, "For Their Own Good: An Historical Analysis of the Educational Thought of Thomas Jesse Jones" (Ph.D. diss., Pennsylvania State University, 1993); Kenneth James King, *Pan Africanism and Education: A Study of Race Philanthropy and Education in the Southern States of America and East Africa* (Oxford, England, 1971), esp. p. 22; Philip Newton, "Dissertation Proposal at Columbia Teacher's College," Apr. 2, 1985.

30. See King, *Pan-Africanism,* pp. 31–43 for a discussion of bias toward the Hampton-Tuskegee model in Thomas Jesse Jones, *Negro Education: a Study of the Private and Higher Schools for Colored People in the United States* (Washington, D.C., 1916).

31. King's *Pan-Africanism* details Jones's work in advancing schemes for the American South. See King, p. 144; Du Bois, "Education in Africa: A Review of the Recommendations of the African Education Committee," *Crisis* 32 (June 1926): 86–89.

32. In February 1941 Jones asked Malcomb McLean of Hampton, "Did you know that the term 'social studies' began with my course at Hampton Institute?" But disputing Jones's outright claim, in 1887 Richard Heber Newton entitled his book *Social Studies* (New York), and Du Bois's Atlanta series used the term. In truth, the term began in England and was popularized by Jones's course and his later role on the Committee on Social Studies. See Jones to McLean, Feb. 23, 1941, in Philip Newton's "Dissertation Proposal."

33. Jones, "Social Studies in the Hampton Curriculum" (hereafter cited as SSHC), part 1, "Why They Are Needed," *SW* 34 (Dec. 1905): 687–89.

34. Materials in the preceding paragraphs all come from Jones, SSHC, part 5, "Sociology and Society," *SW* 35 (Dec. 1906): 687–91 and *SW* 36 (Jan. 1907): 44.

35. King, *Pan-Africanism,* p. 27; Michael Lybarger, "Origins of the Modern Social Studies: 1900–1916," *History of Education Quarterly* 23 (Winter 1983) and Correia, "For Their Own Good."

36. Jones, SSHC, "Sociology," pp. 45–46.

37. Material in last two paragraphs summarized in Jones, SSHC, part 2, "Civics and Social Welfare," *SW* 35 (Jan. 1906): 49–55.

38. Material in last two paragraphs summarized from Jones, SSHC, part 3, "Economics and Material Welfare," *SW* 35 (Mar. 1906): 111–16.

39. Jones, SSHC, part 4, "United States Census and Actual Conditions," *SW* 35 (Apr. 1906): 233 and (May 1906): 313. Jones's computation that 27 percent of Negro farmers owned their own land is misleading. Most southern black land owners were mulattoes who lived in the Upper South: the fewest Negro land owners lived in the black belt. Only 13 percent of blacks in Georgia and 16 percent of them in Mississippi owned land. And while blacks often farmed the best land as sharecroppers, when they were allowed to become owners, they were usually permitted to purchase only the least productive land. See chart, Jones, "Census," *SW* 35 (May 1906): 313.

40. King, *Pan-Africanism,* p. 28–29; Jones, SSHC, "Economics," p. 115.

41. Material in last two paragraphs from Jones, SSHC, part 6, "The Progress of the Indians," *SW* 36 (Mar. 1907): 175–78 and 181–84.

42. King, *Pan-Africanism,* p. 28, points out that if socioeconomic and vital statistics indicated that blacks were "backward," it could be argued that their education should address their weaknesses without raising the sensitive question of whether Negroes ought to be made the recipients of a special type of education.

43. How much impact the educational biases of Jones's SSHC had on the reports of the Committee on Social Studies is being debated. Lybarger's "Origins of Modern Social Studies: 1900–1916" argues that the rationale for subordinating southern Negroes described in SSHC was applied in *Social Studies in Secondary Education* to deal with the similar danger posed to American cities by southern and eastern European immigrants. His major evidence is that the Committee on Social Studies openly acknowledged its pedagogical debt to Hampton Institute, and that the course "Civic Theory and Practice," which Jones described in his *Preliminary Statement* for the committee, was taken verbatim from "Government and the Public Welfare" in SSHC. In turn, with very few further changes, the description for "Civic Theory and Practice" became the better known "Problems in American Democracy" course in the final report. See Lybarger, "Origins," esp. pp. 455, 462–63, 466.

Lybarger's view has been strongly challenged on two major counts, prompting Jones's biographer, Correia, to give Jones less than full credit. First, David Saxe, *Social Studies in Schools* (New York, 1991) holds that it was not Jones but like-minded Indianapolis educator Arthur W. Dunn, who fashioned the final report. Second, Hazel W. Hertzberg viewed the impact of James Harvey Robinson's "new history" as more important to the rise of social studies than either Jones or Dunn. She dismissed any goal of racial or ethnic subordination in *Social Studies and Secondary Education* and saw the social studies movement as growing from a broad consensus of educators who hoped to propound an appropriate curricula for a democratic society. See Hazel W. Hertzberg, *Social Studies Reform: 1880–1980: A Project SPAN Report* (Boulder, 1981), esp. pp. 9–12 and 16–22. One of Hertzberg's students, Michael Whelan, has significantly advanced her perspective in "History and the Social Studies: A Response to the Critics," *Theory and Research in Social Education* 20 (Winter 1992): 2–16. For a general discussion of the "new history," see John Higham, *History* (Englewood Cliffs, 1965), pp. 104–16.

8

As the Years Go By: The Indian Program's Changes and Controversies

As a result of changes both within the Indian education movement generally and at Hampton itself, where challenges to the efficacy and humanity of the program came to threaten its very existence, Hampton's position in Indian education shifted constantly. Not surprisingly, the number of Indian students, their marital status, the tribes from which they came, their prior education, and even the percentage of their Indian ancestry all varied over time and were both products and agents of these changes.

The Indian Student Body's Changing Composition

The 1,388 Indians who attended the institute between 1877 and 1923 belonged to 65 different tribes. But even during years of heaviest enrollment such as 1889, Hampton's pioneering Indian school was only the fourteenth largest. The average enrollment of 96 Indians per year hides the fact that only one year between 1883 and 1902 the school did not finance more Indian students than the 120 provided for in the government contract, hitting a zenith of 160 in 1887. Yet even as Indians began to enter Hampton better prepared, their numbers fell, partly because of Hampton's higher admission standards (albeit only to the upper grades of grammar school). In the decade before the 1912 withdrawal of funding, Hampton averaged only 97 Indians annually; the 81 students enrolled that year plummeted the following year to 41, a figure itself exceeding the average of 31 students per year over the program's final decade.[1]

Throughout the Indian program's tenure, Hampton typically enrolled 3 Indian boys for every 2 girls. But Armstrong continually sought to admit equal numbers of both sexes, having been "forced to the conclusion . . . that only by encouraging, if not arranging [Indian marriages] can we save our work for that race."[2] Thus Hampton faculty and staff actively promoted most of the 31 marriages that occurred among the school's Indian students; no other Indian school attempted to recruit already formed families on the reservations as Hampton did during the 1880s.[3]

In 1882 Commandant Freeland was representing Hampton in Nebraska when anthropologist Alice C. Fletcher first suggested he recruit Indian couples. Fletcher took the initiative by recruiting 2 Indian couples, Noah and Lucy LaFlesche and their relatives Philip and Minnie Stabler, and obtained $400 for the husbands to construct the "Omaha" cottages at Hampton. After the couples had completed their education, Noah LaFlesche helped Philip Stabler construct a home on the agency in 1885, using a $400 loan from Hampton trustee Moses Pierce, under the auspices of Sarah F. Kinney and the Women's National Indian Association (WNIA).[4] In all, Hampton recruited 22 Indian couples (some with children), and housed them in three model cottages behind Winona Lodge.

Following Hampton's example, the WNIA homebuilding department loaned money to 50 or 60 Indian couples to build homes on their allotments. But Hampton stopped admitting married couples about 1890. School officials found recruiting good candidates difficult, and the experiment's very success introduced an anomaly into school life: almost the only married people on campus were Indians, who learned about "proper" family life from a corps of single white women.[5]

While the ratio at Hampton between the sexes of Indian students remained relatively stable, the tribal makeup that prevailed during the 1880s would be radically transformed thereafter, in response to the upgrading of the Indian school system as a whole. This in turn changed Hampton's perception of its role as the capstone of Indian education.

As early as 1880 Pratt's semi-acculturated St. Augustine prisoners began to be replaced by 473 largely "untouched" Sioux (see chap. 2), a bloc more than twice the number of any other tribe at Hampton. Armstrong had originally hoped to show that even the "rudest savages" could be educated, preferring "pupils from the simple, wild, Indian life; pure blood," for whom he would simply "let the light in." Indeed, two-thirds of Hampton's red students during the 1880s (three-fourths among the Sioux) were of wholly Indian ancestry, with 60 percent having slight or no previous exposure to white culture.[6] Their average age was seventeen, although students as old as their early thirties came to Hampton.

Students during this period were typically enlisted by Hampton teachers on visits to agencies along the Missouri River and in Indian Territory. Supportive agents and missionaries helped to recruit them, usually with parental permission, but at times in the beginning with some suggestion of duress or beguilement: in 1887 the *Workman* announced the "discontinuance of all 'coaxing' of Indians to come here."[7]

School representatives themselves recalled dealings with both reluctant and willing families, as students often came from the extreme ranges of Indian society: orphans and other poor children were sent to Hampton because of hard times at home, while the less impoverished or higher placed were sent to be trained as interpreters who would help guide tribal interests. In her recollections of a trip during which Indian children seen at a distance "melted away" at her approach, Folsom reported that one night at Black Wolf's camp, when an Indian named Edward was successfully recruited, "way off in the distance, we heard sounds like the moaning of a giant wind in giant trees. It penetrated our very souls and made creepy shivers run up and down our spines. The teacher said it was Edward's mother and sisters wailing out their sorrow." On another occasion, Reverend J. J. Gravatt recalled having to separate a Sioux child from his grandmother, who "ran screaming into the hut, and getting a knife, cut and slashed . . . her arms and legs" in sign of mourning. But on this same trip, Gravatt reported that another woman traveled seventy miles to have her child enrolled at Hampton, and still another eastern school recruit was told by his father, Chief White Thunder, "If you don't behave yourself [at school] and learn your lessons . . . you will never see the Sioux nation again."[8]

Of those Indians leaving written evidence, most appear to have sent their children to Hampton willingly, even in the early years. Archival records suggest a few Indians were unaware that their destination was a Negro school, or believed they were going to stay three weeks instead of three years. But generally Hampton's methods of recruiting seem to have been more aboveboard than Carlisle's, whose agents sometimes lured otherwise unapproachable children into conversation by giving them candy. Assuming that a willingness to continue schooling indicated an initial willingness to come to Hampton, Cora Folsom proclaimed in 1893 that "of the 460 students (scheduled to return to the reservation) . . . 163 have voluntarily remained at the School after their time had expired; 56 have returned for a second term of years and 70 have gone to other schools after leaving Hampton."[9]

Nevertheless students fresh off the reservations faced a traumatic experience, not only during their first exposure to a "civilized" education, but from the moment they started their journey eastward. Carlisle's Luther Standing Bear, son of a Sioux chief, described what this experience could be like in the years after the Battle of the Little Bighorn. After recruits were herded into a "long row of little houses standing on long pieces of iron stretched away as far as we could see . . . suddenly the whole house started to move." The terrified boy changed seats many times fearing that the telegraph poles would strike the car windows. Going East as a way to count coup, Standing Bear expected "death at the hands of the white people whom we knew had no love for us." The larger boys sang "brave songs," telling the little ones that whites "were taking us to the place where the sun rises, where they would dump us over the edge of the earth." When Ben Brave's party of Hampton recruits lodged overnight at a hotel in Chicago, "young men and boys [in the street outside] hooted as if we were some wild animals."[10] After pulling into the depot at Hampton, male Indians had to walk to the campus while the females rode (in wagons), a disconcerting reversal of tribal custom.

No wonder a teacher found that the newly arrived, culturally shocked Indians were not the "fierce, unmanageable characters we had pictured, [but] timid, observant, silent boys who aroused our immediate pity." An Indian agent commented that their "organs of speech seem unable to form some sounds of the English language." Even as late as 1921 some Indian students at Hampton were "terribly shy . . . the change from the life they have led is so great they are completely dazed and bewildered . . . it is often a year or two before they can bring themselves to recite."[11]

The terror of the journey to Hampton was no wise over when students from the Plains arrived on campus. The male Indian student may have had to sacrifice even more of his traditional life than did the female. One male historian asserted that the Indian female's "already modest dress was approved without change by the missionaries. . . . On the other hand, a man had to have his hair cut, change his style of dress, and adopt new work patterns—in short a whole new role." In any case, fully aware that a male Indian feared that having his long hair cut short would result in the death of near relatives, Hampton staff choose to sever this "connecting link with home . . . a sign of complete surrender to the ways of civilized life."[12] Likewise, the mandatory wearing of the blue school uniform, cap, and uncomfortable brogan shoes cut links to the Indians' spirit world contained in traditional dress and adornment.

In countless other ways, although less completely than government schools, Hampton undermined the culture and sacred beliefs of its Indian students. Indian students were prohibited from speaking their native tongue, except before breakfast and after supper, and on holidays and Sundays. Even on the Sabbath Armstrong advised them to "pray all they can in English and the rest in Indian." They were awarded "pretty badges" called "eagles" if they spoke only English and were fined a quarter and sent to the commandant each time they did not. Nevertheless, Hampton did oppose Commissioner Morgan's policy of English only, since Indian students needed fluency in their native tongue to act as cultural missionaries. (Indeed it appears that some non-Sioux students learned Lakota as well as English.) Neither did Hampton staff change the name of an Indian unless the student "prefers a more euphonious and civilized one."[13] Although Hamptonians inadvertently insulted Sioux warriors by voicing their names in public, by asking reasons for their actions, and by closely questioning them without giving time for reflection, the very frequency with which the staff pointed out such cultural differences suggests that to some extent allowances were made.[14]

Despite such limited concessions to their sensibilities, some Indian students were unable or unwilling to adjust to life at Hampton. An Indian could in extreme cases affect release, as did Sioux Happy Road, her traditional name "an unhappy misnomer" under the circumstances, since she "wept for two months, night and day, [before being] returned home." In another case, Richard Whalen and Sam White Bear got themselves sent back to Pine Ridge by confessing to Moton that "we do not like to spoil the good record of this school. . . . We cannot let up on using tobacco and intoxicating liquor. . . . We are getting wilder every day, and before we get into any mischief we thought we would come out with the truth like men and let you know about it."[15]

———

Perhaps as a result of the problems encountered in fulfilling its mission of civilizing the "rudest savages," Hampton gradually changed its pattern of recruitment after the mid-1880s, and this was soon reflected in the composition of its Indian student body. Once a skeptical public had been persuaded that Indians could indeed learn the ways of whites—which, in turn, fostered a massive school-building program for Indians during the 1880s—the institute proceeded to exclude "uneducated" Indians, "essentially raw material" ("closest to heaven"), and concentrated on the ones who could meet the same entrance requirements as blacks and thus join regular classes.[16]

Hampton became a finishing school for Indians by increasingly recruiting at large missionary stations, reservation boarding schools, and even other nonreservation boarding schools. In 1890 its upgrading of entrance standards was formalized, although at first more in theory than in practice, when Commissioner Morgan arranged the Indian school system hierarchically. Henceforth, instead of all schools competing for all students, agency day schools would form the base of an educational pyramid, with reservation boarding schools in the middle, and nonreservation boarding schools such as Hampton at the top. Indeed around 1900 nonreservation schools began specializing among themselves. Because Hampton was known for trades and teacher training, the Indian Office itself sometimes selected appropriate students for it, especially after the government schools' normal departments were abolished in 1903, leaving Hampton's the only one in the service.[17]

Frissell's annual report for 1895 described the change in Hampton's tribal composition: "In the early days of the school's dealings with the Indians, much the largest number was obtained from the Sioux country and from the Omahas and Winnebagos of Nebraska (the last two tribes providing sixty-four and sixty-three students respectively). A comparatively small number now come from that portion of the country, a large number being taken from the more civilized tribes nearer home."[18]

For example, although a few Winnebagos continued to enter Hampton after 1890, Armstrong told the commissioner that the school had decided not to take any more pupils from that agency because of the "moral corruption of the people and the fact that there was so little good for the children to go back to," in the way of missionaries and agents upholding "civilized" values on the reservations. Conversely, fewer Sioux chose to come from the agency Hampton had once showcased, Crow Creek and Lower Brule; tribal leaders shunned Hampton because so many pupils had died there.[19] Moreover, the Sioux and Omaha now had enough agency schools to make sending students to the East at high transportation (and psychological) costs unnecessary.[20] Whereas Hampton's Indians had once come largely from tribes newly feeling the pressure of whites, tribes whose chiefs, like Omaha Francis LaFlesche, recognized the need for future leaders to acquire some knowledge of English, the new Indians came from tribes already somewhat acculturated.

Although the first Wisconsin Oneida, Richard Powless, came in October 1885, the real influx from this tribe began when Dr. Anna Johnson returned from the West in July 1888 with 8 pupils, and Gravatt brought 10 more in November. Oneidas—49 in 1893—were to provide Hampton with more Indian students (180) than any other tribe for the remainder of the Indian program. Even more than the Omahas the Oneida showed the increasing willingness of partly acculturated tribes to come to eastern boarding schools. Half came from 5 families: there were 14 Powlesses, 12 Doxstaders, 23 Hills, 16 Metoxens (Bairds), and 27 Skenandores. Hampton's training of Oneida pupils centered on the tribe's commitment to dairy farming, which assured its members positions at the agency school, much as Tuskegee employed its black graduates. By 1919 the Oneida's town government was entirely run by Hampton graduates: the head of the tribe, Isaac N. Webster (1902) was married to Josephine Hill (1904), the daughter of the tribe's last hereditary chief, Cornelius Hill, who had also sent his four sons to Hampton.[21]

Onondaga Charles Doxon had come to Hampton as a work student in October 1883, yet the real push for recruiting Indians from New York and North Carolina came in the early 1890s, when the federal government began subsidizing major tribes in these states. In 1893 the Five Nations sent thirty-four Indian students to the institute, becoming its second largest group. Ultimately 169 New York Indians came to Hampton: 112 Seneca, 28 Onondaga, 14 Oneida, 13 Cayuga, and 2 Mohawk. In 1893, Clara Snow, the Hampton teacher who recruited Indians from New York while she was home for the summer, identified their "advantage" over Indian students from other states: they often came specifically to learn industrial trades in the machine shops for the purpose of gaining employment in the factories of Buffalo or neighboring cities.[22]

Six years after the first Eastern Cherokee had come to Hampton in 1890, Frissell proudly announced the presence of 25 students from this tribe that had long associated with whites: "The 1,500 Cherokees of North Carolina are a hopeful tribe. . . . Their reservation is near the school, and it seems eminently proper that Hampton should help them." The next year the Cherokees replaced New York's Indians as Hampton's second largest group behind the Wisconsin Oneidas. A total of 61 Eastern Cherokees attended Hampton.[23]

Thus, during the second half of its government funded program, Hampton would have enrolled more eastern than western Indians were it not for the most easterly and most enthusiastic tribe once from New York—the Wisconsin Oneidas. Even the diminishing numbers of Sioux and Omaha who continued coming to Hampton, often now children of former students, were of a more "easternized," second generation of Indian youth from west of the Mississippi. As the idea of uprooting Indian children from the West and holding them hostage in eastern boarding schools fell into disrepute, Hampton shifted its center of gravity to eastern Indians, many of whom wanted white education.

Hampton's shift toward eastern tribes accelerated a trend already well underway by the mid-1880s: the Indian student body was becoming one of predominantly mixed ancestry. The decreasing number of full-blooded, reservation Indians at Hampton was an inevitable result of the school's rising academic standards coupled with the government's policy of sending only the most "advanced" Indian students to nonreservation schools. Indian children of mixed lineage were more likely to have lived among whites and thus to have acquired formal schooling, a knowledge of English, and Christianity.[24] The cumulative effect of this was to unify the student body. An Indian influenced by a white or black ancestor or coming from an eastern tribe was almost as acculturated as Hampton's Negro students, who came from rural areas and were often of a darker hue: mulattoes more often attended black colleges with classical curricula.[25]

Hampton's enrollment of "white" Indians conflicted with southern segregationist practices in a way that its "black" Indians[26] did not, while both of these racial mixtures reduced cultural differences on campus. As photographs of Hampton's classes—and one of blond Ebenezer Kingsley—confirm, students attended this black school when they had only a trace of Indian ancestry and probably would have been considered white in southern society. Students as much as seven-eighths Caucasian but culturally Indian could attend Hampton at government expense without special permission. Only when a student was fifteen-sixteenths of that race did the Indian Office require verification of a life lived in Indian fashion, and the lack of educational opportunity for such a student without entry to schools under government contract.[27] Hampton's Omahas Amos Lamson and Leta Meyers had to pay their own way: the ruling found them not "Indian" enough. Although some Hampton Indians with mostly white ancestry may have appeared dark enough to fall victim to segregation, government regulations were more concerned about culture than color.

In a case of working at cross purposes to policy, however, a white Indian girl already well adjusted to mainstream society was reassociated with Indian culture at Hampton. Mashpee Eva May Simons attended Indian schools because her father had died and she needed somewhere to stay at government expense. Praised by a school superintendent, A. A. Heath, for her "great refinement," Simons was half Caucasian but appeared able to pass for white in her black-and-white student photograph. Born in Cape Cod, she had received her early education in its public schools, graduating from Wrentham High School in nearby Onset, a "pretty summer resort just off the cape." Simon's rapid promotion at Hampton—from junior to senior middle in three months—was unsurprising, since she had taken the same studies in high school, "so they are not new."[28] After a year at Hampton, Simon moved on to become a model of Indian "progress" at Carlisle.

On the dark side of the color line, but also often acculturated, were Hampton's twenty-five black Indians, ranging from partly to entirely Negro. The chiaroscuro of Hampton Indians—a picture made up of diverse mixes and hues and unique blends of cultural attachments drawn from half a globe—was of course reflected in the differing levels of opportunity open to individual students inside the world of Hampton. For example, Virginia Goings was part African, part Sioux, and part French, while Laura Johnson could claim as her own the traditions of Songhay, the conquistadors, the Blarney Stone, the Rights of Man, and the Sun Dance.[29] But the lever for someone who physically appeared black to receive benefits as an Indian (education at government expense and often an allotment or subsidy as well) was to have one's mother hold membership in a federally recognized Indian tribe, to have been incorporated into one of them as a descendant of its former slaves, or to have been adopted outright by the original people of the land.

Hampton's first black Indian, Frank Black Hawk, came to the institute in November 1881. By the time he departed in July 1885, the Indian Department also included three former slaves of the Seminole; his brother, Peter, would arrive shortly. Raised by a Sioux mother, Black Hawk liked "colored boys [but] mostly associates with Indian boys, who seemed to appreciate him." While popular among both races of students—being versed in both Lakota and English—Black Hawk was termed by *Twenty-Two Years' Work* as Hampton's "Bad Boy," who had "inherited the infirmities of both races." Black Hawk himself blamed his eighteen-month sentence in the State Penitentiary at Sioux Falls (for stealing whiskey from the agency drug store) on his failure to convert Indians to Christianity. He had found his own faith undermined when unable to answer why whites had killed Jesus, or why the Father had not saved His son. Although he deplored "what whiskey will bring on a man" and vowed thereafter "to walk the narrow path," Frank Black Hawk was later convicted of participating in murder.[30]

Another of Hampton's black Indians, William Lone Wolf, epitomized the "tramp student evil," that is, the aimless transfer of "Indian" students from school to school. Lone Wolf was attending the Chilocco Indian School in 1887 when he accompanied the son of the younger Chief Lone Wolf (Mamay-day-Te) home to the Kiowa Reservation. Feeling sorry for a Creek freedwoman's child now an "orphan alone in the world," the chief asked him to be "my adopted son." William Lone Wolf was taken in by the Kiowa nation and placed on the tribal roll. He attended Carlisle from 1892 to 1895 and Hampton from 1897 to 1901, before re-entering Chilocco. Carlisle had declared his competence to live among whites and sent him away eight years before an anonymous Indian complained to Pratt: "William Lone Wolf is a black man. He never was Indian. He is about thirty years old now. . . . You think that right, government educate black man fourteen years in Indian schools?" But Lone Wolf's "negro blood did not matter," retorted *The Chilocco Farmer,* when the government was paying his way at Carlisle. In addition to maximizing his free schooling as an Indian, Lone Wolf also capitalized on his Indian status by investing the money gained from selling his allotment in three houses and an automobile; he rented two of the houses and operated a chauffeur service.[31]

Using his knowledge of the Indian school system, Lone Wolf repaid his debt to the chief by trying to help two other Oklahomans with black ancestry. One day when Virginia Ransom was "coming from the field carrying a very heavy sack of cotton, Mr. W. M. Lone Wolf . . . began to pity my condition of hard labor. He says to me I will write the principal of Hampton school for your admission if you promise me you will put forth every effort to make that favor a success."[32] Acting on this recommendation and the Muskogee agent's listing of her as half Pueblo, apparently on Lone Wolf's word, Hampton's Frederick Gleason sent Ransom a ticket to Hampton.

But soon after Ransom arrived at Hampton in January 1908, the Indian agents at Santa Fe and Muskogee told the Indian Office that her mother was probably not Indian at all but rather white and Mexican, while Frissell preferred that he "would take her for a full Negro." Despite Frissell's rating of her as "rather above average in her school work," Ransom's physical inability to perform hard labor presaged her return to Oklahoma in April. Dismayed that some provision for her had not been made, Ransom charged that Hampton had done a "most horrible thing" in bringing her all the way there only to send her home when the government denied her support.[33]

William Lone Wolf's later protégé, Cynthia Powdrill, went unchallenged by the Indian Office, although some of the Indian students insisted that she was not of their race, despite her tan complexion, straight hair, and high cheek bones. A former Indian student at Hampton, Evelyn Two Guns, told Caroline Andrus that Powdrill was descended from the Indians' former slaves and "hasn't a speck of Indian in her." Two Guns gave Andrus both barrels by telling her that Lydia Shawnee, herself one of Hampton's black Indians, "knows [Powdrill's] people well and Lucy Hunter looked them up too." Eventually Two Guns and Hunter both agreed with Andrus that it was not color but character that mattered, and with Shawnee that Powdrill "ought to give her colored blood some credit."[34] Although such false claims concerned Indian students, none of them sought publicly to remove anyone from the Indian Department on account of color.

Indeed, eight members of the Shawnee family, named after the tribe they belonged to, attended Hampton when it was common knowledge that the family was "colored [and] not Indian at all." The Absentee Shawnee tribe had captured and adopted the children's father, a runaway slave; their mother was a Creek freedman, who Hampton's William Scoville said was "Negro pure and simple." Six of the Shawnee children—Eva, Lafayette, Julia, Emaline, Lydia, and Rebecca—came to Hampton as Indians between 1900 and 1912, and received those things the government provided "for Indians only": dormitories, tables in the dining room, certain social activities, and outing. Conversely, the two Shawnee family members who came after Hampton lost its government subsidy for Indians—Myrtle in 1917 and David in 1920—became part of the Negro student body. Some members of the Shawnee family denied being black while others were ambivalent about it. For example, using a common ruse of blacks living among Indians to mislead the scholarship donors, Julia claimed she was one-fourth Indian, and David that his father was part Cherokee. On the other hand, Eva admitted that "the peculiar circumstances of her life and surroundings give her no settled place in life," and Rebecca displayed no personal allegiance to either Indian or Negro emancipation days. Nevertheless, although all of the Shawnee family would receive allotments, only Rebecca would work her land, marry an Indian, and continue to live among Indians.[35]

Nancy Coleman also denied her black ancestry. While on outing, she claimed superiority to the household's black cook, insisting that she had "not one drop of negro blood" and was "all Indian and white." Before the cook's departure improved Coleman's erratic behavior, her outing matron complained that there were "two Nancys," the one "pleasant, capable, and anxious to please," and the other "sullen, neglectful of duty, and insubordinate." Ironically it was the failed attempt of Nancy's brother Calvin to enroll at Hampton with Indian status that caused the family to be listed as "doubtful" on the Cherokee tribal role, the "book of 'Life and Death.'" As a result Nancy could not work for the Indian Office, the main employer of Indians, because it had become government policy not to employ Indians with black lineage. Andrus attempted to place her as a teacher among the Five Civilized Tribes—some of whose schools mixed black and Indian students—but no positions were said to be available. As a final resort, Nancy was enrolled at the nearby Dixie Hospital, Alice Bacon's training school for black nurses, where Andrus would send four more black Indian girls barred from the greater opportunities open to other "Indians."[36] Having lost her claim to tribal membership, after graduating from Dixie Hospital in 1921, Nancy Coleman moved to Northfield, Massachusetts, with her husband, Georgia black Ernest Thornston (1918).

Hampton was generally regarded as offering opportunities that helped an Indian with black ancestry find a place in American society. For example, Carrie Warren, the orphan of a black father and Arapaho mother, had lived her entire life with the white staff and Indian children of the Cheyenne Mennonite Mission in Cantonment, Oklahoma. Her sponsor, Agnes Williams, wrote Andrus that "in many respects [Hampton] is the place for Carrie." Andrus replied that Warren's Negro blood would make her "happier here than in a strictly Indian school."[37] In the end, Warren married a black, but moved to Oberlin, Ohio, a community with less prejudice than most. Another black Indian, half Sioux and half black, made an even more creative adjustment to prejudice. After finding that her nursing degree from Dixie Hospital consigned her to charity work among Indian people or to the Red Cross, Emma Corn married Felipe Morejon Mella and moved to Matonzas, Cuba, where black and Indian Catholic couples like themselves were more common.[38]

The color line was never more illogical than in its treatment of black Indians. The Indian Office defined a child born of an Indian father and a black mother as Negro unless the mother had been adopted into an Indian tribe, but one with a black father and an Indian mother as Indian, and rewarded the latter with land and free schooling, and often with an annuity and rations as well. Although in some cases coming to Hampton was a black Indian's first exposure to the language and customs of whites, in other cases the monetary benefits of Indian status were added to the familiarity with mainstream culture already imparted by a Negro parent. But any benefits within tribal society that a black Indian might have derived from attending Hampton were negated by the Indian Office's tacit policy, formalized in 1915, of employing no Indians with any black lineage. Thus Hampton's black Indians were typically forced out into the non-Indian world.

In sum, by 1905 Hampton's entering Indian students bore little resemblance to those of the early days, and Hampton had come to welcome that change. At the opening of classes the *Workman* stated that

When one compares a company of the intelligent, self-contained, purposeful young Indians who have gathered at Hampton . . . with a crowd corralled on the reservations twenty years ago, a marked contrast is noticeable. Then the students often came in blankets, with little knowledge of English, with no belongings, and no definite idea of what they were going to obtain in a school. Now many of them travel across the continent alone, usually seeking a trade or preparation for teaching. They are well dressed, have good-sized trunks, and show an excellent command of the English tongue.[39]

Already by the mid-1890s, the makeup of the Indian Department had been so transformed that no more couples came; individual students came from different tribes from different geographical regions, recruited by different methods; more of them were also of racially mixed ancestry, with twice as many black Indians coming after 1900 than came before. However, the school's recruiting methods and educational approach changed not only in response to the general development of the Indian school system already outlined, but also in reaction to a series of troubling controversies that occurred during the 1880s. These controversies themselves—over the lastingness of Hampton's effect on reservation Indians, over the poor health of many western Indian students, and over a method of discipline used only on Indians—influenced the changing perception at the institute of which Indians it was best able to educate.

Returned Students: Debate and Assessment

Almost as soon as Indian students began returning from eastern schools to the reservations, questions arose about the efficacy and permanence of their Anglo ways and skills. The first criticism came in February 1879, soon after the Kiowas from Pratt's St. Augustine prison-school had been returned to Fort Sill. Their agent, C. B. Hunt, claimed that "most of all the Florida boys have gone back to the Indians. [The elder Chief] Lone Wolf is dead, which is a great blessing. He would have caused trouble in the Spring. All the rest of the old men are confirmed Indians. White Horse is the same big lazy Indian that he was in Augustine; he has even forgotten how to put his civilized clothes on anymore." But Comanche Quo-yo-uh defended their situation to Pratt, saying, "You first taught me the white man's road. I am now very poor and disconsolate . . . I never have any money for I cannot earn it here. . . . When you come see us I shall have nothing to show you—no corn, no house, nothing at all. The white people of this country are crazy."[40]

Lacking knowledge on the actual state of affairs in Oklahoma, the *Workman* said that "failures will serve to strengthen future management," and that it may have been "mistaken kindness" to send the "very worst" prisoners back so soon. Then a July article in the New York *Tribune,* "The Effort So Far a Failure," pointed to the collapse of earlier efforts—at Harvard, William and Mary, Dartmouth, and the ABCFM's school at Cornwall, Connecticut—and predicted a similar fate for Hampton's Indian experiment. Hampton replied that because of its emphasis on industrial rather than on classical training, and because it educated both sexes, its project would succeed where these others had failed.[41] This answer, however, did not end the criticisms, and further, more serious charges of ineffectiveness, prompted more specific responses.

————

The most potentially damaging criticisms of returned students surfaced in March 1886 before the House of Representatives, in testimony given by a committee appointed to answer questions about the effectiveness of Indian education at the eastern schools. This committee, chaired by Democrat William S. Holman of Indiana, spent a week visiting the Dakota agencies in the summer of 1885 and concluded that industrial boarding schools on the reservation were satisfactory, but that both reservation day schools and nonreservation boarding schools were unsuccessful. Holman agreed with committee spokesman Joseph G. Cannon (R. Illinois) that not a "single student" educated off the reservations failed to "relapse" unless "supported by government." Several bills were then proposed to withdraw appropriations from eastern boarding schools.[42]

Assisted by Indian agent James McLaughlin and by missionaries Thomas Riggs and Bishop Hare, Hampton, the IRA, and even Carlisle (in Pratt's own idiosyncratic way), marshaled their forces to fight such bills. Using Representative Byron M. Cutcheon (R. Michigan) as their spokesman, they so thoroughly refuted the committee's charges that the House voted 286 to five against abolishing eastern training schools. Although the IRA's Herbert Welsh later contended that eastern schools had really been in "no danger" in the first place, that their supporters had been "over alarmed," he himself had quickly organized the production of a pamphlet entitled "Are Eastern Industrial Schools a Failure?" It relied heavily on a letter from Helen Ludlow, who raised Hampton's standard defense against congressional threats: "The Western work and the Eastern work are one work. This attack upon the Eastern schools does not concern Hampton alone. . . . It is the whole cause of Indian education that is attacked [which] concerns all the friends of the Indian."[43]

Carlisle and Hampton assumed different defensive postures. Pratt's search for doctrinal purity led him to divide eastern from western schools and to attack the latter, causing dissension among Indian reformers. In contrast, Hampton equated the survival of the whole of Indian education with the continuation of its own Indian program, laying the groundwork for coordination among various sectors of the Indian reform movement. Ridiculing the committee's arguments about returned students, Ludlow asked, "Does Judge Holman mean that 'supported by the Government' is a synonym, and a derisive one, for 'employed by the Government?' In that case, every Congressman shares the odium." She pointed out that instead of solving the problem of "reversion to savagery" (i.e., the rejection of white values) by employing greater numbers of returned students, Holman would simply not educate them at all. Moreover, his investigation had no evidence to justify calling for the termination of either eastern boarding or reservation day schools: he had never visited the eastern schools and the day schools had been closed for the summer during his visit.

In the end, Hampton's detailed case studies of its returned students became an effective defense against Holman's critique of eastern boarding schools. Ludlow had recently spent two months at the same agencies that Holman visited. Her statistical analysis of the home conditions of Hampton's 132 students from Dakota found "recidivism" among only 4; of 72 students who were doing "very well indeed," 33 had never worked for the government.[44] Nevertheless her findings alone can not present a fully balanced historical picture, even for the Indians they described, of Indian education's success or failure as a "civilizing" agent.

———

While imperfect, Hampton's record of returned students was the most complete in the Indian reform movement. Indeed Hampton was almost alone in looking at whether these students would live by Anglo rather than Native American values, and so, Indian reformers believed, save the race from extinction. The famous 1928 report by Lewis Meriam of the Brookings Institute pointed out that "the Indian Service has never put into operation an efficient system for getting reliable information regarding the graduates and former students of its schools." The Indian Office had too high a turnover of correspondents with too many systems of record-keeping to do the job properly, even had it really attempted it. Hampton on the other hand had Cora Folsom, who for twenty years gathered reliable, if sympathetically analyzed, information regarding the former Indian students of her school. Between 1884, the time of her first trip to Dakota, and 1903, when her museum duties prevented her from keeping the records up-to-date, Folsom's efforts (supplemented by Ludlow's) led to such important studies of the early history of Indian education as *Ten Years' Work* (1888) and *Twenty-Two Years' Work* (1893). The latter was used by Congress and the Indian Office against critics of Indian education, but its "Instantaneous Views" of individual black students also gave rise to the Hampton Negro Records Office under Myrtilla Sherman.[45]

Indian records enabled Hampton staff to identify prominent students and hold them up as examples of what Indians could attain. Among those about whom books or articles have since been written are Thomas Wildcat Alford (Absentee Shawnee), surveyor; George Bushotter (Sioux), James Murie (Pawnee), and William Jones (Sac and Fox), ethnologists; Anna Dawson Wilde (Arikara), the first Indian field matron; Angel DeCora Deitz (Winnebago), artist; Jacob C. Morgan, Navaho tribal leader; Thomas Sloan (Omaha), federal court commissioner and president of the Society of American Indians (SAI); Susan LaFlesche (Omaha), the first Indian woman physician; and the versatile Owl family (Eastern Cherokee).[46] Other accomplished Hampton Indians include Elizabeth Bender Roe Cloud (Anishinabe), the first Indian to be named Mother of the Year (1950) by the American Mother's Committee and wife of Henry Roe Cloud (the first Indian graduate of Yale and principal of Roe Institute); Benjamin Brave (Sioux), organizer of the Returned Student and Progressive Indian Association at Lower Brule; Frank Hubbard (Penobscot), editor of *The Oglala Light;* Antonio Azul, Pima Chief, and George M. Frazier (Sioux), ophthalmologist.

Of course, individually impressive Hampton records provided no assurance that returnees were trying to share their acquired values and knowledge with other Indians, or might not in some instances be using them to gain selfish advantage. For example, in 1909, just a few years before Hampton's only Indian graduate to become a lawyer, Thomas Sloan, emerged as a leader of the SAI, another equally prominent Hampton graduate, Dr. Susan LaFlesche, charged that he had "defrauded, coerced and exploited the Omaha Indians for a number of years." She claimed that Sloan and others, knowing that the trust period would expire soon, had "formed a syndicate" to acquire Omaha land and removed an honest inspector who was thwarting their plans. LaFlesche asked Hampton to forward her letter to President Taft; it gave details about ten Indians Sloan allegedly cheated and accused him of becoming the guardian of orphans in order to use their land and collect their annuities, of billing a widow half the worth of her allotment ($2,950) to gain its title, of taking a client's land as fee when he had gone to prison, and of inducing an Indian to sign his land away after fellow Hamptonian Garry Myers got him drunk. As Liquor Commissioner Sloan had helped Myers and others bring whiskey onto the reservation for "election purposes," and while acting as tribal attorney he had "betrayed" the Omaha nation by inexplicably withdrawing a treaty claim whose passage by Congress seemed imminent.[47]

While such apparent "failures" were rare, Hampton's returned students often found pleasing whites and serving one's own people to be irreconcilable goals. For example, Thomas Alford acquired names for allotment rolls among traditional Absentee Shawnee by sending a spy into their camp. During his term as secretary of the Sac and Fox Nation, Walter Battice persuaded his tribe to take allotments and sell the "surplus" land to white settlers. A few of Hampton's "civilized" Indians even participated in the capture or death of "renegade" Indians. For instance, Apache Robert McIntosh acted as interpreter for General Nelson A. Miles during Geronimo's "outbreak" in 1886, and Mohave Oliver Eaton's skills in following a "very blind trail" aided in the capture of the last of his band. Sioux John Archambeau was serving in the Twelfth Infantry when Sitting Bull was murdered.[48] Hampton Indians served as allotment agents and scouts, as well as tribal police and judges.

Leaving aside the many Indians who saw absorption *as* extinction, the small number who actually graduated from Hampton—158 out of 1230—throws into question the importance the school attached to individually notable cases.[49] Robert Engs found "more black Hampton alumni professionals in the village of Hampton alone than there were Indian alumni professionals in the West." Indeed the *Workman* in 1920 listed only six returned students as still active in the professions.[50]

Moreover, Folsom's claim that almost 90 percent of the Indian students made "satisfactory" records at home included a group who had "fallen more from force of circumstance and lack of training than from vice." Hampton's measures of "doing well" discounted the returnees' material welfare, while counting such things as entrance into Christian marriage, mode of dress, avoidance of alcohol, and refusal of rations. The school's record of Indian occupations shows that the vast majority of returned students became subsistence farmers or the wives and mothers of such. In 1920, 330 of 526 returned male Indians were farmers or laborers, and 254 of 317 women kept house. While it is not surprising that Hampton's rural and industrial focus produced a lot of farmers, the school was also known for its normal and trades training (almost 90 percent of its black graduates becoming teachers), yet in 1920 had produced only eleven living Indian teachers and sixty-eight independent tradesmen.[51]

On the other hand, Andrus noted that "far too often we expect much more of these students than we do of ourselves. The white boys or girls who have been away at school a short time [typically three years] are not expected to return and reform the whole community; the Indians are." Of course, Armstrong himself had established these unrealistic expectations: "we expect graduates from Hampton Institute to teach the rudiments of knowledge 'in the best manner'; to govern youth and to inspire them with a love for their studies; to acquire the character and behavior fitted to influence the communities in which they live and to destroy prejudice . . . to advocate temperance, thrift, and education." And as Andrus pointed out,

> A white boy who has been to school until he is perhaps twenty, and [has to] master, in addition to the usual studies, a new language, and accept an entirely strange system of living, is not expected to raise the standards of his home community to a very great extent; the Indian is. The Indian must not only have acquired a trade . . . but he must also speak English well enough to act as interpreter, understand the Bible, and teach in a Sunday school, as well as be prepared to advise in the councils of his people regarding various phases of their legal standing and land questions.

To help Indian students understand the Dawes Act alone they needed to be "taken to town and introduced to deeds, banks, mortgages, the post office, marriage records, and etc, including reading newspapers, articles on the Knights [of Labor], boycotts, local option, and tariff." Hampton even held "apron and necktie" parties for them.[52]

Three general obstacles hindered the returned students' retention of European culture. First, the government's policy of supplying agencies with manufactured goods from the outside limited independent economic life, as Hampton-trained Indian tinners, tailors, shoemakers, carpenters, and painters quickly discovered. Other skills withered because agencies lacked an adequate supply of wood for carpentry, or arable land for successful farming. Second, the Indian Office discriminated against Indian workers. Only a quarter to a third of the agency work force was native, despite statutes in 1882 and 1894 stipulating that preference be given to Indians in agency employment "as far as practicable." Omaha Marguerite LaFlesche found this qualification left most whites refusing to be "*beneath*" an Indian.[53] In truth, returned Indian students who were fortunate enough to be hired by the government nevertheless formed an agency subcaste: they seldom became agency clerks, farmers, carpenters, or blacksmiths, as Hampton's listing of occupations might suggest, but merely their assistants. Last, European and native customs often collided. Not only were returned students discouraged from working for wages by traditions of communalism and generosity that allowed relatives and friends to consume their earnings, but the men experienced social ostracism for degrading themselves in labor not compatible with the tribe's warrior traditions.[54]

On the other hand, internalized white standards led Anishinabe Susie St. Martin, while a nurse's trainee at the county hospital at St. Paul, Minnesota, to worry "almost continually" when her mother and brother were in town: "Just imagine . . . if they should come to the hospital inquiring for me. Why I'd die of shame. Every day we see these poor unfortunate beings come here into this place and we pity them. . . . I live in dread waiting for one of my relatives to come in drunk, disorderly, and dirty."[55]

Many returned students faced tribal resistance or alienation and poverty, and before 1886 personal tragedies were not uncommon. Of 304 Indian students, 65 died after returning home and 31 more died at school (discussed in the next section). Don't Know How, a Sioux, had been so elated at the prospect of his daughter's return from Hampton that he built a new cabin, bought a small store, and adopted what he believed were white ways. But he reported that once the girl saw the "desolation" surrounding her, "Ziewie had cried all night because she was civilized, and her sister had cried all night because she was not civilized." Folsom reported that Ziewie Davis soon died of consumption. Shortly thereafter, Ziewie's sister followed her to Hampton and then her "footsteps to the little cemetery on the hill." After his daughters' deaths, Don't Know How changed his name to Mr. D. K. Howe and "kept himself up to the standard that he had raised for their sake."[56]

When Commissioner Morgan introduced to the Senate the text that became *Twenty-Two Years' Work*, he understood that "the good record of a very large proportion [of Indian students] is not in conspicuous acts but in quiet, unobtrusive, patient living-out day by day, amid depressing surroundings and utmost disadvantage, the lessons taught them at school."[57] Of course the frustration of returned students varied greatly in intensity and expression. One former student answered Folsom's inquiry about the welfare of the bright girl who "flashes like a meteor across the eastern sky" by lamenting, "what a thoughtless careless girl I

was. I could never settle myself down to be sober. I only thought of fun
all the time, and now I am a grandmother. . . . Of course I have never
distinguished myself, but in my own quiet unknown way I have tried
to lead those that I have had anything to do with to the right. It isn't
much. I wish I could have done great things when I remember my teachers that tried so hard to educate me, but I have never had time." Less
apologetic, Oneida Richard Powless reminded Hampton that graduates
"need all your influence" to teach in Indian schools: without it we "are
obliged to work the same as [those] who have never been to school.
. . . so small and powerless and unpopular [a minority we] quietly stay
at home and content ourselves by looking at our diplomas."[58]

More generally, in 1920 former student Spencer Fisher Williams told
Hampton what a "successful failure" he had been, claiming that "education was bad for me, because I see through education, what a sham
civilization is." Having had his fill of Booker Washington's saga, the
disillusioned Williams told Andrus that

> There is no such thing as a man starting with a broom sweeping
> around and getting promoted to the top. That's mythology pure
> and simple. . . . Perhaps in my school days I looked at the world
> through *rose colored glasses* but I've had an awful bump and woke
> up. . . . I for one don't wish to be a citizen and be guilty of be-
> ing a "Voter" and say that my vote helped to put so & so [in
> office]. If it's reform, I say, let's have Bolshevism, but of course
> the papers aren't going to tell us the real truth about it because
> our papers are backed by capitalists. How often have you heard
> that an Indian goes back to the blanket. . . . *That's the reason why.*
> I only wish I could have remained a boy all my life, then life would
> have been grand and ideal.[59]

Thus Williams believed that re-embracing Indian culture was the only
course open to an idealistic educated Indian.

Some Indian returnees objected to Folsom's interpretation of individual reports from the reservation. Winnebago Julia De Cora wrote,
"if you or others [at Hampton] want to believe such scandals and petty
gossip, why not take my word. . . . I suppose I ought to let my indig-
nation cool for another twelve hours but I want to let you know about
rumors before judging me." She defended what Folsom called her
"sloven habits" as unavoidable, considering "a person can't dress in
fashion [when one] didn't have a cent." Similarly, Folsom called a "nice
girl" like Sioux Ellen Ellis "too much half-breed and cowboy" and
apparently did not consider that the husband of Sioux Mary Traversie
may have received his name, "Sits Down to Talk," because he was a

good listener rather than because he was "too lazy to stand up." On the other side of the cultural divide, upon seeing his first bicycle one Indian commented, "White man too much lazy, sit down to walk."[60]

Sensitivity to being singled out and a wish for personal privacy made many returned students dislike being held up as standard bearers. A postscript by Oneida Marion Skenandore asked Andrus to "remember this letter is personal. I don't want to see a particle of it in a paper or magazine." Moreover, returned students gave selective reports: although Sioux William Benoist called tribesman William Lavery a "perfect drunkard and no account," he could have told Folsom "about others but do not want to hurt your feelings." In fact many Hampton Indians, especially full bloods, have an empty student file, suggesting they were not comfortable enough with English to write or else were unwilling to do so. Hampton's report on grammar for 1882 commented that "the proportion who can naturally and clearly express themselves is probably never more than twenty-five percent of any senior class."[61] Feedback after 1900 increasingly relied on hearsay from missionaries and former students.

Finally, while the debate about returned students' reversion to tribalism implied that they had left Hampton acculturated, that finding itself rested on unquantifiable emotional and psychological factors. Putting an Indian into an eastern boarding school and making hair, dress, and deportment conform to that of other students could create the illusion that Indian culture had been erased. But evidence that tribal customs survived on campus appears behind the *Workman*'s "amusing and picturesque" descriptions of Indian encounters with "civil living." The Indian boys in the Wigwam slept on verandas in good weather, and when Indian girls were forced to wear feathered hats—having always associated head pieces only with warriors—they removed them at the first opportunity and they were not seen again. Anna Dawson recalled two Indian girls offering the choicest piece of a melon to the "Sun God."[62] Indian students often used native remedies and wore not brogans but moccasins, a footwear eventually adopted by many of the white staff, black students, and local residents.

The *Workman*'s reports of "an occasional mid-night war dance" also treated as merely childlike and colorful what may have been genuine resistance to the eastern school's indoctrination. Resident Hampton physician Martha M. Waldron revealed that Plains Indians sometimes experienced or sought vision quests: "The nervous paroxysms into which the victim is swept, or into which, as it sometimes seems, he throws himself, vary in detail, but in all cases there are pronounced hysterical symptoms. . . . These fits are looked upon with great awe by the more superstitious Indians, and, indeed, with more or less awe by nearly all Indians, and in their camp-life those which are able to throw themselves into such conditions are reverenced as having peculiar relations with the spirit world, and as *medicine-men* exercise a pernicious influence."[63]

During the Ghost Dance and subsequent December 1890 Wounded Knee Massacre in Dakota, Armstrong claimed that Hampton's returned Indians had totally identified with "civilization," since only one of eighty-two from the Dakota agencies—Sitting Bull's son-in-law Andrew Fox—danced with the ghosts. Yet after the massacre, which Armstrong termed a contest between "civilization and barbarism," the Indians on campus boycotted festivities on Indian Emancipation Day, when, as they said, "their own people were bleeding." A prayer meeting had to be substituted for the usual congratulatory speeches.[64]

Even the presumably nontraditional Indians of the school's Wigwam Council adjudicated infractions of campus rules brought before them on a somewhat different basis than did the white staff. In an 1889 case of an Indian stealing the collar from a fellow student's uniform, a minority opinion of councilmen cited the offender's ignorance of property rights as mitigation. The faculty approved this opinion. In another case, when two Indians pilfered potatoes at Shellbanks, the Wigwam Council found that "all of the boys that work on the farm think that while they are working they have the right to eat anything that is raised on the farm. These [Indian] boys thought they had the same right, and the Council does not think that they nor any of the other boys, who are guilty of the same offense, should be punished until [after] it has been thoroughly explained to all of them." However, the white Hampton growers overruled this majority opinion of Indians to argue that the case "seems more serious than the Council considered." Similarly, in two separate cases of Indians cursing a teacher, the council advised private apologies; but the faculty—either disregarding Indian shyness or indeed relying on it to inflict greater shame—insisted that their apologies be made before the entire school. Moreover, the general's boast that the Indian Council's penalties were harsher than the faculty's would have been rings hollow, since only two of the fifteen penalties that the faculty modified between April 1887 and January 1892 were reduced.[65]

In the final analysis, not only were conditions on the reservations out of Hampton's control, but despite the considerable efforts examined here it was not possible to measure either at home or at school, the Indians' internalization of the school's "civilizing" values and habits, much less their transmission of these ideas to others. Hampton portrayed the difficulties optimistically in order to ensure the survival not only of Indian education but of the race itself.

————

Historians of Native Americans have recently utilized models developed for immigrants and blacks to argue that returned Indian students actively and substantially helped their people to subvert the system.[66] But such redirection of protest into institutional channels may serve to underline the marginality of returned students and the lack of Indian self-determination. Many who view returned students as movers and shakers merely tack Indian names onto a pantheon of American heroes, as "cultural brokers" between conqueror and conquered. But emphasis on the "accomplishments" of returned Indian students dismisses the historical context in which they lived and deifies "progressive" Indians whose input to national culture as well as to their own communities was largely cosmetic, and helped to create a new world at odds with that of their ancestors.

For while immigrants and enslaved blacks worked out their destinies in a new country, a handful of educated Indians were returned to their own homelands, assigned to overturn a traditional life not found wanting despite military defeat and economic, cultural, religious, and political assault. Undue emphasis on the "successes" of returned students trivializes both their "failures" and the obstacles they faced.

Hamptonians arguing a hundred years ago that Indian students readily accepted and proselytized the ways of whites captured a constituency for an approach to Indian education that saw Indians who did not adopt these ways as "vanishing." But neither Indian traditions nor Indians have vanished. Elaine Goodale (Eastman), Hampton's former teacher of Indians, perceived not only the reality of gradual acculturation on the reservations, but also the unreality of expecting Hampton's Indians to embrace that process with missionary zeal. At her Indian school in Dakota, she observed the limited cooperation of former Hampton students: they "do not, and they will not, no matter what habits they have learned at school, live or dress or work much better or differently than those about them. . . . the returned student can dress neatly, live honestly, and work well, *up to a certain point,* without making himself conspicuous or exerting himself much beyond his neighbors. *Beyond that point scarcely one can be made to go,* even under the most favorable and encouraging circumstances."[67]

The Childs Investigation

Where the Holman Committee's criticisms had raised the issue of the Indian program's long-term effectiveness, the Childs Report a year or so later forced Hampton to justify its very existence. Reverend Thomas Spencer Childs,[68] chaplain for the Sons of the American Revolution and sometime negotiator for the Indian Office in its dealings with Indian tribes, was commissioned to investigate the treatment of Indians at Hampton after President Cleveland received a letter on September 26, 1887, from Caroline E. G. Colby (the widow of a Confederate veteran of the Old Soldiers' Home). Colby had lived near the Indian cottages for more than eight years, and despite being forbidden to visit townspeople, disgruntled or hungry Indians had often found sanctuary at her residence.[69] Julia St. Cyr (of Winnebago and French descent) was one of at least two Indians who voiced specific complaints to Colby about Hampton's Indian Department.

St. Cyr had attended Hampton twice before, the second time bringing six more pupils with her from Nebraska, and leaving in 1885 as one of its few Indian graduates. She had returned to Hampton as a graduate only two months before Colby's letter; Childs would later attribute St. Cyr's complaints to the fact that she had been readmitted "with no special plan for her return, and no position in view for her to occupy." Although her name was never mentioned in print by any of those involved in the subsequent controversy, St. Cyr herself wrote the Indian Commissioner on October 14, 1887, charging that she had received lower wages than blacks, that Hampton had refused to pay what it owed her, and that she had been made to scrub windows and cut wood, "which is a man's work." The Indian Office would later appoint St. Cyr as a teacher at the Sac and Fox agency although *Twenty-Two Years' Work* went so far as to term her record as "worse than that of any other Hampton student."[70]

Using information provided in large part by St. Cyr, Colby's letter was the outpouring of an uneducated but indignant private citizen on the spot. Her appeal to the ideals of '76 and her humanitarian concern for the Indian co-existed with prejudice against blacks and an institute that she believed favored them over Indians. Colby charged that the more nourishing food was not given to the Indian students; instead, it was sold on the open market or served to teachers. Moreover, Sioux Albert Marshall, a Catholic, had complained to her that for refusing to attend Episcopal services at St. John's, he was exiled to Shellbanks, where overwork had caused his lung to hemorrhage. Colby concluded her remarks to the president by telling him in her own colorful way,

You have spoken brave words for the Indian Race. *Leave them not* to the complete care, irresponsible to no one, to inflict punishment, which is a disgrace to Civilization, a young man put in a Guard House on a sweltering August Saturday afternoon because he wished to rest, no window but holes bored in to admit air the only Ventilation coming through said Holes. Another young man put in that small guard room by the Negro officers of the battallion Maj. Boykin, a stout Negro, black and can outstrut any white officer at Fortress Monroe. the boy had refused to give another indian a chew of tobacco & the one refused reported him. . . . When such earnest efforts are made to grab these indian children & bring them to a school with over five hundred colored students & the indian students made to [clean] grounds under a strutting colored temporary officer with gloves & cane and Umbrella in hot dusty weather thermometer at 104 degrees its time to speak out (and) as the old Liberty bell in "'76" Proclaim "Liberty throughout *all the land*." How quickly one official stroke of your pen, could send a discrete—*wise person* to look . . . how the table is spread . . . your kind heart will surely be mooved to . . . prevent so many deaths, and sanctimonious looks, prayers, & songs, will not hide this outrage enacted in the name of philanthrophy.[71]

President Cleveland instructed Secretary of Interior John W. Noble to research Colby's complaint, and on November 29 Acting Indian Commissioner Alexander Upshaw authorized Childs to "investigate the general management of the Indian Department of [Hampton], and the efficiency and faithfulness of the employees."[72] Childs came to Hampton on the first of December and stayed about a week.

Childs was apparently not predisposed against the school or its students, for he had participated in the Lake Mohonk Conference of 1886, served as a trustee of Tuskegee (1883–90), and claimed to be Armstrong's friend.[73] During his inspection he conferred with Frissell, Business Manager F. C. Briggs, Commandant Curtis, School Physician Martha Waldron, and other school employees (many of whom submitted written depositions). He also conducted two interviews with Indian students, one a large gathering and the other with a few students picked by school officers "with reference to their ability and disposition to give a fair and intelligent representation of the facts." Childs may never have spoken to St. Cyr, for the faculty minutes record without comment that she was "placed in confinement in a comfortably heated room near her own" during his visit.[74]

On his return to Washington, Childs interviewed Armstrong, who unwary of potential trouble continued his fundraising activities in the North. Childs then proceeded on to inspect Carlisle. It is unclear whether Armstrong knew that comparisons were to be made between these rival schools in "The Report on the Indian Schools at Hampton, Va., and Carlisle, Pa.": the examiner's official commission had not mentioned any visit to Carlisle, although Childs had indeed received additional "oral" instruction from Commissioner Atkins.

Later verbal crossfire notwithstanding, the thirty-three page Childs Report did not vilify either Hampton or its Indian program outright. For example, Childs accepted the peripheral but complimentary findings of an 1885 report by the Virginia Assembly, which had probed charges made by white and black mechanics and businessmen of Elizabeth City County that Hampton's tax exempt status was ruinous to local competition. He thus declared that Hampton's work for blacks was "exceptionally important and successful," and its benefits were "hard to exaggerate." Armstrong later wondered why a system so good for blacks was so bad for Indians. But Childs even praised some aspects of Hampton's Indian work, saying that its "most advanced Indians spoke in high terms of their [academic and industrial] instruction," that the methods of the special diet kitchen [for ill students] were "admirable," that medical care was "all that could be desired," and that Hampton's outing system was good, though not as good as Carlisle's.[75]

———

Overall, however, Childs's report not only upheld many of Colby's charges, but went beyond them. While a more objective, quiet, and coherent presentation of facts than Colby's appraisal of Hampton's Indian Department, the report nevertheless began by singling out for criticism the very same items that Colby had questioned: improper diet, the high Indian death rate, the use of a certain guardroom for punishment, and even the very concept of biracial education.

Such criticism, especially coming from another Presbyterian missionary, clearly touched sensitive areas in Armstrong. Although he first responded to Childs's report even before its submission to the commissioner on January 11, 1888, the affair would not be laid to rest for another eighteen months. During this time the principal sent documents supportive of Hampton's position to Chairman of the House Indian Committee Samuel W. Peel, to Commissioner Atkins, and to Albert Smiley and Eliphalet Whittlesey of the Board of Indian Commissioners. Confidential letters were also exchanged within an inner circle of Indian reformers. Specific controversial issues were addressed in the submitted documents, but the underlying meaning of the affair was discussed in the private letters written later, by leaders of public opinion on Indians and by Hamptonians.[76]

Despite having found the "almost universal testimony of pupils was that they had an abundance of food," Childs's report requested a "radical change" in Hampton's bill of fare with "a better supply of beef" and more diversified cooking methods. Like Colby, he also objected that milk, vegetables, and fruits were sold, or served to teachers rather than to students. Armstrong admitted that early vegetables were sold, at high prices, but expressed annoyance that Childs preferred Carlisle's menu. After describing a cornucopia at Hampton, Armstrong nevertheless hired a doctor to improve the diet. When Childs requested further changes, Armstrong replied that the inspector held no "capacity in the matter." This issue became deadlocked, with Childs asserting that Hampton's dietary changes had proven that changes were needed and Armstrong appearing to find Childs's concern for the precise content of the Indian students' diet somewhat bizarre given the actual starvation of many of their families out West.[77]

But the suggestion that poor diet was a cause of the Indians' bad health shocked school officials, who already shared Childs's concern about the high death rate, especially from tuberculosis. As early as 1879 Armstrong's annual report had recognized that the "danger to this experiment is in the matter of health. . . . The change from the cold bracing air of Dakota to this damp seaside air and lower altitude, is a risk."[78] The next year he attempted to improve the Indians' health by hiring Martha Waldron as physician and Cora Folsom as nurse, though the latter moved on to numerous other important duties in Hampton's Indian Department. A few years later Armstrong also built the King's Chapel Hospital primarily to doctor Indians.

Despite such measures, in 1887 Childs found that the thirty-one deaths of Indians at Hampton (more than three per year) represented a ratio of one in fifteen, while only one in twenty died at Carlisle, and that three-fourths of Hampton's Indians actually contracted their disease at school whereas only one-fourth did so at Carlisle. The inspector claimed that ninety-seven of a hundred Indians at Carlisle indicated they were in equal or better health at school than they had been at home, whereas fully two-thirds of Hampton's Indians stated their health was not as good as when they came to the marshy tidewater area. Apparently unimpressed by Dr. Waldron's statement that the death rate of Hampton's Indians was declining, none having died for thirteen months, the Childs Report—with its mild tone and moderate recommendations on the issues Colby had raised—closed with a drastic proposal: "the great fact for which Hampton is not responsible, and which it cannot control, is the climate. . . . But if facts [on the health and death rate of Hampton's Indian] are as stated, the question arises whether . . . it should give itself entirely to the work for which it was founded . . . the education of the colored race—while the Indian is removed to some institution where he may have equal educational advantages at less serious risk of life and health."[79]

Armstrong mockingly told Commissioner Atkins that this "proviso is well put in." He declared that the inspector had failed to catch the spirit of Hampton or to study its charter, since the report assumed the institute was devoted to Negro education through some fundamental law: "Its work for Negroes is incidental, not essential . . . the Indian has as much right here as the Negro and no one class [race] may prejudice the interests of another." Armstrong also questioned Childs's competence. Where, he asked, had Childs earned a degree in medicine? He even let slip that wealthy northerners found Hampton a popular resort area.[80]

Waldron addressed Childs's statement that only one-fifth of the black but fully half of the Indian students required hospitalization during the 1886-87 school year, explaining that this reflected the fact that a black student could be sent to his room to take medicine at prescribed intervals and dosages, while an Indian fresh off the reservation might take it all at once. It was also her opinion that seventeen of the thirty-one deceased Indians should be deleted from Childs's list because three had been infants of Hampton's married couples, not students, and fourteen had come from the Crow Creek and Lower Brule Agency, where tuberculosis was rampant. Hampton's health record would have been better than Carlisle's if Childs had excluded these Indians, but Childs retorted that Hampton's tactic of improving its health rate by striking out over half of the deaths was a "simple and effective" one.[81]

Armstrong asked more generally why Childs called for terminating the Indian program based on health risks, instead of stressing the improvements also noted. He judged that "knowing, as the inspector does, that more than four-fifths of Indian youth in the West have no such chances as are given here, and [that] to break up Hampton['s] Indian work is to destroy the prospects of scores of them, his suggestion that our Indians be removed—where they cannot go—seems hardly a humane one."[82] In retrospect, it appears that Hampton did learn how to compensate for climate and thereby dramatically reduce the Indian death rate. This was done by providing a better diet (as a result of the Childs affair), improving sanitary conditions on campus, more carefully screening the health of recruits in the field, sending sick Indians home, and avoiding high risk agencies, while recruiting from eastern tribes and more "advanced" Indians, who had already withstood the rigors of initial contact in western schools.[83]

Regarding Colby's point about the disciplinary mistreatment of Indian students, Childs from the start criticized Hampton's maintaining a guardroom under the administration building and asked the Indian Office to prohibit its use. Although not elaborating on his charge that it was a "fearful place of punishment," he would later defend this recommendation by asserting that the "dungeon," placed into service in the winter of 1884, only measured 6'6" long, 3'3" wide and 9'6" high, and "had no window or means of light whatsoever. . . . The only ventilation . . . was by some small holes in the [wooden] side wall at the top of the cell. These holes did not connect with fresh air but simply the [basement] area around the cell. On the pavement or floor of the cell was a bed-sacking with apparently a little straw or some such material in it. . . . When a boy was removed from the cell [school officers] stated that 'the stench was awful.'"[84] Forbidding the use of this guardhouse became the government's only official action on the entire Childs Report.

It seems rather quixotic, then, that Armstrong chose to make this dungeon issue the emblem of Childs's false witness against him. In his search for public exoneration, Armstrong slept there himself, and awoke to find the night to have been "uncomfortable, but not excessively severe" and that "very bad air was impossible." When the principal argued in a number of letters that the cell contained 247 rather than 200 cubic feet (at times blaming the inspector for the wrong figure school officers had supplied), Childs replied that "this does not change at all the essential facts."[85] Armstrong asserted that reading could be "done from the bottom as well as top of the door" and added that even he, let alone a sharp-eyed Indian, could see well enough "to make out a few lines." Nevertheless he did "improve" the dungeon's ventilation and lighting. Indeed the general worked tirelessly to overturn Atkin's order prohibiting the use of the cell, insisting that it was needed to fight whiskey, that an inmate was taken out for exercise three times daily and could affect his own release by confessing who sold him liquor, and that Childs's "wholesale condemnation is an exaggeration which seems . . . characteristic of his report."[86]

Although Childs saw no advantage in biracial education at Hampton, he did not disparage Indians associating with blacks, as such. He merely claimed that there were now enough English-speaking Indians to teach others and that blacks might actually make them more self-conscious about using the language. His one potentially damaging criticism of biracial education was that disciplinary regulations were "less strict [at Carlisle] than they possibly must be at Hampton, from the presence and relation of the two races."[87] Childs briefly compared Indians and blacks at Hampton in terms of the discrepancy in wages, the unsuitability of the blacks' diet for Indians and the two races' relative rates of hospitalization. While these comparisons all saw Indians at a disadvantage, and Childs failed to catch Hampton's enthusiasm for using black models in Indian education, his report did not employ race baiting to end the program, a stance that would hardly have befit his position as trustee of Tuskegee.

Therefore it seems baffling at first that Armstrong would write to Congressman Peel that "one of the strongest objections of the inspector to educating Indians at Hampton [was the] low Negro population" residing off campus. Nowhere did Childs mention an adverse effect on Indians by the proximity of blacks either on or off the campus, nor refer to factors good or bad in the surrounding community. Thus the principal lacked cause to tell Peel that "there are many low Negroes around Hampton, [but] our Indians have little or no contact with the outside colored population; considerable however with a fine class of southern people," or elsewhere to term Childs's alleged insinuation "an uncalled for reproach to the noble and friendly white citizens of Virginia."[88]

While Armstrong was thus trying to shift the focus of the debate, he revealed only to his confidants his belief that in back of the Childs investigation stood Richard Pratt, the "gentleman behind the woodpile," as Folsom later called him. The general wrote to Ogden in February that "Pratt recently declared in Washington [to the President and Secretary of War] in the presence of Mr. A. K. Smiley (of Lake Mohonk) and others, his intention to prevent any more Indians being sent to Hampton. Just before that, the Rev. Dr. Childs . . . had been sent to inspect Hampton and Carlisle, had made a report, most unjust to Hampton, inaccurate, professing to be fair, but evidently full of Pratt's ideas and concluded by, in effect, advising the breaking up of the Indian department of the Hampton School."[89] Armstrong inferred that while inspecting Carlisle Childs was poisoned against Hampton by Pratt. The four pages of the report devoted to Carlisle contained not a single negative comment or suggestion for improvement, and all of the advantages mentioned pertained to Carlisle and none to Hampton, even in areas where the latter was plainly superior, such as tracking returned students, medical facilities, and industrial plant. The existence of Pratt's influence on Childs was treated as common knowledge by Albert Smiley of Mohonk, Senator Henry L. Dawes, and Herbert Welsh and C. C. Painter of the IRA. The clearest indication of widespread belief in Childs's collusion with Pratt came from Mary McHenry Cox, principal of Philadelphia's Lincoln Indian School, who said that criticism of Hampton was made by Pratt "through a Dr. Childs."[90]

If indeed Pratt was using Childs to attack Hampton, Armstrong appears to have retaliated by misstating Childs. For it had been Pratt, not Childs, who had recently remarked to Cleveland about Hampton's "low Negro population," in comments made partly to defeat Armstrong's plan to bring Geronimo's Apache prisoners to Hampton (see chap. 3). Childs's investigation gave Pratt an opportunity not only to circumscribe but to kill Armstrong's Indian program, for Pratt continued to fear education with blacks would relegate Indians to a lower form of citizenship. Certainly, Hampton was encircled by politically hostile forces—a Democratic president who had personally asked for the school's investigation; an Indian Office under Atkins and Upshaw, both southerners; and a fiscally conservative House Indian Committee, some of whose members, snubbed by Armstrong at commencement, returned to Washington "full of wrath and ugly as sin."[91]

However much the recent Holman Committee had reminded both pioneers of eastern boarding schools of their common enemies, Pratt was slow to recognize what Senator Dawes now warned of the rivalry between the two schools: "if one breaks down the other will follow very soon. They must stand together."[92] Finding a clear and present danger, Smiley wrote Armstrong on February 14 that the House Indian Committee chaired by Holman's successor, Peel (D. Arkansas), might use Childs's report to withdraw appropriations not only from Hampton but from all eastern schools. Smiley had "hotly discussed" the matter with Childs and with Pratt, who was in Washington, and told Armstrong to proceed to the capital so "that we [might] devise some scheme to counteract the report."[93] The extraordinary "scheme" arrived at was for Smiley and Eliphalet Whittlesey to use their seats on the Board of Indian Commissioners to write a report offsetting Childs's. Although Whittlesey was surprised at being left alone in Washington to compose the March 1888 report while Smiley, "who had taken the lead in all the discussions," went North, he obediently wrote to Armstrong, "My remarks are somewhat repetitious & weaker than yours [of a few days earlier]. If after looking [the report] all over you think it necessary that I do it again I will." Whittlesey also wished he had "seen every Indian student privately & had asked him the same questions that Dr. C. put to them. . . . But it is after all not necessary."[94]

In fact the Smiley-Whittlesey Report made no pretense at neutrality, wanting Hampton's opponents to know that the Childs Report did not represent the views of the Board of Indian Commissioners. The new report relied on the school's principal, staff, and expert witnesses for testimony, and concluded that closing the institute's Indian Department would be a "great calamity . . . followed we fear by the breaking up of all Eastern Indian schools." Leading reformers of Indian affairs thus indicated that they needed Hampton's influence as much as Hampton now needed them, and that saving its Indian program would ultimately save Carlisle from Pratt. Indeed, Pratt later told Childs that he had kept his mouth shut when Smiley and Whittlesey inspected Carlisle, "knowing that if I opened it at all it would be a serious case."

Hampton's Helen Ludlow had correctly perceived that the captain had "o'er leaped his saddle."[95] In the face of well-aimed letters by the commissioners, Welsh, Ogden, and others, the Democratic legislators kept out of the controversy. The House Indian Committee's threat to Hampton's funding withered from the heat, as Peel did not challenge Smiley.[96]

––––––

The Childs controversy then lay dormant from April 1888 to the spring of 1889. Up to this point, little mention of it appeared in the principal's annual reports to the trustees or to the commissioner, or in the *Workman*. Confidential letters had apparently been treated confidentially. Were it not for Atkin's order against the guardroom and for some improvement in the Indians' diet, Childs might as well not have come to Hampton at all, for no one had acted upon his ultimate recommendation. Seemingly content to be repudiated by official silence, Childs had nothing more to say.

Yet with much to lose and only the use of the guardroom to gain, Armstrong once more attempted to dredge up the dungeon. Emboldened by the Republicans' return to power, the general in April 1889 wrote to Indian Commissioner John H. Oberly, who had replaced Armstrong's old adversary, Atkins. The principal's quest to reinstate the guardroom only gained him a new adversary. As if the guardroom issue were the crux of the Childs Report, the next month Armstrong remonstrated with still Interior Secretary Noble that the "offensive and untruthful report of the Rev. T. S. Childs be no longer sustained by the government; its adoption being irritating, humiliating, and against the interest of good discipline in this school." But as one historian has pointed out, "The report had never been 'adopted' by anyone and was in limbo so far as the Bureau and the Department of the Interior were concerned." Armstrong soon learned Noble's real feelings about the guardroom: an acting commissioner wrote the general that, since the secretary considered its use in any form contrary to his "feeling of humanity," any request concerning it must be submitted to him.[97]

The Childs controversy only became public knowledge in June 1889, when the Smiley-Whittlesey Report was included in the annual report of the Commissioner of Indian Affairs. Then on June 17, the Washington *Star* published excerpts from this counter report and the story was given national coverage by the Associated Press. At this point Childs complained to Secretary Noble that his report had been made more than eighteen months ago and "the public knew nothing of it, and would have known nothing of it, if it had not been brought to light by the friends of General Armstrong, by their public attack upon it."[98]

At the same time that Armstrong described Smiley and Whittlesey as "laying low," Pratt remained silent, but privately wrote Childs that their document "is outrageous. I can point out half a dozen absolute lies. Its publication when your report is pigeonholed is one of the most flagrant pieces of chicanery I ever knew."[99] The annual report of the Indian Office to the secretary of interior contained the report of Smiley and Whittlesey but not the one the office itself had commissioned. On June 17, in what Armstrong supporters called "Dr. Childs' Second Attack," the inspector addressed a formal defense to Clinton Fisk, chairman of the Board of Indian Commissioners.[100] Fisk was not likely to give satisfaction to Childs, however, since it was he who authorized the counter report, and who had served, along with Whittlesey, as Armstrong's colleague in the Freedmen's Bureau. Nonetheless Childs gave his version of the events that brought him to Hampton, the conditions under which he completed his task, his findings, and the disposition of his report.

Without backing down on any specific point but not repeating his call to dismantle Hampton's Indian program, Childs spent half of this rebuttal on the guardroom ruling, which Armstrong had made the embodiment of his criticisms of Hampton. Baring his moral fists, the pastor called the dungeon a "place of torment," and said that if "it was not a 'fearful place of punishment' I have failed to hear of one this side of the 'Black Hole' of Calcutta." He found "remarkable" Smiley and Whittlesey's finding that the place "contains more cubic feet than a state-room on a Potomac steamer," since a "tomb may contain more cubic feet than a state-room and not be desirable for a living child." He presented statements from prison wardens who used no like cell for "abandoned criminals," and told Fisk, "the amazing thing to me is that the Board of Indian Commissioners who have no reason for existence unless they stand between the Indian and wrong, can defend and publish to the world their defense of this mode and means of discipline for Indian children."[101]

Childs believed that his report spoke for Hampton's Indian students, and he told Fisk, "That important changes were made as the result of my visit is clear from the fact that [an Indian] representative of the school, standing among the first in the respect and confidence of the officers of the institution, came to Washington bringing me the acknowledgments and thanks of the Indians for their improved condition." Even before Childs so openly asserted to Fisk that most Hampton Indians were on his side of the controversy, Armstrong had essentially admitted the same, by saying that Childs's "seeming acceptance of the complaints of the Indian students [was] unfortunate."[102]

Although Armstrong had called the Indians who complained to Childs of mistreatment at Hampton as "fickle, fertile in grievances," after eighteen months of silence, the *Workman* devoted more than half of its July issue to demonstrating their support in "The Indians Speak for Themselves." It featured a letter of denial from the Indian with whom Childs had spoken in Washington. Omaha Thomas Sloan, the editor of *Talks and Thoughts* and an officer in the student battalion, had just become Hampton's first Indian valedictorian (1889), and would later gain prominence as well as the notoriety discussed earlier, as the only Hampton Indian to become a lawyer. He disputed Childs's description of their encounter, explaining, "I went to Washington to be present at the meeting of the Indian commissioners. Rev. Dr. Childs was present and I went and spoke with him. The meeting was friendly and I told him changes had been made in the diet. I did not go [to Washington] to meet Dr. Childs—neither did I carry any message of thanks or otherwise from the boys to him."[103] Sloan and five other influential Indian students certified that none of Hampton's Indians had thanked the inspector, although conceding that some spoke up at the time of Childs's 1887 inspection, since "complaints were asked for." But they claimed that the inspector gave "a very wrong impression" of an Armstrong policy which in reality treated "us students as men. There is a complaining element among us at all times. Still, these often leave the school with many regrets. . . . Here for the first time many have learned to restrain themselves, and for that of which so much complaint is made they are thankful."

Sloan's statement also defended Hampton's diet and asserted that Childs had misconstrued disciplinary procedures, for it was the Indians' Wigwam Council itself that recommended solitary confinement in the guardroom. As president of the council, Sloan claimed access to prisoners, and the prisoner who had been incarcerated the longest was a relative, whose experience proved that the place "was not 'absolutely' dark for he spent most of . . . the day reading papers which I furnished him." Sloan later secured an affidavit from this relative, Henry Monacravie, who did "truthfully state that there was sufficient light [to read] in the guard house," which he did while confined there. The *Workman* claimed that all fifty of the Wigwam's residents endorsed the published statement so far as they knew the facts. With Indian students rallying behind Hampton in print, Armstrong wrote Ogden that Childs will be "very mad & strike out as hard as he can. He has a ready pen—But he is hit hard by Sloan."[104]

Childs struck back in the Philadelphia *Press* of July 17, and in September the *Workman,* although regretting "the necessity for re-opening this most unfortunate controversy," honored Childs's request for equal time and reprinted his letter to the *Press*. In it he declared that Sloan's statement was "in direct contradiction to all he said to me when [I was] in Hampton"; he was "most severe in his complaints of the treatment of the Indians: he made stronger statements than any other man in respect to the horrors of the dungeon." To Sloan's claim that the guardhouse was light enough to read in Childs retorted that "It would be quite as easy and quite as correct to say . . . that there was no dungeon there." Sloan's "further statement that he never came to see me in Washington is equally wild. He came to see me; he spent more than an hour with me; he dined with me in the presence of several others whose recollections . . . [are] distinct." In what proved to be the last printed round of the controversy, Childs called upon Hampton to join him in asking the Interior Department to publish his own report, and to investigate any inaccuracies; the *Workman* ignored the inspector's request and countered that the entire campus, including the dungeon, was always open to public inspection.[105]

In the end, the Childs-Sloan dispute enabled Armstrong to adopt the position that "If Sloan is not reliable he is not a competent witness against Hampton. If he is reliable . . . we must believe his own voluntary public statement of his position." "Fearfully sat on," as the general said, Childs flailed uselessly; he did not know of private letters suggesting that Sloan was neither a reliable nor willing spokesman for Hampton. For example, Sloan wrote Armstrong on November 28, that "the painful part to me was the attempt [on the part of Hampton staff] to make me write something or I would be held up as a supporter of Mr. Childs' report."[106] Sloan had just responded to Armstrong's earlier request for a second letter by saying that he did "not care to make any reply to Dr. C's letter unless you think it best. I do not deny having dined with him [at Childs's request]. . . . I did not suppose he would make such a rise of that occasion." Armstrong privately conceded that "Sloan's admissions to [Childs] were no doubt the basis of his statements." Indeed, a snookering of Sloan by Childs may have even happened as indirectly as Ludlow speculated: that Sloan "bowed or smiled" when Childs said that Indians ought to be thankful to him.[107] But clearly, Sloan would have had no reason to dine with Childs had he in truth shared Hampton's view of the inspector as a bitter enemy.

———

The salvos that followed the publishing of the counter report gave way to a quiet summer. The mood in the Childs-Pratt camp was one of despair and mutual commiseration. Childs quite probably believed that having reported just what he had seen at Hampton, he was denied final justice. The Democratic administration which had commissioned him had brushed him aside even before the public swept it from office; Secretary Noble was Childs's only remaining champion of any weight. Pratt attempted to explain to Childs the futility of his position in July: "You have given Armstrong the opportunity he is ever seeking and the best he ever had to pose as a martyr. The whole case as far as Hampton and Armstrong are concerned was a shrewd utilization of your report and yourself to catch public attention, sympathy and money. . . . His plans always contemplate owning men and their consciences. . . . You are too straight forward to deal with such a man." Indeed Smiley had suggested this very strategy to Armstrong seventeen months earlier: "We have now a good opportunity for all Friends of [the] School to say a good word for you, which we couldn't have done had you not been attacked."[108]

With the major eastern press swayed by Hampton and its allies—Boston's by Armstrong himself, New York's by Ogden, Philadelphia's by Welsh and John Wanamaker, and Washington's by C. C. Painter—Pratt warned the inspector against taking matters further: "You will not be able I fear to get a fair show under such circumstances." Moreover, Pratt wrote Childs after the Indian Conference in October 1889 that "The situation at Mohonk warranted you staying away. . . . [A full day's proceedings were] manipulated by Armstrong. At the Conference he made a dead set at the politicians and exhibited all the qualities of one of the foremost politicians of the country. This was noted by some of the oldest and wisest heads there. . . . Smiley read your letter, but made a preliminary speech in favor of Armstrong and his school, asserting his own ability to tell a good school, which was applauded all over, inasmuch as everyone was his guest."[109] Smiley then deleted all mention of the Childs controversy from the published proceedings.

Armstrong's ultimate handling of the Childs affair called for public vindication from those "whose souls are lighted." The way Armstrong advertised and profited from the threat of scandal once he isolated and quieted his distractors, Pratt saw as a juncture where politics met psyche. As if the affair could not be reconciled with Armstrong's conscience unless he had the last word by reinstating a guardroom of questionable importance in itself, the general's final public action in the matter was yet another attempt to reverse Noble's prohibition of its use. He told Ogden in the fall of 1889 that the secretary's refusal to acknowledge his letters "confirms the disgrace on the school and me personally: Sec. Noble is bound to be courteous & is not; to be fair & is not. Today he is doing more to mortify me than any man in this country ever did. Childs saw and believed; Mr. Noble has not seen & yet believes. Don't tell him this. I do not need him. In a few years he will be a dead politician. . . . in time, [I] may make some remark in Sec. Noble's political epitaph."[110]

Calling the controversy "one of the harsh cutting things that brands itself into one's life never to be removed," Armstrong thanked Ogden for "doing so much to erase the only stain that my life in this country seems to have brought." He concluded that "The Childs attack has strengthened the inner circle of friends; brought money & helped rather than hurt us financially, but the more remote public is somewhat shaken up & does not distinguish past and present, and, in general, there's a 'bad smell' about the name of Hampton & its work & ideas."[111]

The Widening Controversies of the 1890s

Despite Armstrong's politically successful handling of the Childs's affair, criticisms of eastern Indian schools re-emerged in January 1890 with a very imprecise printed charge attributed to Secretary of the Sioux Commission Irving Miller, that 30 to 70 percent of Indian students from Carlisle and Hampton "die within four years of their return home, die like sheep with the murrain." Armstrong responded in the pamphlet "Another Attack on Eastern Schools," calling attention to the vastly improved health of his Indian students. After pointing out that Hampton's Indian program had experienced a lower death rate over its entire eleven years than the lowest rate—30 percent—claimed by Miller for four years, Armstrong asserted that only three Indians arriving at Hampton since 1885 had died after returning home, and that only four had died at school. The pamphlet also included a letter by Standing Rock missionary Mary C. Collins, who stressed the generally high mortality rate of Indians and said that as many of the students in her own village "die in and from the boarding schools and day schools at home, as from eastern schools."[112] Miller never followed up his charge against Hampton.

Less glancing were the continuing attacks on government funding of eastern schools like Hampton. The Holman controversy of 1886 and the Childs investigation in 1888 were followed in 1892, 1895, 1896, and 1900 by congressional threats to cut off Hampton's funding. In 1892 a newly elected Democratic Congress proposed to eliminate eastern Indian schools as part of a general economic retrenchment. Lobbying by Frissell, Mary McHenry Cox of the Lincoln Institute, and the IRA's C. C. Painter helped to prevent this, as did the Herbert Welsh article, "A Crisis in the Cause of Indian Education." Welsh defended eastern schools with Hampton's now familiar domino principle: "the cause of Indian education is a unit. The western schools stand or fall with the eastern schools."[113]

This argument, so effective against those who would divide and so conquer eastern and western schools, was no longer relevant in the later 1890s, when a new assault arose against schools that contracted with the government to educate Indians.[114] Interestingly, in the late 1880s Armstrong had anticipated the issue that Frissell would face in the mid-1890s: the isolation of Hampton's Indian program if nongovernment, missionary schools were abandoned under Protestant influence to spite the Catholics (see chap. 3). Between 1895 and 1900, at a time when Hamptonians found it necessary to praise Catholic Indian work, Congress was indeed phasing out the contract system with the blessing of Hampton's usual best friends—Protestants, Republicans, and leaders of Indian reform organizations, as well as the Indian Office. Of the seventy-one contract schools that existed in 1889, only Hampton survived the turn of the century.

On each of the three occasions (1895, 1896 and 1900) when Hampton was cut from government appropriations because of its status as a contract school, Frissell won its reinstatement with the nominal support of his old allies. He claimed that although a contract school, Hampton was exceptional since it was not sectarian. Its seventeen trustees represented six different denominations, with none holding a majority; it had

had Catholic teachers, students, and unnamed donors; moreover, Hampton refused help from religious organizations, and received aid from the Peabody Fund, which did not assist sectarian schools.[115]

Catholics, however, were unimpressed by Frissell's statements and chided Protestant Indian reformers and legislators for their inconsistent position. Father Joseph A. Stephens, director of the Bureau of Catholic Missions (1884–1901), complained in 1900 that "Congress has been guilty of the rankest discrimination in renewing the appropriation for the Hampton School [while seeing] sectarianism whenever a Catholic institution is involved."[116] Indeed, Hampton's principal was a Congregational minister, its board had never included a Catholic, it actively trained students as Protestant missionaries, and, under other circumstances, it gloried in its evangelical Protestant charter. Thus Hampton's retention of government funding embarrassed both reformers and the government, and set a precedent for Catholics to resurrect their claim to a contract system.

———

In retrospect, changes in reform thinking as well as the controversies discussed here seriously weakened Hampton's Indian program. On the positive side, the school was forced to find the most suitable Indian candidates for an eastern education, to keep more careful records, to refine and recast its theories on Indian education, to reform real deficiencies in its treatment of Indian students, and generally to become a more cohesive, if less open, institution.

On balance, none of Hampton's victories was clearcut just as none of its defeats cut clear. Indictments made against the institute—and often against eastern schools in general in the 1880s—lingered. Nebulous charges of compulsive recruitment, harsh physical treatment, unhealthy climate, malnutrition, high mortality both at school and at home, and reversion to tribalism (or its opposite, disaffection), became part of the general aura surrounding Hampton. Moreover, the mainstream of Indian education had fallen increasingly out of sympathy with Hampton's philosophy by the arrival of the twentieth century. As a black school, an eastern school, a nongovernment school, a contract school, and a mission school, Hampton could no longer find common cause with other institutions against attacks on all these fronts. Thus its apparent magnanimity was often defensive posturing: Hampton's tolerant acceptance of different types of schools and reform efforts regardless of racial, sectional, political, or religious boundaries was motivated as much by a quest for survival as by a spirit of liberalism.

Notes

1. "Indian Attendance at Hampton Institute," HUA; Jean Scott Sampson, "Hampton Normal and Agricultural Institute: Education of Native Americans, 1878–1923," *Journal of the Afro-American Historical and Genealogical Society* 9 (Summer 1988); *ARCIA* in *The Red Man, His Present and Future* 8 (Oct. 1889): 1.

2. SCA, "Lessons from the Hawaiian Islands," p. 216; *SW* 14 (Feb. 1885): 19; SCA, "Report of Hampton School," *ARCIA* 1883, p. 172. See roster of Hampton's married couples, (n.d.), box 31, Indian Collection, HUA.

3. Wilbert H. Ahern, "'The Returned Indians': Hampton Institute and Its Indian Alumni, 1879–1893," *Journal of Ethnic Studies* 10 (Winter 1983): 108.

4. Folsom, "Indian Days," p. 94; Josephine E. Richards, "The Training of the Indian Girl as the Uplifter of the Home," *NEA* 1900, pp. 701–4; Indian Teachers Faculty, Mar. 12, 1883, HUA; *Twenty-Two Years' Work*, pp. 388–91, 394, shows that Sioux Philip and Kate Counsellor, and their baby Charlie, came about the same time, becoming Hampton's first Indian family.

5. *Twenty-Two Years' Work*, p. 388; Sarah Kinney to SCA, June 24, 1886, HUA; Folsom, "Indian Days," p. 93.

6. SCA, *The Indian Question*, 1883, p. 22; Ahern, "The Returned Indians," p. 104.

7. SCA, "Commencement Address" in *SW* 16 (June 1887): 64. When in June 1880 the *National Republican* charged that there were "no full blood Indians [in government schools] with the free consent of [their] parents," Hampton's response—that its Indians were always obtained with parental permission—was as much an overstatement as the assertion to the contrary. See *SW* 9 (June 1880): 66.

8. Folsom, "Random Recollections," p. 125, in Unsorted Indian Box 3, Indian Collection, HUA; Gravatt, "Some Questions Answered," *SW* 14 (Jan. 1885): 11; "Hampton's Early Indian Days," in *SW* 39 (June 1910): 335; White Thunder to Son, Apr. 17, 1880, box 37, "Letters Related," Indian Collection, HUA.

9. "Incidents," *SW* 10 (Feb. 1881): 19, 10 (Dec. 1881): 122; Luther Standing Bear, *My People the Sioux*, ed. by E. A. Brininstool (Boston, 1928), p. 122; Folsom in *Twenty-Two Years' Work*, pp. 488–89.

10. Standing Bear, *My People the Sioux*, pp. 128–31 and *Land of the Spotted Eagle* (Lincoln, 1933), pp. 231–32; Elaine Goodale Eastman, *Pratt: The Red Man's Moses*, p. 73.

11. Helen Townsend, "Early Indian Outings," p. 2, box 28, Indian Affairs, Hampton Institute Staff, Indian Collection, HUA; Report of Agent John G. Gasmann at Crow Creek, *ARCIA* 1885, p. 21; ? to Gregg, Dec. 12, 1921, box 63, Gregg, Funds for Indian Education, HUA.

12. Editorial remarks, *SW* 16 (Oct. and Dec. 1887): 103, 125; J. C. Robbins, "Incidents," *SW* 8 (Jan. 1879): 7.

13. Minutes of the Indian Teachers Faculty, Oct. 1882 and Dec. 17, 1884, Indian Collection, HUA; Editorial remarks, *SW* 16 (Nov. 1887): 113, 14 (Feb.

1885): 19, and 15 (Sept. 1886): 98; Robert F. Berkhofer, Jr., *Salvation and the Savage* (New York, 1972), p. 114; Muir, "Indian Education," p. 78.

14. Folsom, "Indian Days," p. 56; Charles Eastman, *From Deep Woods to Civilization*, p. 96; Andrus to T. E. Elder, June 29, 1912, in Arphus Watt's student file, HUA.

15. *Twenty-Two Years' Work*, p. 450; Richard Whalen and Sam White Bear to Moton, Dec. 16, 1909, Whalen's student file, HUA.

16. SCA, *SW* 10 (Nov. 1881): 109.

17. R. L. Brunhouse, "A History of Carlisle School: A Phase of Government Indian Policy, 1879–1918" (Ph.D. diss., University of Pennsylvania, 1935), pp. 87–88. Brunhouse argues that the commissioner wanted to halt the growth of nonreservation schools by limiting the number of students eligible to attend them. Commissioner William A. Jones to Superintendent of Indian Schools Estelle Reel, June 27, 1901, RG75, NARA; Minutes of Faculty Meetings, June 15, 1910, HUA.

18. HBF, "Annual Report," *SW* 24 (June 1895): 88.

19. SCA to Commissioner T. J. Morgan, Apr. 14, 1890, RG75, item 25078, NARA. Armstrong said that 33 percent of the Indian students from Winnebago had done "bad" or "poor" compared to 7 percent from all other agencies. See also SCA to Morgan, Aug. 24, 1890, HUA. Agent John Gasmann to SCA, Sept. 19, 1884, HUA; J. J. Gravatt, "Some Questions Answered," *SW* 14 (Jan. 1885): 11.

20. HBF, "Annual Report," *SW* 24 (June 1895): 88.

21. "Roster of Indian Students," HUA; HBF, "Annual Report," *SW* 30 (1901): 288. Hampton worked with Episcopal missionary the Rev. Merrill to train Oneida students for his creamery. See also "Incidents," *SW* 22 (Feb. 1893): 36; and "The Oneida," *SW* 51 (Jan. 1922): 22. Eli Skenandore to Andrus, Jan. 21, 1919, Skenandore's student file, HUA; "Hampton Incidents," *SW* 50 (Oct. 1921): 478; "Onon-gwat-go," *SW* 36 (Mar. 1907): 133; HBF, "Report of Hampton School," *ARCIA* 1888, p. 368; "Sixty-Five Tribes Represented at Hampton, 1878–1923," HUA.

22. HBF, "Report of Hampton School," *ARCIA* 1894, p. 414; "Sixty-Five Tribes Represented," HUA; Clara Snow to SCA, Jan. 30, 1893, HUA; Jeanne Guillemin, *Urban Renegades: The Cultural Strategy of American Indians* (New York, 1975).

23. HBF, "Annual Report," *SW* 24 (June 1895): 88; "Sixty-Five Tribes Represented," HUA; HBF, "Report of Hampton School," *ARCIA* 1896, p. 407.

24. For example, Hampton's Josephine Richards reported in the 1885 *ARCIA*, p. 288, that of seventy-seven Indian boys and forty-one girls, thirty boys and thirty-two girls were between one-fourth and seven-eighths white. In theory at least, even Indians whose white ancestry was not Anglo-Saxon, like Antoine Giard, who was one-eighth Anishinabe but seven-eighths French, or Augustine Gonzales, who was one-fourth Navajo but three-quarters Spanish and Mexican, had more in common with English-speaking culture than did traditional Indians. See the student files of Antoine Giard and Augustus Gonzales, HUA.

25. The Minutes of Faculty Meetings for March 14, 1911, said that black "pupils at Hampton are getting darker. Dr. Frissell explains this by the fact that the lighter students are apt to go to Academic schools and the darker to industrial schools, and that the country Negroes are darker than the city Negroes, and therefore our students are growing darker since it has been our policy to choose them from the country rather than from the city."

26. Throughout this section the term "white Indian" is used to refer to mixed blooded Indians who appeared white and the term "black Indian" is used to refer to both mixed blooded Indians who appeared black or Negroes who were adopted into an Indian tribe.

27. Ebenezer Kingsley's student file, HUA. See the student files of Leta Meyers and Amos Lamson, HUA, and HBF to Superintendent J. A. Buntin, Mar. 15, 1912, HUA, for government regulations on Indian students having a small amount of Indian lineage.

28. See Eva May Simons's student file, HUA.

29. See Virgie Goings's and Laura Johnson's student files, HUA. The black Indians not mentioned in the following pages are Octavene Davis, Louisa Browner, Grace Bunn, Josephine Smith, Henry Thompson and James Prettyhair Williams.

30. "A Black Hawk," *SW* 11 (Jan. 1882): 7; *Twenty-Two Years' Work*, p. 382; "Our 'Bad' Boy," *SW* 17 (Jan. 1888): 11. Several years after his release from prison, Black Hawk, along with four other Indians, was convicted of murdering a white family. See Frank Black Hawk's student file, HUA, for: "Five Men in It," Minneapolis *Tribune*, May 16, 1897, "Five Reds Held for Trial," St. Paul *Globe*, May 17, 1897, and "Black Hawk Dead," Bismarck *Tribune*, Apr. 29, 1901.

31. Lone Wolf (Mamay-day-Te) to Commissioner (William A. Jones), Apr. 13, 1901, RG75, item 21638, NARA; Agent James F. Randlett to Commissioner (Jones), May 15, 1901, RG75, item 26760, NARA. See Lone Wolf's student file, HUA for "Is It Right?," *The Red Man and Helper* 18 (Oct. 16, 1903), for *The Chilocco Farmer and Stock Grower*, Nov. 15, 1903, and for Lone Wolf to HBF, Jan. 15, 1912; *The Indian School Journal* 12 (Oct. 1912).

32. Virginia Ransom to Scholarship Donor, (n.d.), Ransom's student file, HUA.

33. Superintendent C. J. Crandall to Benjamin Mossman, Feb. 29, 1908, Mossman to HBF, Mar. 4, 1908, HBF to Commissioner F. E. Leupp, Mar. 9, 1908, in item 17126, RG75, NARA; Ransom to Gleason, Mar. 6, 1908, Ransom's student file, HUA; Acting Commissioner C. F. Larrabee to HBF, Jan. 25, 1908, RG75, Hampton Box, NARA.

34. See Cynthia Powdrill's student file, HUA, especially Two Guns to Andrus, Aug. 22 and Oct. 15, 1918, and July 20, 1919; Lone Wolf to HBF, Jan. 2, 1911, Lone Wolf's student file, HUA.

35. William Scoville, (n.d.), typewritten letter in Eva Shawnee's student file, HUA; Wilma King, "Multicultural Education at Hampton Institute—The Shawnees: A Case Study, 1900–1923," *Journal of Negro Education* 57 (Fall 1988): 524–35; Hunter (King), "Coming of Age: Frissell," p. 96. Other

members of her family had varying occupations: Eva married a black business-man and became a domestic science teacher at Langston University; Lafay-ette taught black and Indian students among the Seminoles, and then agri-culture at Langston University before becoming a public high school principal; Julia was the housewife of a blind composer, and Lydia married an undertak-er and used her degree from Dixie Hospital to become a nurse serving both black and white patients. Four of the Shawnee family died in an insane asy-lum—Lafayette, Julia, Lydia, and Rebecca. For additional information see the individual student files at HUA.

36. May G. Ellinwood to Andrus, Sept. (?), 1916, in Nancy Coleman's student file, HUA; Eli Bird to Andrus, Sept. 18, 1917, and James Hender-son to Andrus, Jan. 31, 1918, both in Calvin Coleman's student file, HUA. Superintendent of Cherokee Schools James Henderson revealed that the Colemans were "only one-fourth degree Indian blood. The Indians at Cher-okee receive them as Negroes and so do the whites." Andrus to Emma L. Higgins, Mar. 2, 1917, in Nancy Coleman's student file, HUA; Elizabeth Bender Roe to Andrus, May 24, 1915, in Cynthia Powdrill's student file, HUA. For other black Indians refused employment in the Indian Service, see the student files of Emma Corn, Crafton C. Reed, and Henry Thompson. Andrus had also theorized that Coleman might superintend or cook lunches at some Indian school—a waste of her training—or that she might stay at Hampton for a course in graduate sewing. Andrus reported that Coleman had wanted to "stick to her Indian and does not like the idea of Dixie." The oth-er black Indian girls who attended Dixie Hospital were Cynthia Powdrill, Carrie Warren, Lydia Shawnee, and Emma Corn.

37. Bertha Petters, Cheyenne Mennonite Mission, to Andrus, July 17, 1912, Agnes Williams, Cheyenne Mennonite Mission, to Andrus, Apr. 9, 1912, An-drus to Petters, July 25, 1912, all in Carrie Warren's student file, HUA.

38. See Emma Corn's student file, HUA.

39. Editorial, "The Opening of Classes," *SW* 34 (Nov. 1905): 579.

40. "Letter from the Agent at Fort Sill (C. B. Hunt) to Captain (RHP)," in *SW* 8 (Feb. 1879): 19; *SW* 8 (June 1879): 71.

41. "Answer to the N.Y. *Tribune*," *SW* 8 (July 1879): 74.

42. *SW* 15 (Apr. 1886): 37; Muir, "Indian Education," pp. 64–65; Ting-ey, "Blacks and Indians Together," pp. 271–72; Gilcreast, "Pratt," pp. 146–53. Gilcreast shows that committee members, especially Holman, had a fixation about economy; Ryan had earlier opposed the entire idea of Indian education. U.S. House, *Congressional Record* 17 pt. 4 (Mar. 10, 1886), pp. 2264–66 and (Mar. 17, 1886), p. 2464, excerpted in *SW* 17 (Apr. 1888) and *The Morning Star* 6 (Mar. 1886).

43. Welsh to Cutcheon, Mar. 26, 1886, IRA Papers. Opposition to Hol-man from various sources can be seen in *Are Eastern Industrial Schools a Fail-ure?* (Philadelphia, 1886) and *SW* 15 (Apr. 1886). In his own maverick style, Pratt showed up at the congressional hearings with seventeen of his educat-ed Indians. Ludlow in *Are Eastern Industrial Schools a Failure?*, pp. 19–20; Painter to Welsh, May 20, 1886, IRA Papers.

44. Ludlow in *Are Eastern Industrial Schools a Failure?*, pp. 10–14.

45. Lewis Meriam et al, *The Problem of Indian Administration* (Baltimore, 1928), p. 673; Folsom, "Indian Days," p. 133; Elaine Goodale Eastman, *Pratt: The Red Man's Moses*, p. 71. *Ten Years' Work* was assembled to meet an 1888 congressional attack on Indian education similar to Holman's. See Minutes of Faculty Meetings, Jan. 21, 1888, HUA. Andrus, "Changing Indian Conditions," *SW* 51 (Jan. 1922): 25; Folsom, "Random Recollections," p. 138, box on Folsom separate from the Indian Collection, HUA.

46. See Thomas W. Alford, *Civilization;* Raymond J. DeMallie, "George Bushotter: The First Lakota Ethnographer," and Douglas R. Parks, "James Murie: Pawnee Ethnographer," both in Margot Liberty, *American Indian Intellectuals* (St. Paul, 1978); Rideout, *William Jones;* Norma Kidd Green, *Iron Eyes Family: The Children of Joseph LaFlesche* (Chicago, 1969); Sarah D. McAnulty, "Angel DeCora: American Indian Artist and Educator," *Nebraska History* 57 (Summer 1976); Donald L. Parman, "J. C. Morgan: Navajo Apostle of Assimilation," *Journal of the National Archives* 4 (Summer 1972); Valerie Sherer Mathes, "Susan LaFlesche Picotte: Nebraska Indian Physician, 1865–1915," *Nebraska History* 63 (Winter 1982); Jerry E. Clark and Martha Ellen Webb, "Susette and Susan La Flesche: Reformer and Missionary," in James A. Clifton ed, *Being and Becoming Indian: Biographical Studies of North American Frontiers* (Chicago, 1989). Tingey's "Blacks and Indians Together" has sections on Jones, LaFlesche, Dawson, Sloan, and the Owls. For prominent Anishinabes see Paulette Fairbanks Molin, "Training the Hand, the Head, and the Heart: Indian Education at Hampton Institute," *Minnesota History* 51 (Fall 1988).

47. Ogden to HBF, June 28, 1909, HUA; Susan LaFlesche to Secretary of Interior, June 28 and July 7, 1909, LaFlesche's student file, HUA.

48. See Alford, *Civilization,* p. 137 and *Twenty-Two Years' Work*, pp. 256, 363–64, 369.

49. Elaine Goodale Eastman, *Pratt: The Red Man's Moses*, p. 71. Peabody blames the low rate of graduation among blacks and Indians on high mortality at the elementary level and the fact that many students departed as soon as they had gained some competency in trades. See Peabody, *Education for Life*, p. 373.

50. Engs, "Red, Black, and White," p. 260; Gregg, "Annual Report," *SW* 49 (June 1920): 274.

51. Folsom in *Ten Years' Work*, p. 44; Folsom, "Record of Returned Students," *SW* 20 (Mar. 1891): 166; Gregg, "Annual Report," *SW* 49 (June 1920): 274. See also U.S. Department of Interior, Bureau of Education, *Hampton Normal and Agricultural Institute: Its Evolution and Contribution to Education as a Federal Land Grant College,* (Washington, D.C., 1923) p. 91; Ahern, "The Returned Indians," p. 103.

52. Andrus in HBF "Annual Report," *SW* 42 (May 1913): 401; SCA, "Annual Report," 1887, in Aery, "The Hampton Idea: Organizer of Teacher Training," p. 33; Andrus, "Education of Indians at Hampton," (n.d.), typed article in Folsom box, p. 1, HUA; Editorial, "Civilization Class," *SW* 17 (June 1888): 70 and Gregg, "Annual Report," 49 (June 1920): 274.

53. *ARCIA* 1890, p. cxxxix, 1894, p. 347; "The Indian Teachers' Conference," *SW* 25 (June 1896): 178; Schmeckebier, *Office of Indian Affairs,* p. 295; *Procedural Issuances and Orders,* RG75, M1121, reel 10, frame 673, NARA; Marguerite LaFlesche to Commissioner T. J. Morgan, Mar. 12, 1892, in Folsom Letters, p. 70, HUA; Gravatt "Some Questions Answered," *SW* 14 (Jan. 1885): 11.

54. Folsom in *Twenty-Two Years' Work* p. 322; Andrus, "Vacation Days among Hampton's Indians," *SW* 39 (Mar. 1910): 145; "Some Plain Facts," *The Morning Star* 5 (Jan. 1885): 3. The *ARCIA* and NARA's employee rosters seldom list Indians as the agency tradesman; Hampton likely just dropped the prefix "assistant" in rendering the real job title of many students who were employed at the agencies.

55. Susie St. Martin to Helen Townsend, Apr. 5, 1917, St. Martin's student file, HUA.

56. *Ten Years' Work,* pp. 19, 43; *SW* 10 (Oct. 1881): 109; *Twenty-Two Years' Work,* p. 337; Folsom, "Indian Days," p. 110.

57. U.S. Senate, Senate Ex. Doc. 52–31 (Washington, D.C., 1892), serial set 2892, remarks of Commissioner T. J. Morgan; quotation reprinted in *SW* 21 (Feb. 1892): 28. This Senate report later became *Twenty-Two Years' Work.*

58. Folsom, "Three Indian Girls," in Folsom Letters, p. 443, HUA; Hampton's Work for the Indians," *SW* 44 (Feb. 1915): 94; Richard Powless to Mr. Bellows, Jan. 8, 1896, Powless's student file, HUA.

59. Spencer F. Williams to Andrus, Mar. 9, 1920, Williams' student file, HUA.

60. Julia De Cora to Folsom, Nov. 23, 1902, De Cora's student file and notations in Ellen Ellis's and Mary Traversie's student files, all HUA; Editorial remarks, *T&T* 8 (Feb. 1894): 4.

61. Marion Skenandore to Andrus, Oct. 29, 1913, and William Benoist to Folsom, Jan. 18, 1886, both in student files, HUA; "Annual Report," 1882, p. 9.

62. Folsom, "When the Sioux Came to Hampton," *SW* 57 (Feb. 1928): 115–16; Anna Dawson in Folsom, "Three Indian Women," box on Folsom's Indian Letters, p. 443, HUA; *Twenty-Two Years' Work,* p. 373.

63. Isabel Eustis, "Indian Education," *SW* 11 (June 1882): 68; Martha Waldron, "The Indian Health Question," *SW* 19 (Dec. 1890): 127.

64. For the attitudes of Indian students on campus, see "Extracts from Mr. Gravatt's Sermon," *T&T* 5 (Feb. 1, 1891): 1 and "Indian Incidents," *SW* 20 (Feb. 1891): 155. The *Workman* first mentioned the Ghost Dance in September 1890 as "full of romantic interest, almost equal to parts of Ben Hur"; it was called an "encouraging sign of the times, inclined to lead the Indian forward [because its prophet, Wovoca, had arisen as a man of peace]." But after the massacre the paper reversed its stance, claiming Hampton students' nonparticipation in the dance rebuked the "majority of educated people in this country [who] believe that there is no good Indian but a dead one." In fact Armstrong felt he had been placed in the position of having to utilize this

tragedy to defend Indian education. See *SW* 19 (Sept. 1890): 97; SCA, "Annual Report," *SW* 20 (June 1891): 195.

65. See the cases of Bear's Heart and Bagola, Mar. 27, 1889, and Dec. 3, 1890 respectively and the cases of May 18, 1888, and Feb. 19, 1891, Records of the Wigwam Council, HUA.

66. For example, see Ahern, "The Returned Students," and authors mentioned in note 46.

67. Elaine Goodale (Eastman), "The Future of the Indian School System," *Chautauquan* 10 (1889–90): 52. After having looked to returned Hampton students "chiefly for support," she came to see them as "less ready to oblige, more grasping and *selfish & less to be trusted* than the 'wild Indians.'" For similar disillusioned views of returned students see also Goodale to SCA, Feb. 4, 1888, and Mar. 19, 1889, HUA, and Hampton Commandant George Curtis to SCA, Feb. 4, 1888, HUA.

68. Childs received his DD from the University of New York, and taught at the Hartford Theological Seminary (Presbyterian) and Ohio's Wooster College.

69. Ludlow, "Personal Memories," p. 1005, handwritten note appended to Arthur Howe, Jr.'s copy.

70. Childs to Commissioner J. T. B. Atkins, Jan. 11, 1888, RG75, item 1014, NARA, p. 17 (hereafter cited as Childs Report). Many of the documents relevant to this affair can also be found in the box on Childs, Indian Collection, HUA. St. Cyr to Atkins, Oct. 14, 1887, RG75, item 27582, NARA; *Twenty-Two Years' Work,* p. 356. St. Cyr's student file says she would later dress and marry in "Indian fashion," abscond with the spouse of another (as her brother David would also), and gain notoriety as the first Indian woman to act as a lawyer, defending and acquitting herself of extortion against another Indian. See St. Cyr's student file, HUA; "Only One Indian Woman Lawyer," Borlön (Nebr.) *Sunday Herald,* Nov. 3, 1907, for an account of St. Cyr's Trial.

71. In the Childs Report, enclosure 13; Tingey, "Blacks and Indians Together," pp. 282–84. Marshall had complained to Colby in June 1887, but had run away to his home while on outing before Colby wrote her letter. Marshall's religious affiliation is uncertain. Although baptized Catholic at the agency, Marshall had willingly attended Episcopal services at Lincoln Institute and later expressed no religious preference. "Statement of Rev. J. J. Gravatt," in Childs Report, enclosure 11.

72. Alexander B. Upshaw to Childs, Nov. 29, 1887, "Letter of Appointment " in Childs Report.

73. Graham, "Tender Violence: Old Hampton," p. 17; Childs to Clinton B. Fisk, Chairman of the Board of Indian Commissioners, June (?), 1889, RG75, item 15721, NARA, p. 1.

74. Upshaw to Childs, Nov. 29, 1887, in Childs Report; Minutes of Faculty Meetings, Dec. 3, 1887, HUA.

75. "Report of the Special Joint Committee (of the Va. General Assembly) to Examine the Charges Preferred Against the Hampton Normal and

Agricultural Institute," Childs Report, enclosure 44; SCA to Eliphalet Whittlesey and Albert K. Smiley, Mar. 15, 1888, copy in box on Childs Report, Indian Collection, HUA, pp. 1, 5; Graham "Tender Violence: Old Hampton," p. 19; Tingey, "Blacks and Indians Together," p. 288. Childs raised some points without elaborating on them. He included the Indians' complaint that blacks received higher wages, but accepted the school's explanation that the earnings of federally subsidized Indians were given gratuitously and that they still retained more of their wages than their self-supporting black classmates. Again, Childs questioned Hampton's practice of rotating Indian students among different trades in the technical round, and of assigning Indians to an apprenticeship, rather than allowing them to choose or change trades at will. In a similarly almost off-hand manner, he questioned the value of large-scale agricultural operations as preparation for the type of individual farming in which Indians would engage, as well as the need for Indians to "fall in" with Negroes on the march to dinner. See SCA to Whittlesey and Smiley, Mar. 15, 1888, pp. 9, 11, 16, and 27.

76. SCA to Hon. S. W. Peel, Feb. 21, 1888, SCA to Atkins, Mar. 13, 1888, and SCA to E. Whittlesey and A. K. Smiley, Mar. 15, 1888, all in box on Childs Report, Indian Collection, HUA or RG75, NARA.

77. Childs Report, pp. 9–10; SCA to Whittlesey and Smiley, Mar. 15, 1888, pp. 6–7; SCA to Atkins, Mar. 13, 1888, pp. 4, 9.

78. SCA, "Annual Report," *SW* 8 (June 1879): 63.

79. Childs Report, pp. 8, 29–30.

80. SCA to Atkins, Dec. 23, 1887, enclosure 33, Childs Report; SCA to Whittlesey and Smiley, Mar. 15, 1888, p. 10; SCA to Atkins, Mar. 13, 1888, p. 5.

81. Waldron letter dated Dec. 29, 1887, p. 6 in A. K. Smiley and E. Whittlesey to Fisk, Mar. 1888, Childs Report; SCA to Whittlesey and Smiley, Mar. 15, 1888, p. 8. Armstrong retorted that Carlisle's refusal for reasons of health to admit Sioux from Crow Creek "did not mean very much," since eight Apaches, also an unhealthy tribe, had died there in the previous year. See SCA to Atkins, Dec. 23, 1887, p. 11. Childs to Fisk, June (?), 1889, RG75, item 15721, NARA.

82. SCA to Whittlesey and Smiley, Mar. 15, 1888, p. 11.

83. Childs' treatment of the health of Indians at Hampton overlooked two other factors. First, the moral question involved with sending sick and contagious Indians back to their own people without modern medical facilities and where they might infect other tribal members. But Hampton's staff operated a school and not a hospital, and its death rate would have worsened had it cared for stricken Indians, resulting in even more criticism. Waldron revealed that 107 Indians were returned home for physical reasons, sixty-seven with consumption, of whom thirty-six had developed symptoms at school. See *Ten Years' Work*, p. 20.

Second, there was an issue of sanitation. Waldron complained in 1890 that "families living in the Indian cottages [near a 'swampy ditch'] almost invariably contract malaria." Moreover, the school's waterfront received raw sewage from the town of Hampton and especially from the Old Soldiers' Home. In 1879 Armstrong noted that "the forced matter of nearly seven hundred men is daily dropped into Jares Creek." In 1883 Waldron told Armstrong that the "unusual amount of sickness in Virginia Hall" owed to "fecal matter washed by the tide from the soldiers' home." Although in 1897 Waldron got the new breakwater system on campus she said was needed to protect the shoreline from sewage, a better one had to be installed in 1903. For malaria, see Waldron to SCA, Jan. 1, 1890, HUA. For sewage, see SCA to Boutelle, Dec. 5, 1879, HUA; Waldron to SCA, Oct. 9, 1883, HUA and in SCA, *Annual Report,* 1893 and 1897; *SW* 31 (Oct. 1902): 564.

84. Childs to Fisk, June (?), 1889, p. 5; Childs Report, p. 33.

85. SCA in *SW* 18 (July 1889): 77; SCA to Ogden, Oct. 14, 1889, Ogden Papers, Library of Congress; Childs to Fisk, June (?), 1889, p. 5.

86. SCA to Ogden, July 26, 1889, Ogden Papers, Library of Congress; SCA to Smiley and Whittlesey Mar. 15, 1888, p. 4; Editorial remarks in *SW* 18 (Sept. 1889): 77.

87. Childs Report, pp. 6, 25.

88. SCA to Peel, Feb. 21, 1888, p. 6; Graham, "Tender Violence: Old Hampton," p. 22; SCA to J. F. B. Marshall, Feb. 27, 1888, RG75, item 5862, NARA.

89. Folsom to SCA, Aug. 5, 1889, HUA; SCA to Ogden, Feb. 3, 1888, Ogden Papers, Library of Congress.

90. Tingey, "Blacks and Indians Together," p. 303; Mary McHenry Cox to Welsh, Feb. 24, 1888, IRA Papers. See Ludlow to Folsom, Feb. 17, 1888, Pratt Box, Indian Collection, HUA; Dawes to Welsh, Mar. 2, 1888 and Painter to Welsh, Oct. 25, 1888, IRA Papers.

91. Ludlow to Folsom, Feb. 17, 1888, Indian Collection, Pratt Box, HUA; Painter to Welsh, May 26, 1886, IRA Papers.

92. Dawes to Welsh, Mar. 2, 1888, IRA Papers.

93. Smiley to SCA, Feb. 14, 1888, HUA; SCA to Welsh, Feb. 3(?), 1888, in Ogden Papers, Library of Congress. The date of this re-typed letter does not fit the chronology. See also Smiley to SCA, Feb. 14, 1888, HUA.

94. Whittlesey to SCA, Mar. 17 and 14, 1888, HUA. Smiley even arranged a meeting with the president on February 17, 1888, in which Rev. William H. Hare and Rev. J. J. Gravatt supported Armstrong on the issues of the guardroom and race mingling. See Ludlow to Folsom, Feb. 17, 1888, Pratt Box, Indian Collection, HUA.

95. Smiley-Whittlesey Report, p. 10; RHP to Childs, May 27, 1889, box 15, Pratt Papers, Yale University; Ludlow to Folsom, Feb. 17, 1888, Pratt Box, Indian Collection, HUA.

96. Smiley to SCA, Feb. 24, 1888, HUA.

97. SCA to J. H. Oberly, Apr. 9, 1889 and to J. W. Noble, May 18, 1889, HUA; Graham, "Tender Violence: Old Hampton," p. 25; R. V. Belt to SCA, June 25, 1889, quoting Noble to Belt, June 11, 1889, HUA.

98. Childs, "Letter to the Editor," Boston *Evening Transcript,* July 17, 1889; "Indians at Hampton," July 7, 1889, Cincinnati *Commercial Gazette.*

99. RHP to Childs, May 27, 1889, box 15, Pratt Papers, Yale University; SCA in *SW* 18 (July 1889): 77; SCA to Ogden, July 26, 1889, Ogden Papers, Library of Congress.

100. SCA, *SW* 18 (July 1889): 17.

101. Childs to Fisk, June (?), 1889, RG75, item 15721, NARA.

102. Ibid; SCA to Whittlesey and Smiley, Mar. 15, 1888, p. 10.

103. SCA to Peel, Feb. 21, 1888, p. 8; Sloan in "The Indians Speak for Themselves," *SW* 18 (July 1889): 80.

104. Sloan to Ogden, July 31, 1889, Ogden Papers, HUA; SCA to Ogden, July 8, 1889, Ogden Papers, Library of Congress.

105. *SW* 18 (Sept. 1889): 93.

106. Editorial remarks, *SW* 18 (Aug. 1889): 85; SCA to Ogden, July 10, 1889, and Sloan to SCA, Nov. 28, 1889, both in Ogden Papers, Library of Congress. Feeling that Hamptonians regarded him as "very selfish," Sloan did not write to the press as Armstrong directed because it did "no harm" if Childs was "satisfied to vent his wrath on me."

107. Sloan quoted in Business Manager F. C. Briggs to SCA, Aug. 8, 1889, HUA. Briggs wrote SCA that Sloan's letter "seems weak—cannot we write a good letter for him to sign?" SCA to Ogden, July 23, 1889 and Ludlow to Ogden, (?) 1889, both in Ogden Papers, Library of Congress.

108. RHP to Childs, July 10, 1889, Pratt Papers, Yale University; Smiley to SCA, Feb. 24, 1888, HUA.

109. RHP to Childs, July 10, 1889 and Oct. 12, 1889, Pratt Papers, Yale University.

110. SCA to Ludlow, Sept 27, 1872, in Peabody, *Education for Life*, p. 107; SCA to Ogden, Sept. 21 and Oct. 14, 1889, Ogden Papers, Library of Congress.

111. SCA to Ogden, July 10 and Oct. 14, 1889, Ogden Papers, Library of Congress.

112. SCA, *A New Attack on Eastern Schools* (Hampton, 1890), in large part reprinted in *SW* 19 (Jan. 1890). Miller also charged that eastern education "teaches the young Indians to despise their kinsmen, to lose the natural gratitude and affection due their parents, [opening] a gap which cannot be bridged." But Armstrong found sorrow "to have the 'gap' between the old and the new life 'bridged' except by affection leading upward and onward," and recognized that Miller's charge that the educated Indian became alienated from his people was the opposite of Holman's equally erroneous claim that he relapsed to their level.

113. Welsh, *A Crisis in the Cause of Indian Education* (Philadelphia, 1892), pamphlet A-143, p. 3; Welsh to Painter, Jan. 28, 1892, IRA Papers.

114. See *SW* Editorial remarks, 24 (Jan. 1896): 5, 25 (Jan. 1896): 9, 25 (Apr. 1896): 54, 25 (Sept. 1896): 171, 28 (Nov. 1899): 411; 29 (Jan. 1900): 3, and (May 1901): 292; Tingey, "Blacks and Indians Together," pp. 313–20.

115. HBF to ?, Apr. 3, 1896, box on Frissell's Speeches, HUA; Editorial remarks, *SW* 29 (Jan. 1900): 3.

116. Joseph A. Stephens to Henry Elder, May 15, 1890, Bureau of Catholic Indian Missions Records, Marquette University, cited in Prucha, *The Churches,* pp. 43–44.

9

Decline, Demise, and Postmortem of Hampton's Indian Program

In the midst of the 1890s' controversies that limited Hampton's influence on national Indian policy—indeed making school administrators fear national attention brought danger to the Indian program—its founder died. In May 1893 Hollis B. Frissell took full control, having already assumed many of Samuel Armstrong's duties three years earlier, after a stroke partially paralyzed him. Although a skillful administrator, Frissell, with his slouching, unassuming carriage and bald, egg-shaped head, could not match the general's personal magnetism. More important, Frissell could not match Armstrong's political acumen or moral certainty that eastern schools were desirable for Indians or that government paternalism endangered its Indian wards. In fact he supported continued federal guardianship over Indian allotments, to counteract the exploitation unleashed by the Dawes Act. In 1917 Frissell died and James Edgar Gregg, a graduate of Yale Divinity School and a Congregational minister in Pittsfield, Massachusetts, replaced him. Gregg would preside over the Indian program's final, most marginal years, which coincided with a period of virulent racism. In the atmosphere created by past controversies and in the absence of its founder's sustaining energy, the Indian Department experienced continuing decay, particularly after 1900, from a series of relentless pressures applied both inside and outside Hampton.

The Early Decline of the Indian Program

Largely internal factors were already weakening Hampton's Indian program years before the 1912 loss of federal funding. By 1902 the number of Indians at Hampton had fallen below the government quota of 120; it fell below 100 after 1905, and as low as 74 in 1909. This decline reflected several internal developments: the change from Armstrong's style of leadership to Frissell's, as well as their differing attitudes toward Indians; the consequent stiffening of admission standards, coupled with the school's inability to gain the more promising Indian students, and a gradual loss of contact with the reservations and with its returned students. Taken together, these factors rendered Indian concerns ever more peripheral to Frissell's burgeoning industrial and philanthropic complex for blacks.

Although Frissell pledged to grant the founder's last wish that Hampton remain "true to the red and black races of our country," his interest in Indian education did not equal Armstrong's. Frissell did maintain all of Armstrong's organizational ties to Indian reform, and served as head of the National Education Association's Indian Department in 1901, as chair of Mohonk's business committee in 1914 and after 1915 as a trustee of the American Indian Institute of Henry Roe Cloud, but his first concern was always for black—not red—education. Most of Hampton's students were Negroes, he explained, and he possessed a "subtle affinity" for them because of care he received as a child from his black nurse; he believed that freedom and suffrage "imposed a tremendous responsibility upon American citizens for the black people."[1]

Whereas Hampton Indians had had a warrior's respect for the general, it must sometimes have been difficult for them to see the relevance of Frissell's statements. On Indian Days he proclaimed, "You sang together 'My Country 'Tis of Thee.' You were taught something of the blessedness of belonging to this great nation, of coming into possession of this liberty for which our fathers died, of entering into the heritage which has been handed down through the ages." Notwithstanding factors ranging from the slaughter of Indians on the frontier to the cheating by whites of Indians who had indeed become American citizens, the principal went on to say that "wherever a citizen of the United States goes he can appeal to his country's flag for protection. . . . He can appeal to the strong arm of the law to secure to him the enjoyment of home, to secure to him the rightful fruits of his labor, to protect him against the harmful assault of his enemy. . . . The lowest feeble citizen can make his influence felt at the capital." In fact, Cora Folsom, the Indians' correspondent, noted that "Frissell did not like Indians and they did not like him. . . . He was a poor storyteller."[2]

Frissell was also less willing than Armstrong to maintain the Indian program by tolerating a different set of rules for Indians than for blacks. Making "quality and not quantity" his motto, Frissell announced in 1903 that "unless it is possible to obtain Indians who are capable of meeting its requirements for admission, it seems wise that the school should devote itself more to the education of the Negro and less to that of the Indian." Already in 1899 his decision to require prospective Indian students to file application papers just as blacks did, had impeded recruitment: F. D. Gleason would later complain of being expected to forward applications directly to the school for processing and having to return later to collect pupils found eligible. He told Frissell, to no avail, that it was "almost universal testimony" among educators that an agent must get Indians "when they are of a notion of going, [because they] moved along lines of least resistance." Frissell later also refused to admit Indians once a term had begun. Although this ended the resentment of blacks against a double standard, Caroline Andrus (who had succeeded Folsom as Indian correspondent in 1906) maintained that telling an Indian to "wait until next year" insured that he would never come. Her reminder to Frissell, that "colored students . . . apply in such throngs, that we are apt to think that the same methods will work with the Indians," fell on deaf ears.[3]

While the few staff members specifically involved with Indians wanted to maintain the older, more flexible methods of recruitment, the rest had become unhappy that many Indians still were not meeting academic standards. In 1904 principal of the Academic Department Elizabeth Hyde said she and her staff believed that for most Indians, "the civilizing side of our school life at Hampton . . . is the main aim always, and the only side that many of them . . . are able to grasp." Hyde also complained that "our Indians are sometimes in one class for four or five years, although our colored students are allowed only two years in one class. . . . I have never known of an Indian to be returned home for poor scholarship."[4]

After 1897 when special Indian classes were discontinued, meeting the needs of Indian students often became tangential to teaching culturally assimilated blacks. One teacher, Alice M. Price, told Frissell in 1905 that "some of the Indian material is not promising enough to keep the opportunities of Hampton away from more earnest [Negro] students." The same year, another teacher, Flora F. Low, sought to have unpromising Indians removed from her class by telling Frissell, "Elsie Cote, for instance, simply occupies a seat in the classroom. She is idle, uninterested, a demoralizing influence. Esther Moose has been here for years and will still be in preparatory next year. . . . Flannigan Hill is, to my mind, a worse than useless specimen. Cusick seems to have no brains. . . . Is not somebody paying a scholarship for these people? Much as I love the Indian, I wish that every foot of this place be given to the negro, while the government provides such good schools for its wards." Given the fact that many of the Indians were still not fluent in English and were also very different culturally from their teachers, such comments suggest what Andrus would identify seven years later as an "anti-Indian sentiment at Hampton which ought not to exist."[5]

Another measure of the Indian program's decline was the decreasing frequency and duration of recruiting trips to the West, a trend accelerated by Commissioner Francis Leupp's (1905–9) strictures against nonreservation boarding schools. Since the 1890s Hampton had increasingly relied on former students to recruit applicants, and not surprisingly, fewer visits to the reservations also meant less participation in the various Indian teachers' institutes and fewer original articles in the *Workman*. Upon attending St. Paul's Indian Teachers' Meeting in 1896, William Scoville told Frissell that Hampton was "not so much disliked as *unknown*. . . . By half of the [Indian] teachers in the West we are confused with Carlisle. . . . A great many western schools brought class work and pictures and the exhibition room was full, but we did not have so much as a circular." In 1906 Folsom reported, "It is now eleven years since my visit to any of the returned students and now not even the flitting of [Chaplain Herbert B.] Turner or Mr. Gleason through the reservations brings the returned students or the western friends into association with the Hampton family." But it was Leupp who curtailed even this sporadic activity, when in 1908 he prohibited nonreservation boarding schools from soliciting pupils. Calling the schools useless "educational almshouses," he officially terminated their support, which had been waning since Cleveland's first administration. In the future, any initiative would have to come from Indian parents, who could request information regarding climate, distance, and conditions of various schools.[6]

Although this prohibition was not always heeded or enforced, Leupp's policy did reverse Commissioner Morgan's 1890s aim of putting nonreservation training schools at the peak of an educational pyramid. No longer could Hampton and Carlisle expect the Indian Office to send them even the best Indian students passing through day schools and reservation boarding schools. Ironically, however, Leupp's secular policy of pursuing "improvement not transformation" epitomized the Hampton-Tuskegee model; he merely felt that reservation schools best fit this limited vocational emphasis. Representatives from the new western states, who came to dominate congressional committees on Indian affairs, often shared Leupp's "practical" views on Indian potential and objected to federal dollars being spent on expensive eastern schools.[7] Thus, already at a disadvantage beside the western boarding schools its Indian program had inspired, Frissell's Hampton welcomed the curb on aggressive recruiting, charging that two or three schools typically "worked" the same territory and carried off without parental permission students who occasionally contracted fatal illnesses at school.[8]

Even before the 1908 prohibition, western recruiting and visits with returned students was not the only way Hampton's activity for Indians had declined. Hampton's Indian Records Office no longer maintained close ties to former or even current students. After nearly a quarter of a century as Indian correspondent, Folsom found that her new duties after 1903 as head of the Blake Indian Museum increasingly isolated her from other campus activities. Making a "January" letter of her 1906 annual report to the principal, Folsom described the unsatisfactory state of affairs in the office:

> I do not know of anyone connected with the school who has any correspondence with the returned students. . . . With the students [on campus during] the past ten years I have had very little association, with those of the past five almost none. . . . I have tried to have it otherwise, but my own duties [in the museum] have confined me in one place and theirs in another, and since the socials have been given up and even the prayer meetings discontinued, there seems to be almost no point at which I may keep in touch with them. . . . Another difficulty hard to overcome is the fact that I am now in almost every way out of touch with the office or the faculty. Many of the affairs that should become a part of the student's record . . . never reach me or the records. . . . It seems a great pity that we must lose our hold upon these young people upon whose training so much time and labor is being put, but that seems to be the trend.[9]

Hampton staff members who did write to former Indian students received fewer replies. Out of about 780 annual Christmas letters written in 1905, Hampton got 200 replies; it received only 63 in 1906, and just 26 in 1909.[10] Moreover, Folsom pointed out, 47 of the 63 letters that Hampton did receive in 1906 came not from recent students but from those who had attended the school at the Indian program's height during the 1880s and early 1890s. Some letters that Folsom herself received in 1905 and 1906 spoke of growing estrangement. One correspondent charged, "I think school don't care for me"; another asked, "Does Hampton still have an Indian program?"; and a third prompted her to reply, "Your letter asking me not to write again to your husband is received and I have decided that you must be laboring under some curious mistake in regard to my identity."[11] More letters than in the past were also marked "Return To Sender," as reservations were broken up and rural free delivery routes replaced agency postmasters.

By 1912 Folsom and her former Indian students (some now middle-aged) were "far apart, not only in distance and in years, but in that sympathetic knowledge of one another that made our life at Hampton so much like that of one large family." Newer students knew her only as "the old gray haired lady who works in the museum," though Folsom had once been the Indians' favorite Hamptonian.[12] At least a few Indian girls had called her "Ina" (mother). She had been the only faculty member to attempt to learn Lakota; along with Josephine Richards and Martha Waldron she had had the honor of having an Indian baby named for her. Although Andrus came to develop close ties to some of the more recent students, the Indian program ended before their children were of age to attend Hampton.

The Funding Crisis of 1912

The Indian program faced its greatest external threat when Congress withdrew funding in May 1912. Hampton's enrollment of eighty-one Indian students dropped to forty-one, after the school lost $12,519, which had provided for board, room rent, registration fees, clothing, toilet articles, and railroad fares. As a consequence, Frissell had to ask donors of Indian scholarships to switch them into travel grants for Indians, transfer them to blacks, or contribute toward a more general "anti-discouragement" fund for Indians, who received almost no help from home.[13]

———

This funding crisis began when Democrats gained control of the sixty-second Congress. The two previous, sympathetic chairmen of the House Committee on Indian Affairs, Republicans James S. Sherman and Charles H. Burke, were replaced by Democrat John Hall Stephens of Texas, who personally cut the school from the committee's appropriations bill. When the bill reached the House on April 8, Hampton Congressman William Atkinson Jones, himself a Democrat, introduced an amendment attempting to reinstate the tidewater school. He cited as one of his two reasons the fact that the Stephens committee's only witness, Commissioner Robert Valentine, had actually testified on Hampton's behalf. He also labeled as false the committee's only stated grounds for dropping the school—namely the existence of comparable facilities for educating Indians in the West, without the expense of transportation. No other Indian school offered normal training any more, Jones argued, or matched Hampton's industrial or agricultural facilities; moreover, the cost of sending pupils to Hampton was only slightly more than sending them to Carlisle, where Hampton's present Indian students were to be transferred.

But then Jones himself introduced into record the issue that eliminated any remaining chance of federal funding for Hampton. Having heard it "whispered around that there were negroes educated at the Hampton school as well as Indians," he decided to tell uninformed colleagues that Virginia itself had never objected to such a situation, since it had never withheld the school's annual land grant funds. He maintained, "to-day is the first time that I have ever heard this question raised. . . . The Indians have never objected to the presence of negroes at this school. No complaint has ever come from the white inhabitants of Hampton." (He was apparently unaware of Caroline Colby.) Representative Samuel W. McCall (R. Massachusetts) agreed with Jones and interjected that he had not heard this racial question raised in Congress in thirty years. He later asked Stephens to honor state's rights, saying that "if a [southern] State like Virginia does not object [to such mingling] the gentleman from Texas certainly should not object."

Even a visit to Hampton did not change Stephens's position, however. Defending his committee's decision to end federal funding, Chairman Stephens pointed out that Indians had originally come to Hampton involuntarily as prisoners, and claimed that the school was no longer able to fill its government quota of 120 Indians per year because the Indians themselves "do not desire to attend that school and will not do it." Stephens told the House that the government should use its own schools to "separate these two races, and thus elevate the red race to the level of the white race and not degrade and humiliate him by sinking him to the low plane of the negro race."

Stephens's remarks were seconded by Oklahoma's Indian congressman, Democrat Charles D. Carter, a member of the particularly anti-black Chickasaw tribe. Pointing out that Virginia prohibited whites and blacks from mixing in public schools, he pled with his white colleagues to leave his race at least its dignity. Recounting concessions forced upon the Indian until "he has nothing left but his self-respect," he charged, "you come to him with the Hampton school and ask him to surrender his self-respect by placing his children on a social equality with an inferior race, a level to which you yourself will not deign to descend."[14] Jones's easy reply that there was nothing compulsory about Indians going to Hampton, was likely drowned out by the "loud applause" for Carter. Frissell later acknowledged that the Chickasaw's speech did more than anything else to defeat the amendment, effectively ending Hampton's Indian funding.[15]

The House divided along party lines, with sixty-five of the newly elected Democratic majority from the emerging West and Wilsonian South against, and only thirty-three Republicans for Jones's amendment. Although restoring Hampton's usual allotment was supported by the Senate Committee on Indian Affairs, the chairman of a conference committee between the two houses broke an eight to eight tie by voting against funding.[16]

———

Anticipating a partisan attack on its racial policy, Hampton had responded to the imminent and then to the ongoing congressional debate only privately and cautiously. The school administration appeared unwilling to engage in public controversy as it had earlier done on issues raised by Holman, Childs, and Irving Miller. There were no excerpts from the House debate or broadsides against it in the *Workman,* no pamphlets, and no marshaling of forces in newspapers, the IRA, or at Mohonk. Although biracial education at Hampton had been criticized before, Stephens's and Carter's objections were especially dangerous as the first made formally in Congress. On February 17, before Stephens's report had reached the House, the faculty decided "not to fight for the appropriation on the ground that it might be interpreted unfavorably in the South along social lines; and also because we have long felt there should be no distinction [in financing] made between our Negro and Indian students."[17] Thus, by not publicly contesting its loss of federal funding, Hampton apparently capitulated to southern racism and to its own feelings against this treaty right of Indians.

Despite the faculty's stated convictions, Frissell did make quiet efforts to obtain reinstatement of funding. He attempted to persuade white southerners, and to a lesser extent, Indians, that Hampton's racial policies were inoffensive, apparently fearing that any other tactic might antagonize southerners and thus jeopardize Hampton's clearly more important role in black education, without gaining new supporters for its Indian appropriations. Frissell encouraged letters to congressmen by prominent southerners who approved of Hampton's racial mixing, such as Wycliff Rose of Peabody College and J. D. Eggleston, Superintendent of Public Instruction for Virginia. Booker Washington was Hampton's only black spokesman on this issue. In the capital itself, Frissell appealed to Thomas Jesse Jones, whose series of articles on "Social Studies in the Hampton Curriculum" had demonstrated diplomacy in adjusting racial and sectional differences, and to Thomas Sloan, chair of the Executive Committee of the Society of American Indians

(SAI), who had spoken for Hampton's Indian students during the Childs investigation. At Frissell's behest, Jones and Sloan met with members of the House and Senate Indian committees.[18]

Letters of entreaty to congressmen also came directly from Hampton. Instead of opposing segregation as such, Hampton's board chairman, Robert Ogden, assured Stephens that the three southern trustees "are all opposed to amalgamation of the races but are thoroughly in sympathy with the methods of character building and economic progress that prevail at Hampton. . . . your points concerning the race relations of the Indian and the Negro are under careful supervision by excellent southern men." Similarly, Frissell wrote Carter, "I sympathize with you strongly in your earnest desire to keep the Indian on the highest possible plane, and am quite as much opposed as you are to anything which looks like amalgamation of the Indian and Negro races." Boasting that no intermarriage had ever occurred among Hampton students, he even agreed with Carter that it "might be undesirable to establish the precedent of educating the negro and the Indian together" in government schools, but claimed that Hampton was "an exception to the ordinary rule," because it had always practiced such a policy, with a "picked body of negroes" and had ties to influential Americans that had proven useful to Indians.[19]

Unable to budge the Indian representative, Frissell got the first "Indian" senator, Kansas Republican Charles Curtis, who was one-eighth Kaw, to "spring" a petition from all of Hampton's Indians on Carter in Congress.[20] Hampton needed to show, without confronting them directly, that not all educated Indians shared the opinions of Carter or racist southerners. In May 1912 the *Workman* published "Hampton Indians' Petition to Congress": this, its only piece on the matter during the controversy, read in part,

> Not a single Indian boy or girl at Hampton wishes to go elsewhere. . . . We have been reading with deepest interest what the members of Congress have been saying about the educating of Indians and Negroes, and we wish you knew the type of Negro at Hampton Institute as we do. . . . Surely the thrifty, hard-working Negro boys and girls at Hampton have much of good to give us. . . . We know that the average Indian is self-centered, like other men, and needs to know that he is not alone in having to face hard problems. . . . At Hampton we live in the atmosphere of Christian service, and we thoroughly appreciate what we receive and have been receiving from the highly educated men and women . . . we plead again that the Government will not make another

mistake in its Indian policy by taking from us, and those who must follow, the opportunities which Hampton alone offers.

Although Hampton had represented this strong testimonial with its implied reading of the *Congressional Record* as the Indians' own, their real input here is unclear. In prefacing the statement, the *Workman* explicitly claimed only that the Indian students asked to be "allowed" to write to Washington, and that the letter had been "subscribed to" by them. Hampton's Samuel Scoville asserted privately that the Indians' "statements are all their own," but he also revealed that the school's publicity agent, William A. Aery, "put them in shape." Indeed a document entitled "original draft" was signed by Aery and written in his hand.[21] Thus Aery's involvement could have been anything from recording the Indians' remarks verbatim, to selecting and editing the strongest individual statements, to composing the petition himself.

However, Indians outside as well as inside Hampton were not disinterested parties in the debate. They were as powerless as blacks in controlling the color line and even those who personally liked blacks did not want to share their declined status. Charles Williams, the school's black coach, commented on the superficiality of southerners' support for Hampton Indians, saying "they had in mind the complete subjugation of the Negro—they weren't thinking about the elevation of Indians." But the race's larger concern did not change how "hard" staff felt it was on Hampton that "an Indian should have asked to have the help withdrawn, and that other prominent Indians should have used their influence against the school."[22] Representative Carter was also the SAI vice president in charge of legislation, and leaders of the society such as Seneca Arthur C. Parker and Anishinabe Marie L. Baldwin privately opposed Hampton's biracial makeup.[23] Indeed the SAI's secretary treasurer, Peoria Charles E. Dagenett, whose position as supervisor of Indian employment was the highest held by an Indian in the service, had discriminated against Hampton's Indian graduates (prompting the school in 1914 to help secure his removal).[24] This development was unsurprising considering that Dagenett graduated from Carlisle: with Carlisle and Hampton students forming the two largest blocs in the society, the SAI was bound to echo the old Pratt-Armstrong split on whether Indians belonged in black schools.

But neither institute nor SAI records reveal exactly how far the society was involved in the moves against Hampton. Parker and Frissell exchanged guarded notes. The SAI's secretary wrote Hampton's principal first, on May 11, assuring him that Carter was not speaking for the society; he claimed that "Carter and the majority of our members believe in the Hampton ideal but . . . his objection is to the social element of the matter. The Society has not yet expressed itself on the matter nor do I believe that we shall ever discuss the question of color." Although Parker's letter did not endorse Hampton and perhaps hinted that most SAI members would not support the school if anyone there raised the issue, it did imply official neutrality. Frissell responded ambivalently to the sachem four days later: "If Hampton can not be of real service to the Indian we have no desire that the appropriation should be continued, as there is plenty of work for us to do with the negroes. But it seems to me that the Indian needs all the friends he can get, and I believe that Hampton has in the past and may be in the future of great service to him."[25]

Nevertheless, and perhaps without Frissell's knowledge, Hampton graduate Michael Wolfe (Sioux) proposed a resolution at the SAI's annual meeting in October 1913 that called on the government to resume funding to his Alma Mater. Just as quickly, however, Wolfe let the society off the hook on this general question by saying that Hampton's Indians at least desired free transportation. In truth, traveling expenses were now their primary concern. In response, Parker attempted to vitiate the funding proposal by asking whether it would not be "dangerous" to endorse any particular school, and therefore better to endorse all schools. Then, at the urging of Omaha Rosa LaFlesche and Hampton graduate Sloan, the SAI resolved that the government furnish transportation to and from all nonsectarian schools. Most SAI members were probably unaware that Hampton would have been the primary beneficiary. In the end, however, Wolfe's original motion for full funding of Hampton's Indian program was rejected by the society only to have the narrower resolution on transportation rejected by the Indian Office.[26]

While fear of intensifying criticism by southerners appears to have been a major reason for Hampton's halfhearted response to the funding crisis, the Indian program could have ended at once had that been its only concern. Hampton's new treasurer, Frank K. Rogers, even calculated that—owing to the greater productivity of black labor, the elimination of four staff positions, and the fuller utilization of the Indian dormitories—the institute would only lose $2,800 if black students replaced Indians. Yet Hampton did what it pleased on its own grounds, and continued to educate the two races together. Accepting government-provided free food, clothes, and shelter conflicted with the character-building approach to education promulgated at Hampton; its white administrators had thereby seen themselves as undermining the lessons of self-help, personal sacrifice, and sense of obligation they sought to teach their Indian pupils through the example of blacks. The withdrawal of funding ended this inconsistent policy, allowing the *Workman* to proclaim that Hampton's self-supporting Indian students had inaugurated a "new era in Indian education." Indeed this new dispensation did give one boost to the morale of Indian students, who no longer had their "excess" earnings drained off into a tool fund, which Andrus commented had "caused hard feelings first and last."[27]

Overall, the appropriations crisis had set Hampton's economic interest in a federally funded Indian program against its larger interest in maintaining southern support for black education: the forfeiture of $12,519 followed. Frissell dared not reapply for funding even though it had been lost for only one year, but the desire for greater institutional integrity also dictated Hampton's response. There would no longer be the pedagogical contradiction of "special treatment" for Indians, self-help for blacks. But if many Hamptonians were not sorry to see funding go, Andrus noted that the Indians generally "resented" this blessing in disguise: "some who could have perfectly well afforded to pay their own way were unwilling to do so because they felt that the government owed them their education."[28] This Indian summer of self-help (1912–23), during which Hampton's program for Native Americans ran counter to treaty assurances guaranteeing free education, placed the best interests of the school and those of its red students at odds.

Thus the end result of congressional efforts aimed at elevating the Indian by withdrawing funds from a school for blacks was to demote those Indians who nevertheless still came to Hampton. And while Hampton's decision to keep admitting Indians after the loss of funding eliminated most of the distinctions on campus that had in effect placed blacks below Indians, it did little to slow the continued erosion of its program for Indian education.

The Final Chapter

The man who oversaw the final six years of the Indian program, Principal James Gregg, was introduced by the *Workman* in 1917 as a "spiritually minded leader of men, rather than a professional educator or an expert in social problems." Many of the individuals who had given form to Hampton's Indian program, and through whom former students had drawn others to their Alma Mater, were leaving or dying, with each milestone duly noted in the *Workman*. Commandant Moton had already left in 1915 to become principal of Tuskegee. Frissell's death in 1917 was followed the next year by that of Dixie Hospital's Alice Bacon. Folsom retired in 1922, and Helen Ludlow died in 1924. Long departed from Hampton to nearby Richmond, the Reverend Gravatt of St. John's Church died in 1925, as did farm manager Albert Howe. When Charles McDowell, the originator of the Wolfe Indian Training Shop died in 1923 Elizabeth Hyde was retiring as principal of the Academic Department. Writing for Principal Gregg in the annual report for 1918, Vice Principal George P. Phenix was the first to admit publicly that "the indications are that Hampton's work for the Indians is coming to an end, except for a few individuals who for reasons of sentiment may choose to attend from time to time." He emphasized that Hampton's doors "must be kept open" for such students.[29]

As Indian enrollment fell from forty-five in 1915 to sixteen in 1919, Gregg reported that "the war doubtless caused a part of the shrinkage." Since male Indians attending Hampton during World War I were liable to be drafted into Negro units of the Student Army Training Corps, Andrus told those who wanted to join the corps not to come to Hampton. Some Indian parents, for whom armed threats had always come from the East, also worried about sending their children to Hampton during wartime, because it was the scene of intense military activity and very near the coast. But Gregg's concern was long-term: "the steadiness of this decline in numbers leads one to serious queries concerning the future of Hampton's Indian department. For several reasons it seems desirable to maintain it. Many of the missionaries to the Indians are anxious that this shall be done; and the Indian graduates take pleasure in sending their children to their Alma Mater. The closing of the Carlisle Indian School leaves Hampton the principal institution of this type in the East."[30]

Although Gregg made no effort to recruit Carlisle students when in 1918 the War Department requisitioned it as a hospital, he did make one final attempt during the summer and fall of 1919 to revitalize Hampton's Indian program: Gregg and Andrus visited nearly all the Indian agencies where Hampton had returned students or other contacts. Before this trip no one from Hampton had been to Wisconsin for ten years, to Dakota for seven years, nor to Oklahoma and Arizona for five years—or before then to the Southwest for another ten years. In her 1918 report Andrus had stressed the falling morale among Indian students, saying that they "have never been so restless, discontented, and unhappy . . . due to their being so few that they have felt entirely lost in the great numbers of Negro students." In search of fresh recruits, Gregg and Andrus visited Haskell Institute and Santee Indian School, as well as the Winnebago, Omaha, Standing Rock, Cheyenne River, and Eastern Cherokee reservations. Andrus also went to the Crow Creek, Fort Berthold, Pine Ridge, and New York reservations. Returning from the West almost alone, Andrus termed it "humiliating to work for four hard months and produce so little in the way of results. Of the thirteen who I felt might possibly come east with me, only three met me at Sioux City. One of these has since run away, another has been sent [away], and the third is turning out to be a very promising boy."[31]

Andrus's report of 1919 pointed out that race prejudice (building since the 1890s) had become the "greatest drawback" to recruiting Indians. The fact that Congress had divested Hampton's Indians primarily for attending a black school became a signal to Indians not to go there. Although the influence of returned students had once helped to fill Hampton's Indian quota, they were no longer interested in "helping their own or other people's children to come here," reported Andrus in 1916. For example, Absentee Shawnee Pierrepont Alford told her that other former students had "called him to an account" for giving her their addresses, and that he could not blame them because he himself had been fired twice for having attended a "nigger" school. Moreover, Comanche William Sapient advised Andrus that he and other former students could not "conscientiously" recruit for Hampton, explaining that "when [Indians] have been going to public or consolidated schools with white children, of course they naturally hesitate to go to school with negroes."[32] Such attitudes toward association with blacks were more prevalent among Indians in New York, North Carolina, and especially Oklahoma, than among those in Dakota and the Southwest who had less awareness of the social consequences.

Although eleven Indians continued attending his "industrial chapel" the following year, Gregg gave a closing benediction to the Indian program in August 1922. After outlining the Indian program's history, he concluded that "the lack of government aid, the distance of Hampton from the more important reservations, and the fact that this is not distinctly an Indian school . . . operate powerfully to hinder Indian students from coming to Hampton. Further, the strengthening in recent years of the schools in the West [such as Haskell, Bacone, and Roe Institute] has in large measure met the need of such training as Hampton offers." Gregg then broke the bad news that Caroline Andrus would resign the following year and not be replaced. In charge of the Indian Department ever since Gleason's death in 1910, she had assumed new duties recruiting students and making transportation and outing arrangements. With her resignation, the Indian Records Office was absorbed into the Negro Records Office. Although bound to do nothing else, Gregg's announcement was termed "not in the least intended to cut off or discourage the admission of Indian students: all who wish and are qualified to enter the Institute will be welcomed."[33]

Other evidence suggests that Hampton no longer genuinely welcomed Indians. Because their small number had prompted the school to integrate its facilities completely, Indians could no longer maintain the esprit de corps, tribal self-help, and intertribal association they themselves desired. This caused Andrus to resign and dissuade Indians from remaining there, and to rebel against the school's decision to continue biracial education after the loss of federal funding. In effect Andrus joined the segregationists of 1912.

This final chapter came to light on September 3, 1923, when Winnebago Addie Stevens Bouchier, one of Hampton's former Indian students, asked Andrus "why you advise the Indian girls not to return to Hampton? Emma [Henry] received a special delivery letter from Luella [Baird] saying they were not to return because they had been advised by you and Miss Townsend not to." Andrus replied to Bouchier's query three days later:

> Hampton is so changed from the time when you were in school that it hardly seems like the same place. Then the Indians had their own tables, their own dormitories, their own social life and formed a group by themselves. Now they are so few in number that it is utterly out of the question, and they must mix with [the blacks] in every way. It was largely because of Miss [Helen] Townsend's leaving the school [after having been house mother in Winona since 1890] that I said I hoped the girls would not return. Her room has been a refuge at all times . . . some of the other Indian girls flirted so with the colored boys that it made for a good deal of gossip of a kind I hate and despise. Now, there will probably be no Indian boys at the school this year and without Miss Townsend's oversight I am afraid this sort of thing will be worse than before and you know how the Indian people feel about it . . . the changed conditions made me feel I could no longer conscientiously bring children on from the West and that is the reason I resigned.[34]

Thus, Andrus quit largely because she believed that Hampton could no longer prevent amalgamation between Indians and blacks, although she was so little averse to intermarriage between whites and Indians that she mourned the death of her Indian fiancé for the rest of her life. She observed that the knowledge had "spread far and wide" of three marriages between black and Indian students since the loss of the appropriations.[35] Seven of the last eleven Indians had been girls.

Even with this situation, just before her departure Townsend told

Gregg, "Our girls and Emerson Baird had been fully expecting to return to Hampton, although they frequently expressed a dread of going now that so many of their old teachers would not be there."[36] Thus it appears that at least one white teacher, Andrus, and quite possibly Townsend as well, abandoned support for biracial education even before their last Indian students did.

The Fallen Fortunes of Blacks: An External Factor in the Indian Program's Decline

The changing race relations between whites and blacks in the larger society helped shape Hampton's Indian program throughout its history: whereas the better climate of the emancipation era had enabled a black school to admit Indians under a federal contract, the worsened conditions more than thirty years later led to the withdrawal of that contract and to the resignation of the school's last teacher of Indians. The dwindling number of Indians at Hampton compelled greater integration on campus at the same time that it became increasingly difficult to justify educating Indians with blacks at all. For the position of blacks had declined markedly: the defeat of the Blair and Lodge Federal Election bills, the hardened crop lien and debt peonage systems, the increased incidence of lynchings, and the case of *Plessy v. Ferguson*—not to mention the increased imposition of Jim Crow ordinances—all document this downward slide. In addition a series of pogrom-like race riots exploded into the "Red Summer" of 1919.

The times were gone when Indians had asked for and received black roommates, when the AMA had envisioned opposing caste by creating biracial programs in its schools and had lobbied to include Indians in national aid to education, and when the freedom road for blacks had provided paths and momentum alike, however misguided, for Indian reform. Seeing blacks as role models for Indians—in such areas as the denial of rations as well as the granting of immediate citizenship and legal, if not actual, voting rights—had been common earlier because the emancipation of blacks had so closely preceded the defeat of many western tribes, the near extinction of the bison, and the closing of the frontier. As these shaping events receded in memory, Progressivism increased the importance of immigrants as role models for Indians, although analogy to any minority group became less influential with the emergence of cultural anthropology, if not because of progress in Indian education. It was also no longer necessary to promote sectional reconciliation by emphasizing that blacks were more "civilized" than Indians because of slavery: the spread of conservative southern views made northerners more ready to believe that slavery had been a positive good.

Armstrong's belief that black schools should limit themselves to teaching basic industrial and academic skills had spawned the corollary that those same schools would prove most practical for "civilizing" Indians. His idea, however, became increasingly unpopular toward the end of the century when predominantly black missionary schools became virtually all black at the same time that the number of Indians and whites in school together mushroomed. Although no more than 413 Indian children were enrolled in public schools in any one year from 1891 to 1908, historian Laurence Schmeckebier has shown that by 1916 there were more Indians (28,463) in public schools than there were in schools of their own, despite the fact that many white parents still refused to educate their children with Indians.[37] At the same time, tuition-paying whites were admitted into the government's boarding and day schools for Indians; indeed these often provided a nucleus around which frontier public school systems developed. Coexistent with all the abuses that one might expect in consolidated schools— rank discrimination against Indian pupils, the presence of a large number of mixed bloods while purebloods clustered in Indian schools, and the use of what were supposed to be Indian schools to benefit whites— integration between whites and Indians expanded at a time when caste had tightened around blacks even in the more egalitarian denominational schools.[38]

The relative status of blacks to Indians also declined where such relations were most important, among the previously slaveholding Five Civilized Tribes, in what was called Indian Territory before it became the state of Oklahoma. The historian Angie Debo has argued that the Indians' freedmen had been "the special favorites of the government from the negotiations of the peace treaties in 1866, through an entire generation of threatened division of land, to the compulsory allotments to freedmen provided by . . . the Dawes Commission [1893–1905]."[39] Having earlier abandoned southern tribes to the Confederacy, the United States followed the most contradictory policy after the war of forcing the Cherokees, Creeks, and Seminoles to adopt their freedmen while offering to remove them from among the Choctaw and Chickasaw, an option that once exercised, Washington failed to honor. The Choctaw eventually chose to adopt their freedmen (1885) but the Chickasaw refused. All freedmen on the rolls of the Civilized Tribes received allotments when preparatory to statehood the Dawes Commission transformed Indian Territory from five separate Indian nations holding land communally into individual landholdings. Thus Congress mandated a sharing of these nations' land with their former slaves both before and during allotment, while refusing to confiscate and redistribute the plantations of Confederates.

Yet in the end, Congress did not follow through in its protective stance toward the Indians' freedmen: in 1904, after only two years, it withdrew its ban on the conveyance of their allotments, except for their homesteads, because of, Debo argues, a growing conviction that Negroes had never been entitled to Indian land in the first place. Indeed by 1912 Indian reformer Warren Moorehead found few freedmen still residing on their homesteads, even as Indians were losing their own allotments.[40]

Moreover, Daniel F. Littlefield, Jr., has shown that, although the Indians' freedmen had played a significant role in all of the governments of the Five Civilized Tribes except the Chickasaw's—by voting, sitting on juries, being elected to office, and enjoying tax-free use of land—they lost these rights in 1907 after tribal governments were abolished and Oklahoma became a state. Thus "racial hatred was a basic issue in the founding of the State of Oklahoma." The Sooners quickly passed sweeping Jim Crow laws, segregating public institutions and prohibiting interracial marriages with blacks; their infamous grandfather clause effectively disfranchised the Negro population in 1910. Oklahoma also segregated the Seminole schools, the only ones among the Civilized Tribes that had been integrated. A "Young Seminole" faction came of age under Jim Crow, challenging traditional Seminoles who had valued black allies and absorbed black culture. The legal position of blacks deteriorated even among the Chickasaws, whose views on blacks had long approximated those of most white southerners, and whose freedmen lived from Reconstruction to statehood without schools and without legal status as "a people without a country." Although the Chickasaw nation had granted its freedmen no rights, neither had it passed legislation against them, as did the new state.[41]

The Indian Office in Washington itself was often hostile toward Hampton's Indian graduates because of their association with blacks, and it increasingly discriminated against the latter race, despite Commissioner Valentine's support of Hampton during the funding crisis. In 1930 Lucy Hunter Kennedy wrote Andrus, her former teacher, "Indian Service people have not been very cordial to Hampton [Indian] graduates, and whenever one got into the 'Service' life was made rather unpleasant for him, and it was seen to it that he had not much time to put into practice his Hampton principles and ideals." But a more comprehensive idea of the Indian Office's attitude toward Hampton's biracial focus is suggested by its employment practices toward blacks at the agencies. The employee rosters of the Indian Office indicate that only about 226 black citizens worked at agencies or schools from 1877 to 1909. Adding figures given in its internal correspondence up to 1929 reveals that during a period of over fifty years blacks averaged only 15 out of some 3,000 field positions a year (see table). The Indian Office was less and less open to blacks after the Wilson administration, although the *consistently* small number hired obscures the increasing discrimination, since the office's total work force *grew* from 723 in 1877 to 5,050 in 1912.[42]

Of Indian Service jobs open to blacks, the highest positions awarded were civil service appointments. Four black physicians made $1,000 a year, but were placed among the more "remote" and unassimilated tribes: Nathaniel J. Kennedy at Mescalaro, New Mexico (1892–95); Simeon L. Carson at Lower Brule, South Dakota (1903–9); Edward J. Davis at Zuni, New Mexico (1904–12); and Charles F. Maxwell at Tulalip, Washington (1902–6). Maxwell was fired soon after he was transferred south to Santee in 1906.[43] The only other black to earn $1,000 a year was John Taylor, for two decades the interpreter for the Southern Ute. The middle level black employees of the Indian field service earned just over $700 per year and included another interpreter,

Indian Office Employment Practices
with Regard to Blacks, 1877–1928

Year	Number	Year	Number
1877	17	1898	13
1878	6	1899	13
1879	17	1900	8
1880	10	1901	13
1883	24	1902	19
1884	24	1903	19
1886	13	1904	23
1888	17	1905	21
1890	8	1906	17
1891	10	1907	33
1892	11	1908	32
1893	11	1912	23
1894	14	1916	14
1895	10	1923	11
1896	10	1925	11
1897	11	1928	5

a teacher, a field matron, a financial clerk, a stenographer, a tailor, and an engineer. Twenty-two of the twenty-eight blacks who earned over $700 annually in desirable positions had had to move farther west than Indian Territory or the equally prejudiced state of Nebraska. However, most of the Indian Office's black employees worked near their original homes, at agencies adjoining the South; they earned less than $400 per year in unskilled jobs traditionally assigned to Negroes such as herder, butcher, cook, janitor, stableman, messenger, night watchman, laborer, and laundress.[44]

Although blacks already tended to work only at certain agencies, even greater segregation within the Indian Service, albeit veiled with a promise of certain advantages for them, was contemplated. In 1907, citing the "danger of friction" between black and white agency employees and the "objection the Indians themselves had to negroes," Commissioner Leupp asked once Hampton Indian house father Booker Washington his opinion of "grouping all the negroes we have . . . at one point. If we found a certain negro man capable in our judgment of handling the affairs of a school or agency, and gathered around him a corp of assistants of his own race, placing all this group . . . where we discover perhaps the least objection on the part of the Indians to negroes in authority do you believe success would follow? . . . The trouble with our present mixed system is not only the friction . . . but the failure of the negro to get his full credit." The Tuskegeean replied that the experiment might succeed if undertaken "in connection with Indians who had been trained at Hampton and [thus] would not share any prejudice against colored people." But he advised against "any radical change . . . until the feeling had passed on the part of the colored people over the Brownsville affair" (i.e., the court-martial of 167 blacks by Leupp's boss, President Theodore Roosevelt). Leupp agreed to wait for the right "psychological moment," but reiterated that "a school in which the Hampton-trained Indians and the very best of our black employees could be brought together, would offer a very interesting field in the humanities."[45]

Of course the increasing discrimination against blacks at the agencies occurred against the backdrop of discrimination in the Indian Office's Washington headquarters. Records beginning in 1912 show that out of a total work force of 289, the home office employed only six blacks; in 1923 and 1928 the numbers held steady at eight, out of totals numbering 222 and 191 respectively. Only three of the Indian Office's eleven divisions—administrative, land, and mail—hired blacks at all.[46] Except for a handful of clerks and subclerical employees, most black employees in the Indian Office from 1912 to 1922 were messengers (segregated in an area of the mail room), charwomen, and "laborers" whose regular duties were listed as filling water coolers, collecting waste paper, and cleaning windows and cuspidors.[47] Seen in perspective, employment practices in the central office were no worse than in most other divisions of the Interior Department, perhaps no worse than in other departments and branches of government; however, they are consistent with the increasing prevalence, even within an agency "serving" a racial minority, of prejudice against blacks, and therefore against Indians educated with blacks.[48]

Hampton's Role in Indian Education: An Overview

In the long view, despite being gradually overtaken by the pressures discussed in this chapter, Hampton's Indian program influenced national Indian affairs in several important, concrete ways, especially during its first ten years. Initially, Hampton's admission of Pratt's St. Augustine prisoners generated public sentiment for educating Indians in the East. Several of the nation's chief executives credited Hampton with inspiring the establishment of Carlisle, and credited both with having encouraged the founding of major western boarding schools at Forest Grove in 1880 (renamed Chemewa), and at Haskell, Chilocco, and Albuquerque in 1884. Hampton's industrial and vocational emphasis was not only adopted in all these schools but also influenced Indian education in Canada: the Davin Report of 1879 set up boarding schools in the provinces modeled after those in the states.[49]

Hampton also established itself in Indian affairs by initiating the standard yearly government contract of $167 to educate each Indian in the East; by pioneering Pratt's outing system, the education of Indian girls, and coeducation; and by pushing the government to purchase schoolmade goods and employ returned students. Further, by admitting married couples with children and placing them in cottages, Hampton began the Women's National Indian Association's (WNIA) homebuilding program, even though its proposal to resettle either the entire Nez Perce or Apache tribe near the school proved impractical. Armstrong helped to organize the IRA and place C. C. Painter and J. B. Harrison on its staff, and he joined forces with other leading Indian reformers to pass the major legislation of the acculturationist Vanishing Policy and to appoint the agents and commissioners who would implement it. Even after Hampton's influence on Indian reform began to wane, the school inaugurated an Indian Emancipation Day of sorts and editorialized against the exploitation of Indians in wild west shows.

Moreover, during the Indian program's peak of activity in the 1880s, Hampton's Indian Records Office provided the most systematic evidence available that Indians educated in European ways did not "go back to the blanket." Folsom had some reason to assert in 1904 that there "was a time when [our] figures and facts . . . saved, not only Hampton, but all non-reservation schools from being closed." She added in 1911 that "these figures were printed in our reports, copied in papers and magazines, used by General Armstrong and others in public addresses, printed in government reports, adopted by the Indian societies, and used in many other helpful ways. . . . [They] were all the time influencing public opinion, starting Indian societies, increasing government appropriations, and, year by year, building up the Indian school system."[50]

Two of Hampton's monthlies broke new ground in Indian affairs. The *Southern Workman* became one of the longest running periodicals regularly to cover Indians; it exposed all kinds of people involved with the affairs of blacks to Indian affairs, even as this breadth reduced its focus on black issues. The paper provided a forum for leading Indian reformers without their own organs, and listed among its regular contributors Herbert Welsh, anthropologist Alice Fletcher, Amelia S. Quinton of the WNIA, Reverend Sheldon Jackson of the Presbyterian missions in Alaska, and reformer William Harsha, in addition to a staff of Folsom, Ludlow and other faculty writers who ranked among the movement's best. The *Workman* drew source material from as many as twenty-three Indian papers and regularly printed excerpts from the commissioners' annual reports, IRA publications, Mohonk conference proceedings, WNIA reports, and yearly meetings of the SAI. Moreover, beginning from a debating society established in 1882 by Thomas Tuttle and Joseph Estes (both Sioux), and from a modest periodical called *Speeches, Talks and Thoughts* (1886–1907) became one of the first newspapers and at times the only newspaper in the country whose editors and contributors were Indian students. Much of its content, however, like many black and Indian student speeches, was "censored and directed" by Hampton's white staff.[51]

One apparently unforeseen and uncontrived effect at Hampton of black influence on Indian culture deserves mention. The Negro spirituals usually first heard by Indians at the institute added to native musical traditions. For example, Jacob C. Morgan, Hampton's Navajo assimilationist, translated "plantation" hymns into Navajo religious services in 1940. In 1969 David Owl sang with the "Cherokee Indian Singers," an impromptu group of seven alumni that performed whenever a quartet was present. The Wisconsin Oneida singers of Ruth Baird are still singing the gospel songs they had learned at Hampton. And Sioux Henry Leeds, when reviewing the events of his life, wrote to Folsom, "I had some good lucks as well as some bad ones. . . . I am like that dear old plantation song we used to sing while at Hampton, 'Sometimes I'm up sometimes I down, Oh yes Lord sometimes I'm almost to the ground, oh yes lord.'"[52]

Finally, Hampton's efforts for Indians also provided a reservoir of personnel who went on to work for Indian acculturation at other places and times. For example, Treasurer J. F. B. Marshall became head of the American Unitarian Association's Bureau of Southern and Indian Educational Work in 1886, the same year that teachers Elaine Goodale (Eastman) and Laura E. Tileston established the White River Camp School among the Lower Brule. Tileston headed a committee that built a hospital among these Indians in 1891, while her better known co-worker, Goodale, became in 1890 the first field supervisor of the Sioux's schools, as well as an author and co-author with her prominent husband, Charles Eastman. Moreover, Armstrong's son-in-law's sister, Annie Beecher Scoville, who had grown up at Hampton, became an interim superintendent of Indian schools in 1905. Decades later, Vice Principal J. Henry Scattergood became assistant commissioner of Indian Affairs in the Hoover administration.

Despite what white policymakers saw as significant accomplishments, however, Hampton did not speak for minority groups themselves when it failed to combat racial prejudice and discrimination. Instead, and especially regarding Indians, the school attempted to inculcate Eurocentric ideas of civilization into minority representatives of its own choosing, while denying full expression to their opinions and values. Its arguments were nevertheless convincing enough—and often useful and clever enough—to help black accommodationists gain primacy in black thought during a discouraging period, and to help create English-speaking Indian leaders in the West who fashioned nontraditional survival strategies after their own peoples were disarmed.

Even though black precedents for Indian reform were less common and effective after 1900, the age of Booker T. Washington had made its mark on the general discussion of the Indians' personal habits, rural economy, and political stance. *Up from Slavery* was read in many Indian schools and part of it was even translated into Lakota, in Santee Indian School's *Iapi Oaye*. Moreover, returned Sioux students at Lower Brule patterned an Indian Business League on the Tuskegeean's National Negro Business League. Educated Indian leaders such as those in the SAI stressed themes of duty and obligation to the United States as well as rights of citizenship, rights understood not to include self-determination. For example, Henry Roe Cloud, who patterned his American Indian Institute on Hampton and Tuskegee, told an audience at Hampton's Indian Day that "the Indians of old had to prove themselves worthy before they enjoyed the privileges of braves; similarly the Indians of today must show themselves able to perform the duties of citizenship before they demand its rights."[53]

Indeed Hampton sometimes offered both Indians and blacks even less than they already possessed: it compared their histories in public and utilized their interaction on campus in ways at odds with their apparent best interests. Thus Hampton opposed the Indians' treaties, particularly annuities and rations, and would have preferred that Indians not be given land in severalty, while it advised blacks to forego for the time being the constitutional protections resulting from the Civil War and Reconstruction. Because Armstrong held that such benefits had come to both minorities without the spiritual wellspring of self-initiated labor and sacrifice, he deemed it morally correct to deny these races legal and material advantages that were not yet "theirs." Although his strategic initiative challenged "them" rather than "us," it expressed less simple racism than confidence in his own methods and underlying beliefs, a complex of puritanical ideas that viewed industrious habits as the basis for morality: only such habits could earn political privileges and advance civilization. All of this was captured and perpetuated in Frissell's repetition of the words of an unnamed black preacher who prayed to "make the unfit fit and the fitter more fitting."[54]

Armstrong's attempt to place the acquisition of political rights and economic justice on a moral foundation itself never open to question, grew not from contempt for those he believed in need of his help but from the thoroughly internalized conservative social values associated with rugged individualism. Consequently, far from questioning his moral ascendancy over blacks and Indians, he viewed their surrender to his higher law as the basis for their ultimate moral regeneration. While all other measures were seen as artificial, "it would be as impossible to control the tides of the sea as to prevent real worth and moral force in this country from finally taking the place for which it is fitted. Opposition would strengthen it, persecution tremendously stimulate it. Legislation cannot help it."[55]

It was a shame that Armstrong did not view as equally providential his rare insights into the excesses generated by the very values he represented. For example, while patrolling the Mexican border in 1865, he had philosophized that "men are as a rule heathen. We adore as many absurdities as the Hindoos—society impels us to a false manhood ... here [near the Rio Grande] it is easier to be manly, to cultivate noble aspirations than in the most pious New England village—a greasy, dirty Mexican fighting for the liberty of his country inspires me more than the whole faculty of Andover Theological Seminary would. Don't let us pity the Zulus and the Esquinmaux [*sic*] too much—we are almost as blind as they—they by darkness—we by too much light."[56] Clearly, for Armstrong it was the struggle, the ongoing fight for freedom, equality, and respect, not the complacent enjoyment of them, that God had bestowed upon man, as his obligation rather than his inalienable right. In peacetime he saw the struggle as that of proving one's worthiness to advance through the ranks of the "Grand Army of God's Workers."

Even as worsening race relations thrust Hampton into the forefront of black education, precisely because the school was making it palatable for some blacks to articulate the new American mainstream's separatist position on the "Negro problem," its Indian Department increasingly diverged from the new mainstream of the Indian movement. Paradoxically, the Indian program died once it had generated a social acceptance of Indian schools. Far from reaping its own irrepressible moral rewards, because of the pre-existing treaty system and the unforeseen withdrawal of many Protestants from Indian contract work in order to force a similar withdrawal by Catholics, Hampton's effort for Indian education ultimately inspired the development of an increasingly centralized, professional, and bureaucratic national system. It was a system bereft of the strong religious input that had prevailed in Indian affairs under Grant's Peace Policy, and which had built southern schools including Hampton itself. Although affiliation with Hampton embarrassed the modernizing Indian Office, it often envied the school's equipment, copied its methods, and imbibed its practical philosophy.

Hampton was a missionary school that became isolated in a more secular age, a contract school outside the governmental civil service, an eastern boarding school in a system beginning to emphasize reservation day schools, and a black school whose Indian students experienced all of the vicissitudes of declining white-black relations. Armstrong's "moral force" had not ensured that Hampton's Indian program would "finally [take] the place for which it is fitted." In recalling her sister-in-law's father and his friends, Annie Beecher Scoville reflected, "Every reformer who is brought face to face with the results of his own enthusiasm at some time in his career echoes Browning's, 'Tis dangerous work to meddle with souls / And trouble enough to save one's own.'"[57] Armstrong's vision was too limited to address the challenges that the twentieth century would bring to red, black, and white Americans.

Notes

1. Frissell served on the business committee of the 1897 Capon Springs Conference for the Negro as well as on the Southern and General Education Boards (the latter organization coming to serve mostly whites), and would be instrumental in the establishment of the Hampton Farmers' Conferences (1896), the Hampton Negro Conferences (1897) and the Negro Organizational Society for civic improvement (1912). HBF, no title, (n.d.), box 3 in HBF "To Be Typed," HUA.

2. HBF, "Speech on Indian Day," (n.d.), unnumbered box of his speeches, HUA; Folsom, "Notes on Dr. Frissell," typewritten reminiscences, Indian Collection, HUA. Similarly, in 1880 when Frissell applied for the position of Hampton's chaplain, the AMA's Michael Strieby told Armstrong that Frissell "lacked the snap which I had expected of him, and I have learned . . . he has not much imagination or energy. I think we better wait before moving on him." See Strieby to SCA, May 14, 1880, HUA.

3. HBF, "Annual Report," *SW* 32 (May 1903): 244; F. D. Gleason to HBF, Feb. 10, 1904, HUA; Andrus, "Report of Indian Records Office," Feb. 15, 1918, p. 3, box 31, Indian Records, Indian Collection, HUA.

4. Elizabeth Hyde to Joseph C. Hart, Superintendent of Indian Schools at Oneida, Wisconsin, June 22, 1904, box 28, Indian Affairs, Hampton Institute Staff, Indian Collection, HUA.

5. Alice M. Price to HBF, May 29, 1905, Flora F. Low to HBF, May 16, 1905, C. Augustus Adams to HBF, May 8, 1905, all HUA; Andrus, "Report of Indian Records Office," Jan. 1912, p. 12, box 31, Indian Records, Indian Collection, HUA.

6. HBF, *Annual Report*, 1905, p. 3; Editorial remarks, *SW* 37 (Dec. 1908): 646; William Scoville to HBF, Sept. 10, 1896, HUA; Folsom, "Report of the Indian Records Office," 1906, p. 1, Folsom box, Indian Collection, HUA. Editorial remarks, *SW* 37 (Dec. 1908): 646.

7. Hoxie, *A Final Promise*, pp. 198–204.

8. Editorial remarks, *SW* 37 (Dec. 1908): 646; HBF, Dec. 1910, Indian Affairs Box, Indian Collection, HUA.

9. Folsom, "Report of Indian Records Office," 1906, p. 1, Folsom Box, Indian Collection, HUA.

10. Ibid., p. 1; Andrus, "Report of Indian Records Office," 1909, p. 327, box on Indian Letters, Folsom, Indian Collection, HUA.

11. Andrus to unknown, Feb. 27, 1920, p. 4, HUA; Folsom to Mrs. Chavez, Feb. 23, 1905, box on Indian Letters, Folsom, p. 286, Indian Collection, HUA.

12. Folsom, "Letters to Returned Students," Dec. 1912, box on Indian Affairs, Indian Collection, HUA.

13. Tingey, "Blacks and Indians Together," pp. 320–26 and King, "Color and Race," pp. 15–17 discuss the withdrawal of funds issue.

14. HBF, untitled letter on appropriations, Dec. 1912, box on Indian Affairs, Letters from Hampton Institute to Returned Students, Folsom, In-

dian Collection, HUA; U.S. House, *Congressional Record* 48 part 5 (Apr. 8, 1912), pp. 4454–59. Many in Congress were apparently not aware that Hampton was primarily a school for blacks. When a congressional committee decided to abolish the Hampton "Indian school" in 1907, Commissioner Leupp was forced to tell it, "Don't sell what you haven't got. . . . Not a man in the room did not express . . . surprise." Francis E. Leupp, *The Indian and His Problem* (New York, 1910), pp. 200–01.

15. HBF, untitled typed letter on appropriations, incorrectly dated Dec. 1912, box on Indian Affairs, Letters from Hampton Institute to Returned Students, Folsom, Indian Collection, HUA.

16. Albert Smiley to Mrs. M. E. Wickham, Aug. 19, 1912, Smiley Papers, Haverford College; U.S. Congress, Indian Appropriation Bill, 1912, Senate Committee Hearing, M43652, p. 59, Library of Congress; T. J. Jones to HBF, Mar. 28, and Apr. 15 and 19, 1912, Jones's box, Trustee's Section, HUA; Indian Affairs—H of R., Senate, and Booker T. Washington, box 86, Indian Collection, HUA.

17. Minutes of Faculty Meetings, Feb. 17, 1912, HUA.

18. HBF to Stephens, Feb. 8, 1912, p. 3, HUA; Jones to HBF, Apr. 8 and 15, 1912, Jones's box, Trustee's Section, HUA, names the congressmen that Jones visited. For Sloan's efforts on behalf of Hampton see Sloan to Arthur C. Parker, Feb. 19, 1912, Parker Papers, New York State Museum, Albany (hereafter cited as NYSM).

19. Robert Ogden to Stephens, Feb. 12, 1912, box 22, Indian Affairs, Indian Collection, HUA; HBF to Charles Carter, May 10, 1912, box 42, Appropriations and Funds for Indian Education at Hampton, Indian Collection, HUA.

20. Minutes of Faculty Meetings, May 8, 1912, HUA. Curtis would later sponsor antilynching legislation, report the Indian Citizenship bill out of the Senate Committee on Indian Affairs, and serve as Herbert Hoover's vice president. See Robert L. Zangrando, *The NAACP Crusade against Lynching, 1909–1950* (Philadelphia, 1980), pp. 54–56, 67, 69, 71; Hazel W. Hertzberg, *The Search for an American Indian Identity*, p. 206; William E. Unrau, *Mixed-Bloods and Tribal Dissolution: Charles Curtis and the Quest for Indian Identity* (Lawrence, 1989).

21. "Hampton Indians Petition Congress," *SW* 41 (May 1912): 265; Samuel Scoville to T. J. Jones, May 3, 1912, HUA; William Aery, "Original Draft" of Hampton's Indians Petition to Sen. Charles Curtis, box 29, Staff, Indian Collection, HUA. Jones and the staff also decided that "it would not be best to send the Indian boys to appear in person before the [Senate] Committee." See Minutes of Faculty Meetings, May 8, 1912, HUA.

22. Tingey, interview with Charles Williams on Aug. 27, 1974, in "Blacks and Indians Together," pp. 325–26; HBF, untitled typed letter on appropriations, incorrectly dated Dec. 1912, box on Indian Affairs, Letters to Returned Students, Folsom, Indian Collection, HUA.

23. Hertzberg, *The Search for an American Indian Identity*, pp. 81, 99.

24. See Parker to Fayette A. McKenzie, Sept. 26, 1914, Parker Papers, NYSM.

25. Parker to HBF, May 11, 1912, Parker Papers, NYSM; HBF to Parker, May 15, 1912, HUA.

26. *Quarterly Journal of the Society of American Indians* 1 (Jan. 1913): 213–15, cited without author in Hertzberg, *The Search for an American Indian Identity,* pp. 99–100.

27. Frank K. Rogers to HBF, Feb. 21, 1912, box 22, Indian Collection, HUA. Andrus, "Hampton's Work for the Indians," *SW* 44 (Feb. 1915): 89; Hyde in HBF, "Annual Report," *SW* 42 (June 1913): 294; Andrus to Mrs. Pierrepont Alford, Apr. 10, 1914, box on Indian Letters, Andrus, Indian Collection, HUA.

28. Andrus, "For Dr. Hanus," box 31, Indian Records, Indian Collection, HUA.

29. Editorial, "Hampton's Principal Elect," *SW* 47 (Feb. 1918): 51; Vice Principal George P. Phenix, "Annual Report," *SW* 47 (June 1918): 286.

30. Gregg, "Annual Report," *SW* 48 (June 1919): 322; Andrus to Charles E. Emory, Oct. 9, 1918, Emory's student files, HUA; Gregg, "Annual Report," *SW* 48 (June 1919): 322.

31. Andrus to unknown, Feb. 27, 1920, box 31, Indian Records, Indian Collection, HUA. Although one or two unrecorded western trips may have been made after Armstrong's death, Hampton's personnel only seem to have gone West in 1894, 1904, 1915, and 1919. Andrus, "Report of the Indian Records Office," Feb. 15, 1918, p. 3, box 31, Indian Records, Indian Collection, HUA; "Incidents," *SW* 48 (Sept. 1919): 465.

32. Andrus, "Report of Indian Records Office," Feb. 15, 1919 and Jan. 15, 1916, box 31, Indian Records, Indian Collection, HUA; Pierrepont Alford to Andrus, Jan. 3, 1915, Alford's student file, HUA; William Sapient to Andrus, Aug. 10, 1920, Sapient's student file, HUA.

33. Gregg, "Regarding Hampton Indians," *SW* 51 (Aug. 1922): 393.

34. Addie Stevens Bouchier to Andrus, Sept. 3, 1923 and Andrus to Bouchier, Sept. 6, 1923, Bouchier's student file, HUA.

35. Andrus, "Report of Indian Records Office," Feb. 15, 1919, box 31, Indian Records, Indian Collection, HUA.

36. Helen L. Townsend to Gregg, Sept. 13, 1923, box 28, Indian Affairs, Hampton Institute Staff, Indian Collection, HUA.

37. Schmeckebier, The *Office of Indian Affairs,* p. 216.

38. Acting Commissioner F. H. Abbott to the Superintendents, Aug. 21, 1909, RG75, circular 335, NARA; Editorial, "Schools for White Children," *Indian School Journal* 5 (Sept. 1905): 48; Schmeckebier, The *Office of Indian Affairs,* p. 482; Evelyn C. Adams, *American Indian Education,* pp. 63–65.

39. Angie Debo, *And Still the Waters Run: The Betrayal of the Five Civilized Tribes* (Princeton, 1940), p. 135; Debo, *A History of Indians in the United States* (Norman, 1970), p. 279.

40. Debo, *And Still the Waters Run,* p. 135; Warren Moorehead, *Our National Problem: The Sad Condition of the Oklahoma Indians* (Philadelphia, 1912), p. 32, pamphlet A-238, roll 127, IRA Papers.

41. Daniel F. Littlefield, Jr., *The Chickasaw Freedmen: A People without a Country* (Westport, 1980), pp. 225–27; Rebecca Bateman, "Jim Crow Comes to Indian Territory: Racism and Relations between Blacks and Indians of the Oklahoma Seminole Tribe after Statehood" (Paper presented before the American Society for Ethnohistory, Toronto, Canada, Nov. 2, 1990).

42. Lucy Hunter Kennedy to Andrus, May 8, 1930, Kennedy's student file, HUA; Employee Rosters, 1877–1909, RG75, NARA. See RG48, file 15-15-14, Appointment Division, Colored Employees, NARA. In 1918 applicants had to include a picture. See *Procedural Issuances and Orders*, Feb. 13, 1918, RG75, M1142, NARA. Stuart, *The Indian Office*, p. 130 and Chief Clerk C. F. Hauck to the Secretary of the Interior, July 9, 1912, RG75, file 160, Central Superintendency, item 68840, NARA.

43. Employee Rosters, 1892–95 and 1902–9, RG75, NARA. The Indian Office's treatment of Dr. Maxwell had racial overtones. Although Maxwell had received good reports at Tulalip, Washington, soon after he went to Santee, Nebraska, Agent W. E. Megley charged him with neglecting to make house calls, disposing of a syphilitic Indian's dirty linen on the lawn, permitting unsanitary conditions in his office, and allowing an Indian with tuberculosis to remain in the Santee Indian school. Maxwell countered that his actions were really reactions to specific cases of discriminatory treatment and general disrespect that he had suffered at the agency: he had been denied a team of horses, refused such matron services as collecting and laundering hospital linen and office cleaning, and the school had not utilized his services. For Maxwell's record at Tulalip, see Superintendent Charles M. Buchanan to Commissioner, June 15, 1903, RG75, item 38850, NARA; for the trial transcript, see Megley to Commissioner, Feb. 9, 1907, RG75, item 15495, NARA.

One other lengthy transcript exists, describing the Indian Office's discharge of a black nurse for apparently racial reasons—her alleged sexual relationship with a local white man—see Lillian N. Henry, Jan. 1907, RG75, items 5290 and 3483, NARA.

44. Employee Rosters, RG75, NARA. These rosters furnish information on race, age, birthplace, position, and the agency of employment. Blacks systematically received the same wages as nonblacks for the same job.

45. F. E. Leupp to BTW, Jan. 10, 1907, BTW to Leupp, Jan. 16, 1907, and Leupp to BTW, Jan. 21, 1907, all in box 303, General Correspondence, BTW Papers, Library of Congress.

46. Chief Clerk of the Indian Office F. M. Conser to Chief Clerk of the Department of Interior E. M. Dawson, May 15, 1908; Interior Department memo dated July 6, 1912; Chief Clerk of the Department of Interior W. B. Acker to Commissioner of Conciliation Philip H. Brown, Department of Labor, Aug. 3, 1923; Chief Clerk of the Indian Office C. F. Hauke to Miss Atwood, Apr. 7, 1928. All items are in RG48, file 15-15-14, Appointment Division, Colored Employees, NARA.

47. See records for Aug. 1927, RG48, file 15-15-14, Appointment Division, Colored Employees, NARA.

48. For example, in 1929 the National Park Service had twenty-nine whites and one black, the Bureau of Education had ninety-eight whites and three blacks, the Bureau of Pensions had 521 whites and sixty blacks, and the Geological Survey 457 whites and twenty blacks. The only office in which blacks outnumbered whites was, not surprisingly, the Freedmen's Hospital, which employed 169 blacks and eight whites. See Memorandum, Apr. 11, 1929, RG48, file 15-15-14, Appointment Division, Colored Employees, NARA.

49. President Rutherford B. Hayes, "Annual Message," Dec. 2, 1878 and Dec. 1, 1879, in James D. Richardson, *Messages and Papers*, 10: 4455 and 4527–29 respectively; President James Garfield, "Speech of July 5, 1881 at Hampton Institute," *SW* 10 (July 1881): 74; President Chester A. Arthur, "Annual Message," *Messages and Papers*, 10: 4642–44. All in Muir, "Indian Education," pp. 56–59. Jean Barman, Yvonne Hebert, and Don McCaskill, *Indian Education in Canada*, 2 vols. (Vancouver, 1986) 1: 6.

50. Folsom, "Letters from Hampton Institute to Returned Students," Dec. 1904 and Dec. 1911, in box on Indian Affairs, Folsom, Indian Collection, HUA.

51. Folsom, "Activities of the Boys," loose typed materials not included in the final draft of "Indian Days," in Folsom Box on "Indian Days," Indian Collection, HUA; *T&T* 22 (Dec. 1906): 2 and 20 (Nov. 1904): 2; Daniel F. Littlefield, Jr., and James W. Parins, *American Indian Newspapers and Periodicals, 1826–1924* (Westport, 1984), pp. 356–58. The short-lived *Cherokee Rose Buds* and the *Sequoyah Memorial* of the 1850s were the first Indian student newspapers.

52. Joseph Morgan to Hampton Institute, Jan. 3, 1940, Morgan's student file, HUA; David Owl to Eleanor Gilman, Sept. 30, 1969, box on Prominent Students, Indian Collection, HUA; Jack Campisi and Laurence M. Hauptman, "Talking Back: The Oneida Language and Folklore Project, 1938–41," *Proceedings of the American Philosophical Society* 125 (Dec. 1981): 446 and 448n; Henry Leeds to Folsom, Dec. 28, 1913, Leeds's student file, HUA.

53. *T&T* 20 (Dec. 1904): 2; Henry Leeds to Folsom, Apr. 8, 1905, Leeds's student file, HUA; Henry Roe Cloud in "Hampton Incidents," *SW* 42 (Mar. 1913): 185. See also Roe Cloud to Gregg, Apr. 3, 1923, Elizabeth Bender's student file, HUA; "History Making News," *Quarterly Journal of the Society of American Indians* 3 (June 1915): 137; *LMC* 1914, p. 82. Hampton staff members attended SAI meetings and published its proceedings in the *Workman*, while publicly ignoring the NAACP, which had recognized that, by any objective measurement, segregation and discrimination had grown in spite of the school's conciliatory approaches towards race relations.

54. HBF, "Indian Education at Hampton," typed article, (n.d.), p. 17, Seely Mudd Library, Yale University.

55. SCA, "Annual Report," *SW* 20 (May 1891): 195.

56. SCA to Mrs. E. G. Beckwith, Aug. 23, 1865, Ludlow "Personal Memories," pp. 470–71.

57. Annie Beecher Scoville, "The Field Matron's Work" *SW* 20 (Aug. 1901): 975.

Works Cited

Archival Collections (in order of importance)

Hampton University, Hampton.
    Hampton University Archives
    Peabody Collection, Collis P. Huntington Memorial Library
    Hampton Institute Museum
Williams College, Williamstown, Mass., Stetson Library, Williamsiana Collection
    Armstrong Family Papers
National Archives and Research Administration, Washington, D.C.
    Record Group 75, Office of Indian Affairs
    Record Group 48, Office of the Secretary of Interior
Library of Congress, Manuscript Reading Room, Washington, D.C.
    Papers of Robert Curtis Ogden
    Papers of Booker Taliaferro Washington
    Papers of Henry Laurens Dawes
    Papers of Carl Schurz
    Papers of George Foster Peabody
    Papers of William Edward Burghardt Du Bois
    Papers of Richard Armstrong
Yale University, Beinecke Rare Book and Manuscript Library, Western Americana Collection, New Haven, Conn.
    Papers of Richard Henry Pratt
U.S. Army Military Research Institute, Carlisle Barracks, Pa.
    Richard Pratt Collection
State Museum of New York, Albany, N.Y.
    Papers of Arthur C. Parker (relative to the Society of American Indians)
Haverford College, Haverford College Library, Quaker Collection, Philadelphia.
    Smiley Family Papers (Lake Mohonk Conferences)

Microform Collections

American Missionary Association records, 281 rolls. Microfilmed by the Tennessee Microfilm Corporation, Nashville, Tenn., used with permission of the Amistad Research Center, Tulane University, New Orleans, La.

The Council Fire and Arbitrator. Philadelphia and Washington: A. B. Meacham and T. A. Bland, 1878–87 (1878–87). Microfilmed by the Brookhaven Press, LaCrosse, Wis.

Indian Rights Association Papers, Historical Society of Pennsylvania, microfilm ed. and *Indian Rights Association Papers: A Guide to the Microfilm
Edition, 1864–1973,* 236 rolls. Microfilmed by the Microfilming Corporation of America, Glen Rock, N.J.
The Indian School Journal. Chilocco, Okla.: Chilocco Indian School, 1901–
80, (1901–13). Microfilmed by Clearwater Publishing, New York, N.Y.
The Native American. Phoenix, Ariz.: Phoenix Indian School, 1900–1931
(1900–1916). Microfilmed by the Library of Congress Photoduplication Service, Washington, D.C.
The Papers of Carlos Montezuma, M.D., ed. by John W. Larner, 9 rolls. Microfilmed by Scholarly Resources, Inc., Wilmington, Del.
Quarterly Journal of the Society of American Indians, renamed *American Indian Magazine.* Washington, D.C.: Published by the Society of American Indians, 1913–20 (1913–20). Microfilmed by Clearwater Publishing, New York, N.Y.
Southern Workman, 1872–1939 (1872–1928). Hampton Institute, 68 rolls.
Microfilmed by the Library of Congress Photoduplication Service, Washington, D.C.
U.S. Indian Industrial School, Carlisle, Pa.: *Eadle Keahtah Toh* 1880–82. Microfilmed by the Oklahoma Historical Society, Oklahoma City. *The
Morning Star* 1882–87, *The Red Man* 1888–1900, and *The Red Man
and Helper* 1900–1904. Microfilmed by Clearwater Publishing, New
York, N.Y.
Wowapi: A Magazine Devoted to the Cause of the Indians. Boston: *Wowapi,*
1883 (1883). Microfilmed by the Historical Society of Wisconsin, Madison, Wis.

Privately Held Papers

Armstrong, (Samuel Chapman). "Breadbox" Papers, in possession of Dr.
Arthur Howe Jr., Lyme, Conn.
Graham, Edward Kidder. "A Tender Violence: The Life of Hampton Insti-
tute in Relation to Its Times, 1868–1968," 1968, copy provided by Julia
Graham Lear, Washington, D.C.
Newton, Philip. "Dissertation Proposal on Thomas Jesse Jones at Columbia
Teacher's College." Apr. 2, 1985. Dissertation Proposal, Columbia
Teacher's College. Copy provided by Newton, Altanta, Ga.

Newspapers

Bismarck *Tribune,* N.Dak.
Borlön *Sunday Herald,* Nebr.
Boston *Daily Advertiser*
Boston *Evening Transcript*
Boston *Journal*
Chicago *Defender*
Chicago *Interior*

Cincinnati *Commercial Gazette*
Denver *Republican*
Indianapolis *Freeman*
Minneapolis *Tribune*
New York *Age*
New York *Evening Post*
New York *Independent*
New York *Post*
New York *Sun*
New York *Tribune*
People's Advocate, Alexandria and Washington, D.C.
Philadephia *Inquirer*
Richmond *Daily Dispatch,* Va.
Richmond *Virginia Star*
St. Paul *Globe,* Minn.
Springfield *Republican,* Mass.

Periodicals and Series

American Missionary Magazine. New York: American Missionary Association, 1846–1933, (1872–1917).
Annual Reports of the Commissioner of Indian Affairs to the Secretary of the Interior. Washington, D.C.: Government Printing Office, 1824–present, (1877–1913).
Annual Reports of the Principal to the Board of Trustees. Hampton Institute Press, 1868–present, (1868–1928).
Annual Reports of the Women's National Indian Association. Philadelphia: The Executive Committee of the Women's National Indian Association, 1883–1912, (1883–1912).
The Chilocco Farmer. Chilocco, Okla.: Chilocco Indian School, 1903, (1903).
The Journal of Proceedings and Addresses of the National Educational Association. Washington, D.C.: NEA, 1857–present, (1878–1923).
Lend a Hand. Boston: J. Stillman Smith, 1886–97, (1886–97).
Proceedings of the Annual Meetings of the Lake Mohonk Conference of Friends of the Indian. New Paltz, N.Y.: Published by the Lake Mohonk Conferences, 1883–1914, 1929, (1883–1914, 1929).
Proceedings of the Annual Meetings of the Lake Mohonk Conference of Friends of the Negro. New Paltz, N.Y.: Published by the Lake Mohonk Conferences, 1890–91, (1890–91).
Proceedings of the Capon Springs Conferences for Education in the South. Capon Springs, W.V.. Published by The Capon Springs Conferences, 1898–1900, (1898–1900).
Proceedings of the Conferences for Education in the South. Washington, D.C.: Southern Education Board, 1901–17, (1901–17).
Talks and Thoughts of the Hampton Indian Students. Hampton: Hampton Institute Press, 1886–1906, (1886–1906).
U.S. *Congressional Record.*

Books

Adams, Evelyn C. *American Indian Education: Government Schools and Economic Progress.* Morningside Heights, N.Y.: King's Crown Press, 1946.

Alford, Thomas Wildcat. *Civilization and the Story of the Absentee Shawnee.* As told to Florence Drake. Norman: University of Oklahoma Press, 1936.

Anderson, James D. *The Education of Blacks in the South, 1860–1935.* Chapel Hill: University of North Carolina Press, 1988.

Armstrong, Samuel C. *Indian Education at the Hampton Normal and Agricultural Institute.* New York, N.Y.: George F. Nesbit & Son Printers, 1881.

———. *The Indian Question.* Hampton: Normal School Steam Press, 1883.

———. *Report of a Trip Made on Behalf of the IRA to Some Indian Reservations of the Southwest.* Philadelphia: Indian Rights Association, 1883. Pamphlet A-4, roll 102, IRA Papers.

———. *A New Attack on Eastern Schools.* Hampton: Hampton Institute Press, 1890.

———. *The Ideas on Education Expressed by Samuel C. Armstrong.* Hampton: For the Armstrong League of Hampton Workers by the Hampton Institute Press, 1909.

———. *Armstrong's Ideas on Education for Life.* Hampton: Press of the Hampton Normal and Agricultural Institute, 1926.

Barman, Jean, Yvonne Herbert, and Don McCaskill. *Indian Education in Canada.* 2 vols. Vancouver: University of British Columbia Press, 1986.

Barrows, William. *The Indians' Side of the Indian Question.* Boston: D. Lothrop, 1887.

Bear, Luther Standing. *My People the Sioux.* Ed. E. A. Brininstool. Boston: Houghton Mifflin, Riverside Cambridge Press, 1928.

Berkhofer, Robert F., Jr. *Salvation and the Savage.* New York, N.Y.: Antheneum, 1972.

Berry, Brewton. *The Education of the American Indian: A Survey of the Literature.* Washington, D.C.: Government Printing Office, 1968.

Burlin, Natalie Curtis. *Negro Folk Songs.* New York, N.Y.: George Schirmer, 1919.

———. *Songs and Tales from the Dark Continent.* New York, N.Y.: George Schirmer, 1920.

Carter, Forrest. *The Education of Little Tree.* Albuquerque: University of New Mexico Press, 1976.

Church, J. W. *The Regeneration of Sam Jackson.* Hampton: Hampton Institute Press, 1911.

Cohoe, with commentary by E. Adamson Hoebel and Karen Daniels Peterson. *A Cheyenne Sketchbook.* Norman: University of Oklahoma Press, 1964.

Debo, Angie. *And Still the Waters Run: The Betrayal of the Five Civilized Tribes.* Princeton, N.J.: Princeton University Press, 1970.

———. *A History of Indians in the United States.* Norman: University of Oklahoma Press, 1970.

Denison, John. *Mark Hopkins: A Biography.* New York, N.Y.: Charles Scribner's Sons, 1935.

Dockstader, Frederick J. *The American Indian in Graduate Studies: A Bibliography of Theses and Dissertations.* New York, N.Y. Museum of the American Indian, Heye Foundation, 1957.

Dyson, Walter. *Howard University: The Capstone of Negro Education.* Washington, D.C.: The Graduate School of Howard University, 1941.

Eastman, Elaine Goodale. *Pratt: The Red Man's Moses.* Norman: University of Oklahoma Press, 1935.

Engs, Robert Francis. *Freedom's First Generation: Black Hampton, Virginia, 1861–1890.* Philadelphia: University of Pennsylvania Press, 1979.

Fletcher, Alice C. *Indian Education and Civilization.* Sen. Ex Doc. 95, 48th Cong., 2nd sess. ser. 2264. Washington, D.C.: Government Printing Office, 1885.

Frissell, Hollis B. *The Work and Influence of Hampton.* New York, N.Y.: Armstrong Association, 1904.

Fritz, Henry E. *The Movement for Indian Assimilation.* Philadelphia: University of Pennsylvania Press, 1963.

Green, Norma Kidd. *Iron Eyes Family: The Children of Joseph LaFlesche.* Chicago: Johnson Publishing, 1969.

Guillemin, Jeanne. *Urban Renegades: The Cultural Strategy of American Indians.* New York, N.Y.: Columbia University Press, 1975.

Hagan, William T. *Indian Police and Judges: Experiments in Acculturation and Control.* New Haven, Conn.: Yale University Press, 1966.

———. *The Indian Rights Association: The Herbert Welsh Years, 1882–1904.* Tucson: University of Arizona Press, 1985.

Hailmann, William N. *Education of the Indian.* Monographs on Education in the U.S., no. 19. St. Louis, Mo.: Division of Exhibits, Department of Education, Universal Exposition, 1904.

Hall, Charles Lenox. *Forty Years in the Wilderness.* New York, N.Y.: Frederick A. Stokes, 1916.

Hampton Institute. *Ten Years' Work for Indians at Hampton, Virginia, 1878–1888.* Hampton: Hampton Institute Press, 1888.

———. *Twenty-Two Years' Work of the Hampton Normal and Agricultural Institute at Hampton Va., Record of Negro and Indian Graduates and Ex-Students.* Hampton: Normal School Press, 1893.

Harlan, Louis R. *Booker T. Washington: The Making of a Black Leader, 1856–1901.* New York, N.Y.: Oxford University Press, 1972.

Harlan, Louis R., ed. *The Booker T. Washington Papers.* 13 vols. Urbana: University of Illinois Press, 1972.

Harrison, J. B. *The Latest Studies on Indian Reservations.* Philadelphia: Indian Rights Association, 1886.

Hertzberg, Hazel W. *The Search for an American Indian Identity: Modern Pan-Indian Movements.* Syracuse, N.Y.: Syracuse University Press, 1971.

———. *Social Studies Reform: 1880–1980.* A Project SPAN Report. Boulder, Colo.: Social Science Consortium, 1981.

Hewitt, John H. *Williams College and Foreign Missions.* Boston: Pilgrim Press, 1914.

Higham, John. *History.* Englewood Cliffs, N.J.: Prentice-Hall, 1965.

Hopkins, Alphonso A. *The Life of Clinton Bowen Fisk.* New York, N.Y.: Funk and Wagnalls, 1910.

Hoxie, Frederick E. *A Final Promise: The Campaign to Assimilate the Indians, 1880–1920.* Lincoln: University of Nebraska Press, 1984.

Hughes, William Harden. *Robert Russa Moton of Hampton and Tuskegee.* Chapel Hill: University of North Carolina Press, 1956.

Hyde, George E. *A Sioux Chronicle.* Norman: University of Oklahoma Press, 1956.

Jones, Thomas Jesse. *Negro Education: A Study of Private and Higher Schools for Colored People in the United States.* Department of Interior, Bureau of Education, Bulletin, 1916, Nos. 38, 39, Washington, D.C.: Government Printing Office, 1917.

Keller, Robert H, Jr. *American Protestantism and United States Indian Policy, 1869–1882.* Lincoln: University of Nebraska Press, 1983.

Kelly, Lawrence C. *The Assault on Assimilation: John Collier and the Origins of Indian Policy Reform.* Albuquerque: University of New Mexico Press, 1983.

King, Kenneth James. *Pan-Africanism and Education: A Study of Race Philanthropy and Education in the Southern United States of America and East Africa.* Oxford, England: Clarendon Press, 1971.

Leupp, Francis E. *The Indian and His Problem.* New York, N.Y.: Charles Scribner's Sons, 1910.

Littlefield, Daniel F., Jr. *The Chickasaw Freedmen: A People without a Country.* Westport, Conn.: Greenwood Press, 1980.

Littlefield, Daniel F., Jr., and James W. Parins. *American Indian Newspapers and Periodicals, 1826–1924.* Westport, Conn.: Greenwood Press, 1984.

Logan, Rayford W. *Howard University: The First Hundred Years, 1867–1967.* New York, N.Y.: New York University Press, 1969.

Ludlow, Helen W. *The Hampton Institute: Its Work for Two Races.* Hampton: Hampton Normal and Agricultural School Steam Press, 1885.

Malval, Fritz J. *A Guide to the Archives of Hampton Institute.* Westport, Conn.: Greenwood Press, 1985.

Mardock, Robert W. *The Reformers and the American Indian.* Columbia: University of Missouri Press, 1971.

Massachusetts Indian Association. *Twelfth Annual Report of the Massachusetts Indian Association.* Boston: J. Stillman Smith, 1894.

Meriam, Lewis, et al. *The Problem of Indian Administration.* Baltimore, Md.: Johns Hopkins University Press, 1928.

Moorehead, Warren. *Our National Problem: The Sad Condition of the Oklahoma Indians.* Philadelphia: Indian Rights Association, 1912. Pamphlet A 238, IRA Papers.

Morgan, Thomas J. *The Negro in the Ideal American Republic.* Philadelphia: American Baptist Publishing, 1885.

———. *Reminiscences of Service With Colored Troops in the Army of the Cumberland.* Providence, R.I.: Soldiers' and Sailors' Historical Society Publishing, 1885.

Moton, Robert Russa. *Finding a Way Out.* College Park, Md.: McGrath Publishing, 1920.

Newton, Richard Heber. *Social Studies.* New York, N.Y.: G.P. Putnam & Sons, 1887.

New York Evening Post. *A Bill to Promote Mendicancy, Further Exposition of its Demoralizing Tendencies* (citing Armstrong). New York: New York Evening Post Publishing, 1889.

Peabody, Francis Greenwood. *Education for Life: The Story of Hampton Institute.* 1918. Reprint, College Park, Md.: McGrath Publishing, 1969.

Peets, Isaac L. *Language Lessons: Designed to Introduce Young Learners, Deaf Mutes and Foreigners to a Correct Understanding of the English Language.* New York, N.Y.: Baker & Taylor, 1875.

Petersen, Karen Daniels. *Plains Indian Art from Fort Marion.* Norman: University of Oklahoma Press, 1971.

Pratt, Richard H. *American Indians, Chained and Unchained, Address before the Pennsylvania Commandery of the Military Order of the Royal Legion, at the Union League, Philadelphia, Oct. 23, 1912, Entitled "One of General Sheridan's Ways with Indians and What Came of It," by R. H. Pratt, Brig. Gen., U.S.A.* n.p. 1912. Washington, D.C.: Library of Congress, Class E. Misc. Microfilms, 41000-41046.

———. *Negroes and Indians. Address of Brigadier General Richard H. Pratt Made before the Pennsylvania Commandery, Military Order of Foreign Wars of the United States at the Bellevue-Stratford Hotel, Philadelphia, January 14, 1913.* Pamphlet A 258, IRA Papers.

———. *Battlefield and Classroom: Four Decades with the American Indian, 1867–1904.* Ed. Robert M. Utley. New Haven, Conn.: Yale University Press, 1964.

Priest, Loring. *Uncle Sam's Stepchildren: The Reformation of United States Indian Policy, 1865–1887.* Camden, N.J.: Rutgers University Press, 1942.

Prucha, Francis Paul. *American Indian Policy in Crisis: Christian Reformers and the Indian, 1865–1900.* Norman: University of Oklahoma Press, 1976.

———. *A Bibliographical Guide to the History of Indian-White Relations in the United States.* Chicago: University of Chicago Press, 1977.

———. *The Churches and the Indian Schools, 1888–1912.* Lincoln: University of Nebraska Press, 1979.

———. *The Great Father: The United States Government and the American Indian,* 2 vols. Lincoln: University of Nebraska Press, 1984.

Richards, Thomas C. *Samuel J. Mills: Missionary Pathfinder, Pioneer and Promoter.* Boston: Pilgrim Press, 1906.

Richardson, James D. *A Compilation of the Messages and Papers of the Presi-

dents, 1789–1897. 20 vols. New York, N.Y.: Bureau of National Literature, 1897.

Rideout, Henry M. *William Jones: Indian, Cowboy, Scholar, and Anthropologist in the Field.* New York, N.Y.: Frederick A Stokes, 1912.

Rose, Willie Lee. *Rehearsal for Reconstruction: The Port Royal Experiment.* New York, N.Y.: Oxford University Press, 1964.

Rudolph Frederick. *Mark Hopkins and the Log: Williams College, 1836–1872.* New Haven, Conn.: Yale University Press, 1956.

Rules for Indian Schools, with Course of Study, Lists of Text Books, and Civil Service Rules. Washington, D.C.: Government Printing Office, 1892.

Saxe, David. *Social Studies in Schools.* New York, N.Y.: SUNY Press, 1991.

Schmeckebier, Laurence. *Office of Indian Affairs.* Baltimore, Md.: Johns Hopkins University Press, 1927.

Sheppard, William H. *Pioneers in Congo.* Louisville, Ky: Pentecostal Publishing, 1923.

Stuart, Paul. *The Indian Office: Growth and Development of an American Institution, 1865–1900.* Ann Arbor, Mich.: University Microfilms International, 1979.

Supress, Burton, and Ann Ross. *Bear's Heart: Scenes from the Life of a Cheyenne Artist.* New York, N.Y.: J.B. Lippincott, 1977.

Szasz, Margaret Connell. *Indian Education in the American Colonies.* Albuquerque: University of New Mexico Press, 1988.

Talbot, Edith Armstrong. *Samuel Chapman Armstrong: A Biographical Study.* New York: Doubleday, Page, 1904.

Tomlinson, Everette T., and Paul G. Tomlinson. *A Leader of the Freedmen: The Life and Story of Samuel Chapman Armstrong.* Army and Navy edition. Philadelphia: American Sunday School Union, 1917.

Trennert, Robert A., Jr. *The Phoenix Indian School.* Norman: University of Oklahoma Press, 1988.

Unrau, William E. *Mixed-Bloods and Tribal Dissolution: Charles Curtis and the Quest for Indian Identity.* Lawrence: University of Kansas Press, 1989.

Washburn, Wilcomb. *Assault on American Tribalism: The Dawes Act.* New York, N.Y.: J.B. Lippincott, 1975.

Washington, Booker T. *Up from Slavery.* New York, N.Y.: A.L. Burt, 1901.

———. *The Story of the Negro: The Rise of the Race from Slavery.* New York, N.Y.: Doubleday, Page, 1909.

Welsh, Herbert. *Are Eastern Industrial Schools for Indian Children a Failure?* Philadelphia: Indian Rights Association, 1886.

———. *A Crisis in the Cause of Indian Education.* Philadelphia: Indian Rights Association, 1892. Pamphlet A 143, IRA Papers.

Whelan, Michael. "History and the Social Studies: A Response to the Critics." *Theory and Research in Social Education* 20 (Winter 1992): 2–16.

Williams, Walter L. *Black Americans and the Evangelization of Africa, 1877–1900.* Madison: University of Wisconsin Press, 1982.

Wilson, Gilbert L. *Buffalo Bird Woman's Garden: Agriculture of the Hidatsa*

Indians. 1917. Reprint. St. Paul: Minnesota Historical Society Press, 1987.

Zangrando, Robert L. *The NAACP Crusade against Lynching.* Philadelphia: Temple University Press, 1980.

Articles

Abbott, Lyman. "Snapshots of My Contemporaries: General Samuel Chapman Armstrong—Educational Pioneer." *Outlook* (Aug. 17, 1894).

Adams, David Wallace. "Education in Hues: Red and Black at Hampton Institute, 1878–1893." *South Atlantic Quarterly* 76 (Spring 1877).

Ahern, Wilbert H. "'The Returned Indians': Hampton Institute and Its Indian Alumni, 1879–1893." *Journal of Ethnic Studies* 10 (Winter 1983).

Anderson, James D. "The Hampton Model of Normal School Industrial Education, 1868–1900." In *New Perspectives on Black Educational History.* Ed. James D. Anderson and Vincent P. Franklin. Boston: G. K. Hall, 1978.

Armstrong, Samuel Chapman. "Educational Work among the Freedmen." *American Missionary Magazine* 1 (Dec. 1877).

———. "A Paper Read at the Anniversary Meeting of the AMA." *American Missionary Magazine* 1 (Dec. 1877).

———. "Work and Duty in the East." *American Missionary Magazine* 4 (Dec. 1881).

———. "The Hemenway Farm." *American Missionary Magazine* 6 (Feb. 1883).

———. "Indian Education at the East." *Pamphlets in American History,* Washington, D.C.: Library of Congress (1883).

———. "The Indian Work at Hampton." *Wowapi* 1 (Nov. 7, 1883).

———. "Lessons from the Hawaiian Islands." *Journal of Christian Philosophy* 3 (Jan. 1884).

———. "A Letter from General Armstrong." *Council Fire and Arbitrator* 8 (Jan. 1884).

———. Education of the Indian." *Proceedings of the National Educational Association.* (1884).

———. "The Future of the American Negro." *Proceedings of the Fourteenth Annual Conference on Charities and Corrections* 14 (1887).

———. "Industrial Work." In *Proceedings of the Lake Mohonk Conference on the Negro,* New Paltz, N.Y.: Lake Mohonk Conferences, 1890.

Bacon, Alice M. "Work and Methods of the Hampton Folk-lore Society." *Journal of American Folk-Lore* 11 (Jan.–Mar. 1898).

Bacon, A. M., and E. C. Parsons. "Folk-Lore from Elizabeth City County Virginia." *Journal of American Folk-Lore* 35 (Jan.–Mar. 1922).

Bateman, Rebecca. "Jim Crow Comes to Indian Territory: Racism and Relations between Blacks and Indians of the Oklahoma Seminole Tribe." Paper presented before the American Society for Ethnohistory, Toronto, Canada, Nov. 2, 1990.

Bourke, George. "From the Report of Captain Bourke." *Annual Report of the Indian Rights Association* 7 (1889).

Brackett, Anna C. "Indian and Negro." *Harper's New Monthly Magazine* 61 (Sept. 1880).

Campisi, Jack, and Lawrence M. Hauptman. "Talking Back: The Oneida Language and Folklore Project, 1938–1941." *Proceedings of the American Philosophical Society* 125 (Dec. 1981).

Clark, Jerry E., and Martha Ellen Webb. "Susette and Susan LaFlesche: Reformer and Missionary." In *Being and Becoming Indian: Biographical Studies of North American Frontiers*. Ed. James A. Clifton. Chicago: Dorsey Press, 1989.

Cowger, Thomas W. "Dr. Thomas A. Bland, Critic of Forced Assimilation." *American Indian Culture and Research Journal* 16 (Fall 1992).

DeMallie, Raymond J. "George Bushotter: The First Lakota Ethnographer." In *American Indian Intellectuals*. Ed. Margot Liberty. St. Paul, Minn.: West Publishing, 1978.

Du Bois, W. E. B. "Education in Africa: A Review of the Recommendations of the African Education Committee." *Crisis* 32 (June 1926).

Eastman, Elaine Goodale. "The Future of the Indian School System." *Chautauquan* 10 (1889–90).

Engs, Robert Francis. "Red, Black, and White: A Study of Intellectual Inequality." In *Region, Race and Reconstruction: Essays in Honor of C. Vann Woodward*. Ed. James M. McPherson and J. Morgan Kouss. New York, N.Y.: Oxford University Press, 1982.

Foster Addison P. "The Hampton Anniversary." *American Missionary Magazine* 3 (July 1880).

Frissell, Hollis Burke. "A Survey of the Field." *Proceedings of the First Lake Capon Conference.* (1898).

———. "Negro Education." *New World* 9 (Dec. 1900).

———. "Hampton Institute." In *From Servitude to Service*. Ed. Kelly Miller. Boston: American Unitarian Association, 1905.

Giles, Susan M. "May Day at Hampton." *Lend a Hand* 5 (Sept. 1890).

Harlan, Louis R. "Booker T. Washington in Biographical Perspective." *American Historical Review* 75 (Oct. 1970).

"History Making News." *Quarterly Journal of the Society of American Indians* 4 (June 1915).

Hopkins, Mark. "The Living House or God's Method of Social Unity." *Twentieth Baccalaureate Sermons.* (Aug. 3, 1862). Cited by Robert E. Schneider, "Samuel Chapman Armstrong and the Founding of the Hampton Institute." Honors thesis, Williams College, 1973.

King, Wilma. "Color and Race: Multicultural Education at Hampton Institute—The Shawnees: A Case Study, 1900–1923." *Journal of Negro Education* 57 (Fall 1988).

Lybarger, Michael. "Origins of the Modern Social Studies: 1900–1916." *History of Education Quarterly* 23 (Winter 1983).

Mathes, Valerie Sherer. "Susan LaFlesche Picotte: Nebraska Indian Physician, 1865–1915." *Nebraska History* 63 (Winter 1983).

McAnulty, Sarah D. "Angel DeCora: American Indian Artist and Educator." *Nebraska History* 57 (Summer 1976).

Molin, Paulette Fairbanks. "Training the Hand, the Head, and the Heart: Indian Education at Hampton Institute." *Minnesota History* 51 (Fall 1988).

Ogden, Robert C. "Samuel Chapman Armstrong: A Sketch." New York, N.Y.: Fleming H. Revell, 1894.

Parkhurst, W. H. "General A. Reviewed." *Council Fire and Arbitrator* 9 (June 1885).

———. "Part Two. General A. Revisited." *Council Fire and Arbitrator* 9 (July 1885).

Parks, Douglas R. "James Murie: Pawnee Ethnographer." In *American Indian Intellectuals*. Ed. Margot Liberty. St. Paul, Minn.: West Publishing, 1978.

Parman, Donald L. "J. C. Morgan: Navaho Apostle of Assimilation." *Journal of the National Archives* 4 (Summer 1972).

Porter, Kenneth Wiggins. "Notes Supplementary to Relations between Negroes and Indians." *Journal of Negro History* 18 (July 1933).

Pratt, Richard H. "Address of Captain Pratt before the National Education Convention at Ocean Grove, New Jersey, Aug. 11, 1883." *The Morning Star* 4 (Dec. 1882): 2.

———. "The Advantages of Mingling Indians with Whites." In *Proceedings of the Nineteenth Annual Conference on Charities and Corrections, at the Nineteenth Annual Session held in Denver, Colorado.* (1892).

———. "The Solution to the Indian Problem." *Quarterly Journal of the Society of American Indians* 3 (Apr. 1915).

———. "What Is the Matter with Our Indians?" *Quarterly Journal of the Society of American Indians* 3 (Apr. 1915).

Richards, Josephine E. "The Training of the Indian Girl as the Uplifter of the Home." *Proceedings of the National Educational Association* (1900).

Sampson, Jean Scott. "Hampton Normal and Agricultural Institute: Education of Native Americans, 1878–1923." *Journal of the Afro-American Historical and Genealogical Society* 9 (Summer 1988).

Schall, Larryetta M. "William H. Sheppard: Fighter for African Rights." In *Stony the Road: Chapters in the History of Hampton Institute.* Ed. Keith Schall. Charlottesville: University of Virginia Press, 1977.

"Schools for White Children." *Indian School Journal* 5 (Sept. 1905).

Sherman, Richard B. "The 'Teachings at the Hampton Institute': Social Equality, Race Integrity, and the Virginia Public Assemblage Act of 1926." *Virginia Magazine of History and Biography* 95 (July 1987).

Stowe, Harriet Beecher. "The Indians at St. Augustine." *Christian Union* 15 (Apr. 25, 1877).

"Training Primitive Peoples." *Indian School Journal* 5 (Jan. 1905).

U.S. House, *Congressional Record* 17, part 4 (Mar. 10, 1886).

U.S. House, untitled text of Commissioner T. J. Morgan, House Ex. Doc. 51-1 Washington, D.C.: Government Printing Office, 1891. Serial Set 2725.

U.S. Senate, Senate Ex. Doc. 52-31. Washington, D.C.: Government Printing Office, 1892. Serial Set 2892.

U.S. House, *Congressional Record* 48, part 5 (Apr. 8, 1912).

U.S. Department of Interior, Bureau of Education, *Hampton Normal and Agricultural Institute: Its Evolution and Contribution to Education as a Federal Land Grant College*. Bulletin No. 27, 1923. Washington, D.C.: Government Printing Office, 1923.

Welsh, Herbert. "Some Present Aspects of the Negro Problem." An Address delivered in the Coulter Street Meeting House, Germantown, Philadelphia, Mar. 18, 1907 (copy in possession of author).

Williams, Walter L. "The Merger of Apaches with Eastern Cherokees: Qualla in 1893," *Journal of Cherokee Studies* 2 (Spring 1977): 240–45.

Winnemuca, Sarah. "Letter to Senator Logan." *Council Fire and Arbitrator* 7 (Feb. 1883).

Dissertations, Theses, and Unpublished Manuscripts

Adams, David Wallace. "The Federal Indian Boarding School: A Study of Environment and Response." Ph.D. diss., Indiana University, 1975.

Aery, William Anthony. "The Hampton Idea of Education, 1868–1893, with Special Reference to the Contributions of Samuel Chapman Armstrong." n.d. Hampton Institute Archives.

Ayers, Solon G. "An Investigation of Terminal Vocational Education at Haskell Institute." Ph.D. diss., University of Kansas, 1952.

Brunhouse, R. L. "A History of Carlisle School: A Phase of Government Indian Policy, 1879–1918." Ph.D. diss., University of Pennsylvania, 1935.

Carson, Suzanne C. "Samuel Chapman Armstrong: Missionary to the South." Ph.D. diss., Johns Hopkins University, 1952.

Correia, Stephen. "For Their Own Good: An Historical Analysis of the Educational Thought of Thomas Jesse Jones." Ph.D. diss., Pennsylvania State University, 1993.

Folsom, Cora M. "Indian Days at Hampton." n.d. Hampton Institute Archives.

Gilcreast, Everette A. "Richard Henry Pratt and American Indian Policy, 1877–1906: A Study of the Assimilation Movement." Ph.D. diss., Yale University, 1967.

Goodman, David M. "The Apache Prisoners of War, 1886–1894." Ph.D. diss., Texas Christian University, 1969.

Hunter, Wilma King. "Coming of Age: Hollis B. Frissell and the Emergence of Hampton Institute, 1893–1917." Ph.D. diss., Indiana University, 1982.

Ludlow, Helen W. "The Personal Memories and Letters of General S.C. Armstrong." 1898, Williams College, Williamsiana Collection, 1408 pages.

Muir, Margaret R. "Indian Education at Hampton Institute and Federal Indian Policy: Solutions to the Indian Problem." Master's thesis, Brown University, 1970.

Robinson, William. "The History of Hampton Institute." Ph.D. diss., New York University, 1959.

Ryan, Carmelita S. "The Carlisle Indian Industrial School." Ph.D. diss., Georgetown University, 1962.

Schneider, Robert F. "Samuel Chapman Armstrong and the Founding of Hampton Institute." Honors thesis, Williams College, 1973.

Tingey, Joseph Willard. "Blacks and Indians Together: An Experiment in Biracial Education at Hampton Institute (1878–1923)." Ph.D. diss., Columbia Teacher's College, 1978.

White, William B. "The Military and the Melting Pot: The American Army and Minority Groups, 1865–1924." Ph.D. diss., University of Wisconsin, 1968.

Index

Robertson, Charles, 19
Robinson, James Harvey, 195–96n43
Robinson, William, 149n31, 150n37
Roe Cloud, Elizabeth Bender, 212
Roe Cloud, Henry, 212, 248, 269–70
Rogers, Frank K., 125, 184–85, 257
Rolfe, John, 31
Romeyn, Lt. Henry, 31, 33, 39, 47n37
Roosevelt, Theodore, 266
Rose, Wycliff, 254
Royal School (Honolulu), 2–3
Ruffner, William H., 16n24
Rulo, Cora, 169

St. Augustine: prisoners at, 27–33,
   48n41, 96, 198, 209, 267
St. Cyr, Julia, 162, 220, 221, 242n70
St. Martin, Susie, 215
Sale, William H., 85n35
Sanitation, 243–44n83
Santee Indian School, 95, 113n15, 259,
   265, 269, 275n43
Sapient, William, 260
Sawyer, Allen, 157
Saxe, David, 195n43
Scales, Alfred, 21
Scattergood, J. Henry, 269
Schmeckebier, Laurence, 112–13n9, 263
Schneider, Robert, 5–6
Schurz, Carl, 21, 34, 35, 39, 42, 54–55
Scott, Emmett J., 177
Scoville, Annie Beecher, 269, 271
Scoville, Samuel, 256
Scoville, William, 207, 250
Sectarian issues, 36, 67–70, 234–35
Sectionalism: post–Civil War, 70–73
Segregation: in Indian Office employ-
   ment, 265–66; and mixed-ancestry
   students, 204; in society as a whole,
   46n23, 154n97, 204
—at Hampton Institute: in classrooms,
   118–20, 147nn5,6,9,11,12; in dining rooms, 136–45, 153nn75,77,81,
   153–54n88, 154nn89,91; in discipline structure, 125–27, 128; in extracurricular activities, 132–36; in
   housing, 125, 127–31, 151n51; in
   productive industries, 43–44, 120–
   25, 148nn17,18,20, 149nn30,31,33;
   summary, 117–18, 145–46

Self-help: in system of education, 109–
   11, 145; in theory of reform, 74–80,
   100, 103
Selon, Balany, 147n9
Senecas, 203
Shawnee, Lydia, 206, 239n36
Shawnee family, 207, 238–39n35
Sheppard, William H., 177
Sheridan, Gen. Philip Henry, 27–29, 39
Sherman, James S., 252
Sherman, Myrtilla, 162, 167, 212
Sherwood Farm: and plan for Apaches
   at Hampton, 62–65, 85n47,
   86nn54,55,58, 267
Showers, Susan H., 109
Simmons, David, 102–3
Simons, Eva May, 204
Sioux: at Carlisle, 199–200; at Hamp-
   ton, 34–36, 42, 60, 198, 201, 202;
   national policy on, 60, 61, 90n103;
   views on white culture, 92–93
Sits Down to Talk, 216–17
Skenandore, Marion, 217
Skenandore family, 203
Slavery: Native American slaveholders,
   158; opinions on, 4–5, 24–25, 71–72
Sloan, Thomas: charges of land fraud
   against, 212–13; and Childs investi-
   gation, 230–32, 245nn106,107; and
   discipline, 128, 150n39; and funding
   crisis of 1912, 254–55, 257
Smiley, Albert: Armstrong's influence
   on, 58, 64, 89n99; and Childs inves-
   tigation, 222, 227–28, 229–30, 232,
   233, 244n94
Smith, Edward Parmelee, 19
Smith, J. E., 97, 123, 149n29
Smith, Capt. John, 18
Smith, Josephine, 238n29
Smith, Sidney, 159
Smithsonian Institution Bureau of Eth-
   nology, 20
Snow, Clara, 203
Snowball fights, 158–59
Social organizations: at Hampton, 133–
   34
Social studies curriculum, 186–91,
   194n32, 195nn39,42, 195–96n43
Social Studies in Secondary Education
   (NEA), 191, 195–96n43

Books in the Series Blacks in the New World

REPRINT EDITIONS

King: A Biography
Second Edition
David Levering Lewis

The Death and Life of Malcolm X
Second Edition
Peter Goldman

Race Relations in the Urban South, 1865–1890
Howard N. Rabinowitz; foreword by C. Vann Woodward

Race Riot at East St. Louis, July 2, 1917
Elliott Rudwick

W. E. B. Du Bois: Voice of the Black Protest Movement
Elliott Rudwick

The Negro's Civil War: How American Negroes Felt and Acted during the War for the Union
James M. McPherson

Lincoln and Black Freedom: A Study in Presidential Leadership
LaWanda Cox

Slavery and Freedom in the Age of the American Revolution
Edited by Ira Berlin and Ronald Hoffman

Diary of a Sit-In
Second Edition
Merrill Proudfoot; introduction by Michael S. Mayer

They Who Would Be Free: Blacks' Search for Freedom, 1830–61
Jane H. Pease and William H. Pease

The Reshaping of Plantation Society: The Natchez District, 1860–80
Michael Wayne

Rice and Slaves: Ethnicity and the Slave Trade in Colonial South Carolina
Daniel C. Littlefield

WIDENER UNIVERSITY
WOLFGRAM
LIBRARY
CHESTER, PA.

NOV 2 4 1998

DATE DUE

NOV 2 4 1998			
ILL 72513668			
LZN Nigro			
due 3-16-00			

Demco, Inc. 38-293